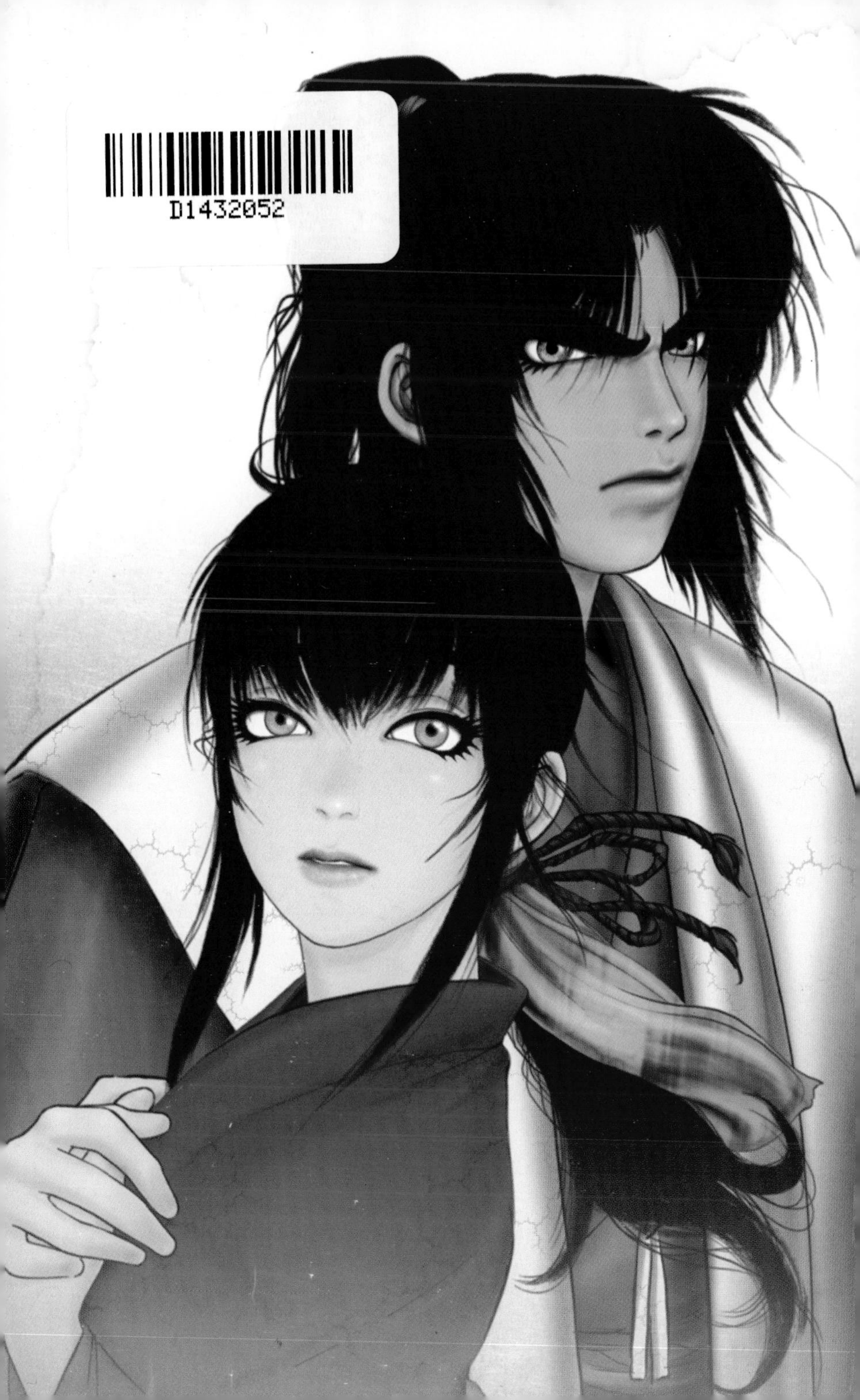

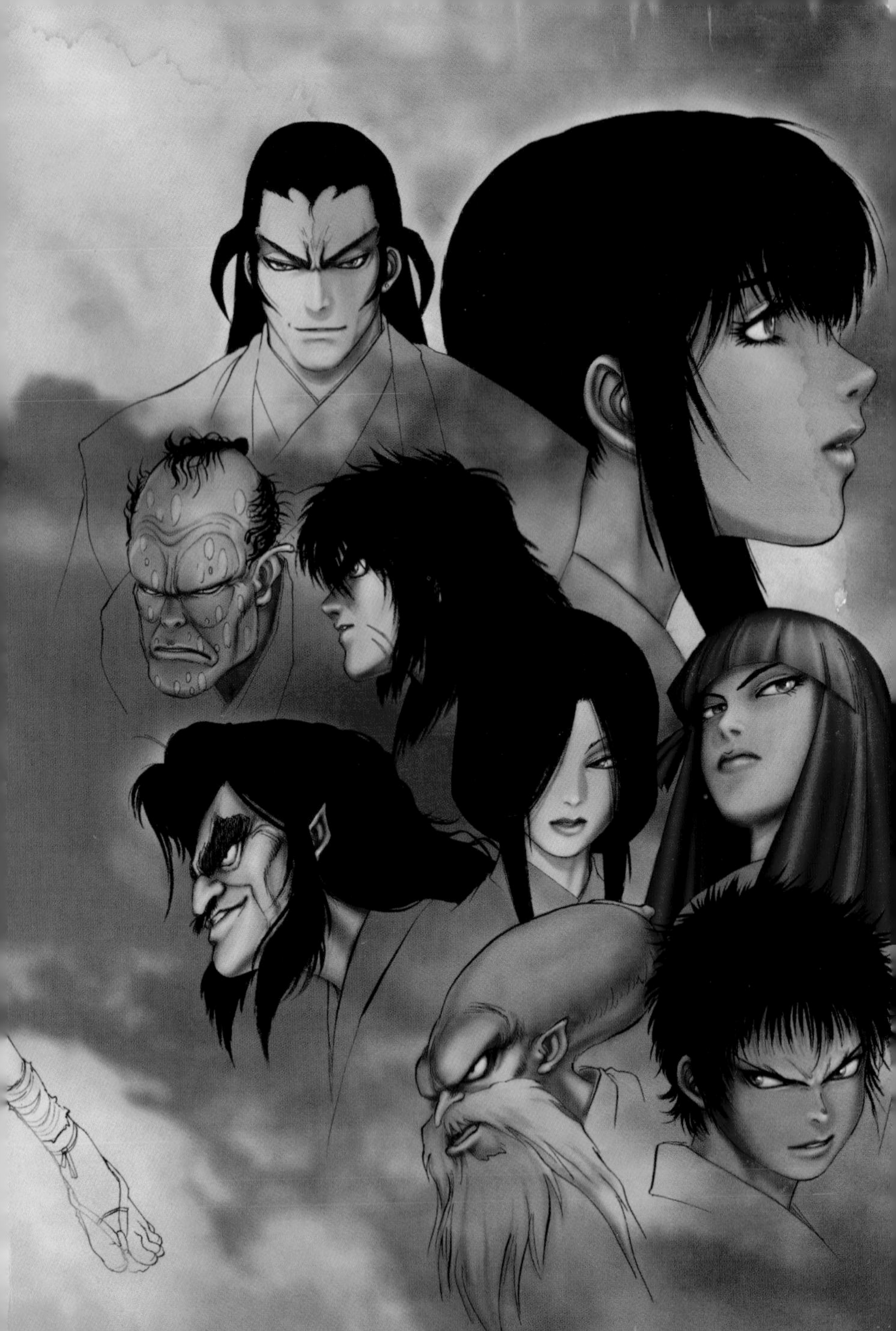

原作 **山田風太郎** 漫画 **せがわまさき**

講談社文庫『甲賀忍法帖』より

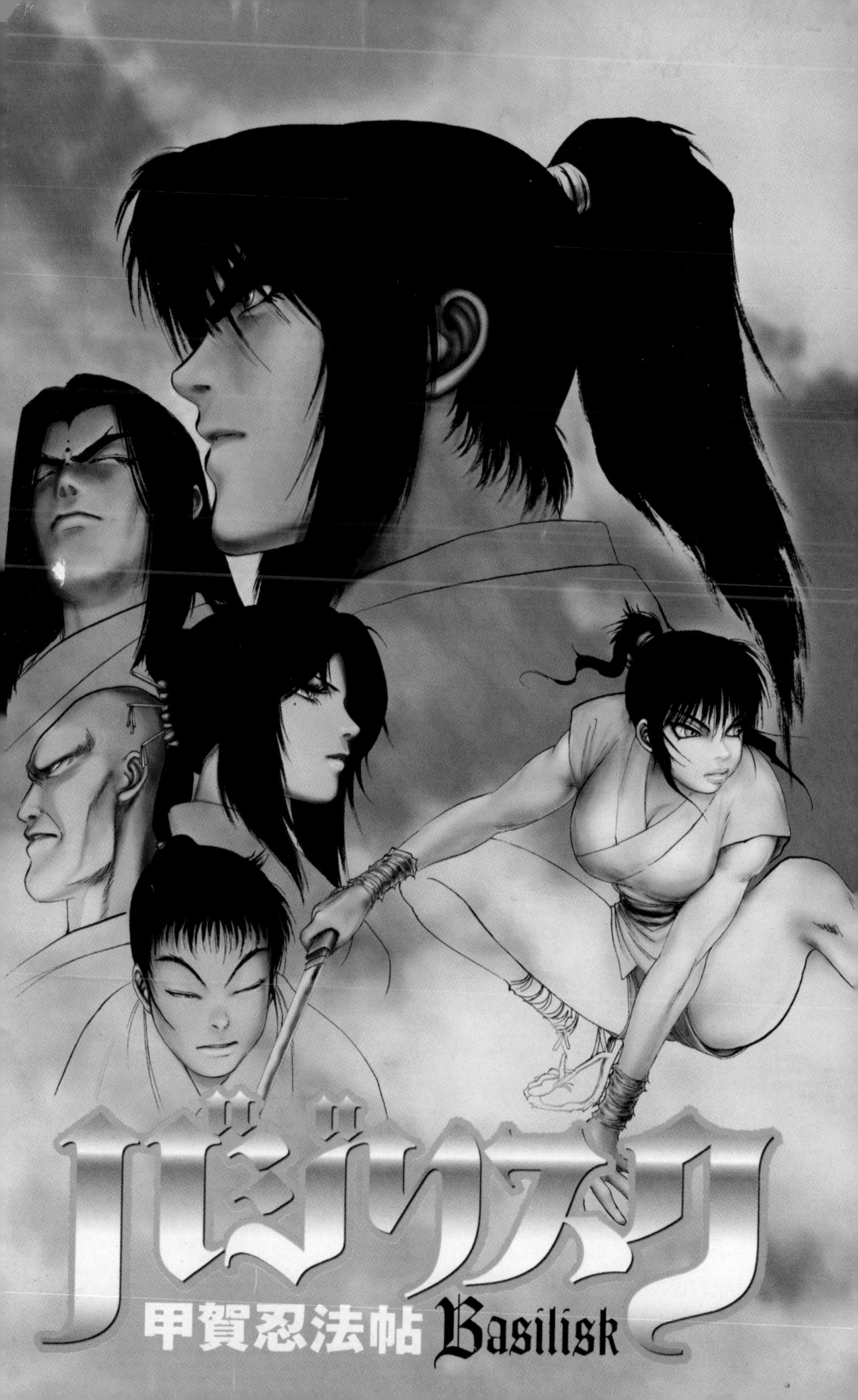
バジリスク
甲賀忍法帖
Basilisk

甲賀組十人衆

甲賀弾正

甲賀弦之介

地虫十兵衛

風待将監

霞刑部

鵜殿丈助

如月左衛門

室賀豹馬

陽炎

お胡夷

伊賀組十人衆

お幻

朧

夜叉丸

小豆蝋斉

薬師寺天膳

雨夜陣五郎

筑摩小四郎

簑念鬼

蛍火

朱絹

Basilisk

ORIGINAL STORY BY FŪTARO YAMADA

BASED ON THE KODANSHA NOVEL *THE KOUGA NINJA SCROLLS*

MANGA BY MASAKI SEGAWA

TRANSLATED AND ADAPTED BY DAVID URY
LETTERED BY FOLTZ DESIGN

2

DEL REY
BALLANTINE BOOKS • NEW YORK

SR

Basilisk volume 2 is a work of fiction. Names, characters, places, and incidents are the products of the author's imagination or are used fictitiously. Any resemblance to actual events, locales, or persons, living or dead, is entirely coincidental.

A Del Rey Trade Paperback Original

Published in the United States by Del Rey Books, an imprint of The Random House Publishing Group, a division of Random House, Inc., New York.

DEL REY is a registered trademark and the Del Rey colophon is a trademark of Random House, Inc.

Publication rights arranged through Kodansha Ltd.

First published in Japan in 2003 by Kodansha Ltd., Tokyo.

ISBN 0-345-48271-9

Printed in the United States of America

www.delreymanga.com

9 8 7 6 5 4 3 2 1

Translator and adaptor: David Ury
Lettering: Foltz Design

Contents

Honorifics Explained

Throughout the Del Rey Manga books, you will find Japanese honorifics left intact in the translations. For those not familiar with how the Japanese use honorifics, and, more important, how they differ from American honorifics, we present this brief overview.

Politeness has always been a critical facet of Japanese culture. Ever since the feudal era, when Japan was a highly stratified society, use of honorifics—which can be defined as polite speech that indicates relationship or status—has played an essential role in the Japanese language. When addressing someone in Japanese, an honorific usually takes the form of a suffix attached to one's name (example: "Asuna-san"), as a title at the end of one's name, or in place of the name itself (example: "Negi-sensei," or simply "Sensei!").

Honorifics can be expressions of respect or endearment. In the context of manga and anime, honorifics give insight into the nature of the relationship between characters. Many English translations leave out these important honorifics, and therefore distort the feel of the original Japanese. Because Japanese honorifics contain nuances that English honorifics lack, it is our policy at Del Rey not to translate them. Here, instead, is a guide to some of the honorifics you may encounter in Del Rey Manga.

-SAN: This is the most common honorific and is equivalent to Mr., Miss, Ms., or Mrs. It is the all-purpose honorific and can be used in any situation where politeness is required.

-SAMA: This is one level higher than "-san" and is used to confer great respect.

-DONO: This comes from the word "tono," which means "lord." It is an even higher level than "-sama" and confers utmost respect.

-KUN: This suffix is used at the end of boys' names to express familiarity or endearment. It is also sometimes used by men among friends, or when addressing someone younger or of a lower station.

-CHAN: This is used to express endearment, mostly toward girls. It is also used for little boys, pets, and even among lovers. It gives a sense of childish cuteness.

BOZU: This is an informal way to refer to a boy, similar to the English terms "kid" or "squirt."

SEMPAI/ SENPAI: This title suggests that the addressee is one's senior in a group or organization. It is most often used in a school setting, where underclassmen refer to their upperclassmen as "sempai." It can also be used in the workplace, such as when a newer employee addresses an employee who has seniority in the company.

KOHAI: This is the opposite of "-sempai" and is used toward underclassmen in school or newcomers in the workplace. It connotes that the addressee is of a lower station.

SENSEI: Literally meaning "one who has come before," this title is used for teachers, doctors, or masters of any profession or art.

-[BLANK]: This is usually forgotten on these lists, but it is perhaps the most significant difference between Japanese and English. The lack of honorific means that the speaker has permission to address the person in a very intimate way. Usually, only family, spouses, or very close friends have this kind of permission. Known as *yobisute,* it can be gratifying when someone who has earned the intimacy starts to call one by one's name without an honorific. But when that intimacy hasn't been earned, it can be very insulting.

Basilisk
2

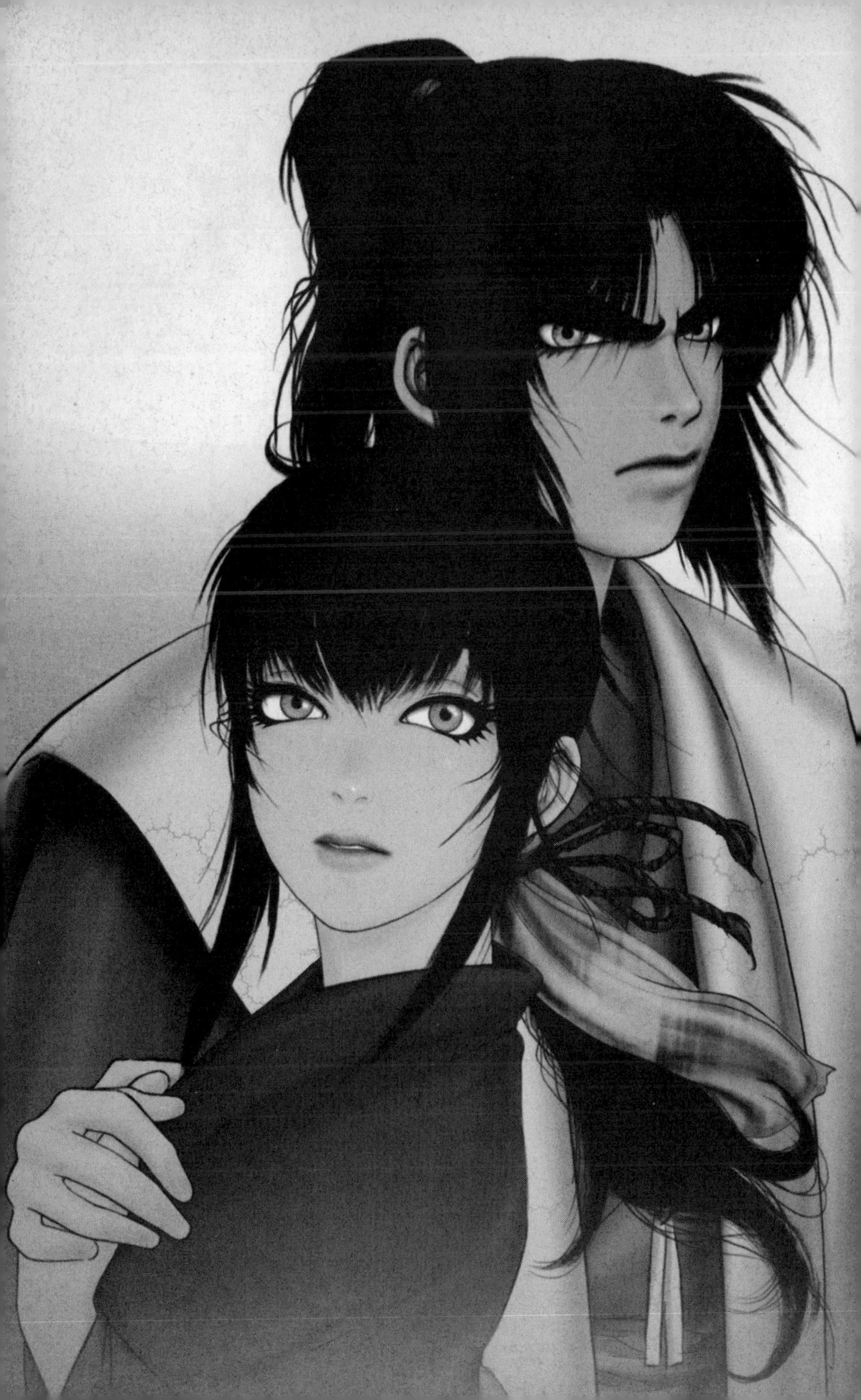

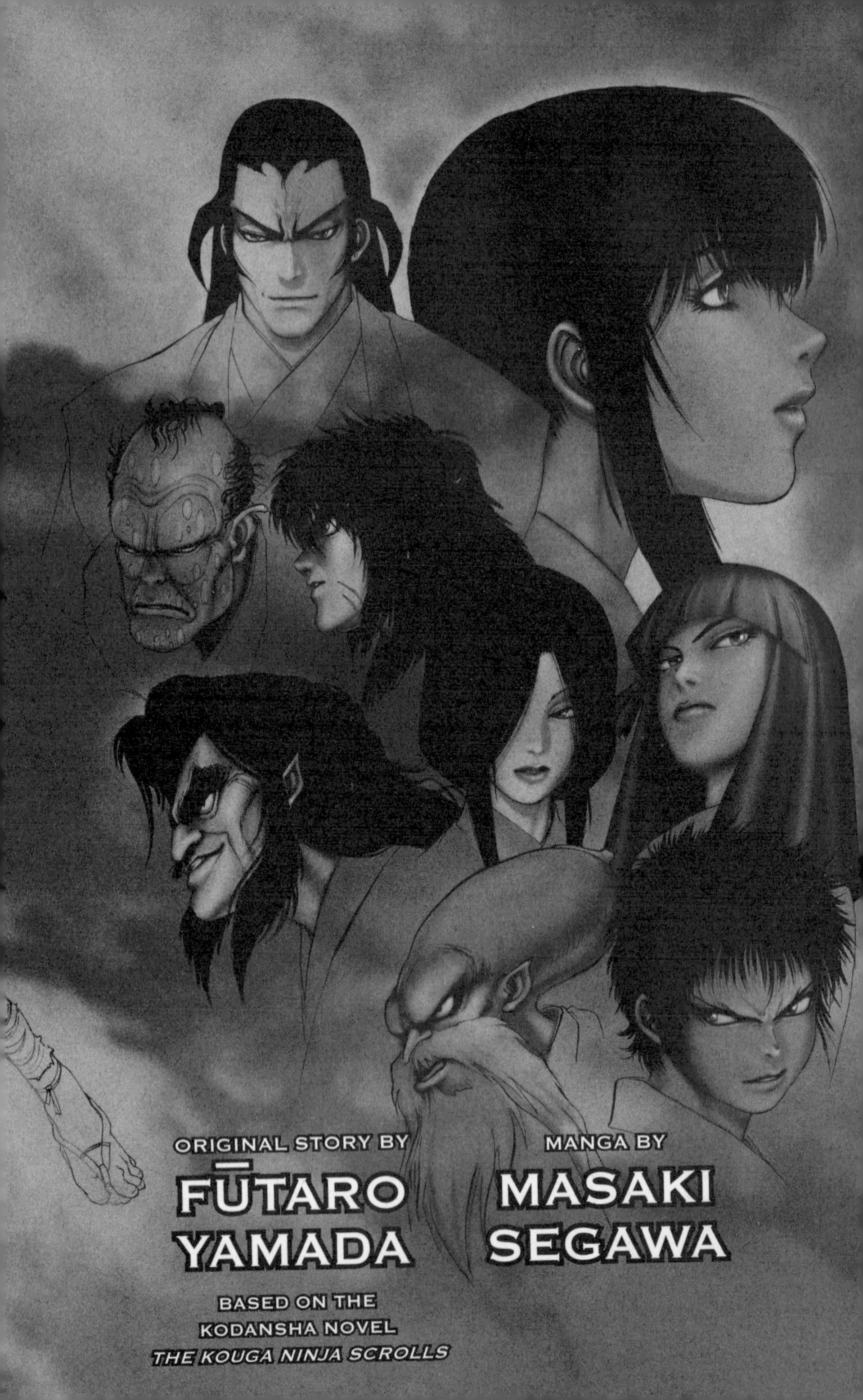

ORIGINAL STORY BY

FŪTARO YAMADA

MANGA BY

MASAKI SEGAWA

BASED ON THE KODANSHA NOVEL *THE KOUGA NINJA SCROLLS*

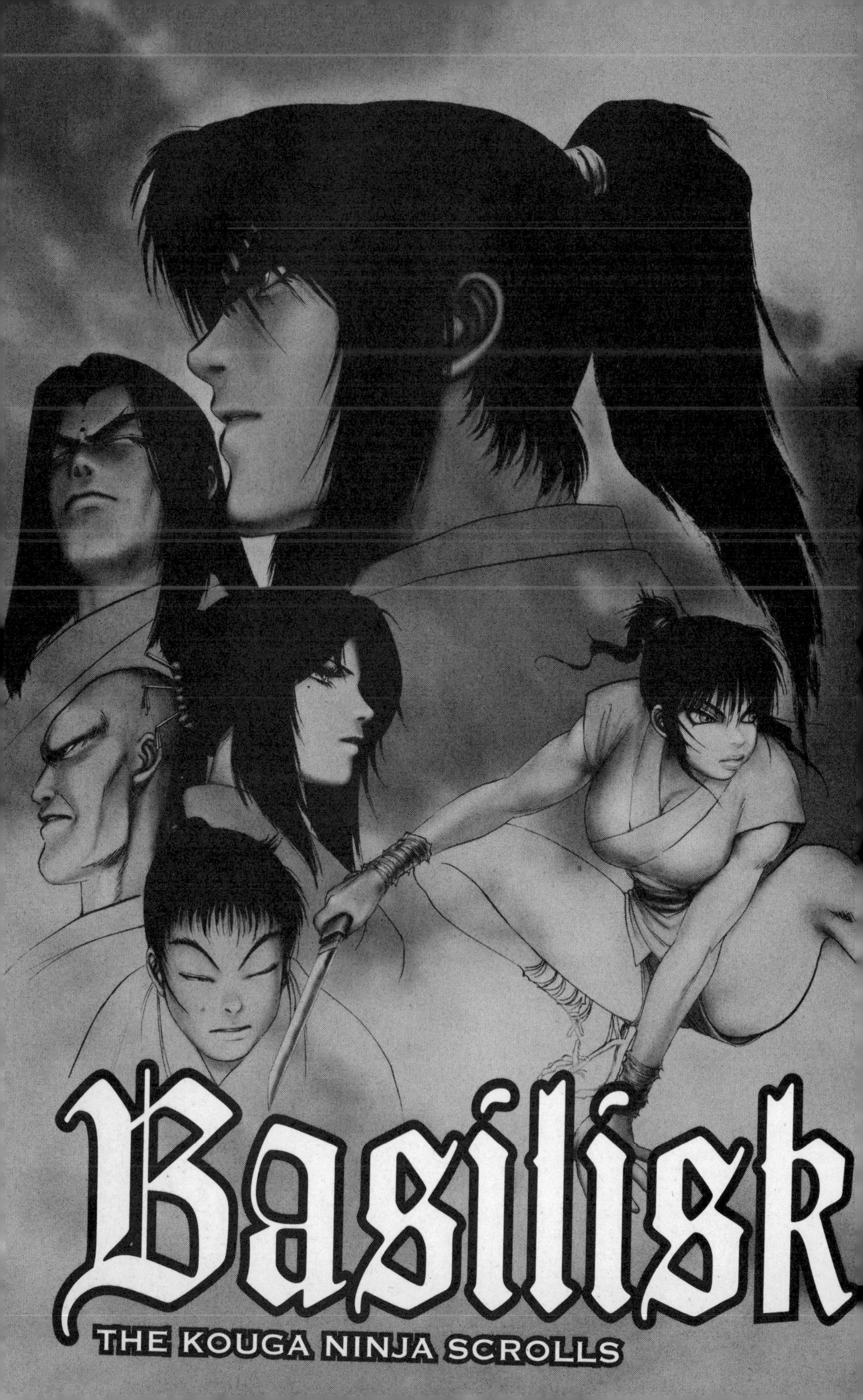
Basilisk
THE KOUGA NINJA SCROLLS

HE TEN COMBATANTS OF THE IGA CLAN

OGEN

OBORO

YASHAMARU

ROUSAI AZUKI

JINGOROU AMAYO

KOSHIROU CHIKUMA

NENKI MINO

HOTARUBI

TENZEN YAKUSHIJI

AKEGINU

THE TEN COMBATANTS OF THE KOUGA CLAN

DANJOU KOUGA

GENNOSUKE KOUGA

JUUBEI JIMUSHI

SHOUGEN KAZAMACHI

GYOUBU KASUMI

JOUSUKE UDONO

SAEMON KISARAGI

HYOUMA MUROGA

KAGEROU

OKOI

THE STORY SO FAR

UNDER THE ORDER OF RULER IEYASU TOKUGAWA, THE THIRD TOKUGAW SHOGUN SHALL BE DECIDED BY A BATTLE OF 10 VS 10 BETWEEN THE KOUGA AND THE IGA NINJA. THE BLOODBATH BETWEEN THESE TWO NINJA CLANS BEGINS WHEN THE TWO CLAN LEADERS, OGEN OF THE IGA AND DANJOU OF THE KOUGA CLAN TAKE EACH OTHER'S LIVES.

BOTH LEADERS DIE BEFORE THEY CAN TELL THEIR FELLOW CLAN MEMBERS ABOUT IEYASU'S ORDER. HOWEVER, THE IGA CLAN MANAGES TO GET HOLD OF THE BATTLE SCROLL BEFORE THE KOUGA CLAN KNOWS OF ITS EXISTENCE. SOON, THE IGA CLAN VANQUISHES JUUBEI JIMUSHI, SHOUGEN KAZAMACHI, AND JOUSUKE UDONO. THE ONLY NINJA WHO DON'T KNOW THAT WAR HAS BEEN DECLARED ARE OBORO OF IGA, GENNOSUKE KOUGA, AND THE KOUGA CLAN.

THE IGA CLAN HAS THE ADVANTAGE, BUT WILL THE KOUGA CLAN STRIKE BACK?

AND WHAT OF GENNOSUKE AND OBORO'S LOVE AFFAIR?

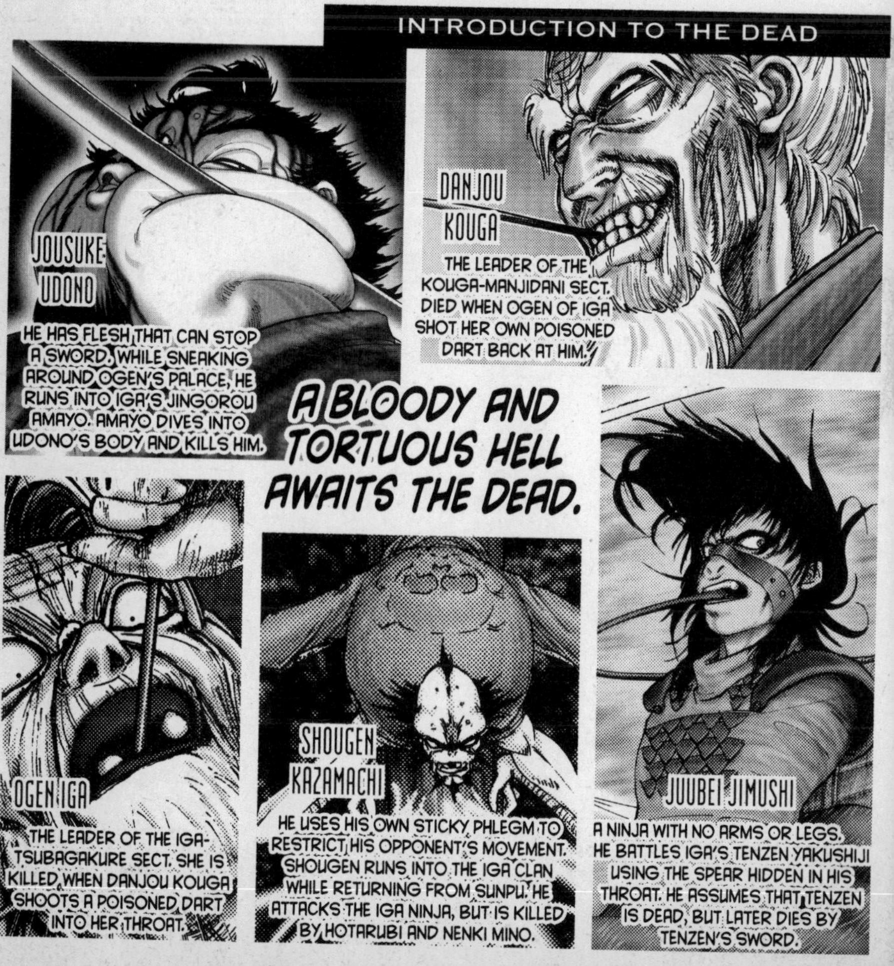
INTRODUCTION TO THE DEAD
DANJOU KOUGA
THE LEADER OF THE KOUGA-MANJIDANI SECT. DIED WHEN OGEN OF IGA SHOT HER OWN POISONED DART BACK AT HIM.
JOUSUKE UDONO
HE HAS FLESH THAT CAN STOP A SWORD. WHILE SNEAKING AROUND OGEN'S PALACE, HE RUNS INTO IGA'S JINGOROU AMAYO. AMAYO DIVES INTO UDONO'S BODY AND KILLS HIM.
A BLOODY AND TORTUOUS HELL AWAITS THE DEAD.
JUUBEI JIMUSHI
A NINJA WITH NO ARMS OR LEGS. HE BATTLES IGA'S TENZEN YAKUSHIJI USING THE SPEAR HIDDEN IN HIS THROAT. HE ASSUMES THAT TENZEN IS DEAD, BUT LATER DIES BY TENZEN'S SWORD.
SHOUGEN KAZAMACHI
HE USES HIS OWN STICKY PHLEGM TO RESTRICT HIS OPPONENT'S MOVEMENT. SHOUGEN RUNS INTO THE IGA CLAN WHILE RETURNING FROM SUNPU. HE ATTACKS THE IGA NINJA, BUT IS KILLED BY HOTARUBI AND NENKI MINO.
OGEN IGA
THE LEADER OF THE IGA-TSUBAGAKURE SECT. SHE IS KILLED WHEN DANJOU KOUGA SHOOTS A POISONED DART INTO HER THROAT.

Contents

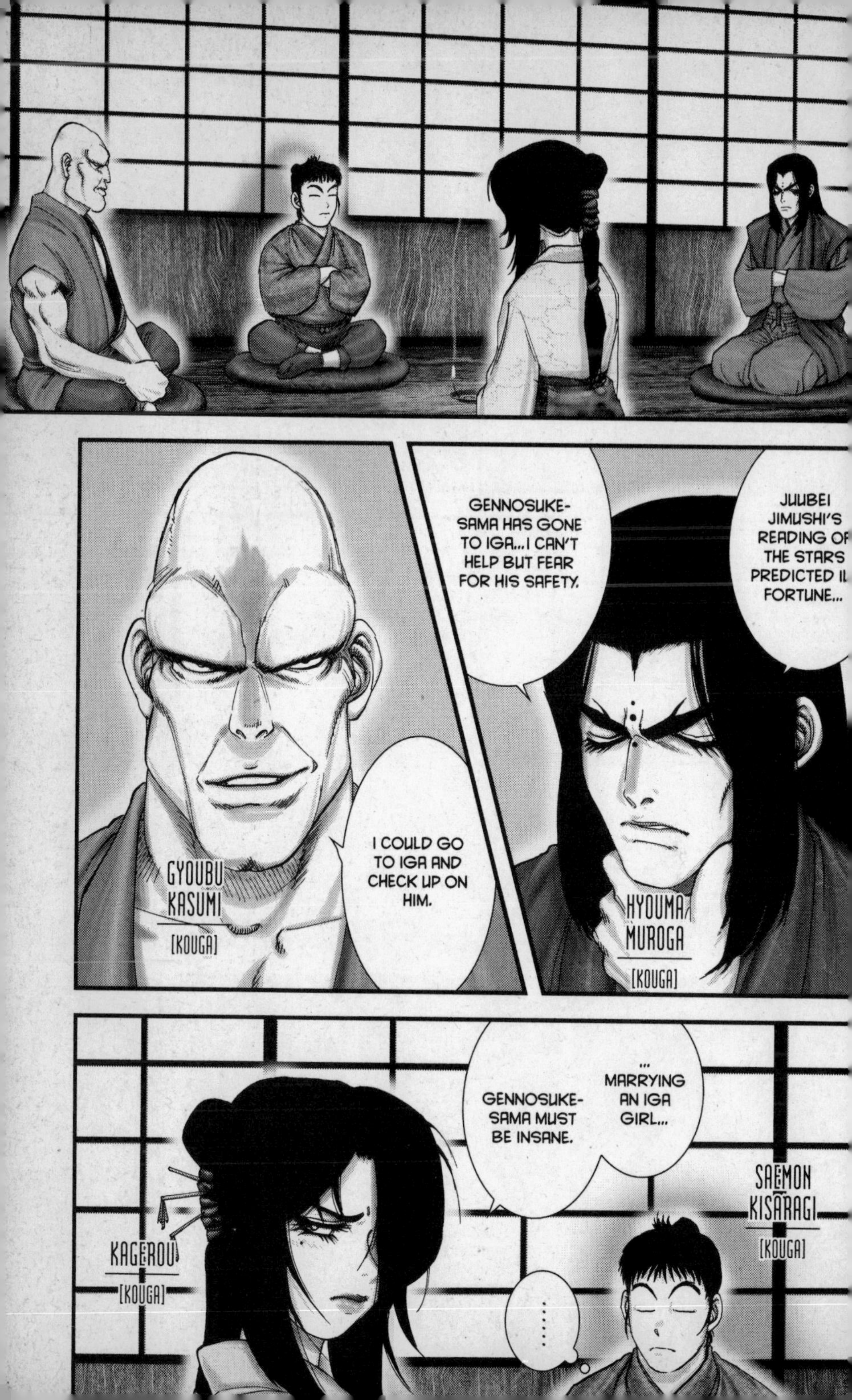
JUUBEI JIMUSHI'S READING OF THE STARS PREDICTED IL FORTUNE...
GENNOSUKE-SAMA HAS GONE TO IGA...I CAN'T HELP BUT FEAR FOR HIS SAFETY.
HYOUMA MUROGA
[KOUGA]
GYOUBU KASUMI
[KOUGA]
I COULD GO TO IGA AND CHECK UP ON HIM.
... MARRYING AN IGA GIRL...
GENNOSUKE-SAMA MUST BE INSANE.
SAEMON KISARAGI
[KOUGA]
KAGEROU
[KOUGA]
......

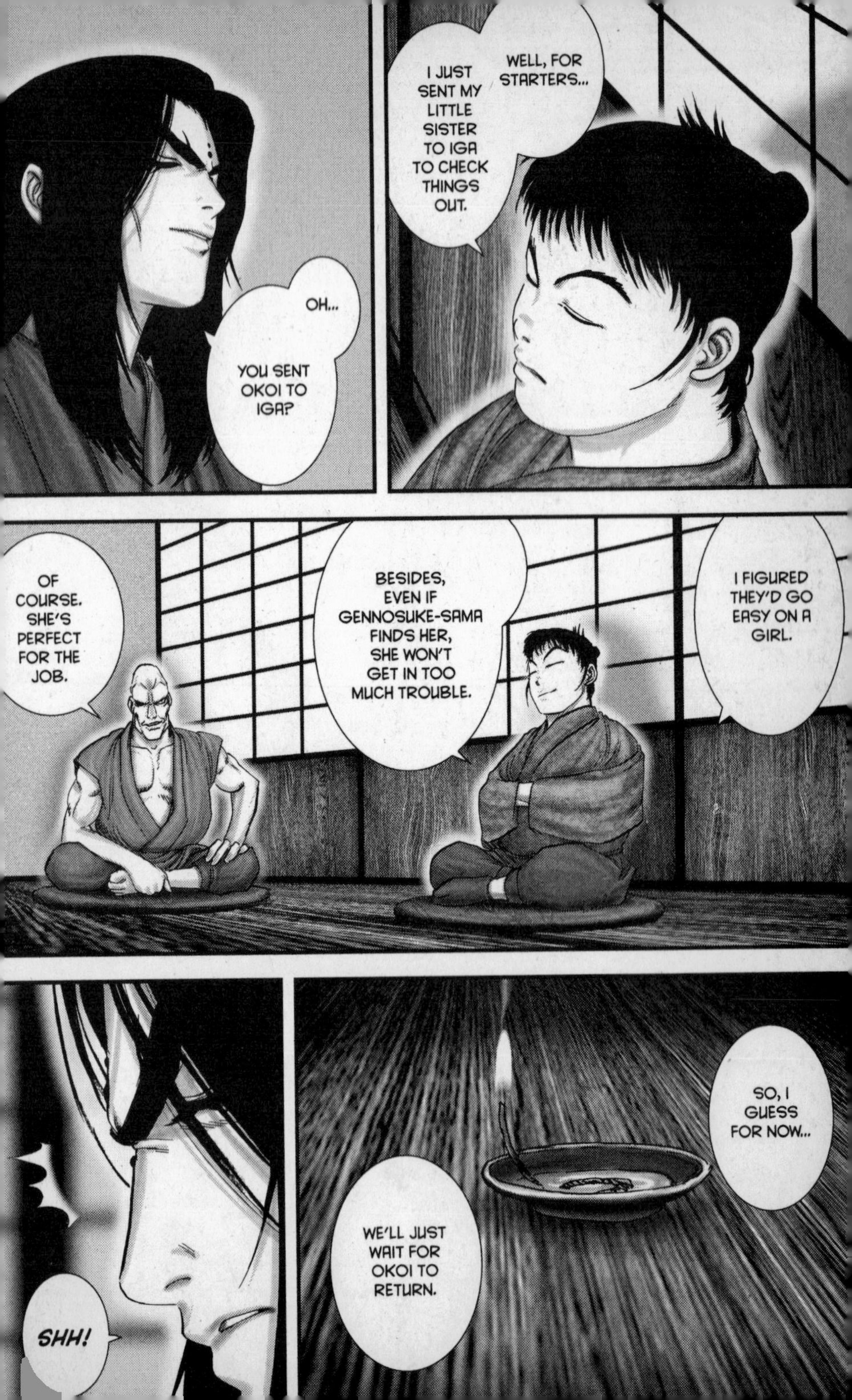
WELL, FOR STARTERS...
I JUST SENT MY LITTLE SISTER TO IGA TO CHECK THINGS OUT.
OH...
YOU SENT OKOI TO IGA?
I FIGURED THEY'D GO EASY ON A GIRL.
BESIDES, EVEN IF GENNOSUKE-SAMA FINDS HER, SHE WON'T GET IN TOO MUCH TROUBLE.
OF COURSE. SHE'S PERFECT FOR THE JOB.
SO, I GUESS FOR NOW...
WE'LL JUST WAIT FOR OKOI TO RETURN.
SHH!

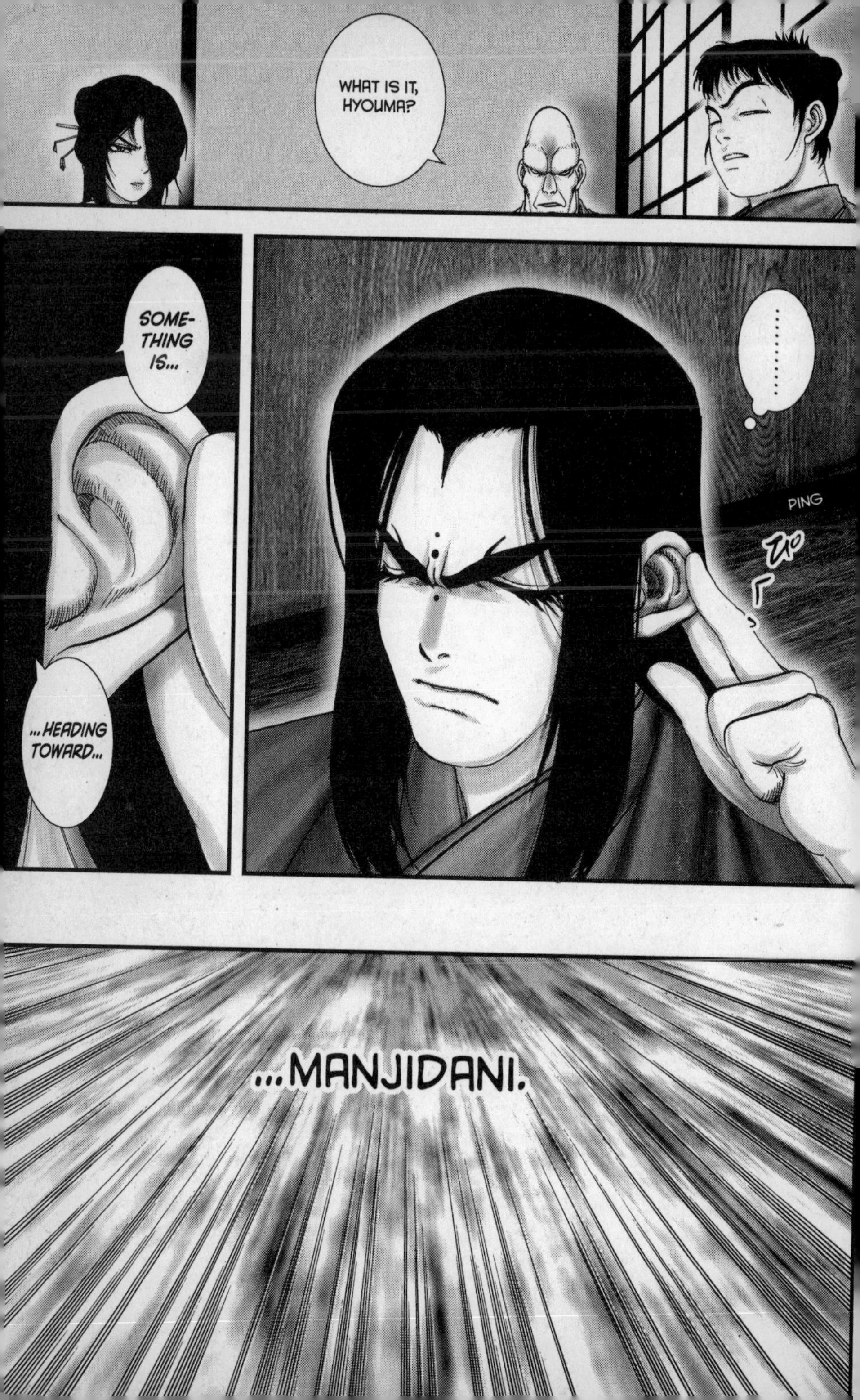
WHAT IS IT, HYOUMA?
......
PING
SOME-THING IS...
...HEADING TOWARD...
...MANJIDANI.

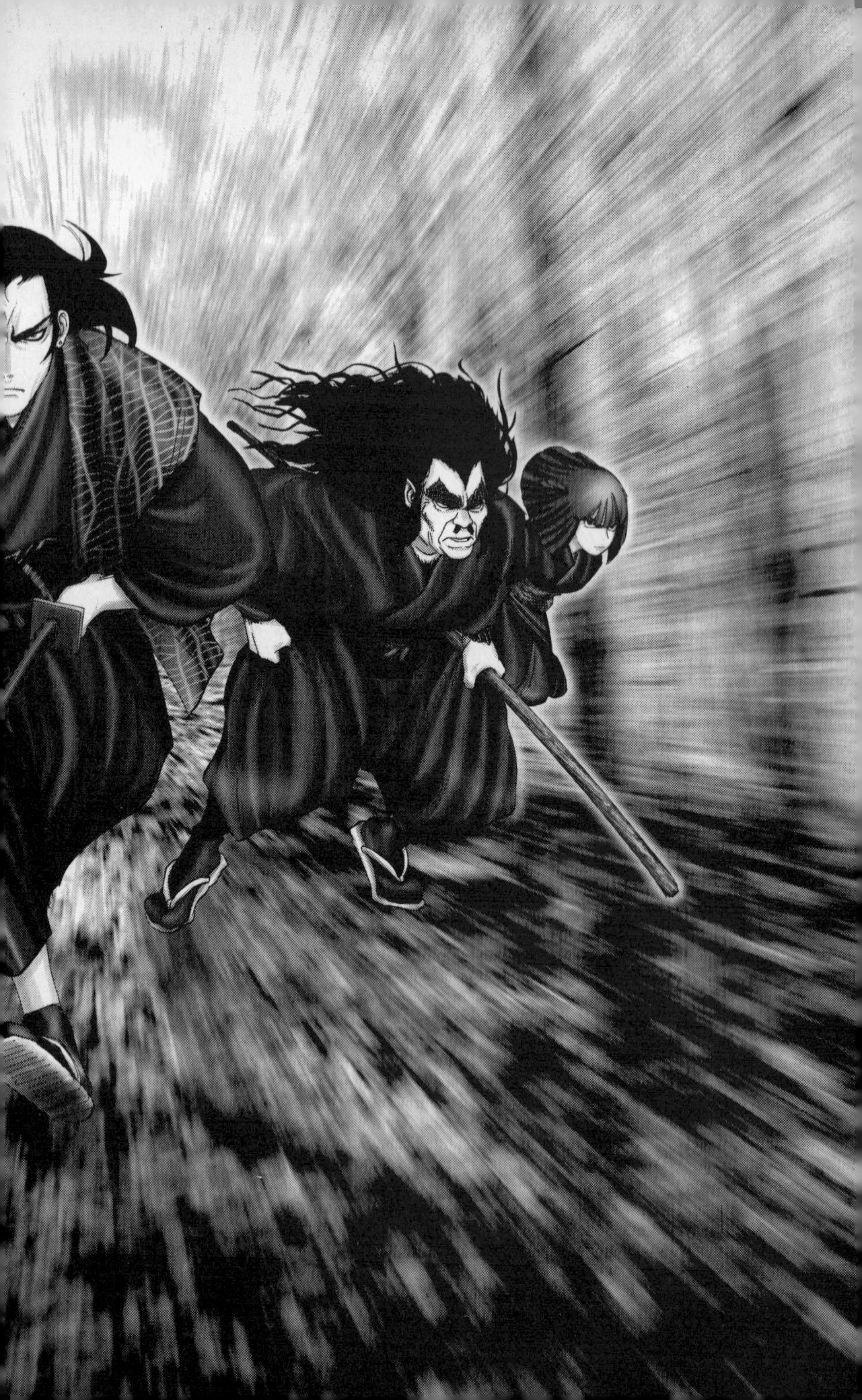

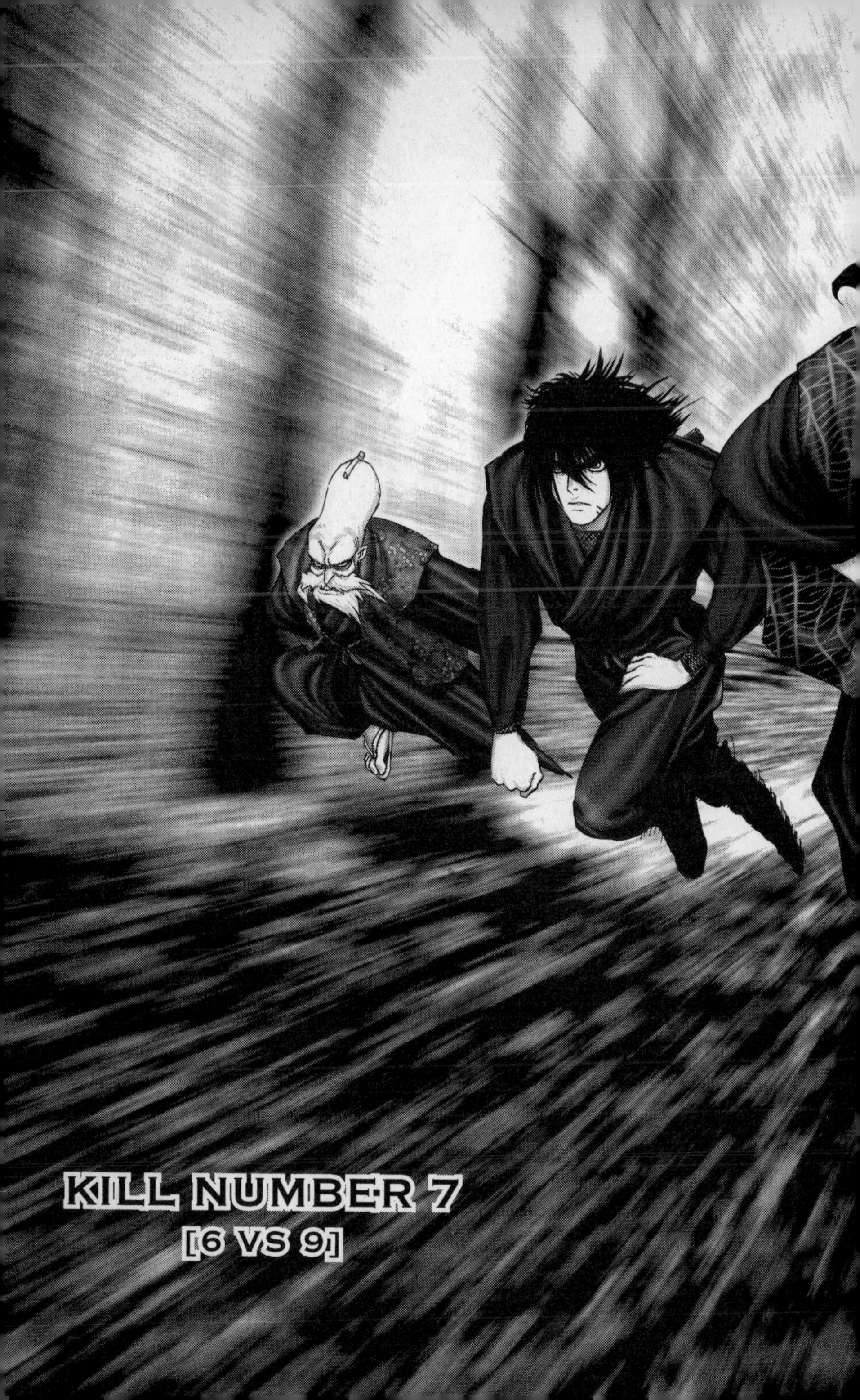
KILL NUMBER 7
[6 VS 9]

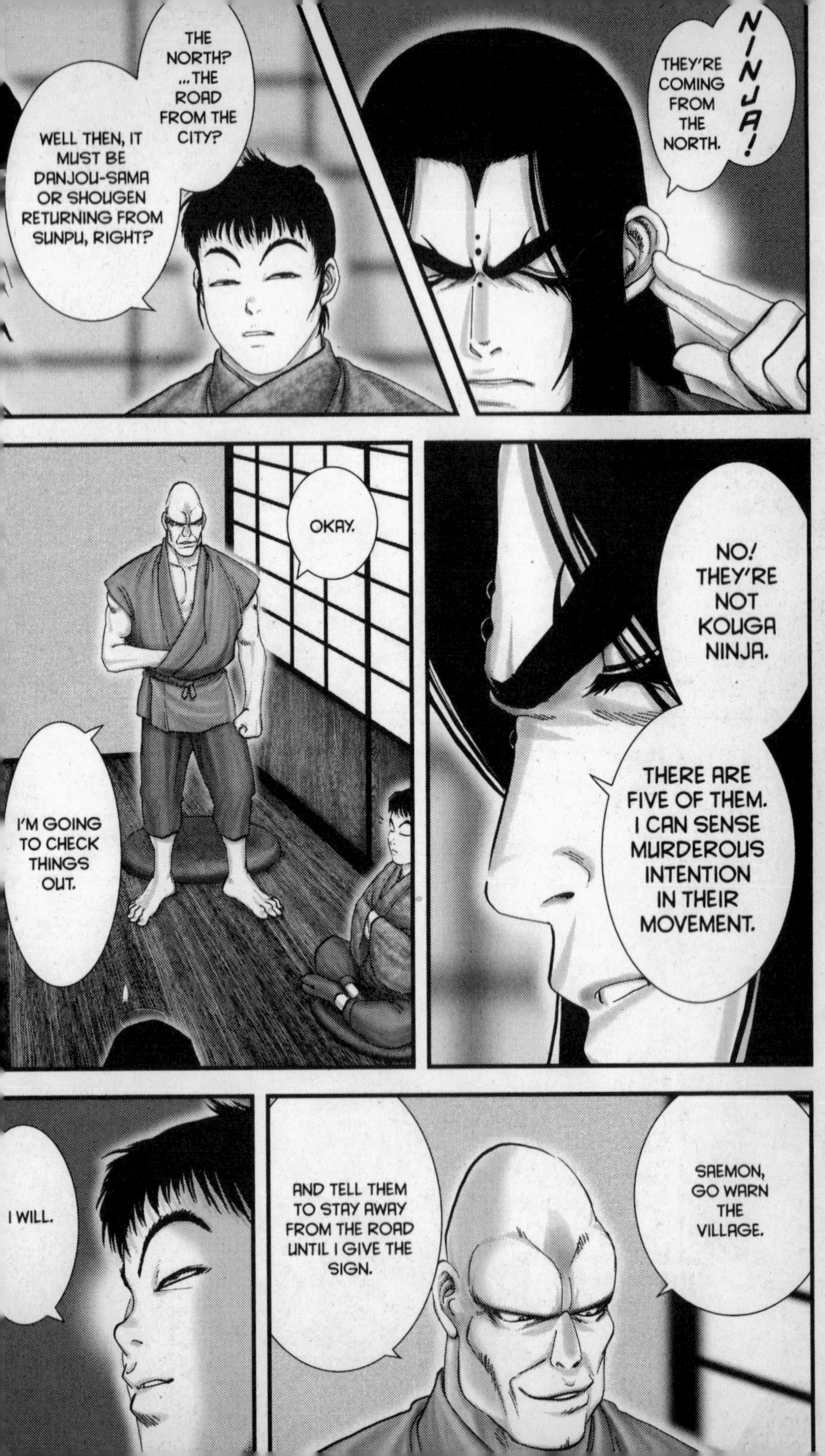
NINJA!
THEY'RE COMING FROM THE NORTH.
THE NORTH? ...THE ROAD FROM THE CITY?
WELL THEN, IT MUST BE DANJOU-SAMA OR SHOUGEN RETURNING FROM SUNPU, RIGHT?
NO! THEY'RE NOT KOUGA NINJA.
THERE ARE FIVE OF THEM. I CAN SENSE MURDEROUS INTENTION IN THEIR MOVEMENT.
OKAY.
I'M GOING TO CHECK THINGS OUT.
SAEMON, GO WARN THE VILLAGE.
AND TELL THEM TO STAY AWAY FROM THE ROAD UNTIL I GIVE THE SIGN.
I WILL.

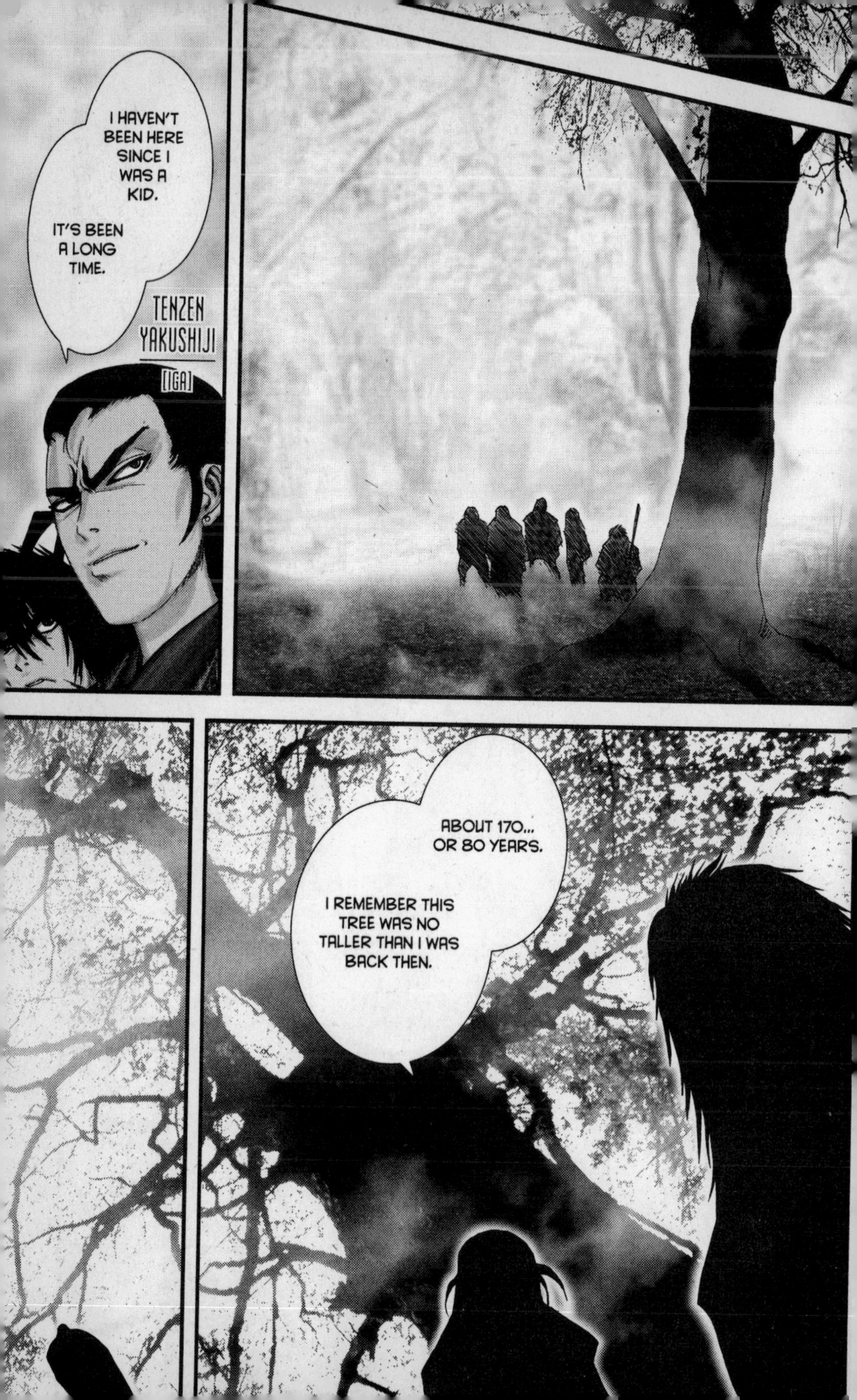
I HAVEN'T BEEN HERE SINCE I WAS A KID.
IT'S BEEN A LONG TIME.
TENZEN YAKUSHIJI
[IGA]
ABOUT 170... OR 80 YEARS.
I REMEMBER THIS TREE WAS NO TALLER THAN I WAS BACK THEN.

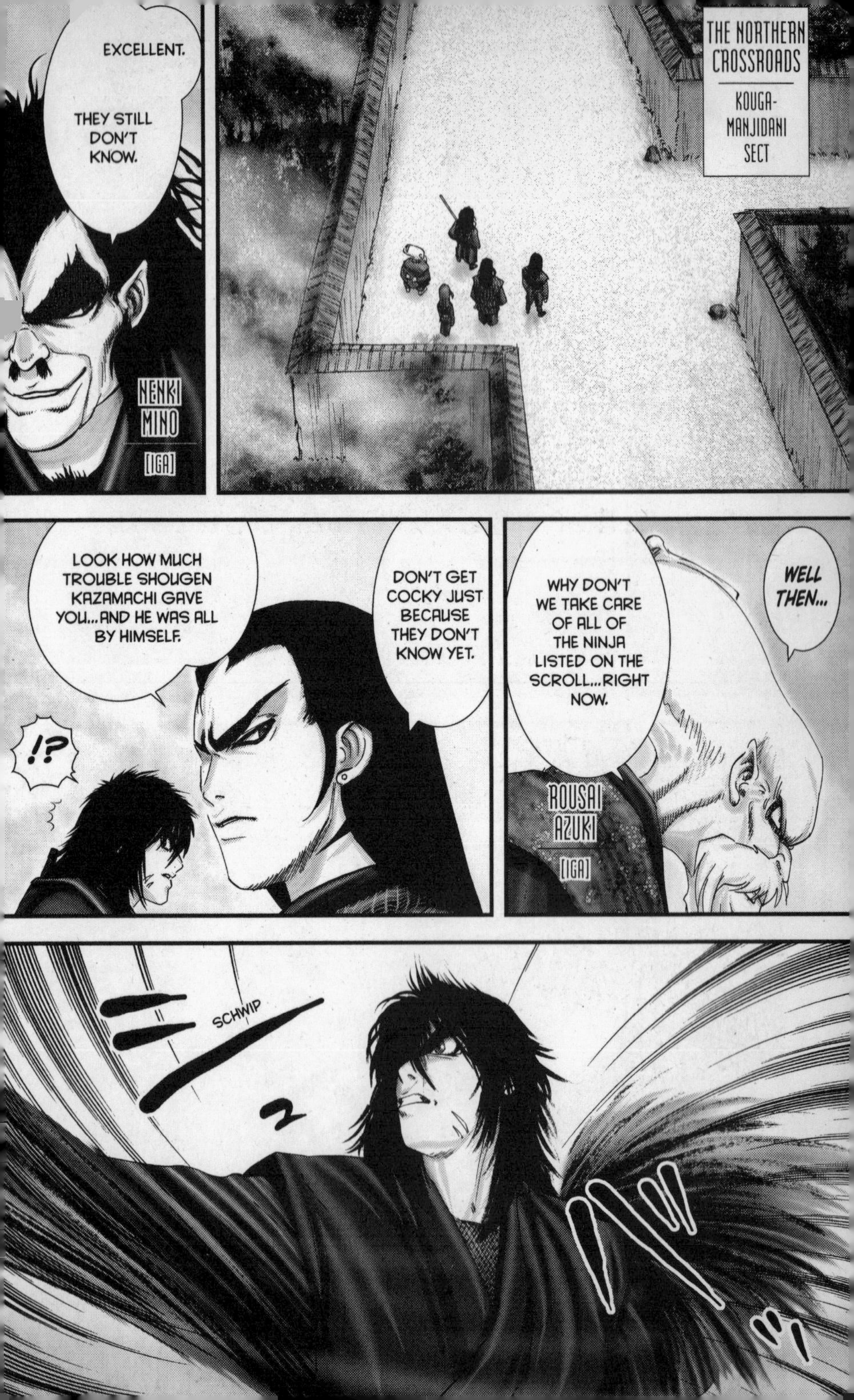
THE NORTHERN CROSSROADS
KOUGA-MANJIDANI SECT
EXCELLENT.
THEY STILL DON'T KNOW.
NENKI MINO
[IGA]
WELL THEN...
WHY DON'T WE TAKE CARE OF ALL OF THE NINJA LISTED ON THE SCROLL...RIGHT NOW.
ROUSAI AZUKI
[IGA]
DON'T GET COCKY JUST BECAUSE THEY DON'T KNOW YET.
LOOK HOW MUCH TROUBLE SHOUGEN KAZAMACHI GAVE YOU...AND HE WAS ALL BY HIMSELF.
!?
SCHWIP

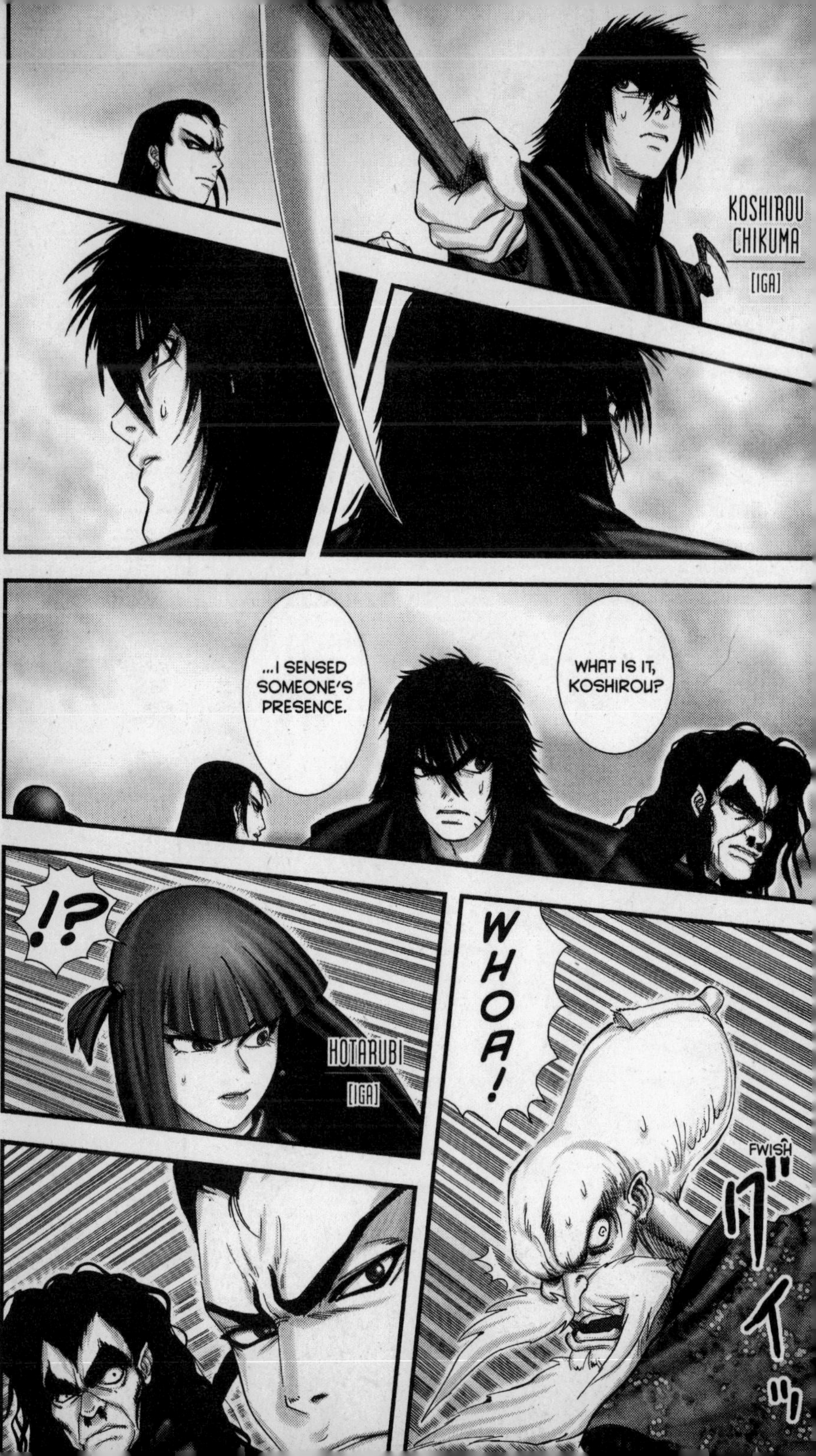
KOSHIROU CHIKUMA
[IGA]
WHAT IS IT, KOSHIROU?
...I SENSED SOMEONE'S PRESENCE.
WHOA!
FWISH
!?
HOTARUBI
[IGA]

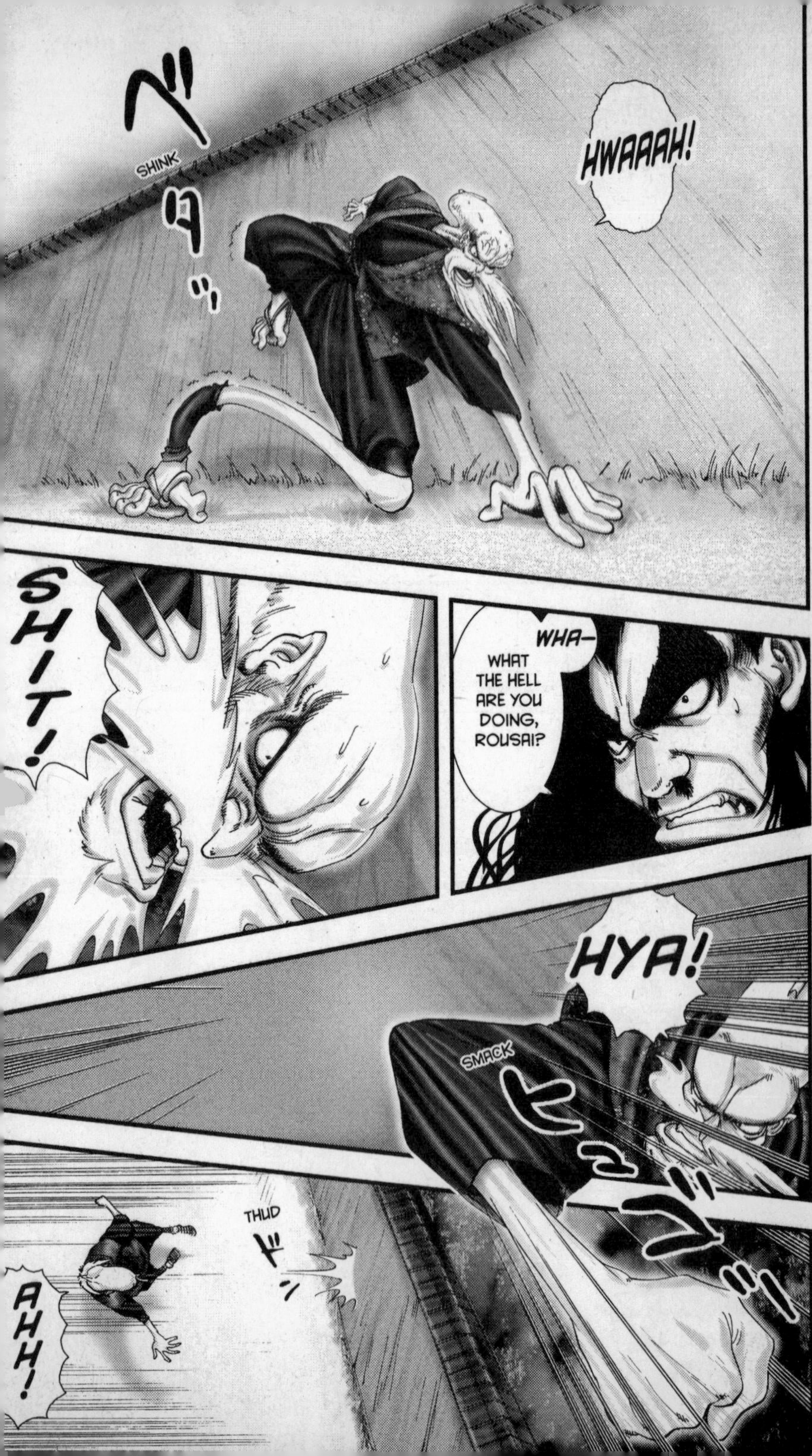
HWAAAH!
SHINK
WHA—
WHAT THE HELL ARE YOU DOING, ROUSAI?
SHIT!!
HYA!
SMACK
THUD
AHH!

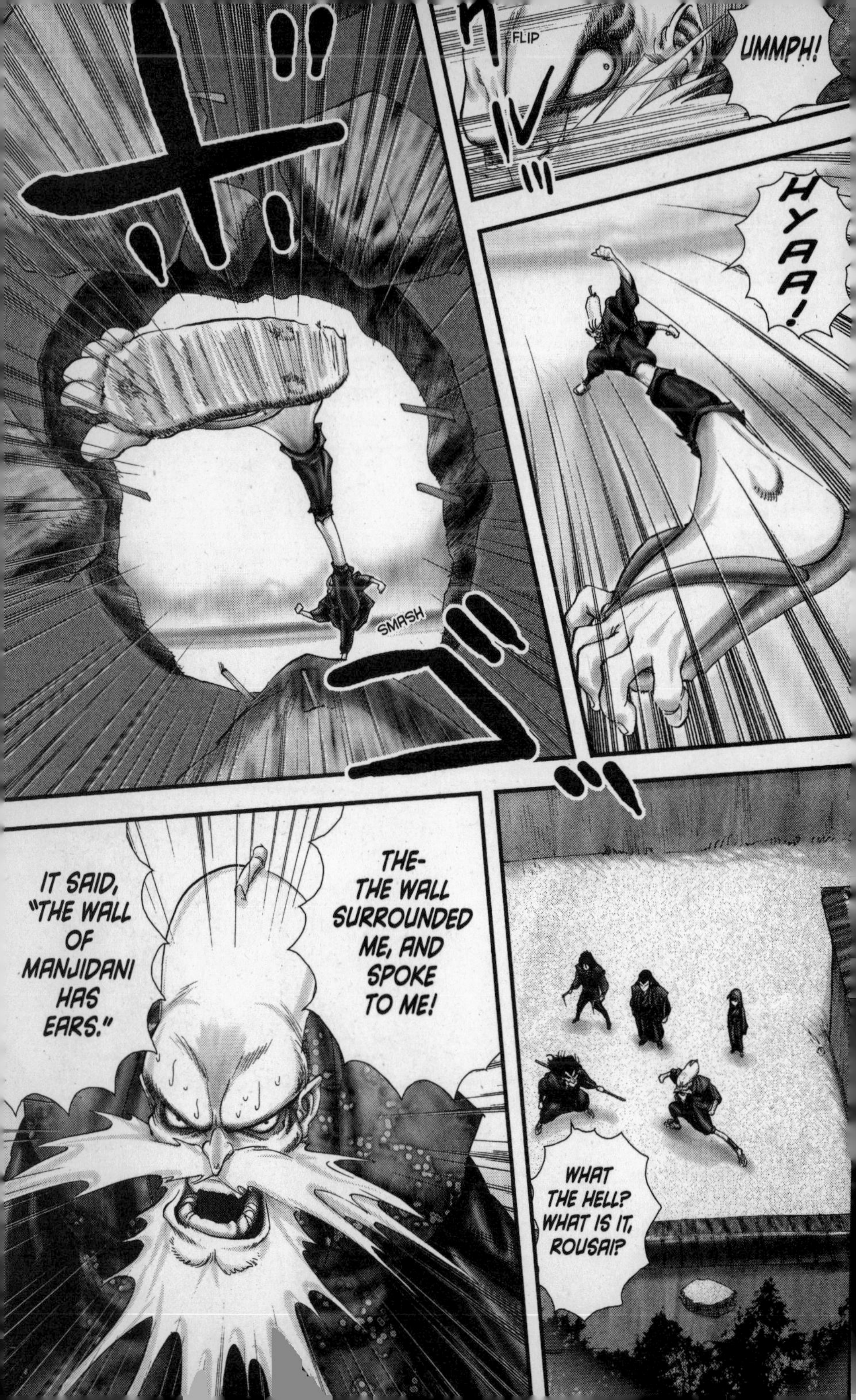
FLIP
UMMPH!
HYAA!
SMASH
WHAT THE HELL? WHAT IS IT, ROUSAI?
THE- THE WALL SURROUNDED ME, AND SPOKE TO ME!
IT SAID, "THE WALL OF MANJIDANI HAS EARS."

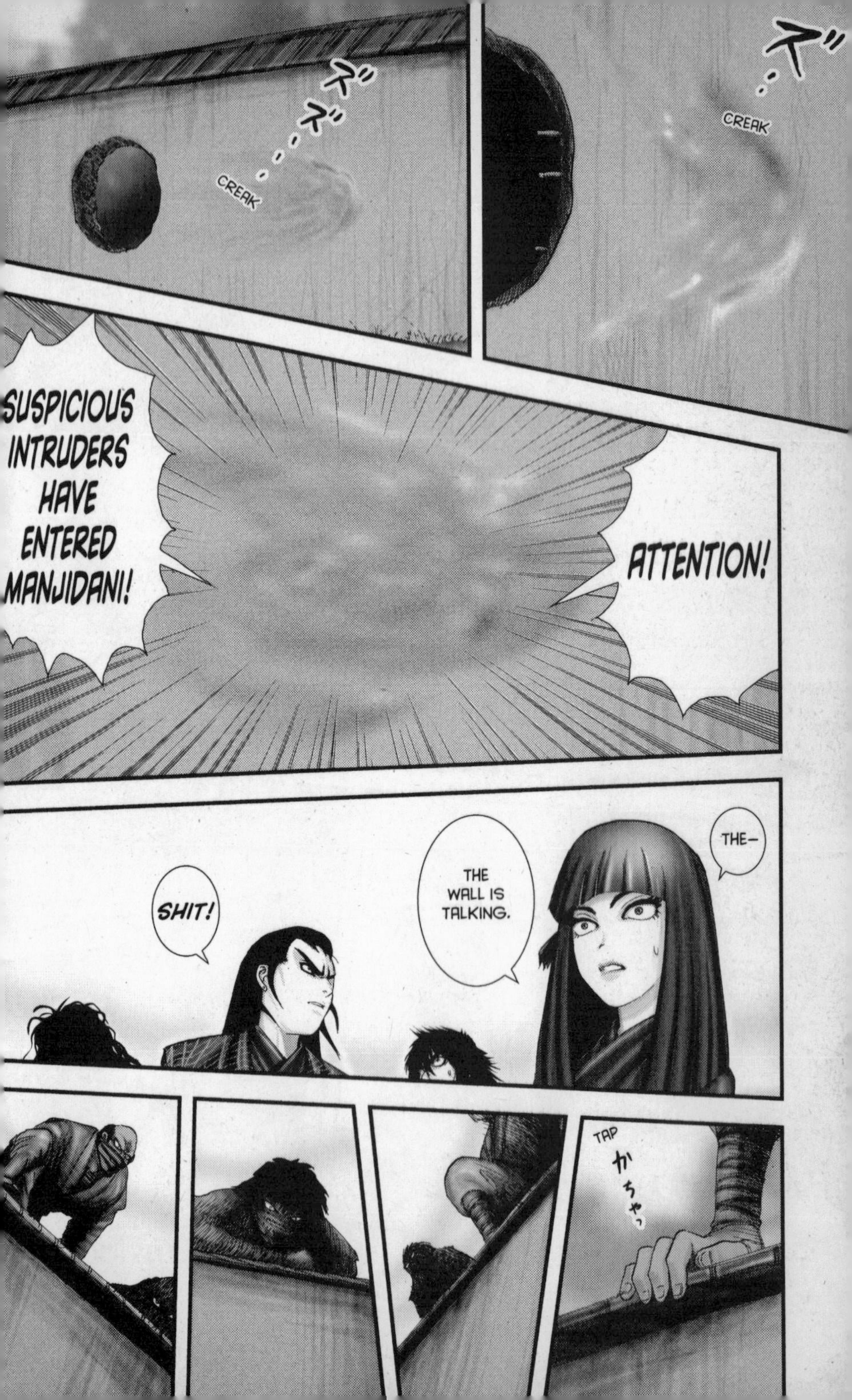
ズ・・
CREAK
ズズ・・・
CREAK
ATTENTION!
SUSPICIOUS INTRUDERS HAVE ENTERED MANJIDANI!
THE—
THE WALL IS TALKING.
SHIT!
TAP
かちゃっ

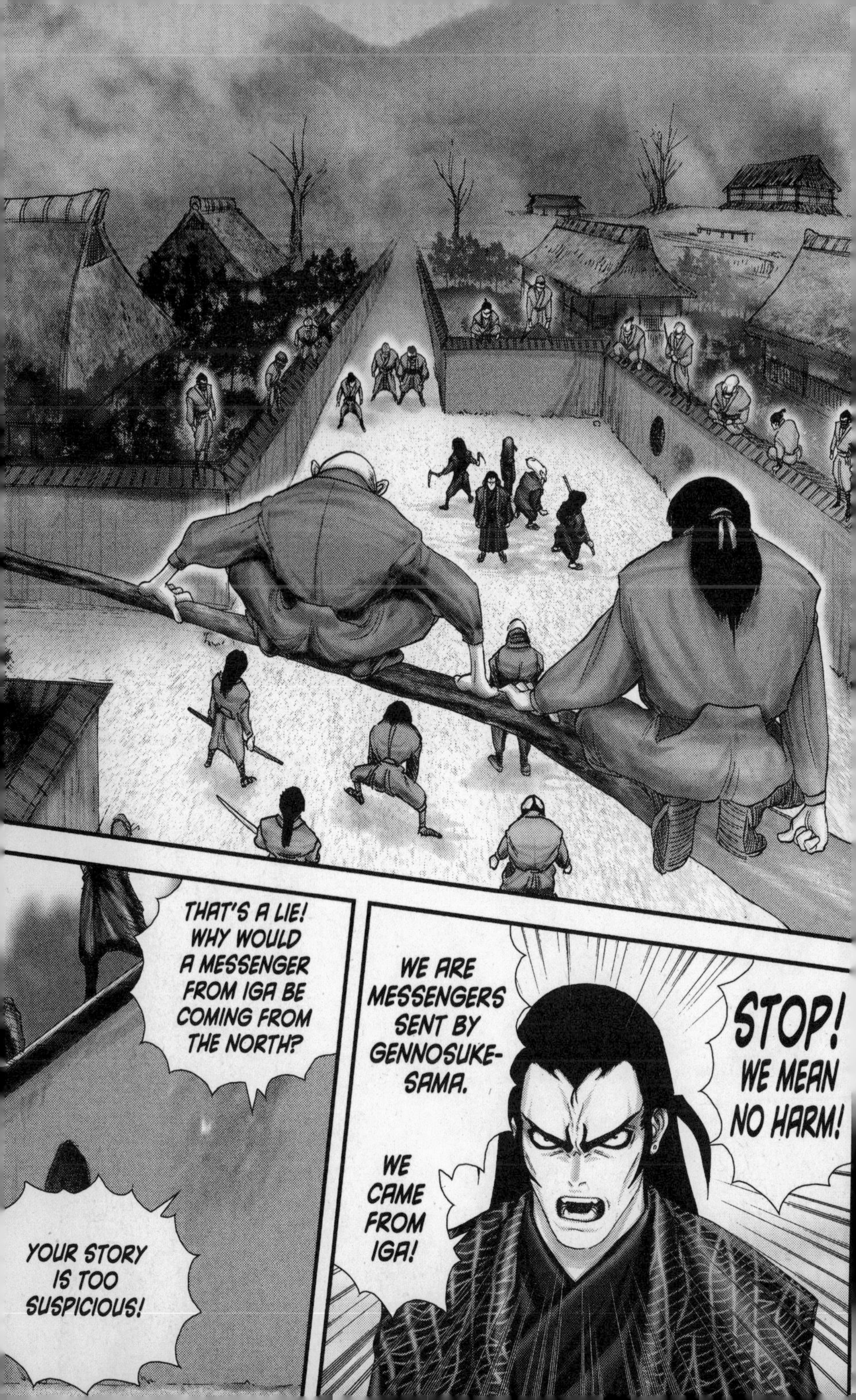
STOP! WE MEAN NO HARM!
WE ARE MESSENGERS SENT BY GENNOSUKE-SAMA.
WE CAME FROM IGA!
THAT'S A LIE! WHY WOULD A MESSENGER FROM IGA BE COMING FROM THE NORTH?
YOUR STORY IS TOO SUSPICIOUS!

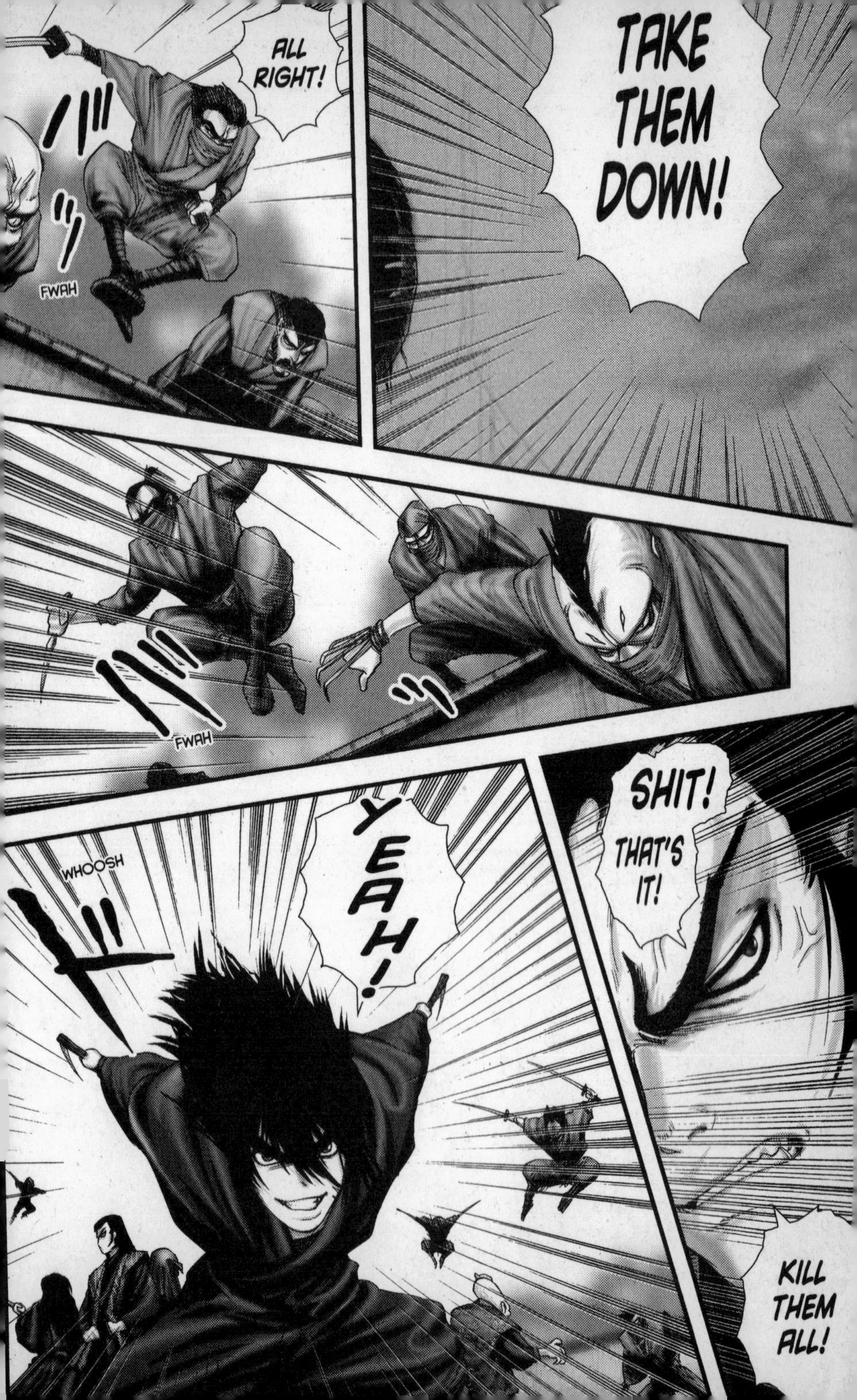
TAKE THEM DOWN!
ALL RIGHT!
FWAH
FWAH
SHIT!
THAT'S IT!
KILL THEM ALL!
YEAH!
WHOOSH

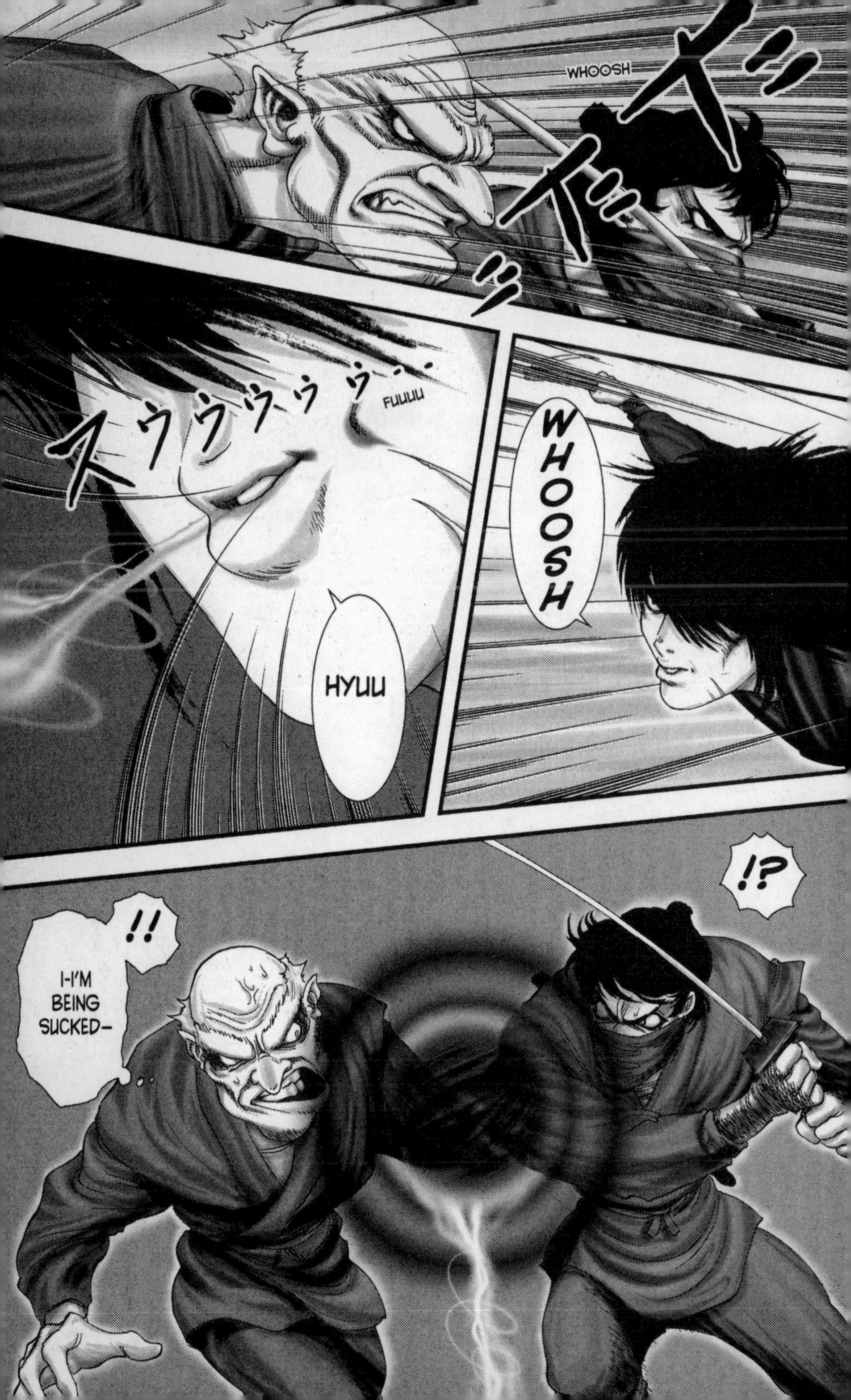
WHOOSH
WHOOSH
スウウウウウ
FUUUU
HYUU
!?
!!
I-I'M BEING SUCKED—

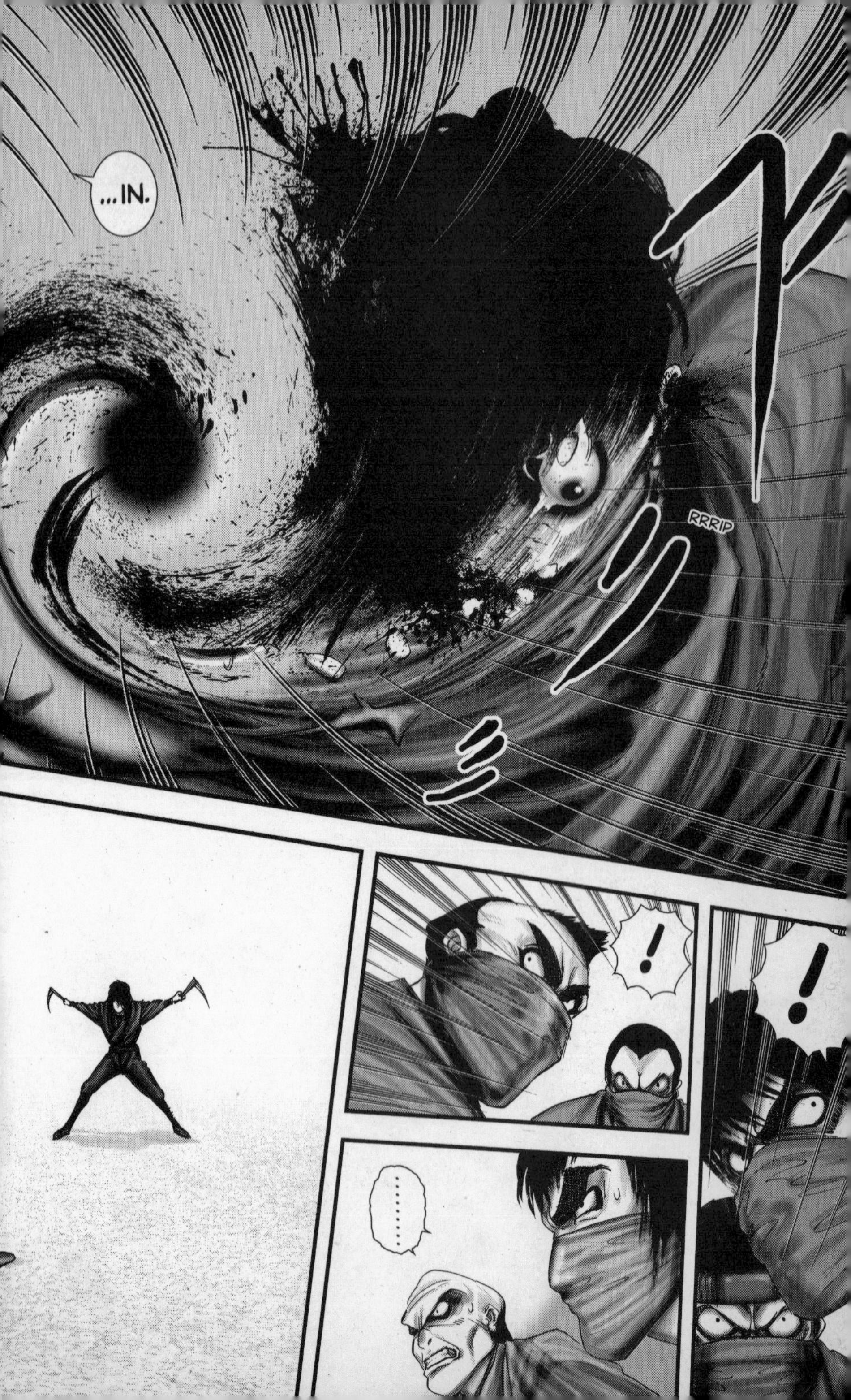
...IN.
RRRIP
!
!
......

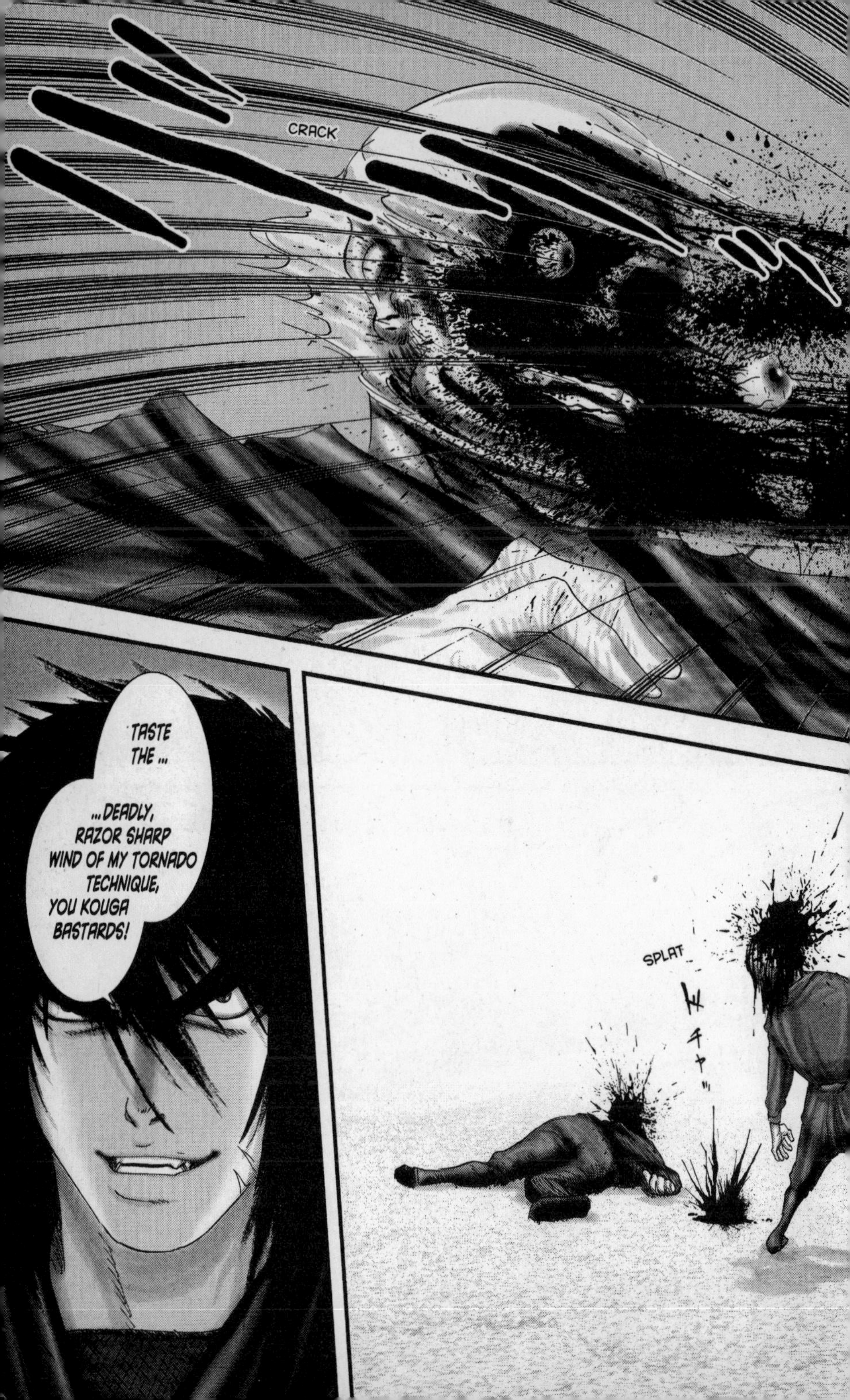
CRACK
SPLAT
ドチャッ
TASTE THE ...
...DEADLY, RAZOR SHARP WIND OF MY TORNADO TECHNIQUE, YOU KOUGA BASTARDS!

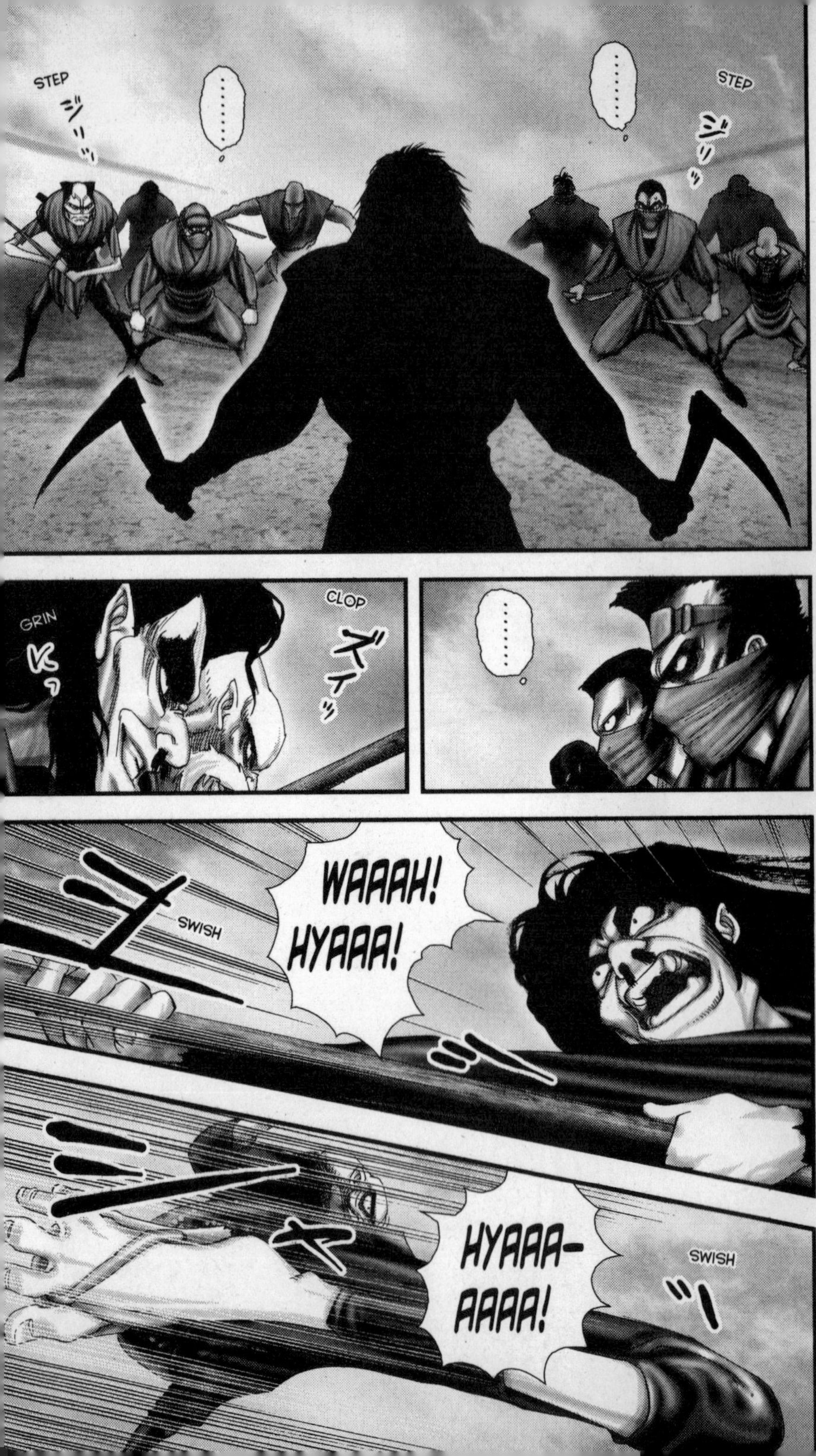
STEP
……
……
STEP
……
CLOP
GRIN
WAAAH! HYAAA!
SWISH
SWISH
HYAAA-AAAA!

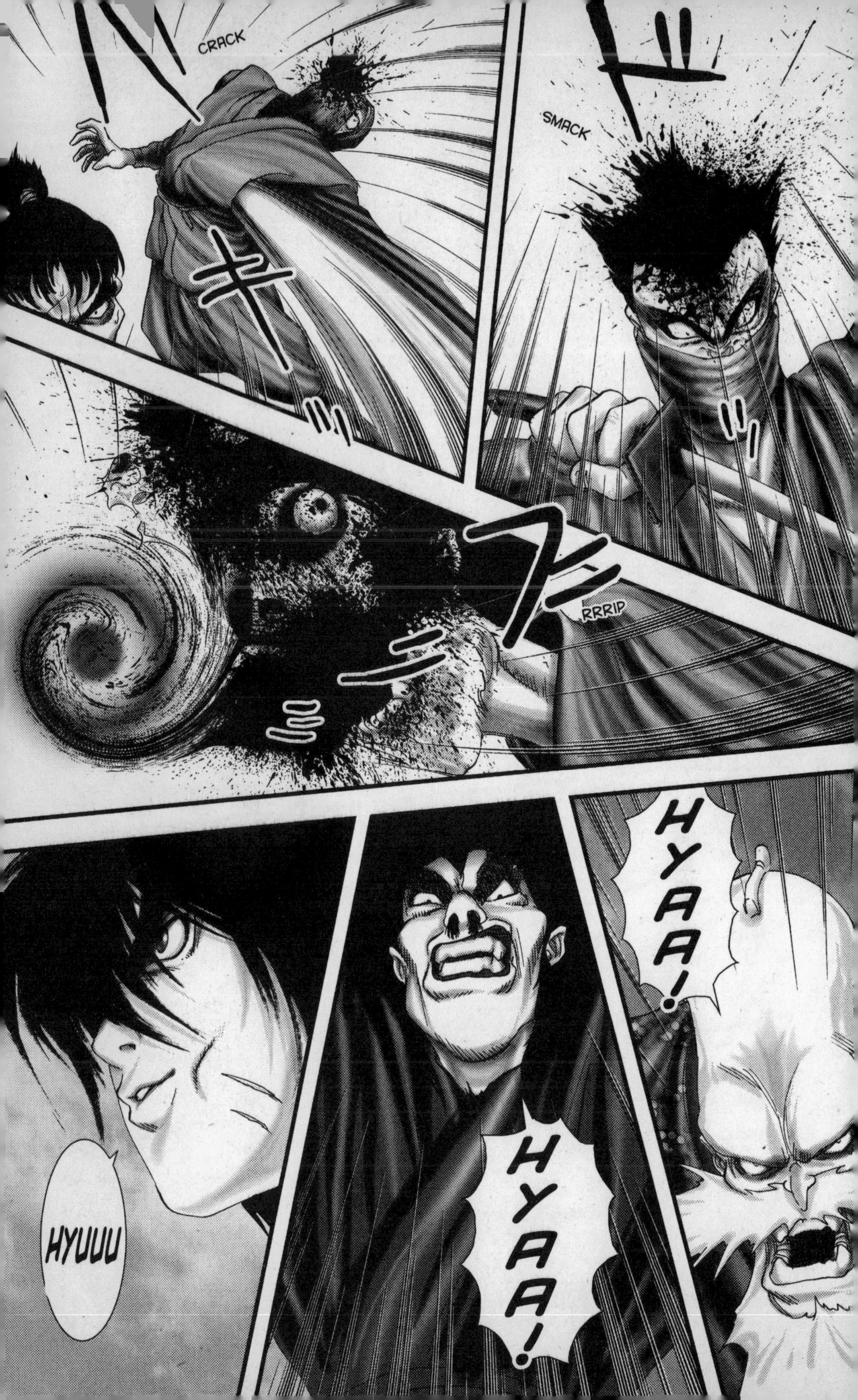
SMACK
CRACK
RRRIP
HYAAA!
HYAAA!
HYUUU

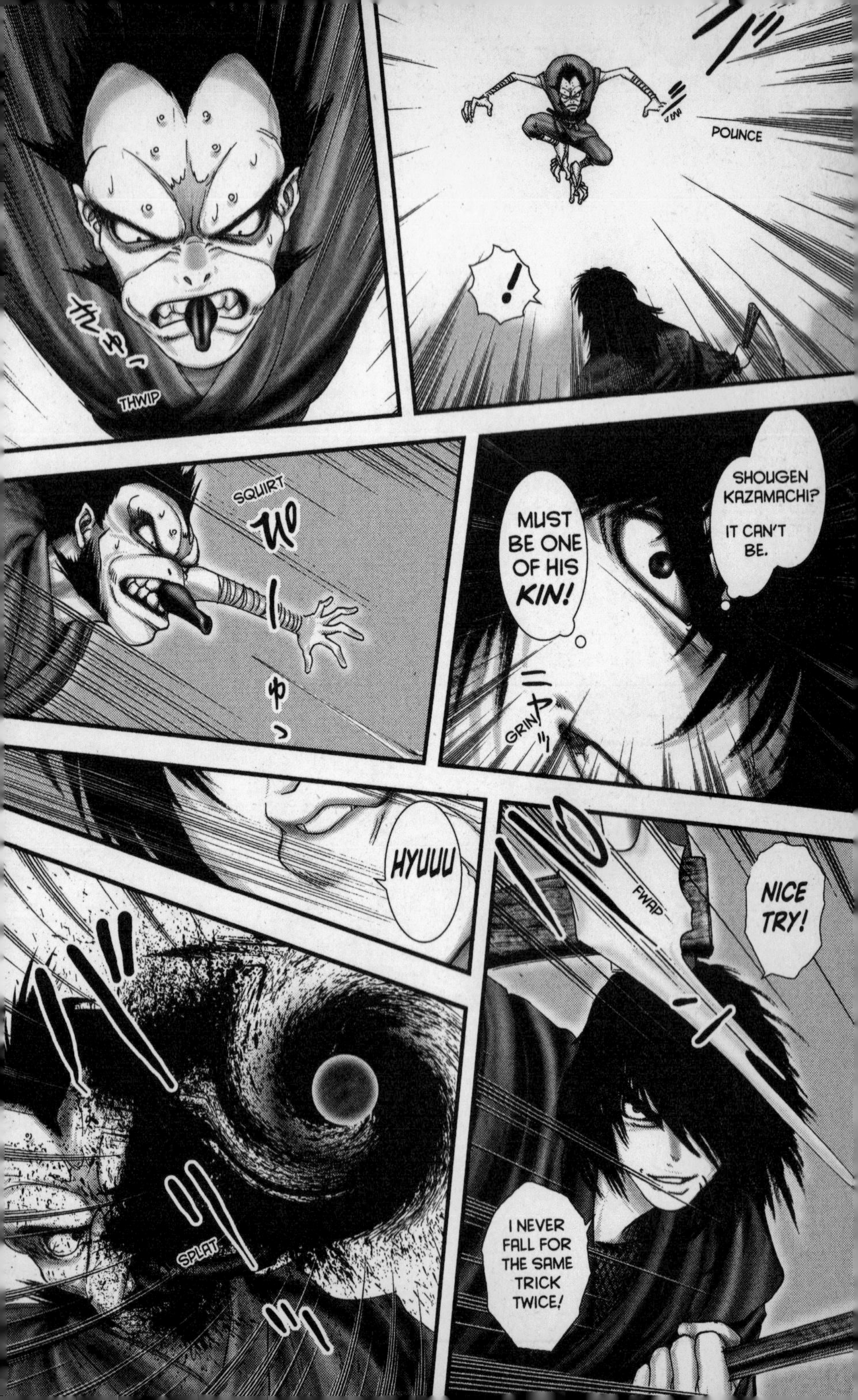
POUNCE
!
THWIP
SHOUGEN KAZAMACHI? IT CAN'T BE.
MUST BE ONE OF HIS *KIN!*
GRIN
SQUIRT
NICE TRY!
FWAP
I NEVER FALL FOR THE SAME TRICK TWICE!
HYUUU
SPLAT

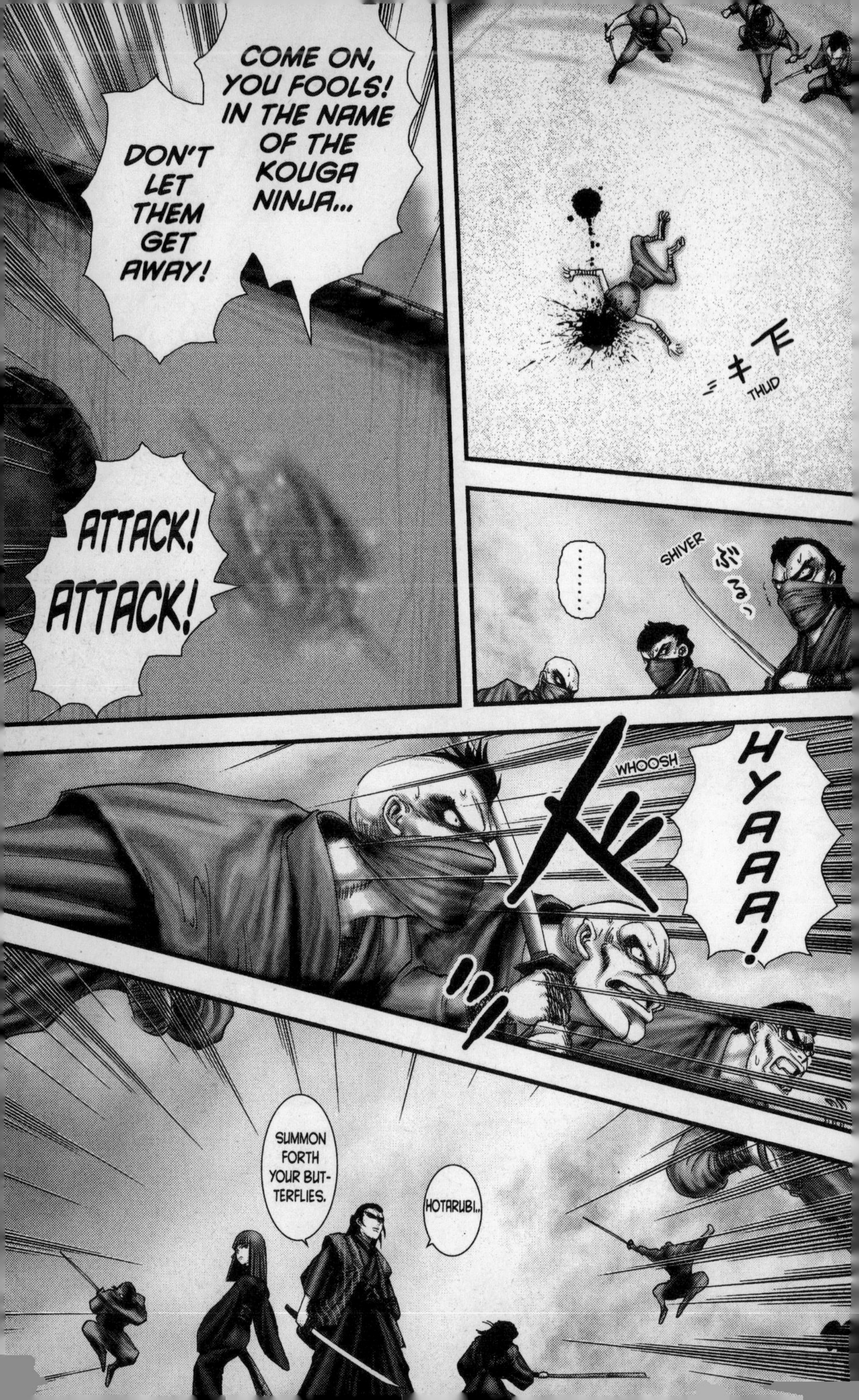

THUD
......
SHIVER
ぶるっ
COME ON, YOU FOOLS! IN THE NAME OF THE KOUGA NINJA...
DON'T LET THEM GET AWAY!
ATTACK! ATTACK!
HYAAAA!
WHOOSH
HOTARUBI...
SUMMON FORTH YOUR BUT-TERFLIES.

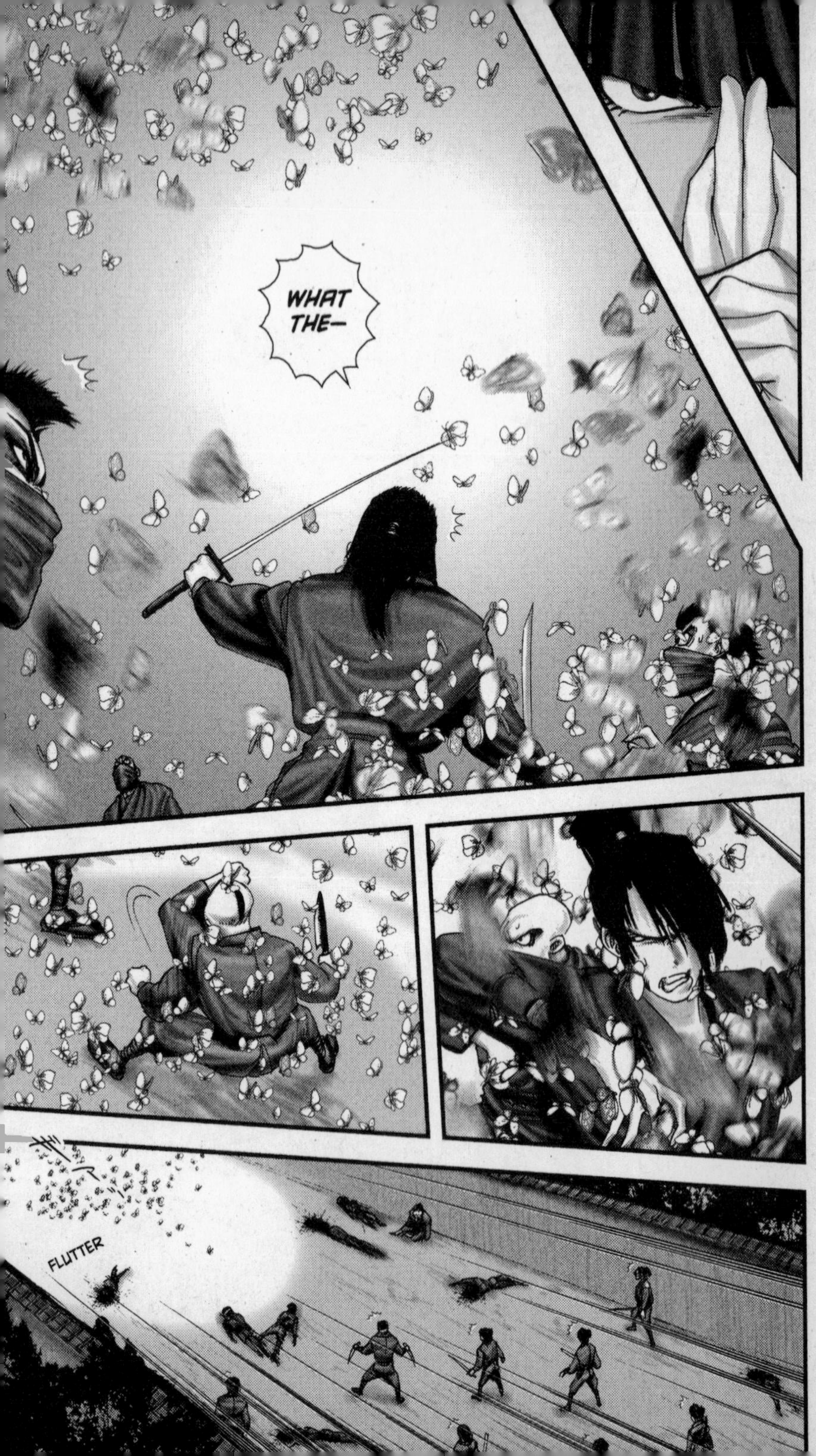
WHAT THE—
FLUTTER

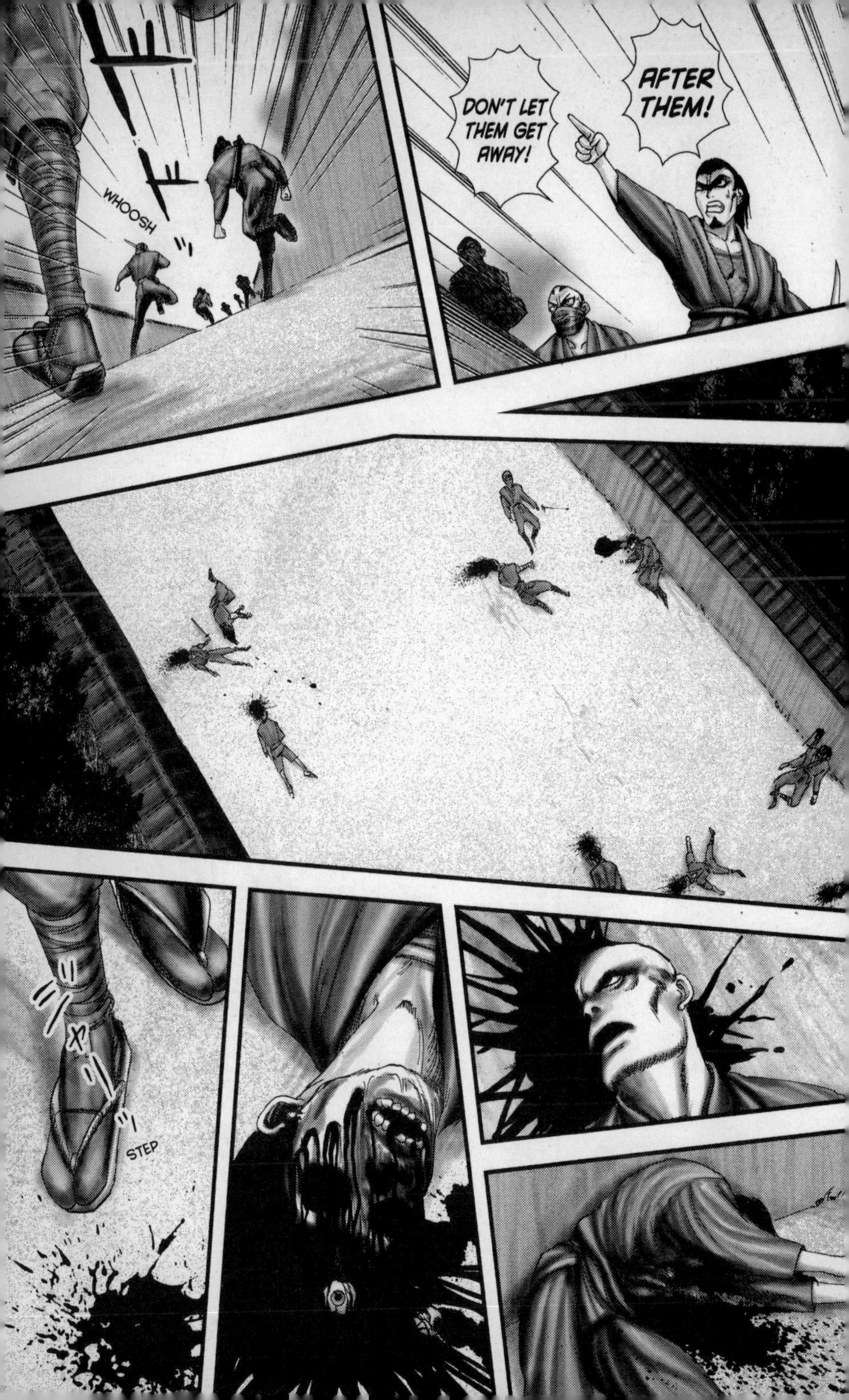
AFTER THEM!
DON'T LET THEM GET AWAY!
WHOOSH
STEP

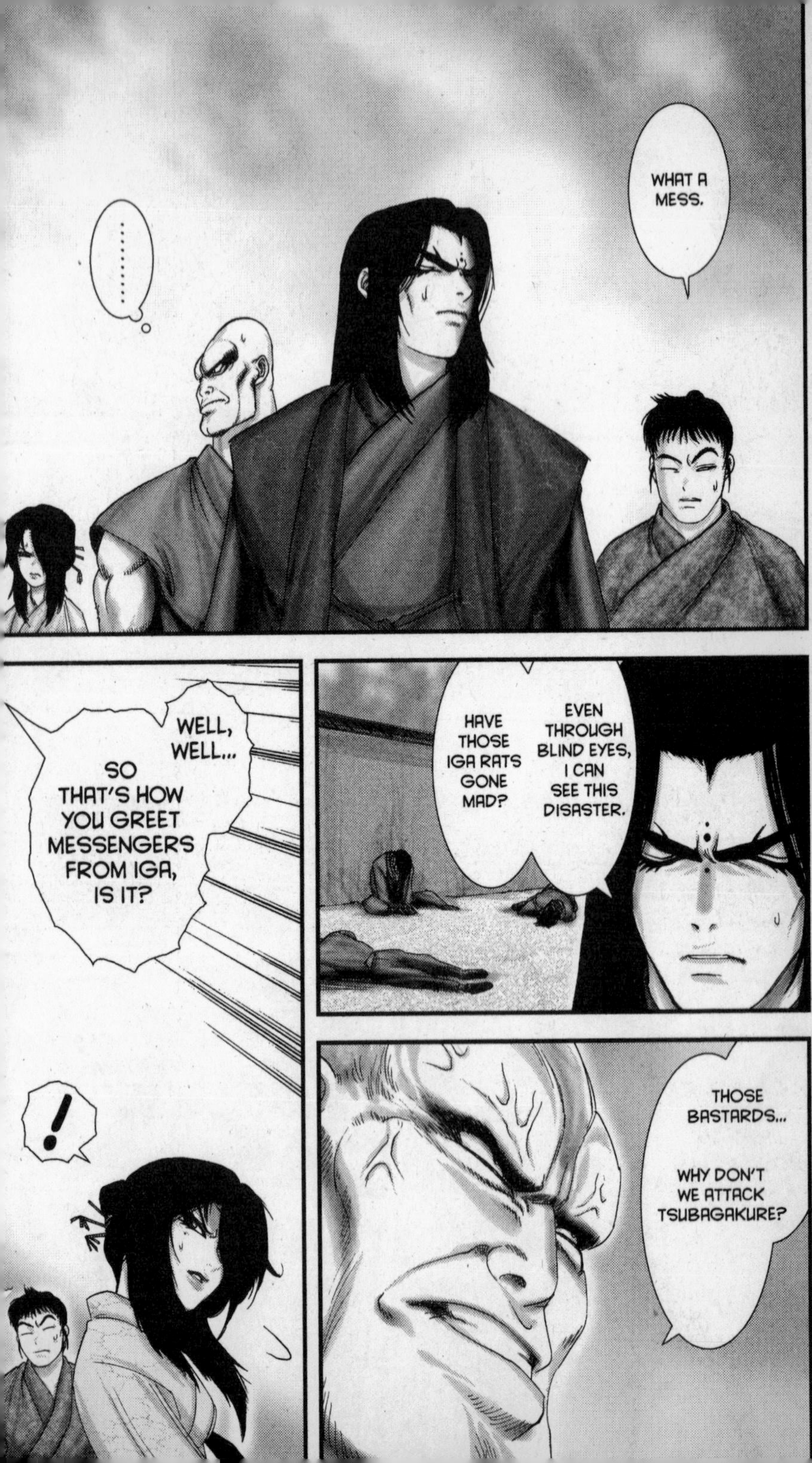
WHAT A MESS.
......
EVEN THROUGH BLIND EYES, I CAN SEE THIS DISASTER.
HAVE THOSE IGA RATS GONE MAD?
THOSE BASTARDS...
WHY DON'T WE ATTACK TSUBAGAKURE?
WELL, WELL...
SO THAT'S HOW YOU GREET MESSENGERS FROM IGA, IS IT?
!

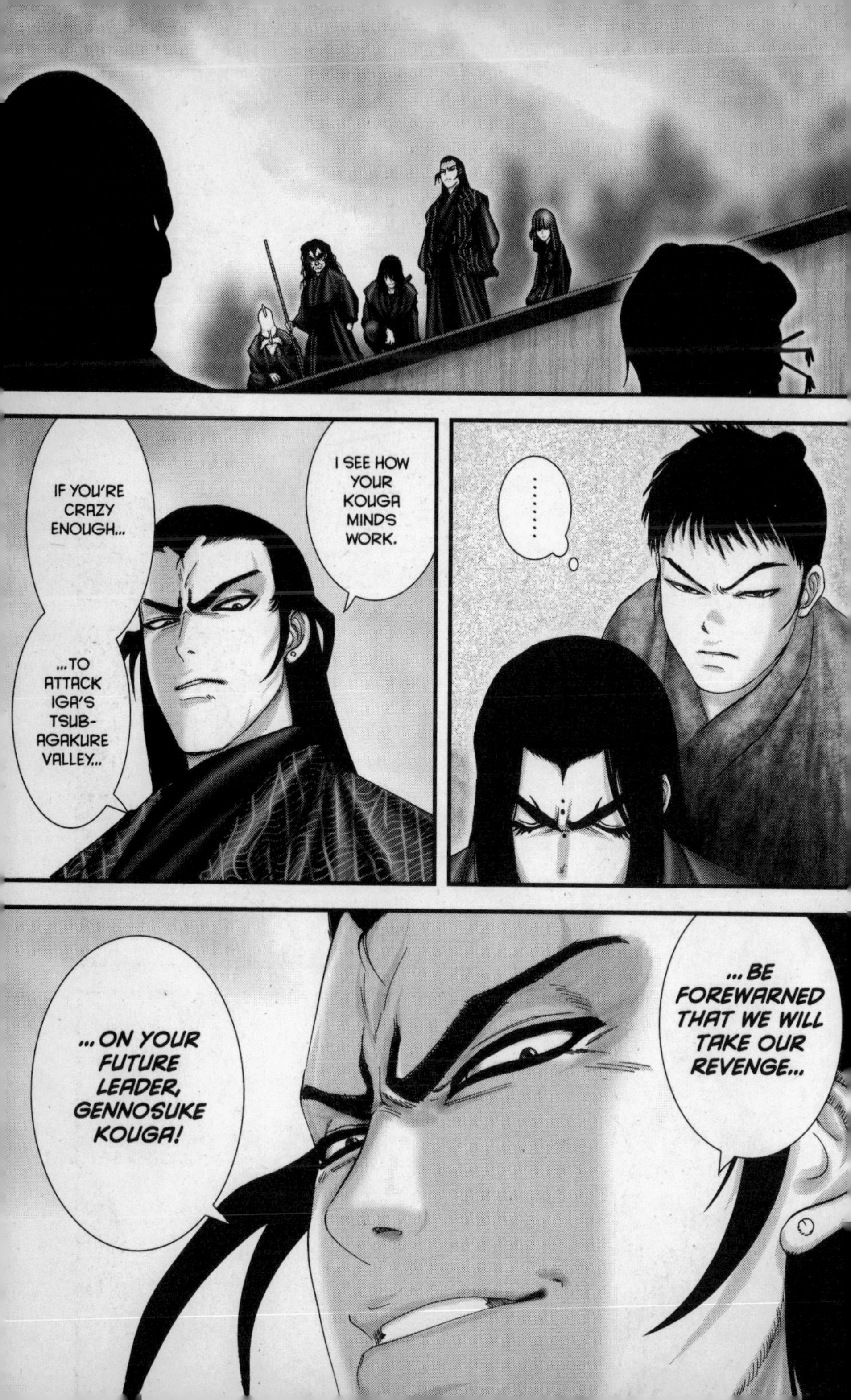
......
I SEE HOW YOUR KOUGA MINDS WORK.
IF YOU'RE CRAZY ENOUGH...
...TO ATTACK IGA'S TSUB-AGAKURE VALLEY...
...BE FOREWARNED THAT WE WILL TAKE OUR REVENGE...
...ON YOUR FUTURE LEADER, GENNOSUKE KOUGA!

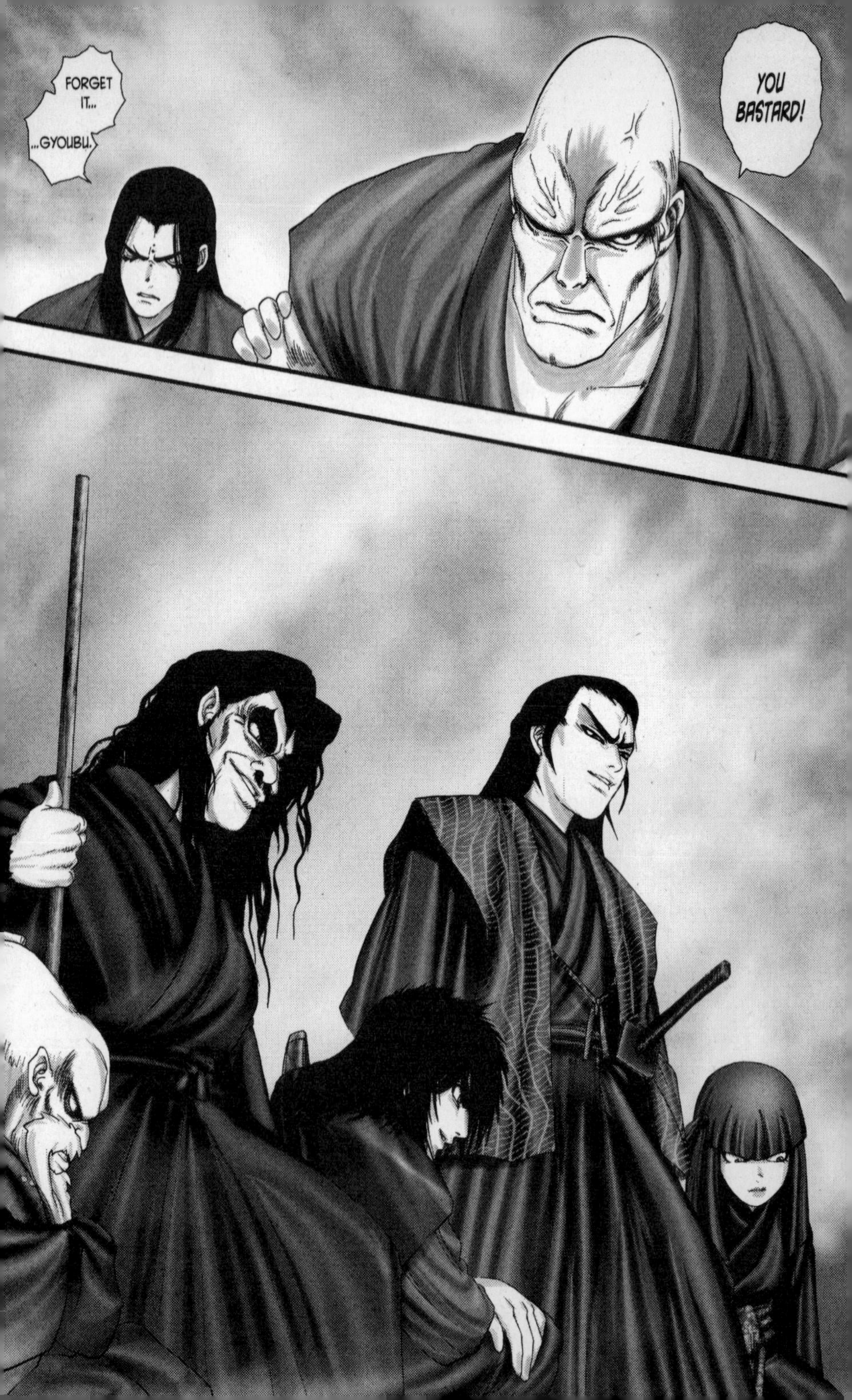
YOU BASTARD!
FORGET IT...
...GYOUBU.

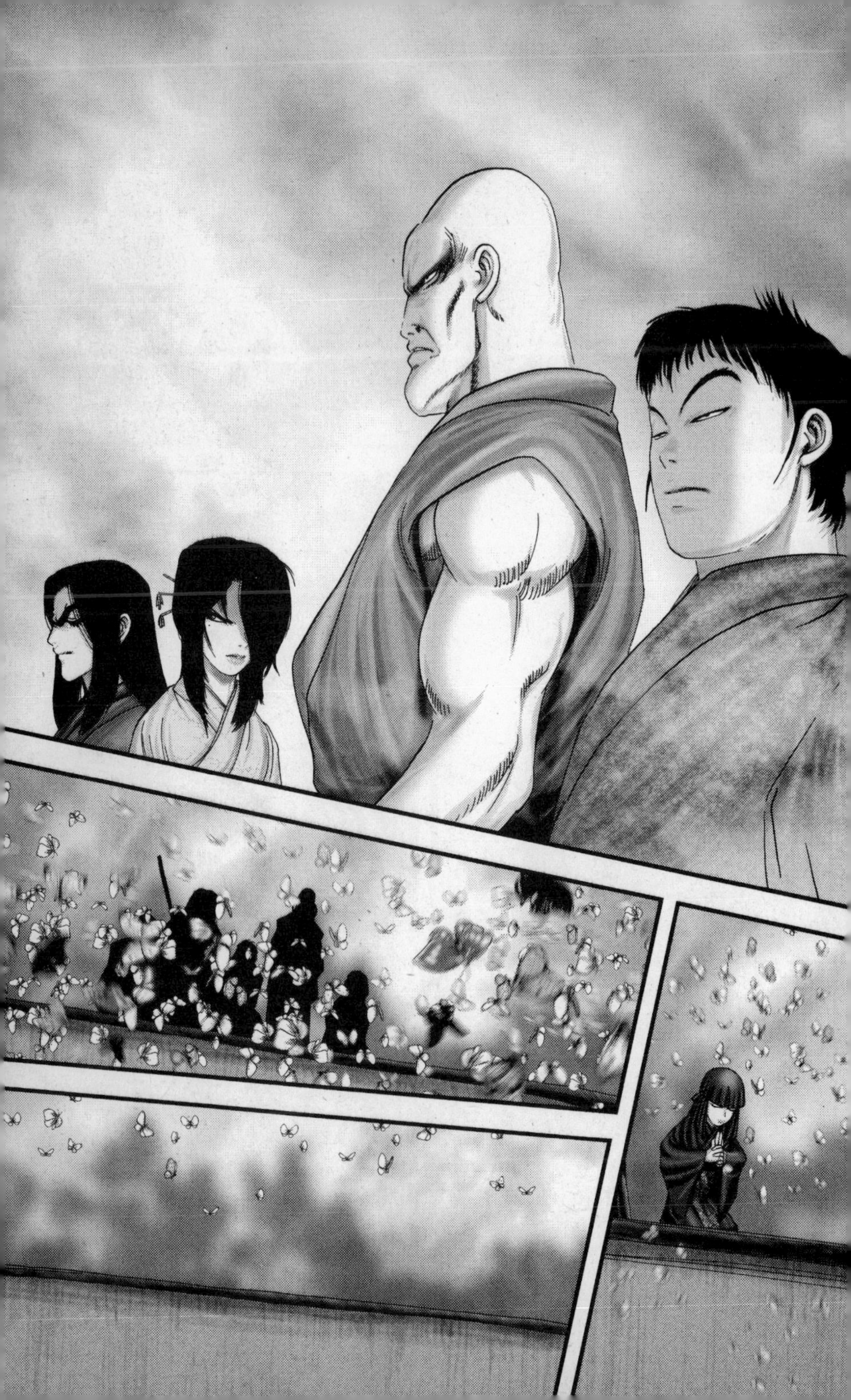

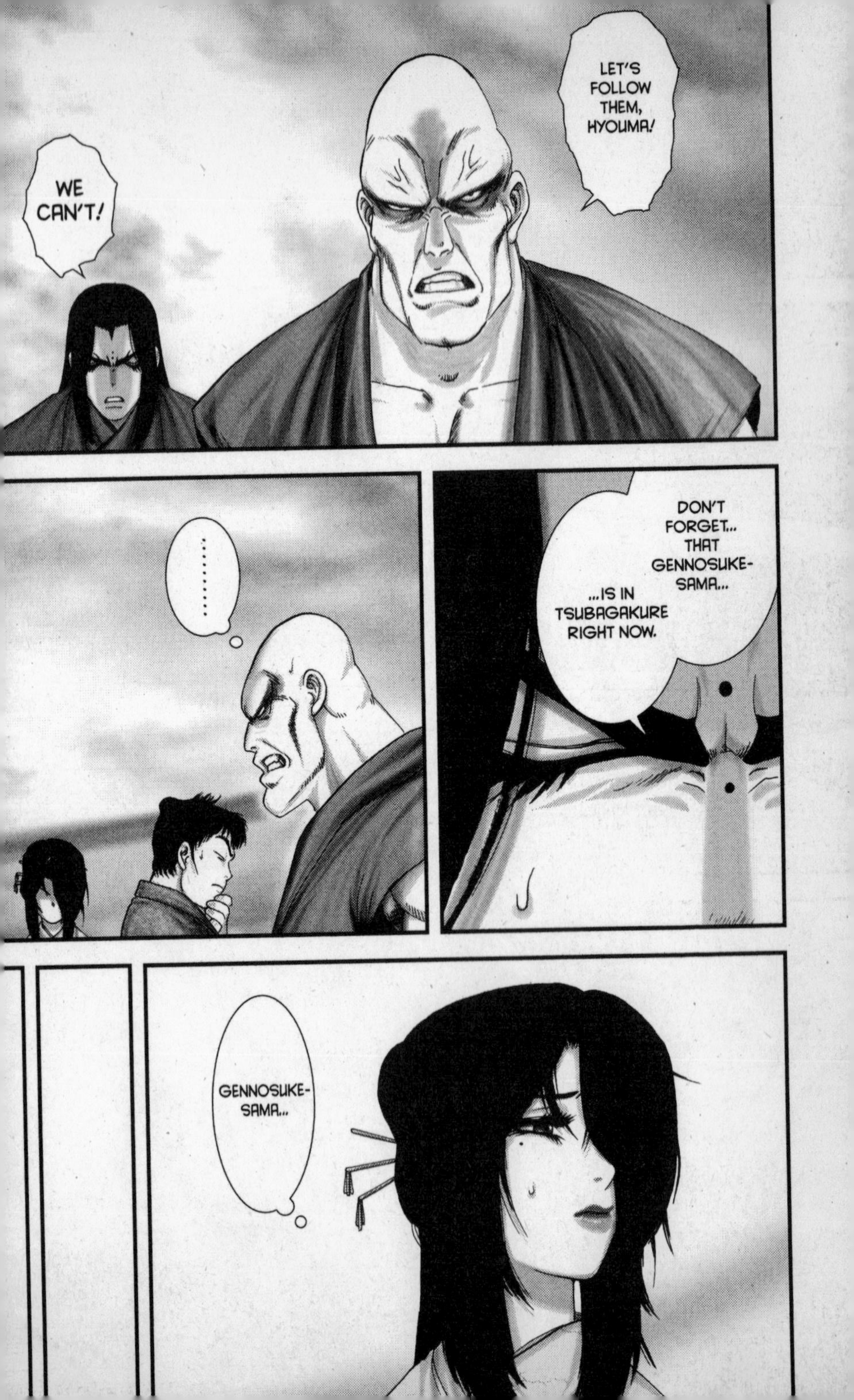
LET'S FOLLOW THEM, HYOUMA!
WE CAN'T!
DON'T FORGET... THAT GENNOSUKE-SAMA...
...IS IN TSUBAGAKURE RIGHT NOW.
....
GENNOSUKE-SAMA...

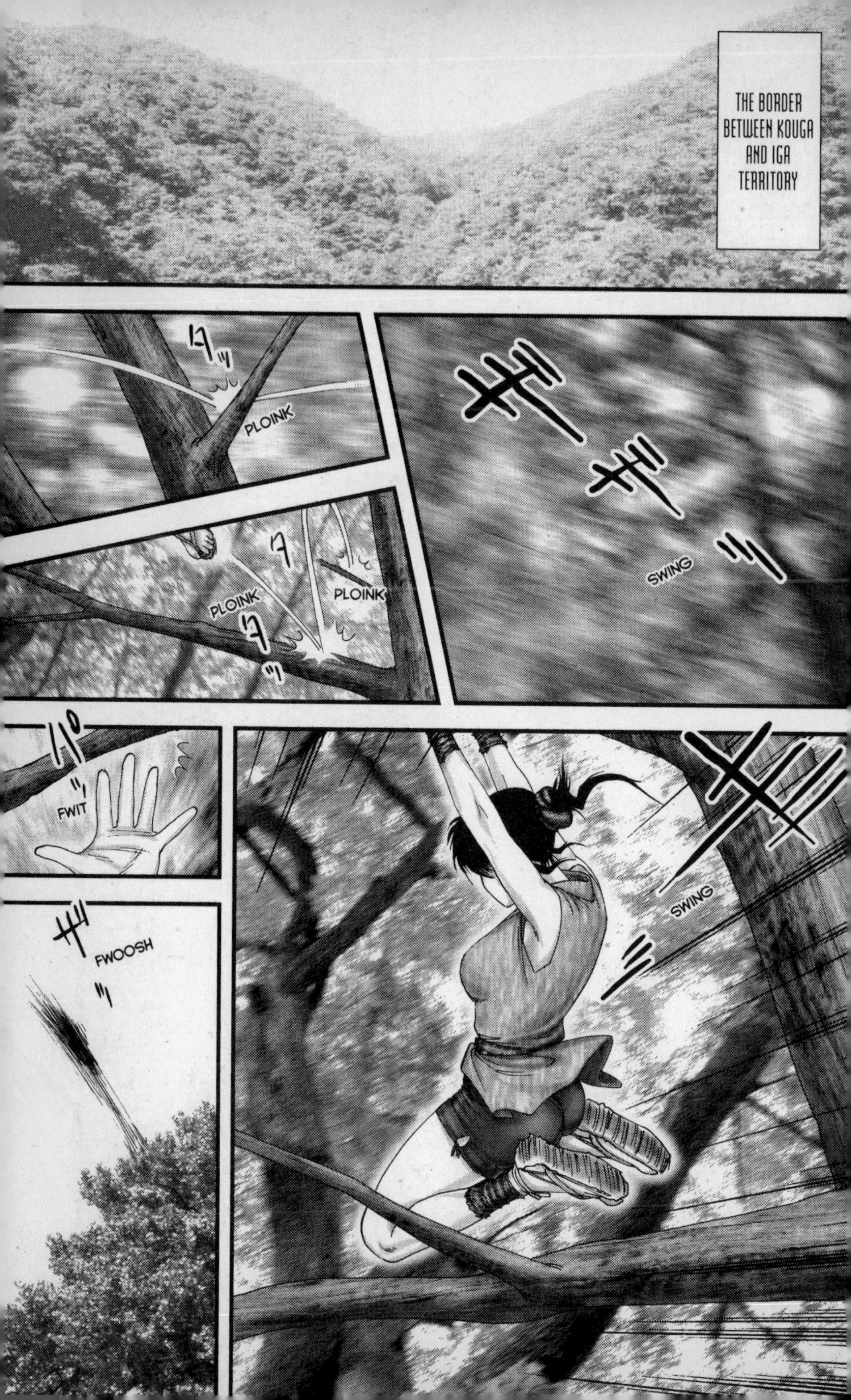
THE BORDER BETWEEN KOUGA AND IGA TERRITORY
SWING
PLOINK
PLOINK
PLOINK
SWING
FWIT
FWOOSH

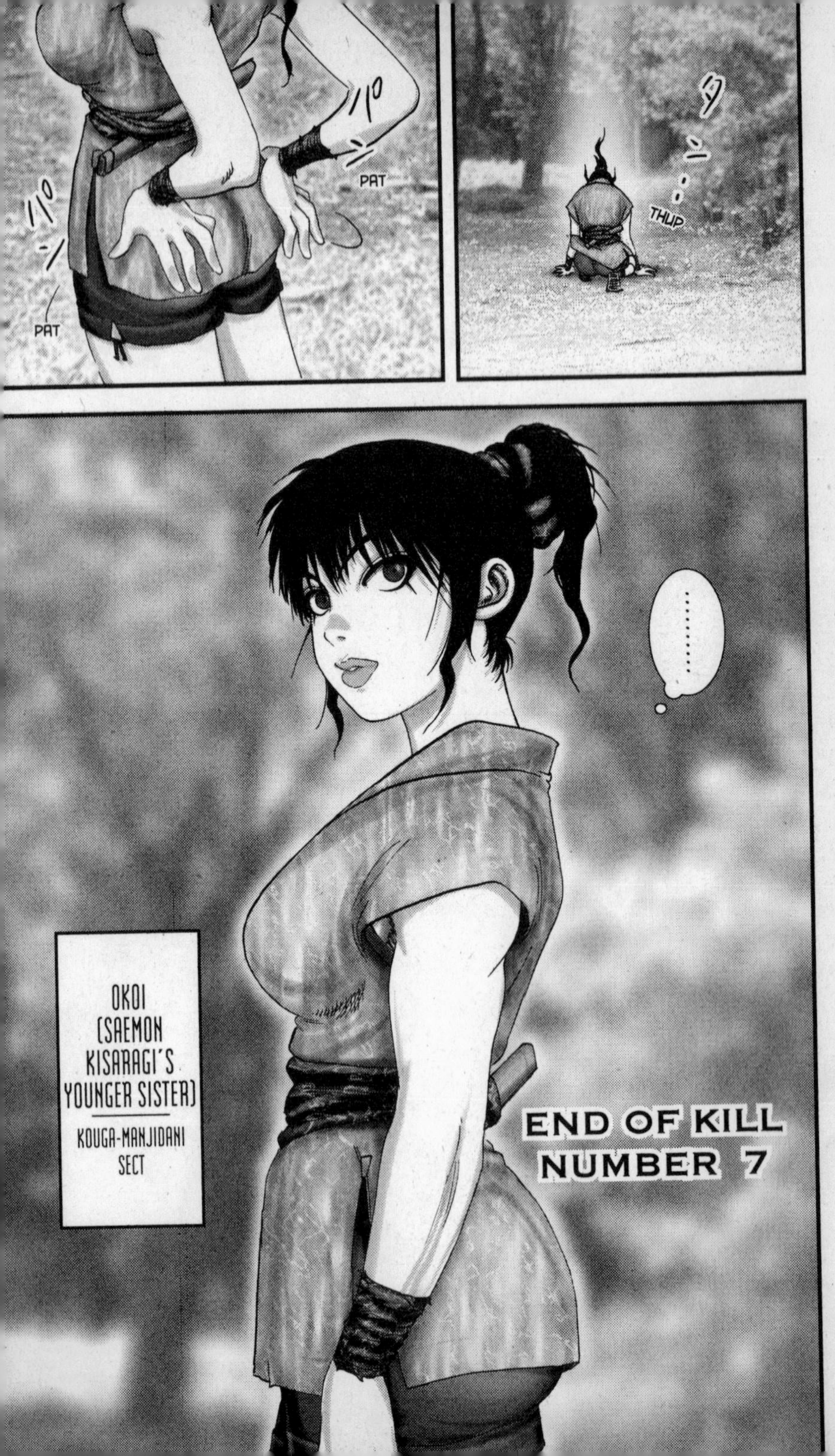
THUP
PAT
PAT
....
OKOI (SAEMON KISARAGI'S YOUNGER SISTER)
KOUGA-MANJIDANI SECT
END OF KILL NUMBER 7

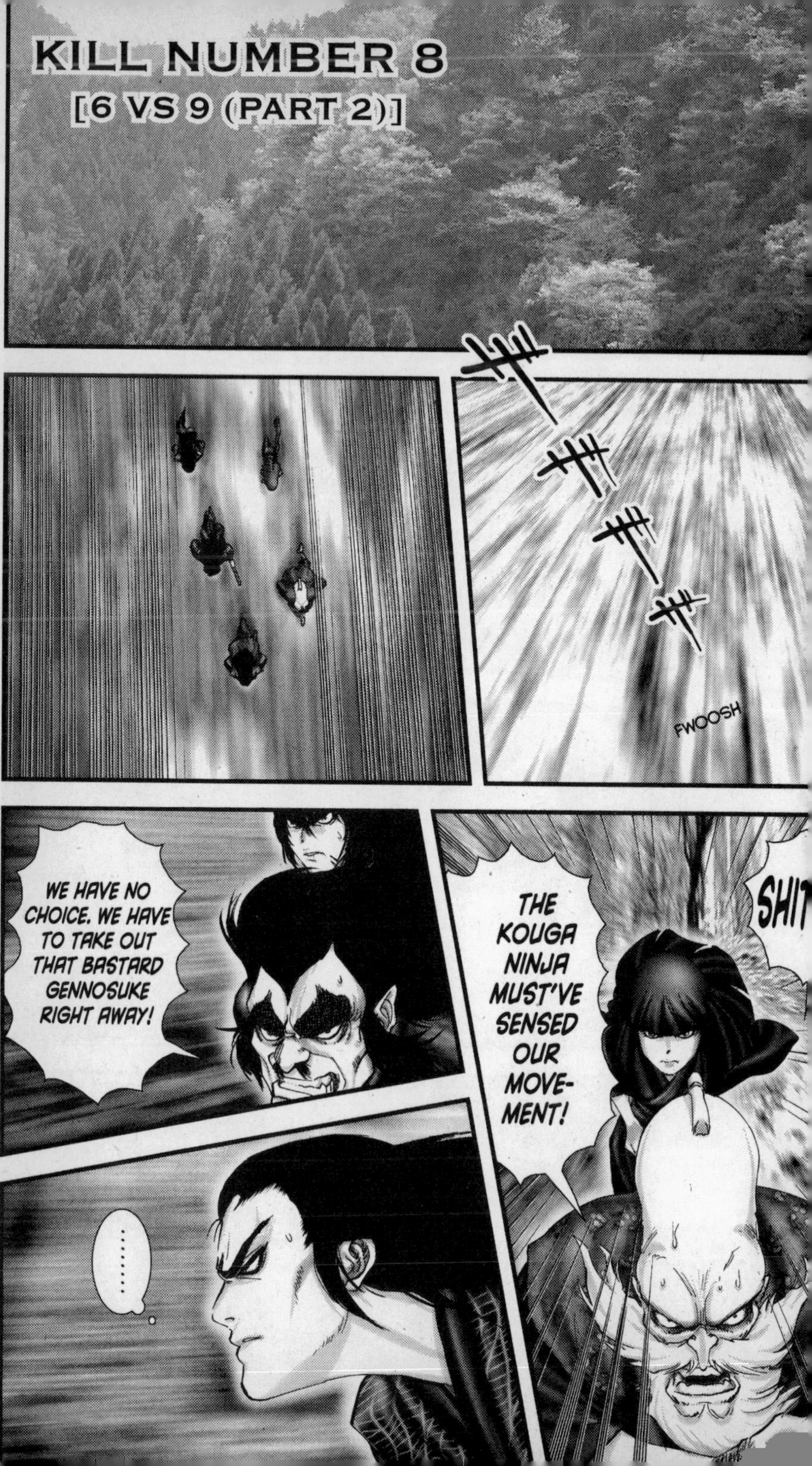
KILL NUMBER 8
[6 VS 9 (PART 2)]
FWOOSH
SHIT
THE KOUGA NINJA MUST'VE SENSED OUR MOVE-MENT!
WE HAVE NO CHOICE. WE HAVE TO TAKE OUT THAT BASTARD GENNOSUKE RIGHT AWAY!
....

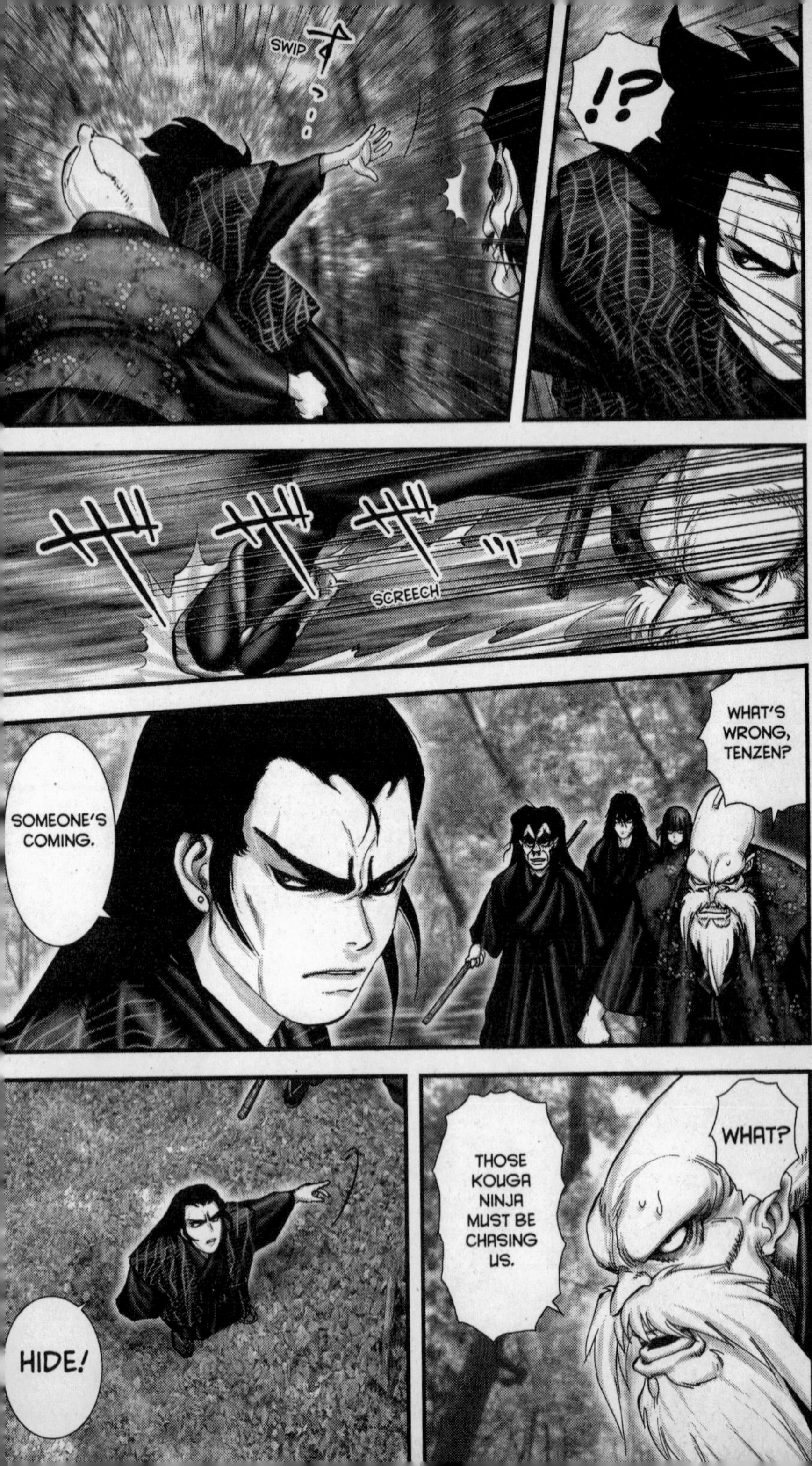
!?
SWIP
SCREECH
WHAT'S WRONG, TENZEN?
SOMEONE'S COMING.
WHAT?
THOSE KOUGA NINJA MUST BE CHASING US.
HIDE!

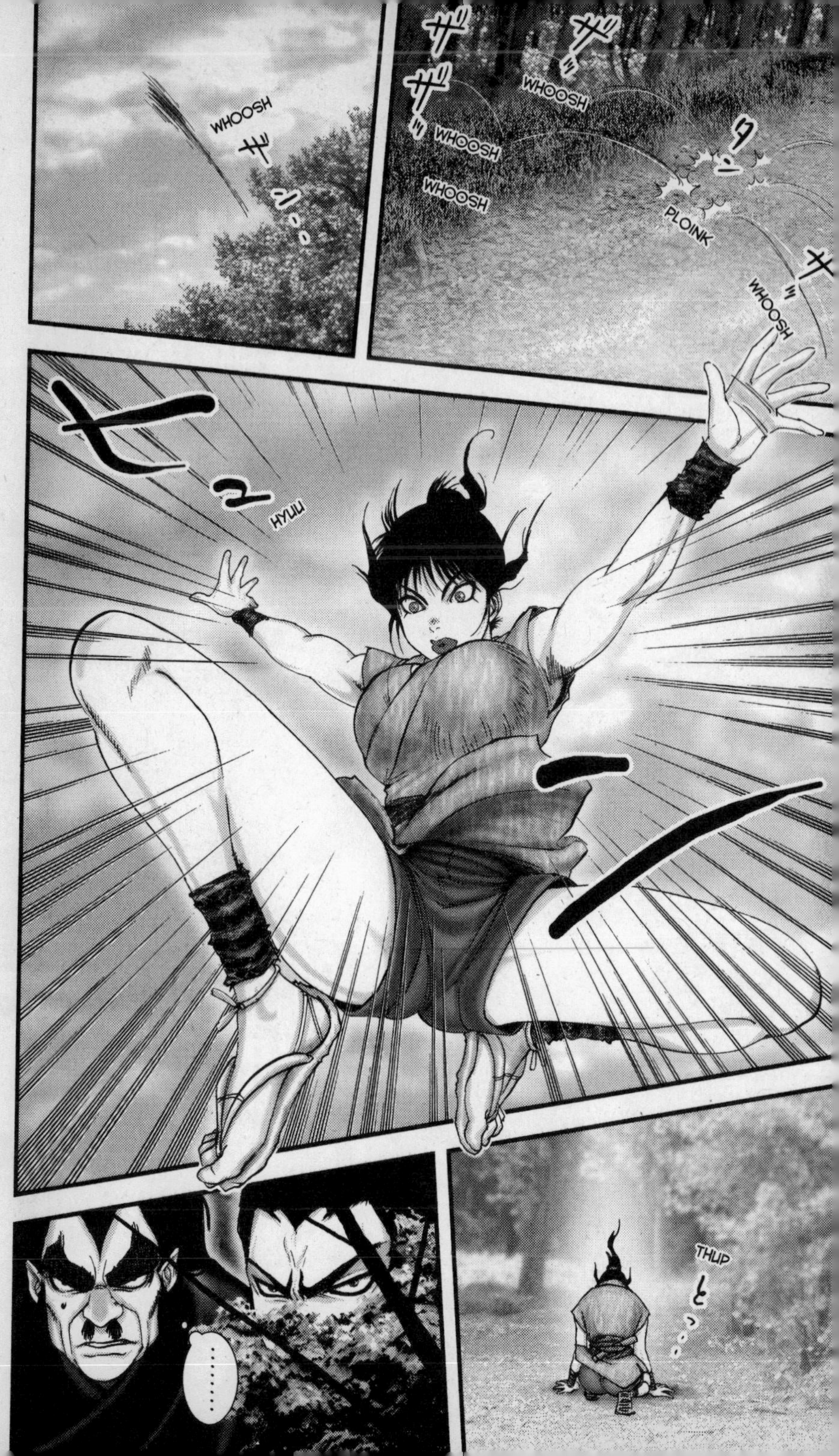
WHOOSH
WHOOSH
WHOOSH
PLOINK
WHOOSH
WHOOSH
HYUU
THUP
......

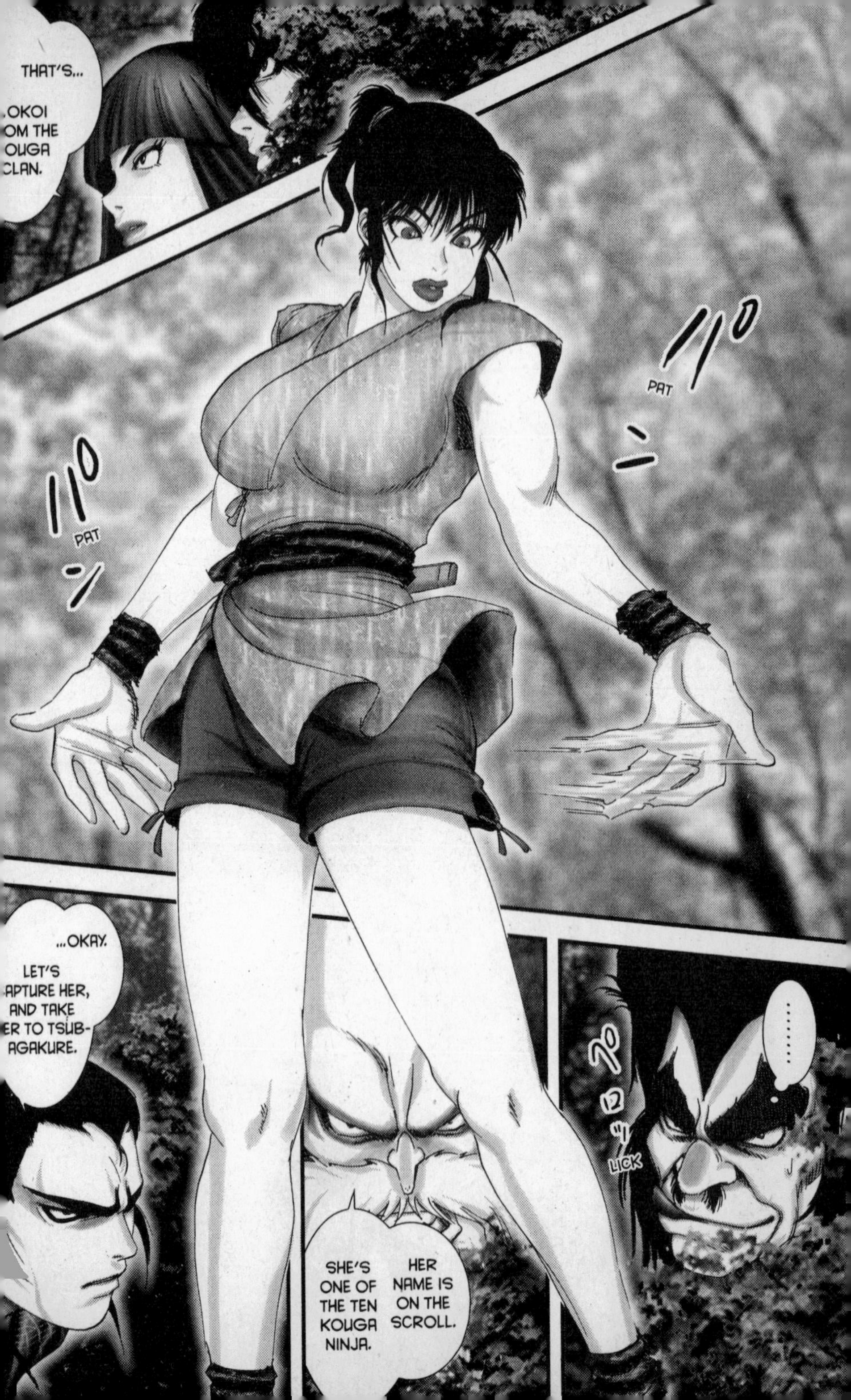
THAT'S...
.OKOI
OM THE
OUGA
CLAN.
PAT
PAT
......
LICK
HER NAME IS ON THE SCROLL.
SHE'S ONE OF THE TEN KOUGA NINJA.
...OKAY.
LET'S
APTURE HER,
AND TAKE
ER TO TSUB-
AGAKURE.

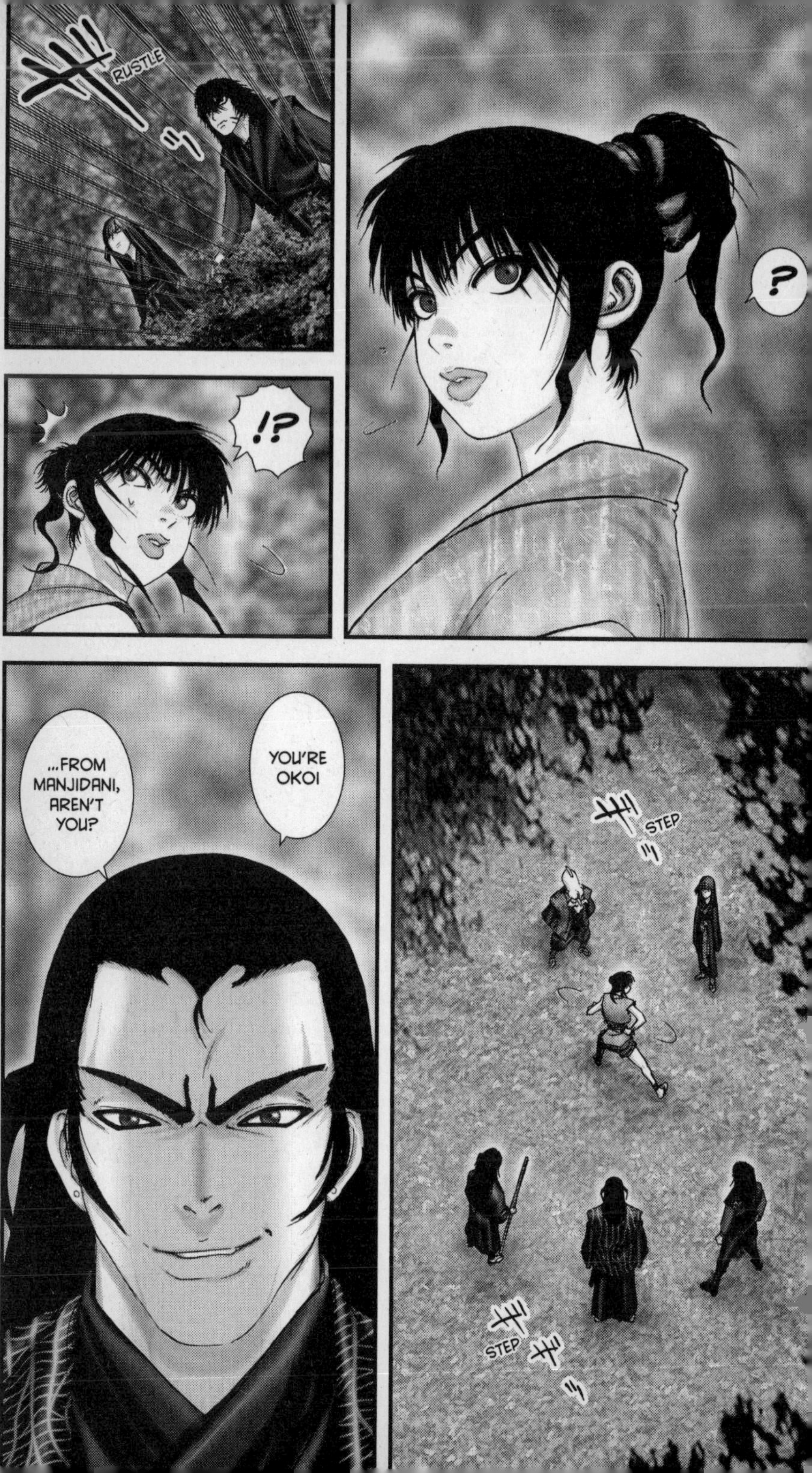
?
RUSTLE
!?
STEP
STEP
YOU'RE OKOI
...FROM MANJIDANI, AREN'T YOU?

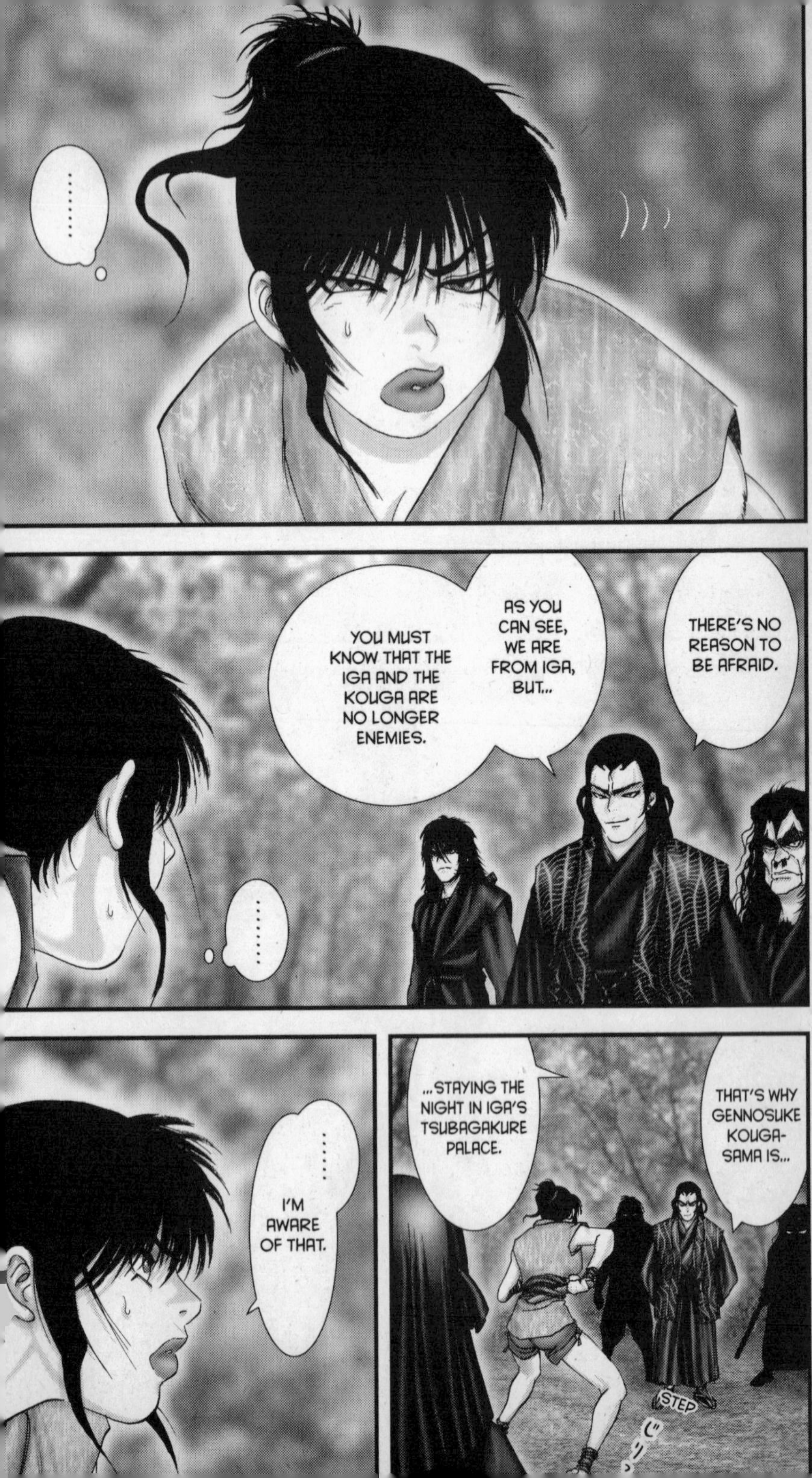
......
THERE'S NO REASON TO BE AFRAID.
AS YOU CAN SEE, WE ARE FROM IGA, BUT...
YOU MUST KNOW THAT THE IGA AND THE KOUGA ARE NO LONGER ENEMIES.
......
THAT'S WHY GENNOSUKE KOUGA-SAMA IS...
...STAYING THE NIGHT IN IGA'S TSUBAGAKURE PALACE.
STEP
......
I'M AWARE OF THAT.

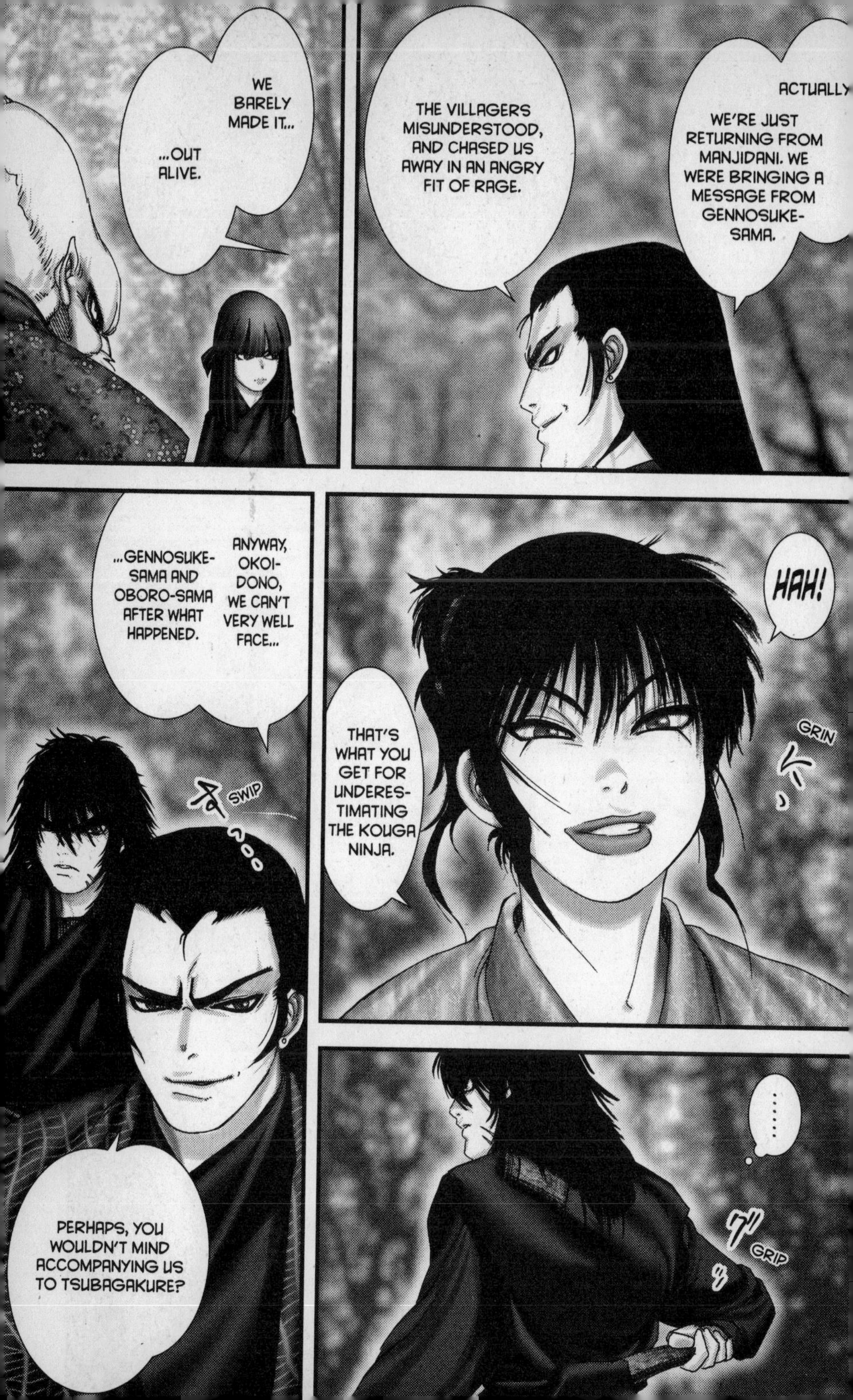
ACTUALLY
WE'RE JUST RETURNING FROM MANJIDANI. WE WERE BRINGING A MESSAGE FROM GENNOSUKE-SAMA.
THE VILLAGERS MISUNDERSTOOD, AND CHASED US AWAY IN AN ANGRY FIT OF RAGE.
WE BARELY MADE IT...
...OUT ALIVE.
HAH!
GRIN
THAT'S WHAT YOU GET FOR UNDERES-TIMATING THE KOUGA NINJA.
......
GRIP
ANYWAY, OKOI-DONO, WE CAN'T VERY WELL FACE...
...GENNOSUKE-SAMA AND OBORO-SAMA AFTER WHAT HAPPENED.
SWIP
PERHAPS, YOU WOULDN'T MIND ACCOMPANYING US TO TSUBAGAKURE?

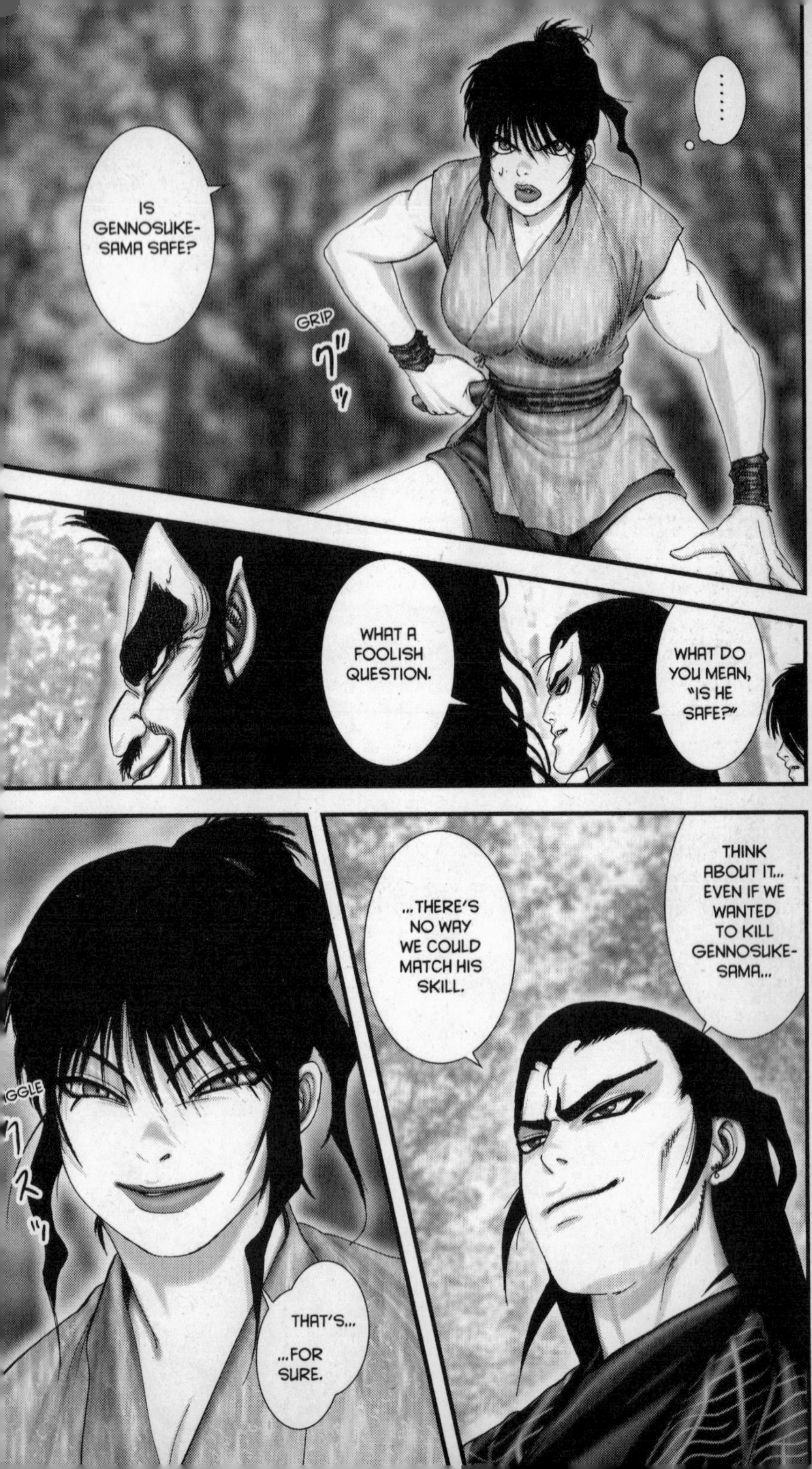
......
IS GENNOSUKE-SAMA SAFE?
GRIP
WHAT DO YOU MEAN, "IS HE SAFE?"
WHAT A FOOLISH QUESTION.
THINK ABOUT IT... EVEN IF WE WANTED TO KILL GENNOSUKE-SAMA...
...THERE'S NO WAY WE COULD MATCH HIS SKILL.
IGGLE
THAT'S...
...FOR SURE.

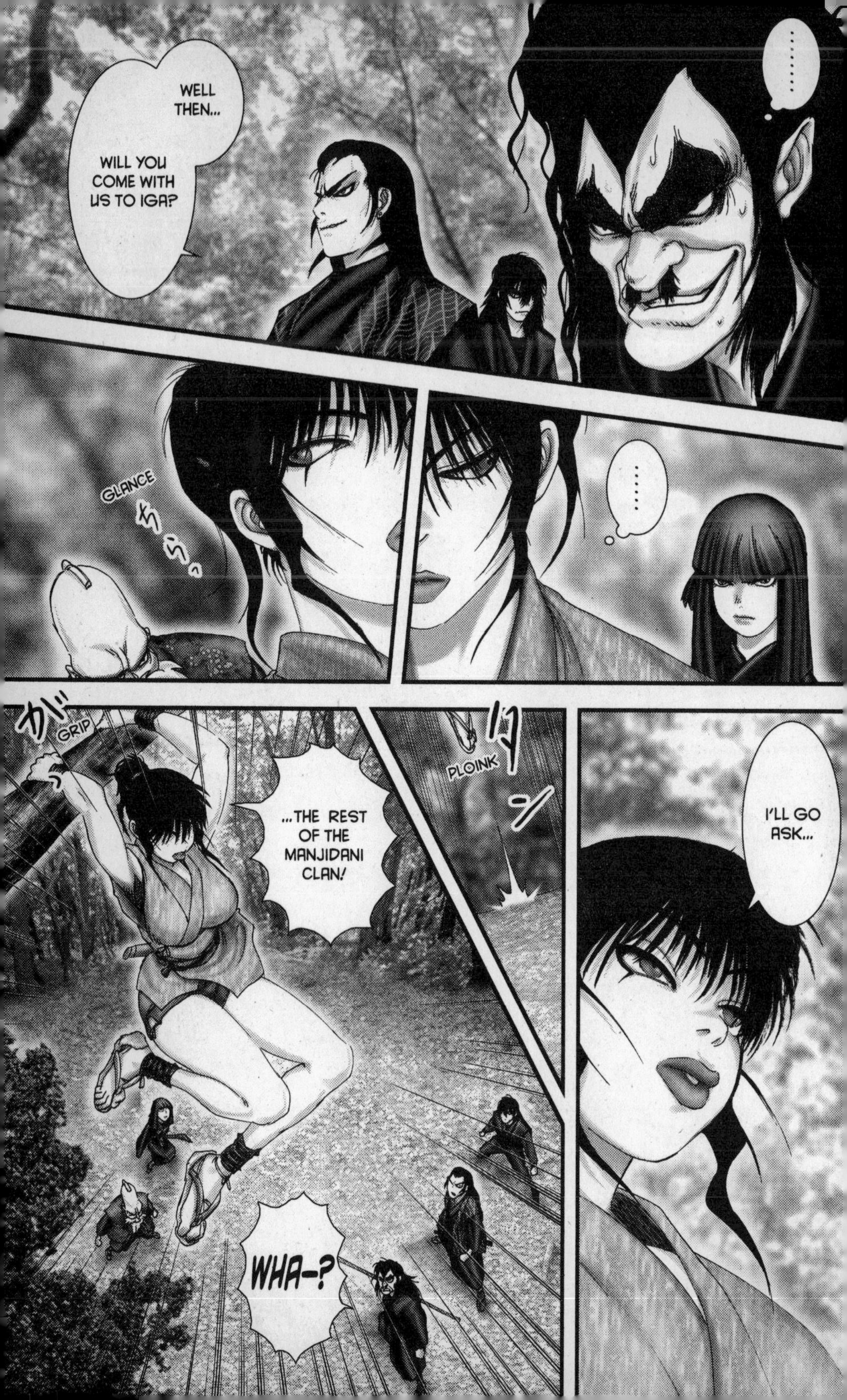
......
WELL THEN...
WILL YOU COME WITH US TO IGA?
......
GLANCE
I'LL GO ASK...
PLOINK
GRIP
...THE REST OF THE MANJIDANI CLAN!
WHA-?

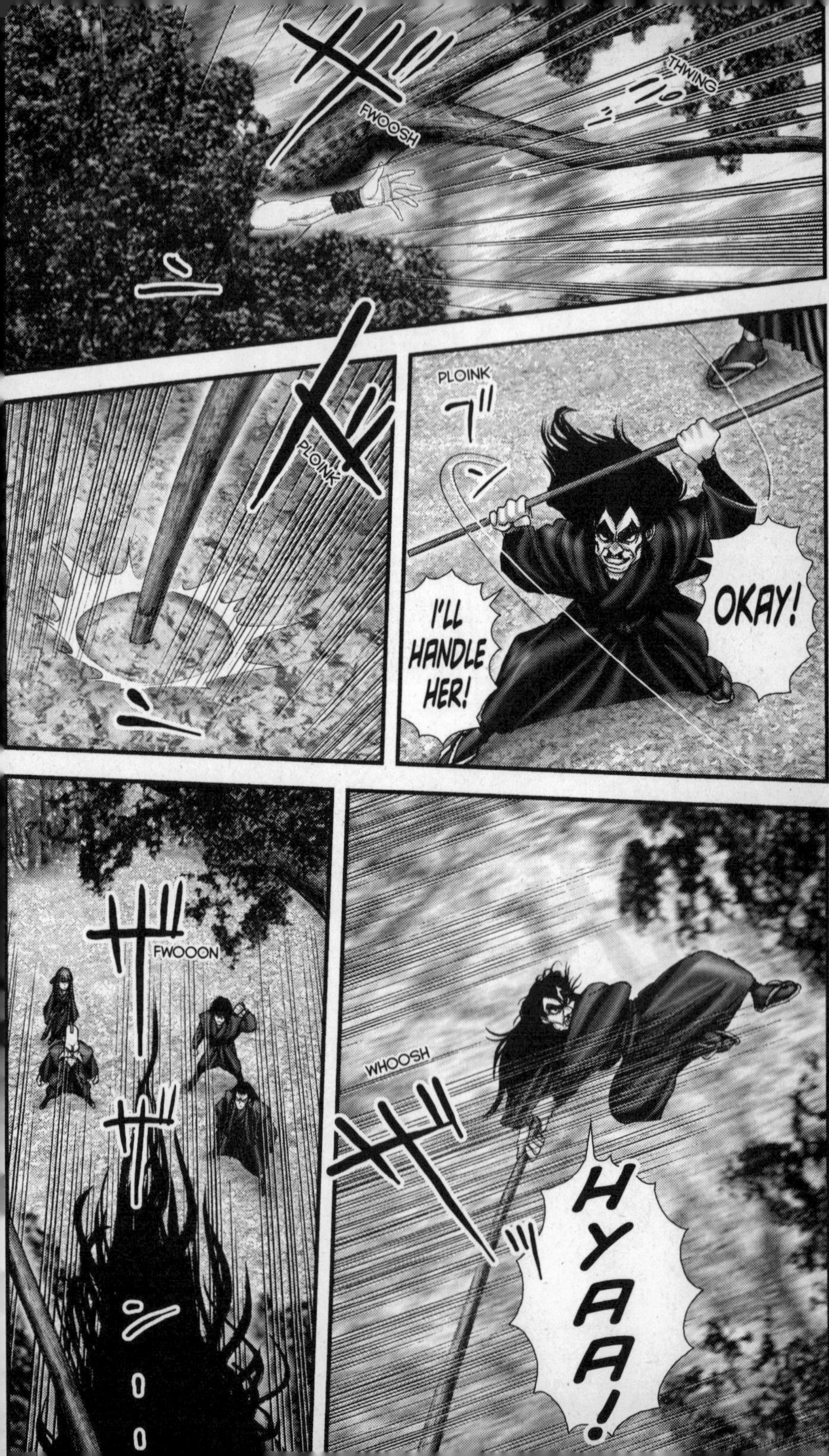
THWING
FWOOSH
PLOINK
OKAY!
I'LL HANDLE HER!
PLOINK
WHOOSH
HYAA!
FWOOON

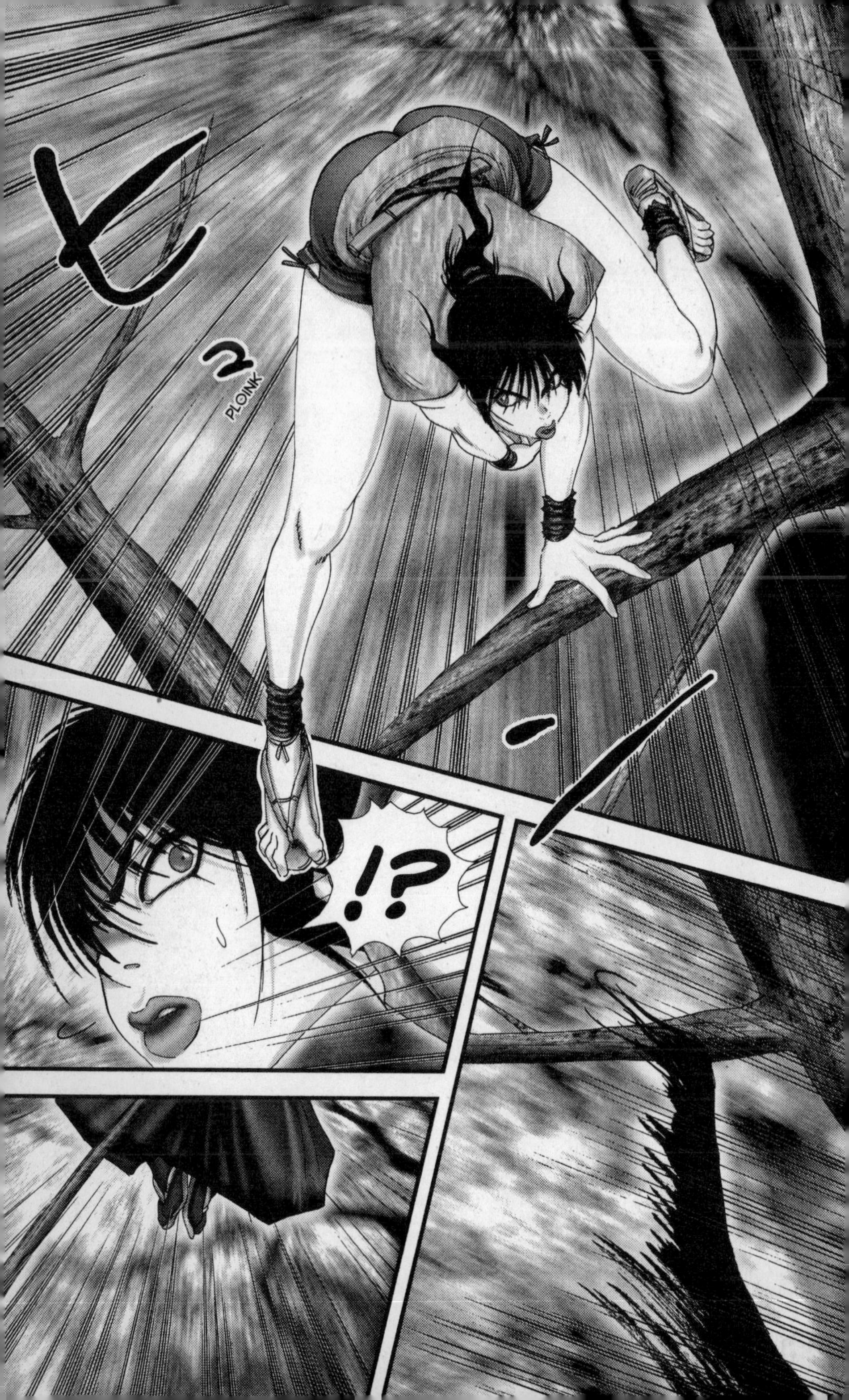
PLOINK
!?

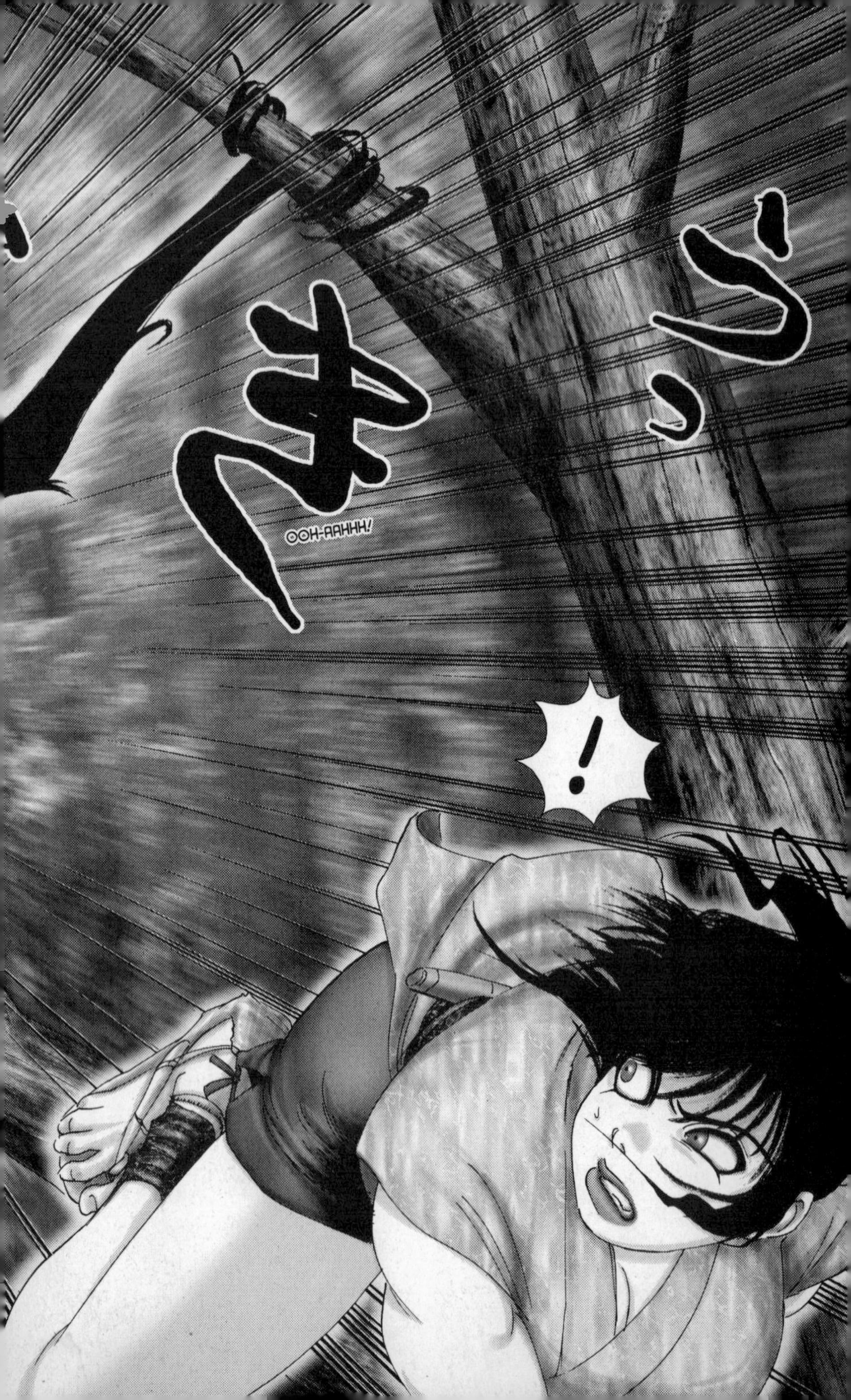
ぎ、きぃ
OOH-AAHHH!
!

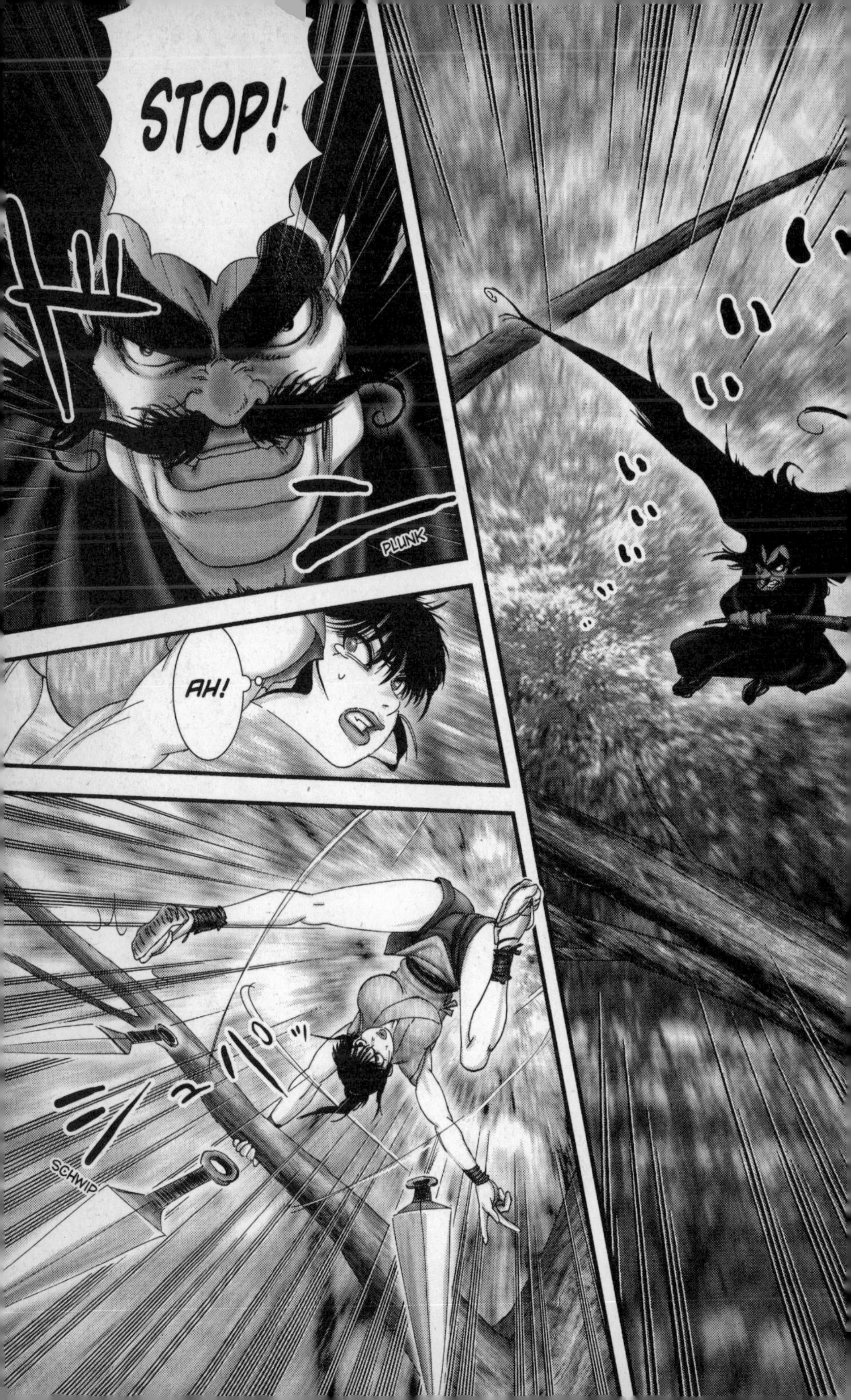
STOP!
PLUNK
AH!
SCHWIP

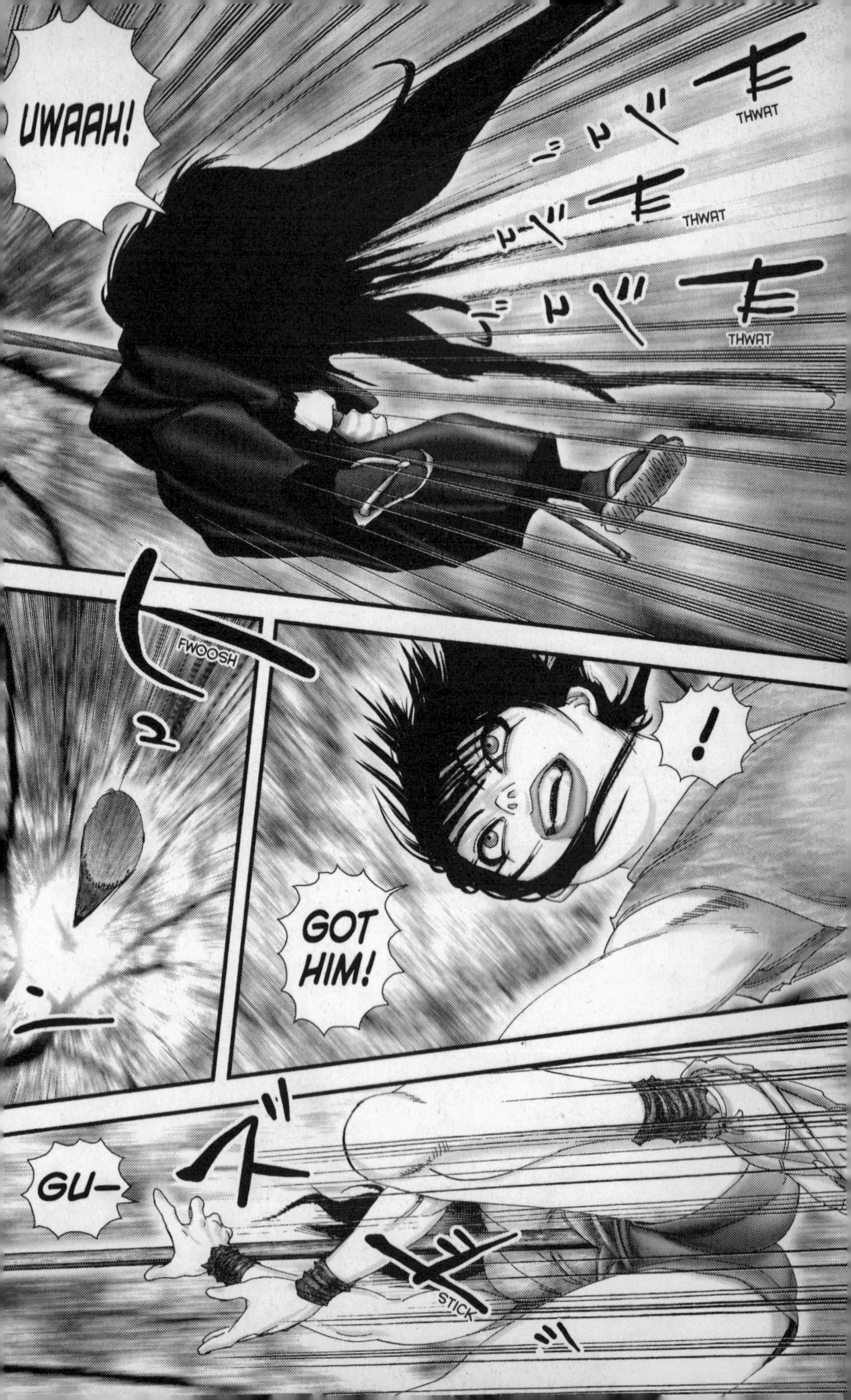
THWAT
THWAT
THWAT
UWAAH!
!
GOT HIM!
FWOOSH
STICK
GU-

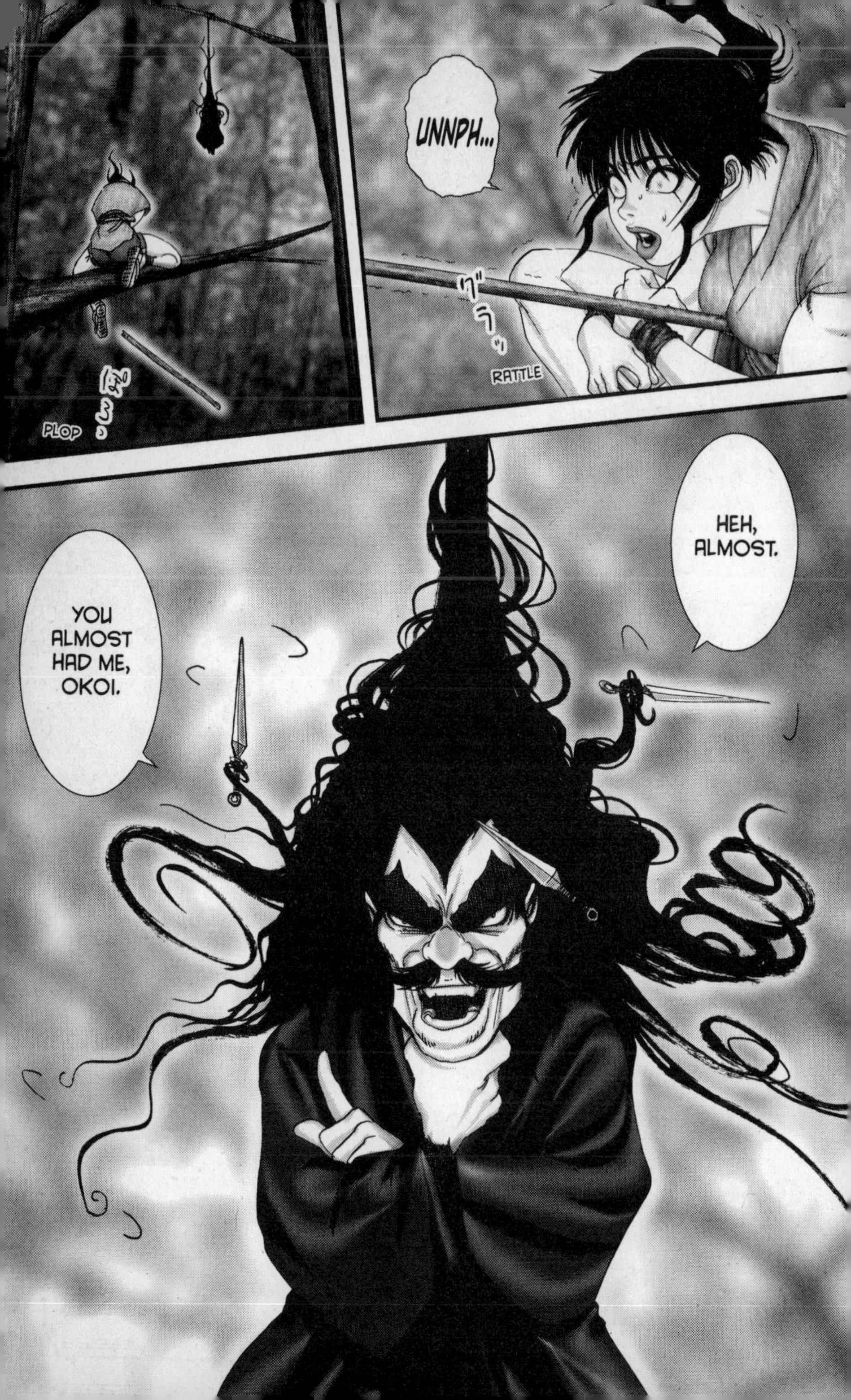
UNNPH...
ガラッ
RATTLE
PLOP
HEH, ALMOST.
YOU ALMOST HAD ME, OKOI.

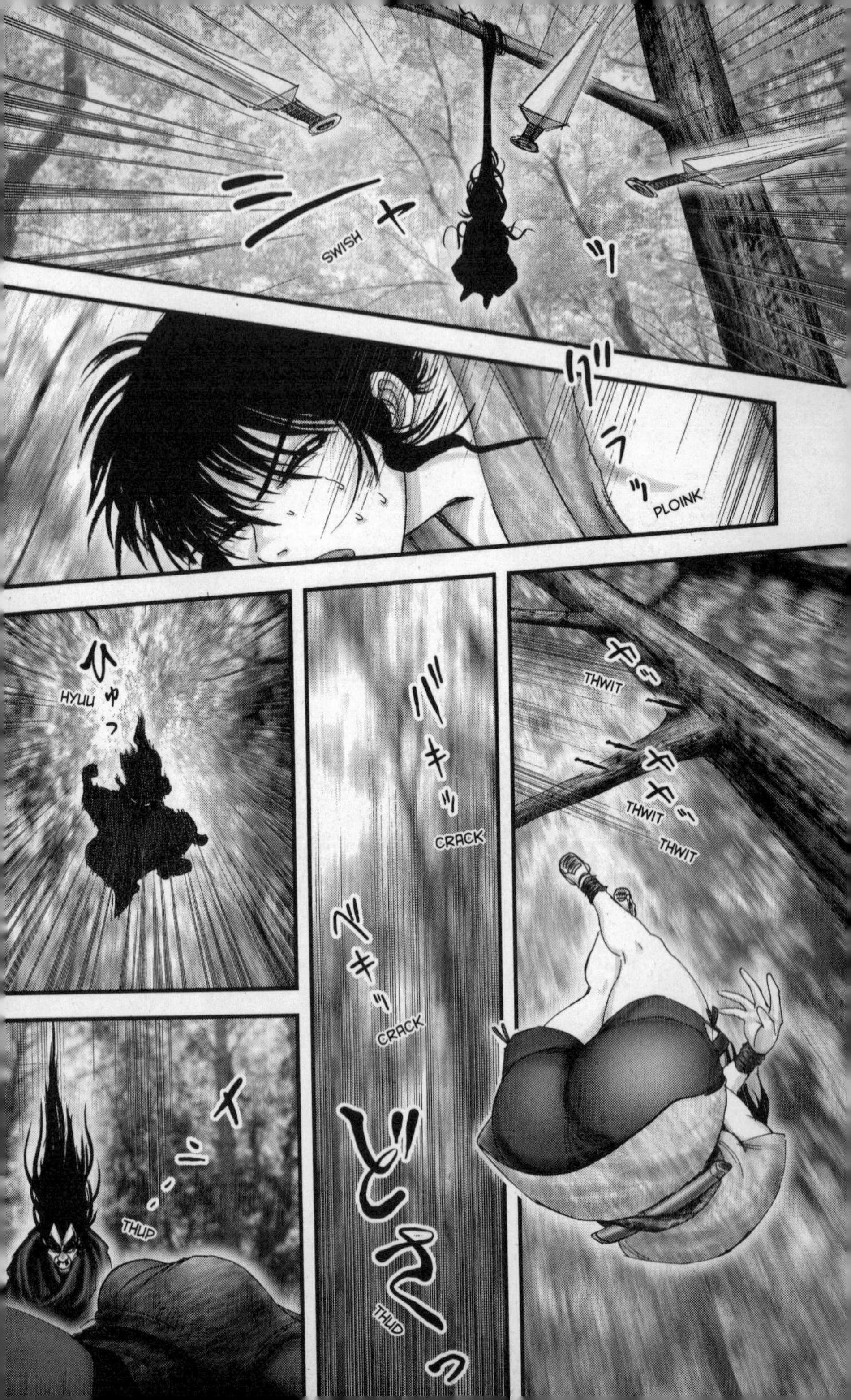
SWISH
PLOINK
THWIT
THWIT
THWIT
CRACK
CRACK
THUD
HYUU
THUP

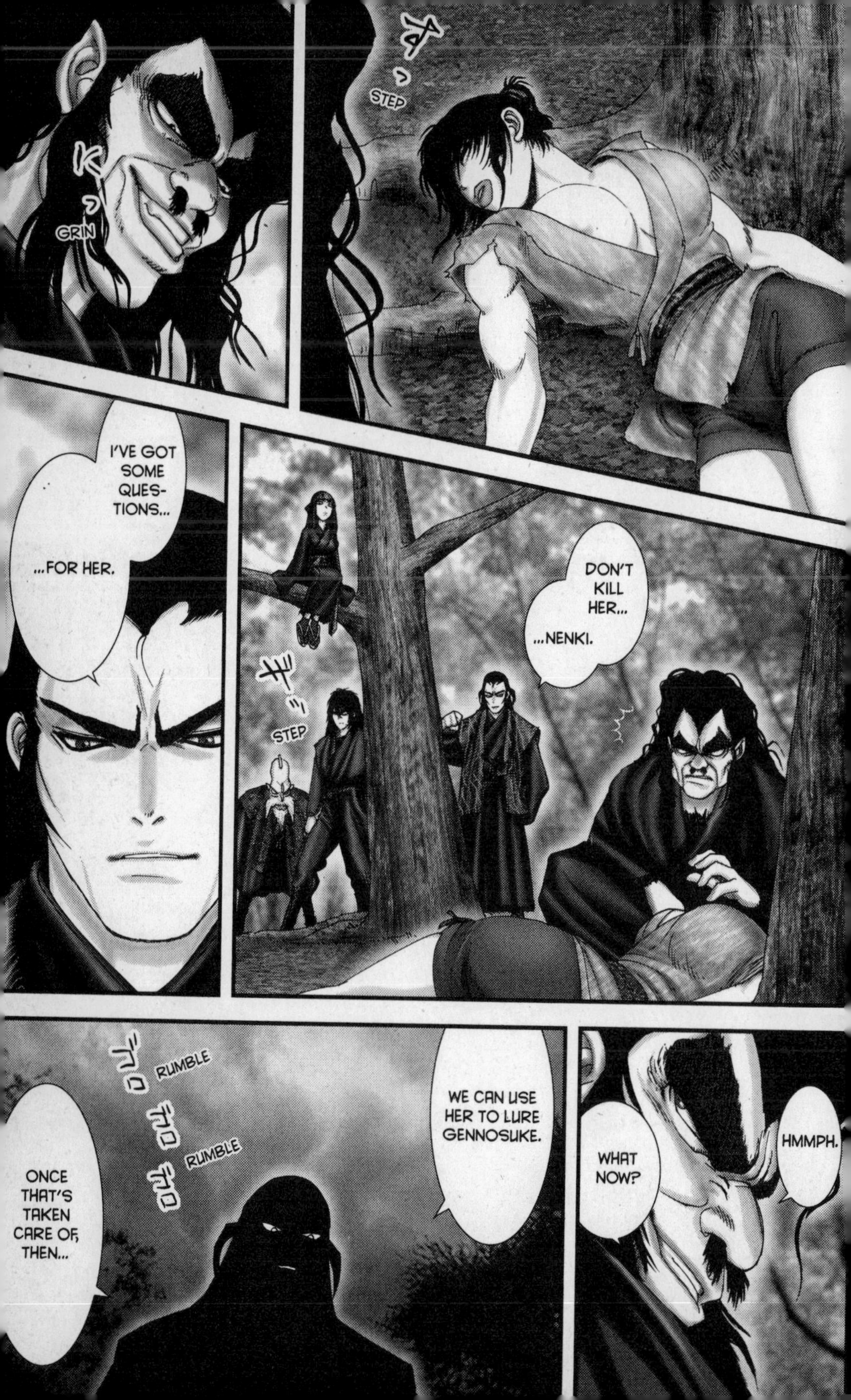
STEP
GRIN
DON'T KILL HER...
...NENKI.
STEP
I'VE GOT SOME QUES-TIONS...
...FOR HER.
HMMPH.
WHAT NOW?
WE CAN USE HER TO LURE GENNOSUKE.
RUMBLE
RUMBLE
ONCE THAT'S TAKEN CARE OF, THEN...

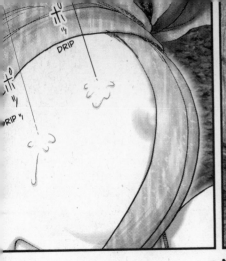

DRIP

WE CAN CROSS HER NAME OFF THE LIST.

SMACK

TSSSS

DANJOU KOUGA'S PALACE

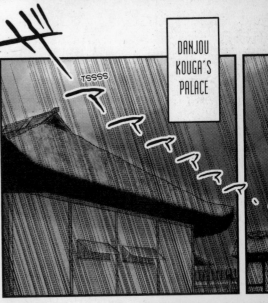

WE MUST ATTACK IGA!

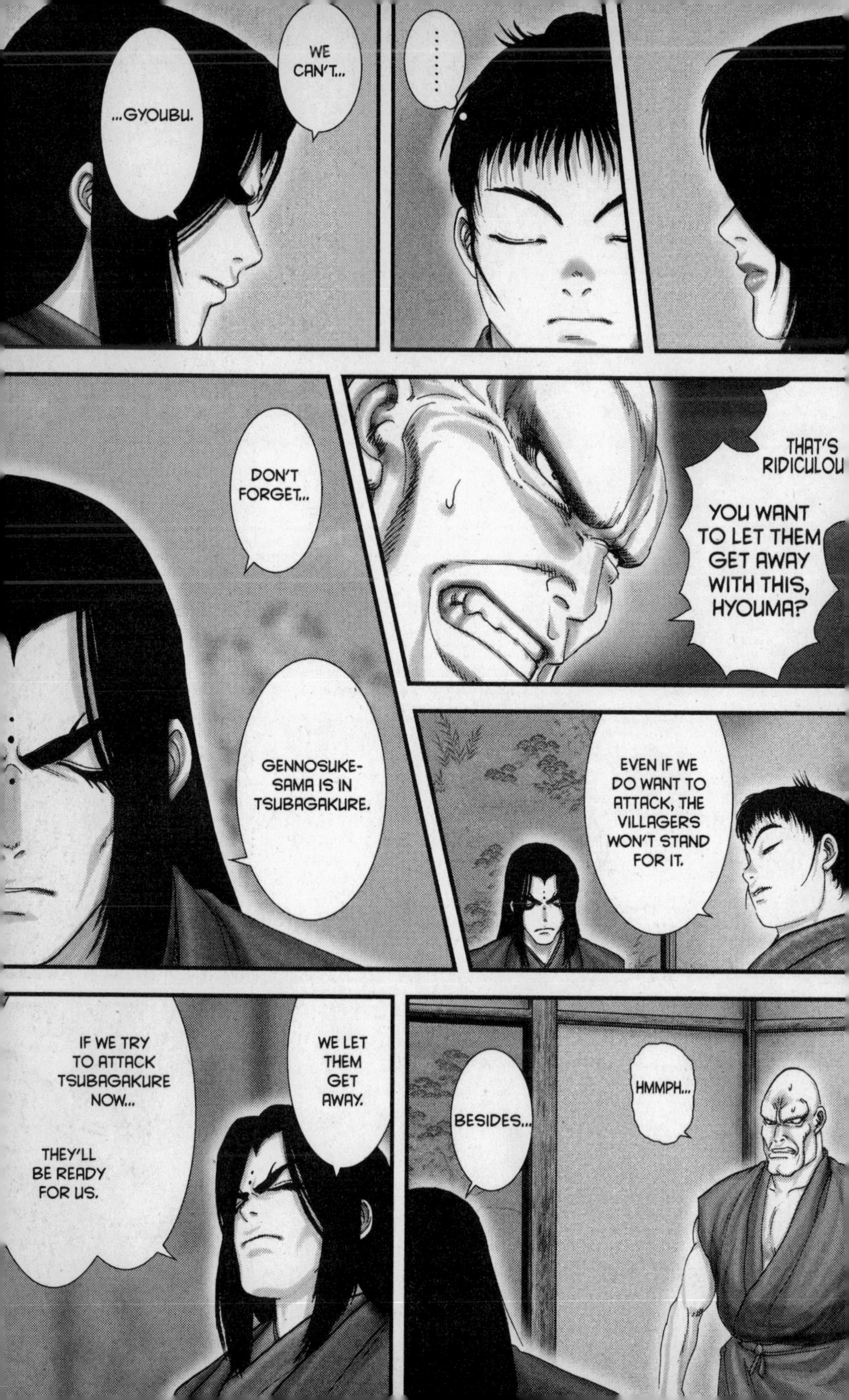

......
WE CAN'T...
...GYOUBU.
THAT'S RIDICULOU
YOU WANT TO LET THEM GET AWAY WITH THIS, HYOUMA?
EVEN IF WE DO WANT TO ATTACK, THE VILLAGERS WON'T STAND FOR IT.
DON'T FORGET...
GENNOSUKE-SAMA IS IN TSUBAGAKURE.
HMMPH...
BESIDES...
WE LET THEM GET AWAY.
IF WE TRY TO ATTACK TSUBAGAKURE NOW...
THEY'LL BE READY FOR US.

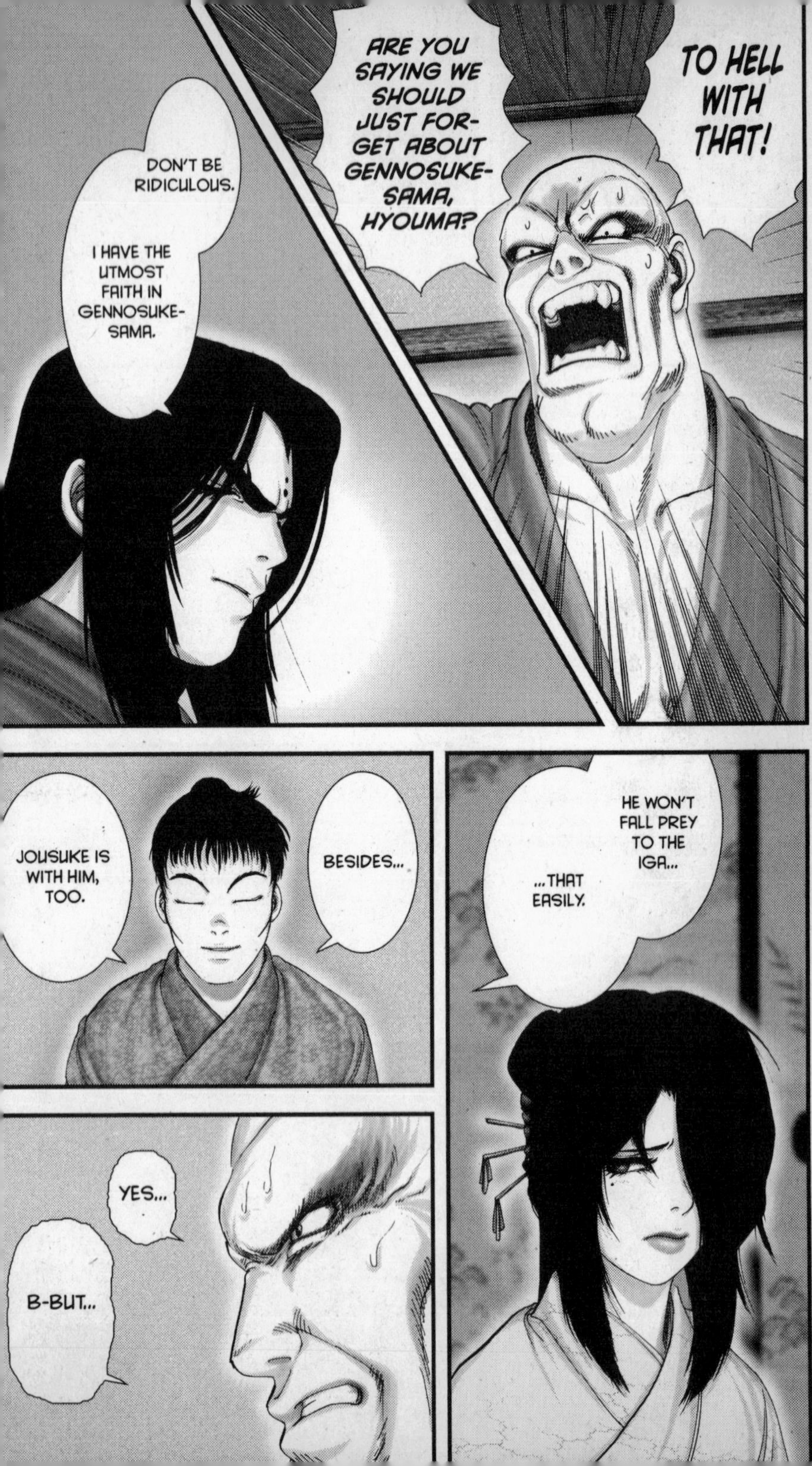
TO HELL WITH THAT!
ARE YOU SAYING WE SHOULD JUST FORGET ABOUT GENNOSUKE-SAMA, HYOUMA?
DON'T BE RIDICULOUS.
I HAVE THE UTMOST FAITH IN GENNOSUKE-SAMA.
HE WON'T FALL PREY TO THE IGA...
...THAT EASILY.
BESIDES...
JOUSUKE IS WITH HIM, TOO.
YES...
B-BUT...

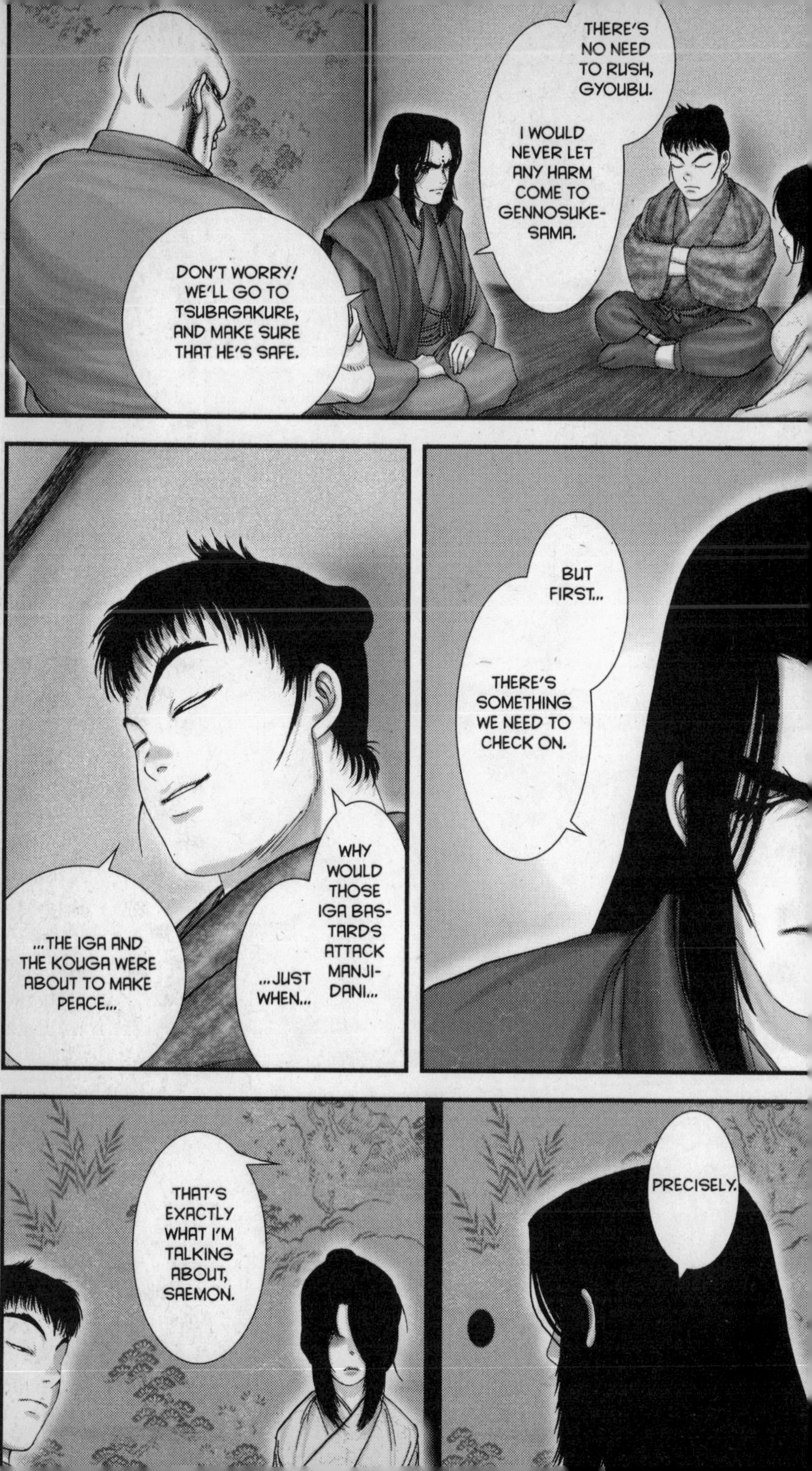
THERE'S NO NEED TO RUSH, GYOUBU.
I WOULD NEVER LET ANY HARM COME TO GENNOSUKE-SAMA.
DON'T WORRY! WE'LL GO TO TSUBAGAKURE, AND MAKE SURE THAT HE'S SAFE.
BUT FIRST...
THERE'S SOMETHING WE NEED TO CHECK ON.
WHY WOULD THOSE IGA BAS-TARDS ATTACK MANJI-DANI...
...JUST WHEN...
...THE IGA AND THE KOUGA WERE ABOUT TO MAKE PEACE...
PRECISELY.
THAT'S EXACTLY WHAT I'M TALKING ABOUT, SAEMON.

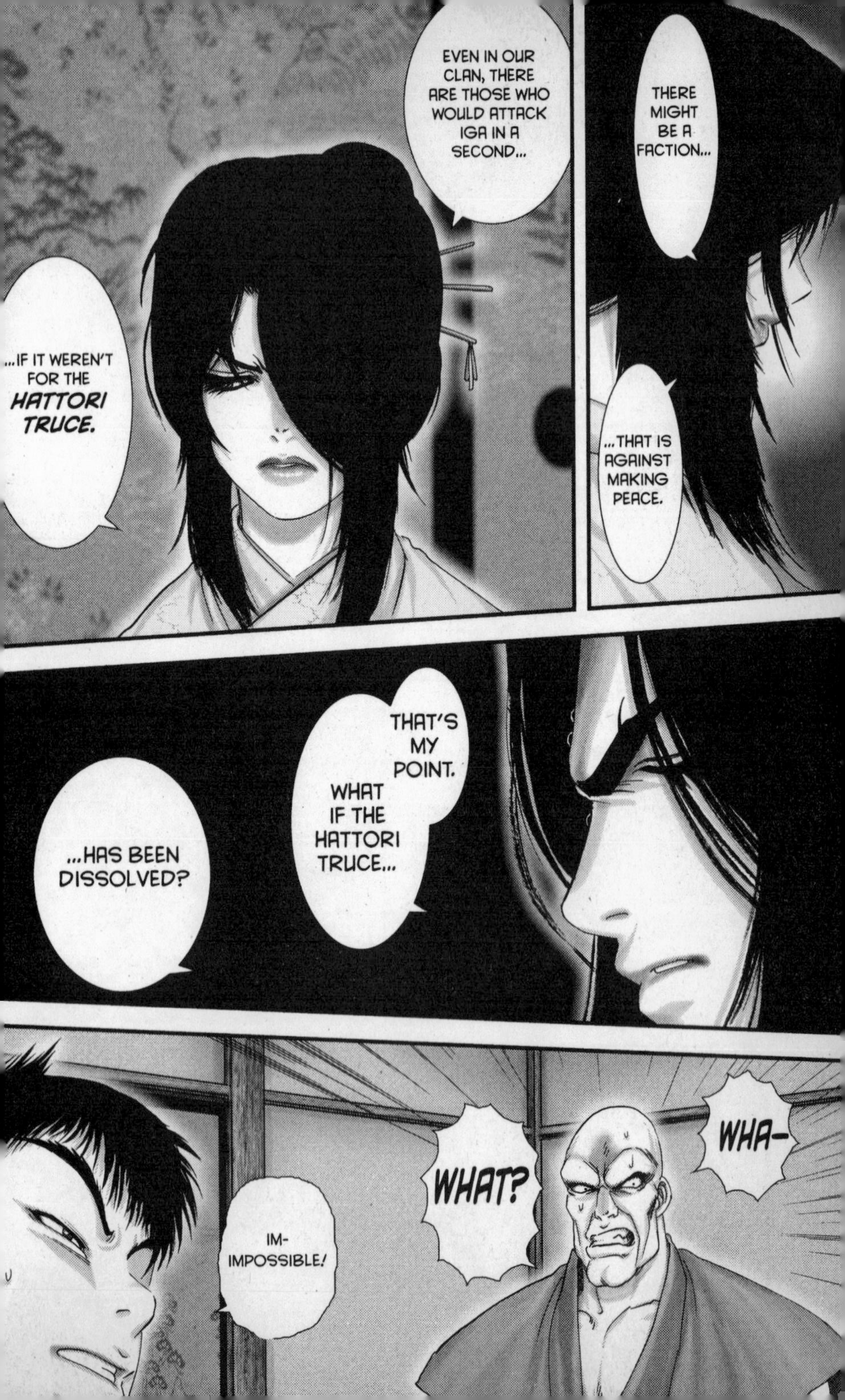
THERE MIGHT BE A FACTION...
...THAT IS AGAINST MAKING PEACE.
EVEN IN OUR CLAN, THERE ARE THOSE WHO WOULD ATTACK IGA IN A SECOND...
...IF IT WEREN'T FOR THE *HATTORI TRUCE.*
THAT'S MY POINT. WHAT IF THE HATTORI TRUCE...
...HAS BEEN DISSOLVED?
WHA-
WHAT?
IM-IMPOSSIBLE!

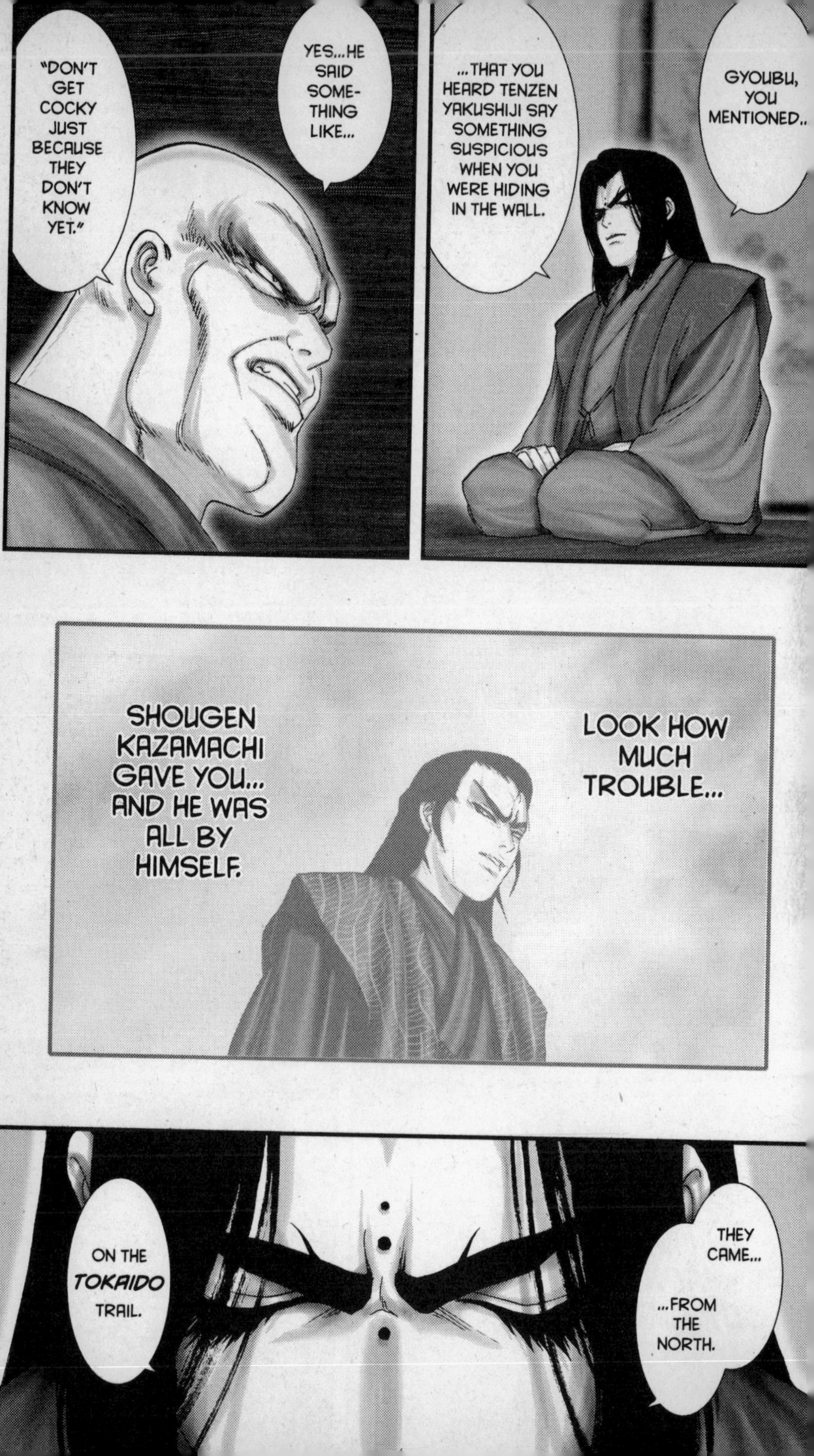
GYOUBU, YOU MENTIONED...
...THAT YOU HEARD TENZEN YAKUSHIJI SAY SOMETHING SUSPICIOUS WHEN YOU WERE HIDING IN THE WALL.
YES...HE SAID SOME-THING LIKE...
"DON'T GET COCKY JUST BECAUSE THEY DON'T KNOW YET."
LOOK HOW MUCH TROUBLE...
SHOUGEN KAZAMACHI GAVE YOU... AND HE WAS ALL BY HIMSELF.
THEY CAME...
...FROM THE NORTH.
ON THE *TOKAIDO* TRAIL.

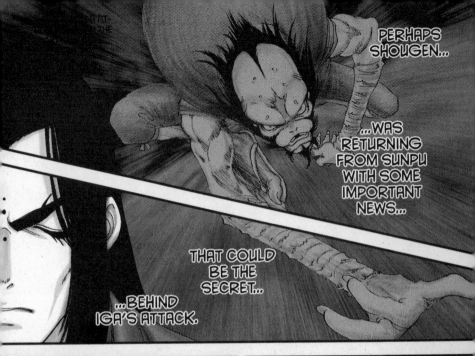

PERHAPS SHOUGEN...

...WAS RETURNING FROM SUNPU WITH SOME IMPORTANT NEWS...

THAT COULD BE THE SECRET...

...BEHIND IGA'S ATTACK.

ALL RIGHT!

WHAP

I'M HEADING OUT ON THE TOKAIDO TRAIL.

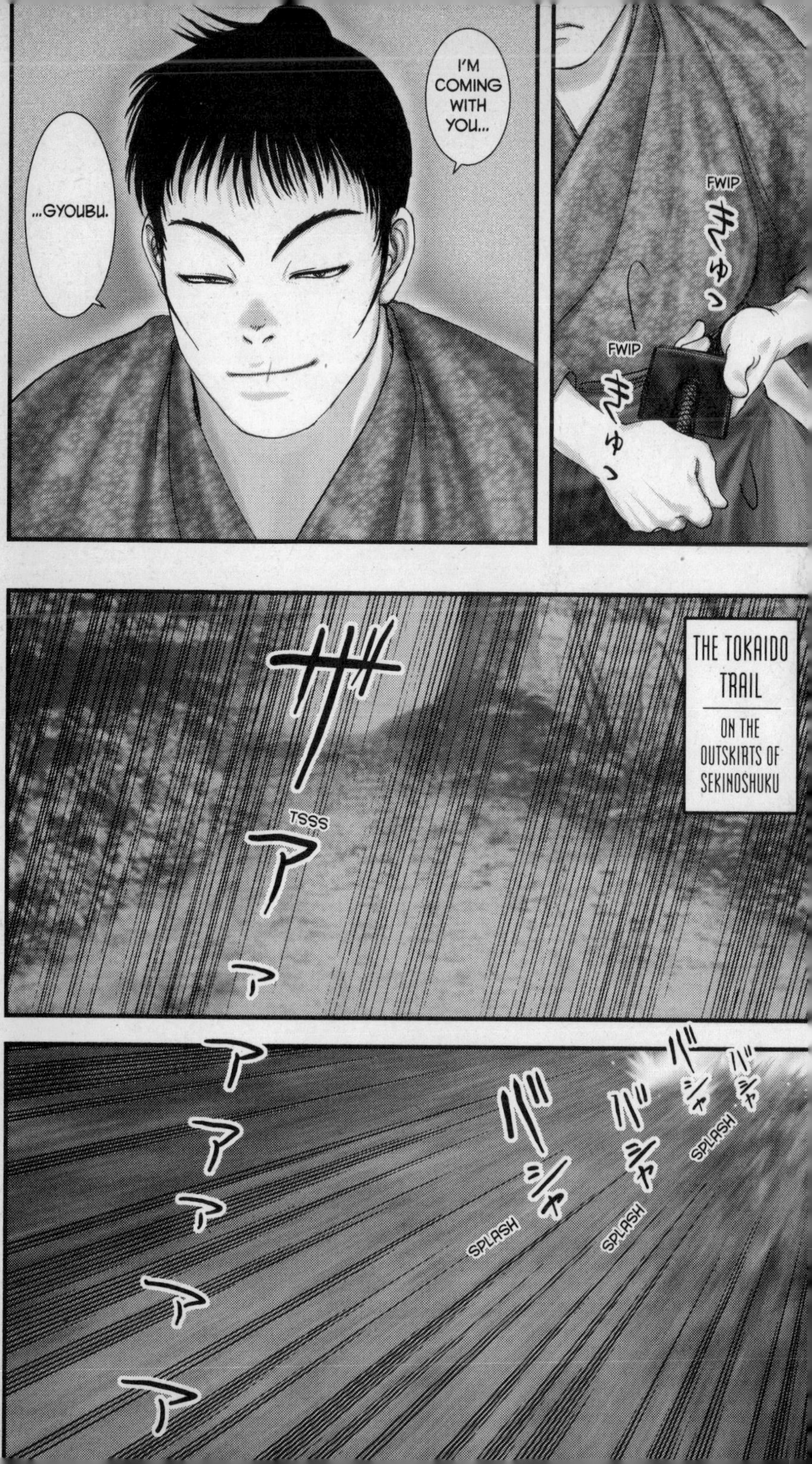
FWIP
きゅっ
FWIP
きゅっ
I'M COMING WITH YOU...
...GYOUBU.
THE TOKAIDO TRAIL
ON THE OUTSKIRTS OF SEKINOSHUKU
ザァァァァァァァァ
TSSS
バシャ
SPLASH
バシャ
SPLASH
バシャ
SPLASH

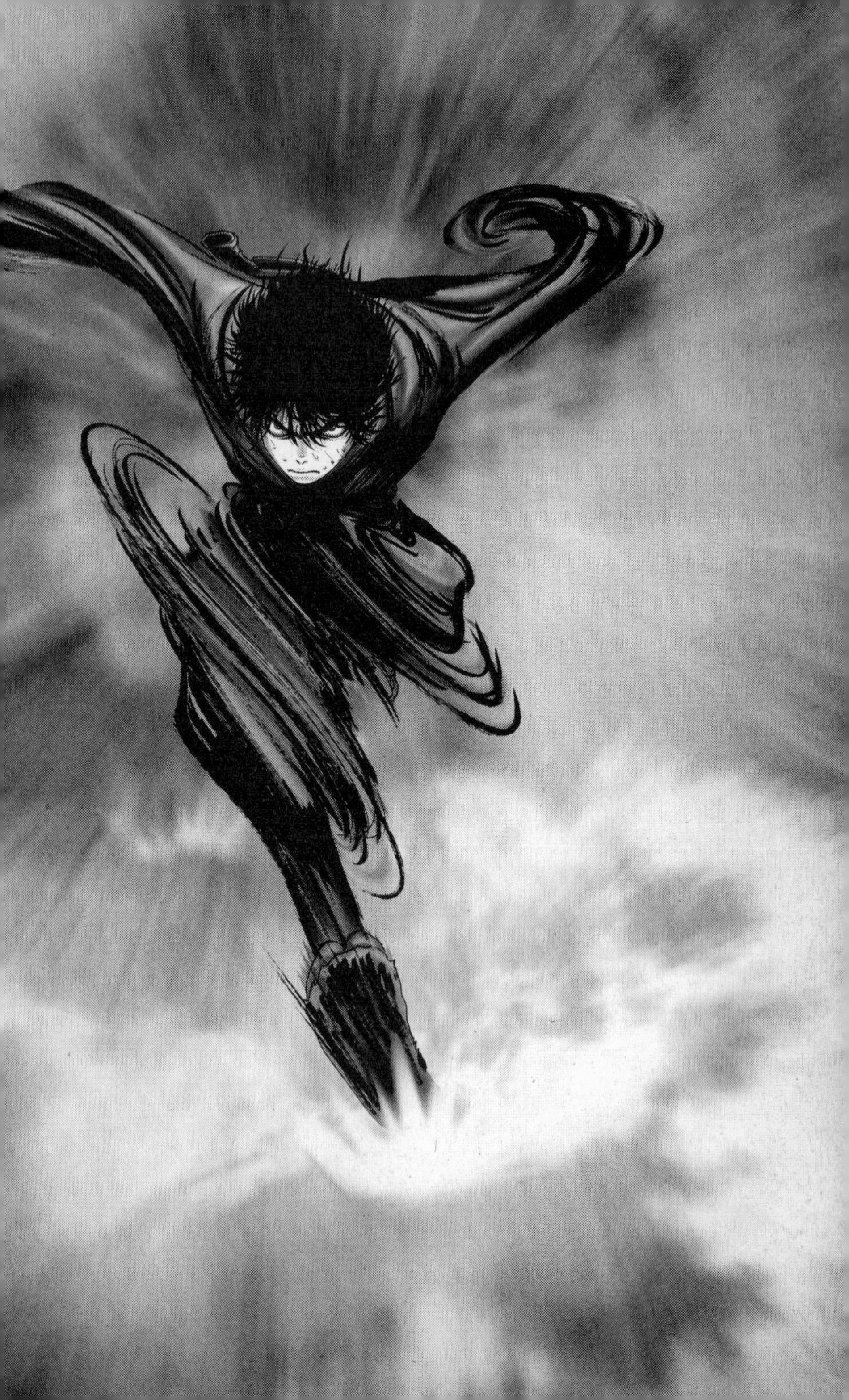

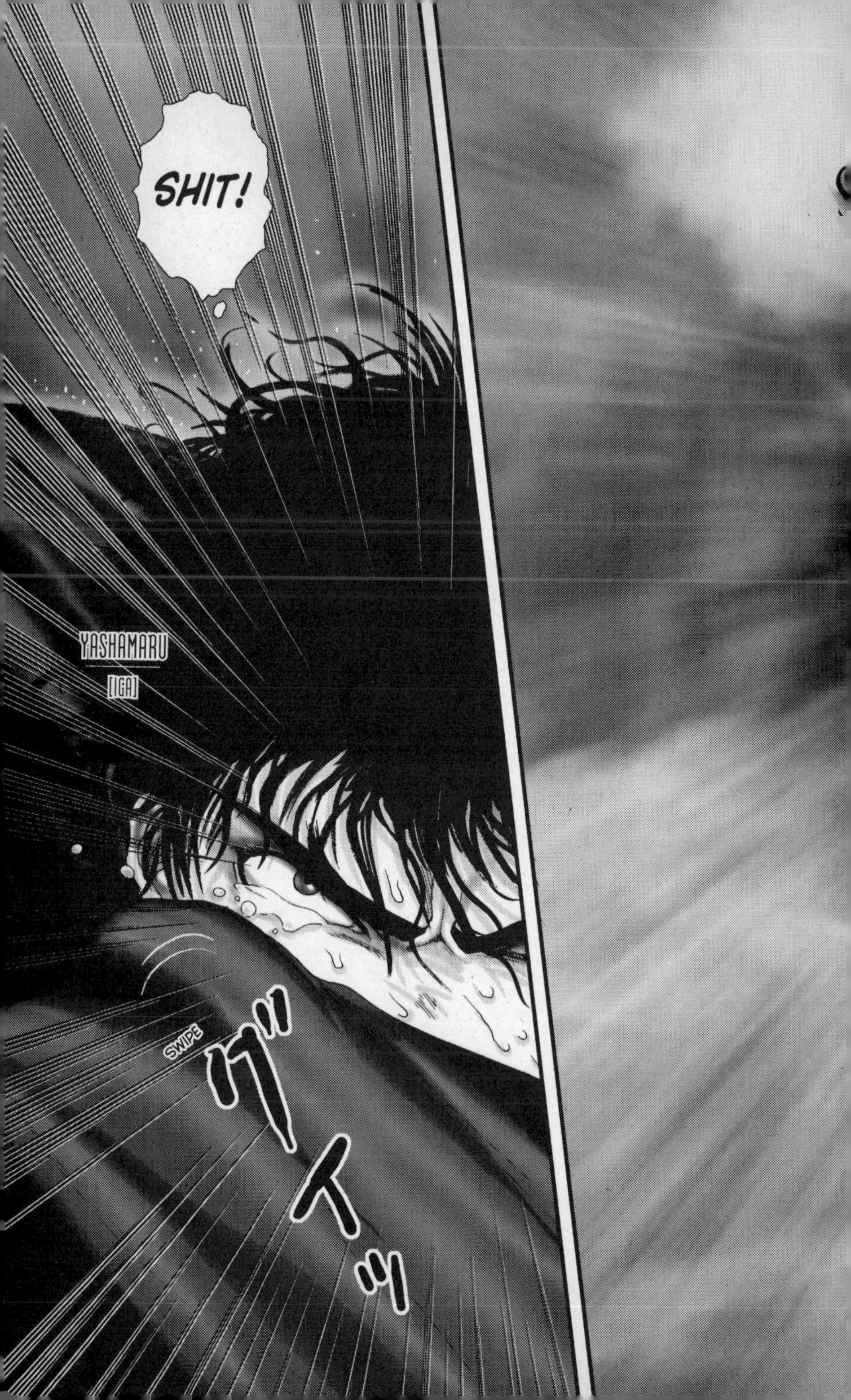
SHIT!
YASHAMARU
[IGA]
SWIPE
グイッ

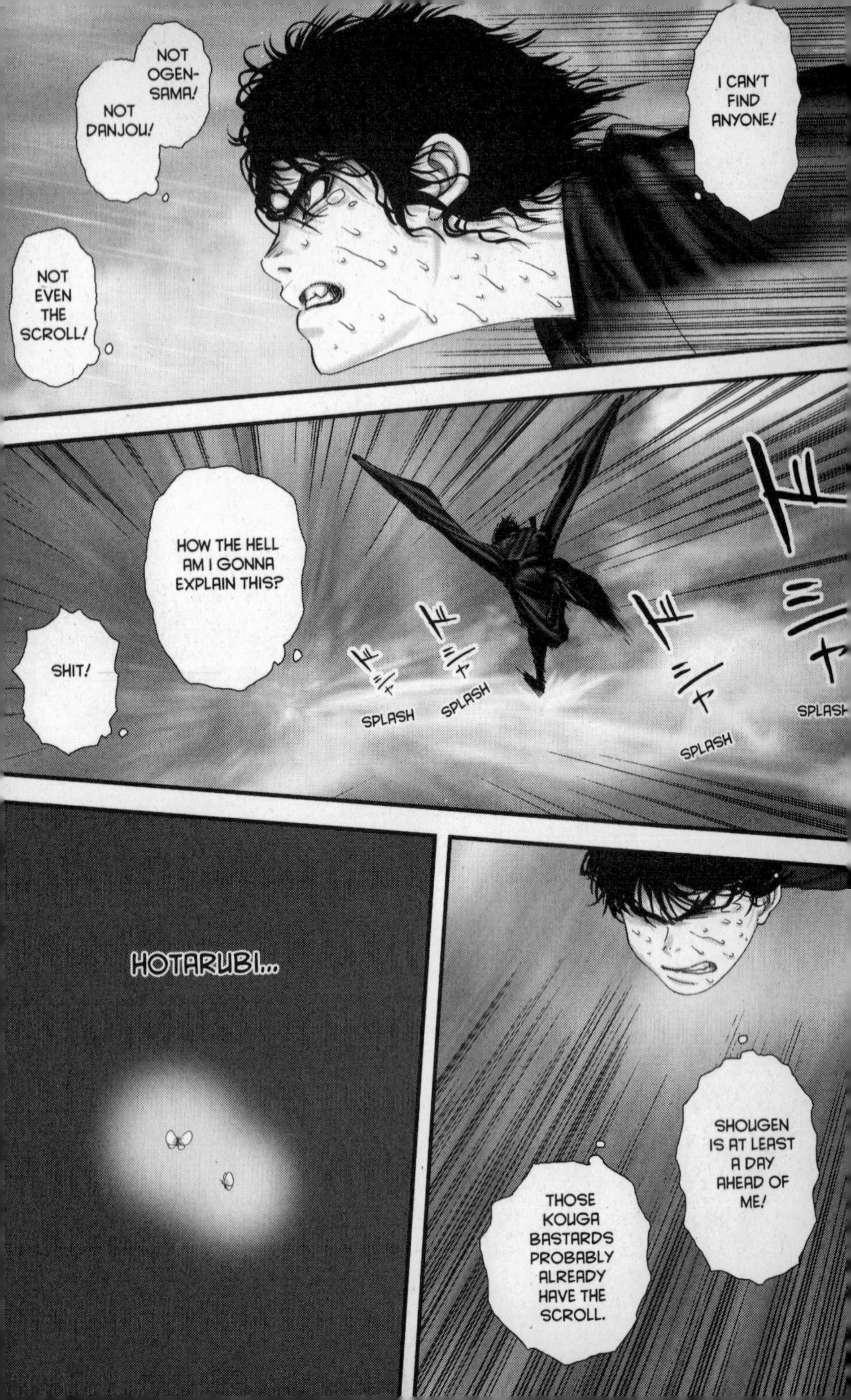
I CAN'T FIND ANYONE!
NOT OGEN-SAMA!
NOT DANJOU!
NOT EVEN THE SCROLL!
SPLASH
SPLASH
SPLASH
SPLASH
HOW THE HELL AM I GONNA EXPLAIN THIS?
SHIT!
SHOUGEN IS AT LEAST A DAY AHEAD OF ME!
THOSE KOUGA BASTARDS PROBABLY ALREADY HAVE THE SCROLL.
HOTARUBI...

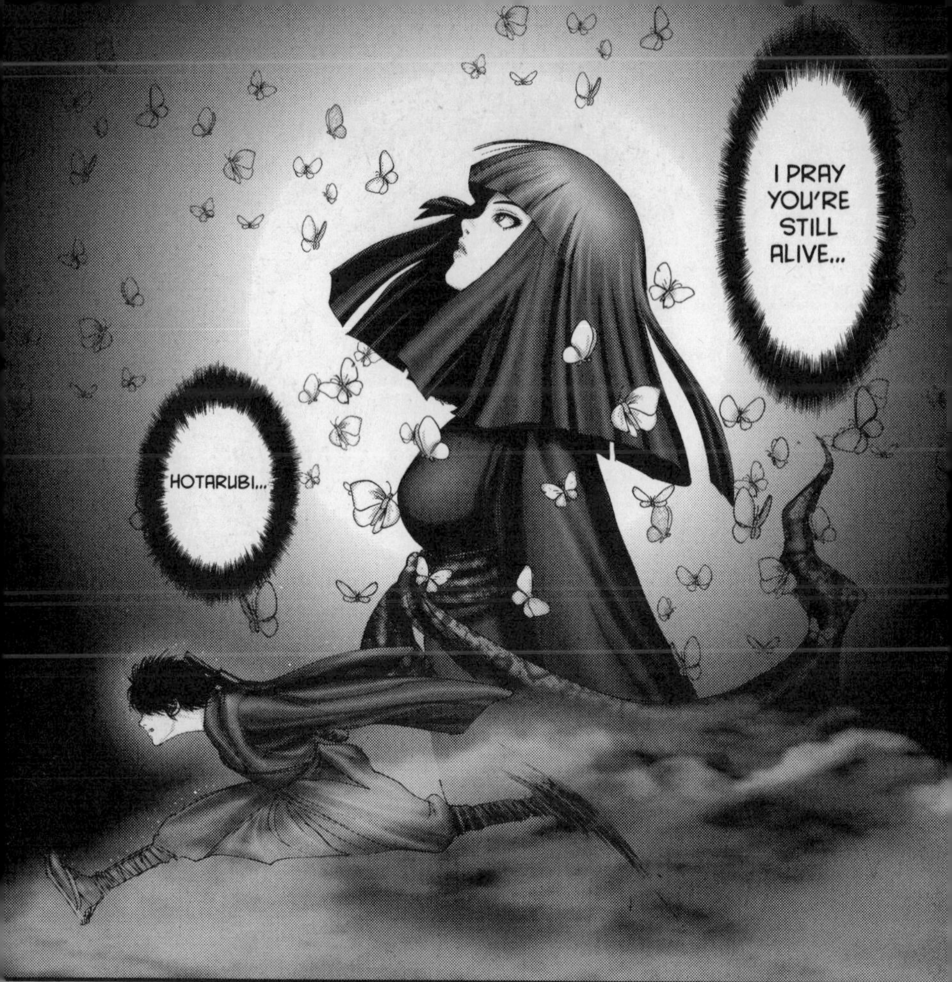
I PRAY YOU'RE STILL ALIVE...
HOTARUBI...

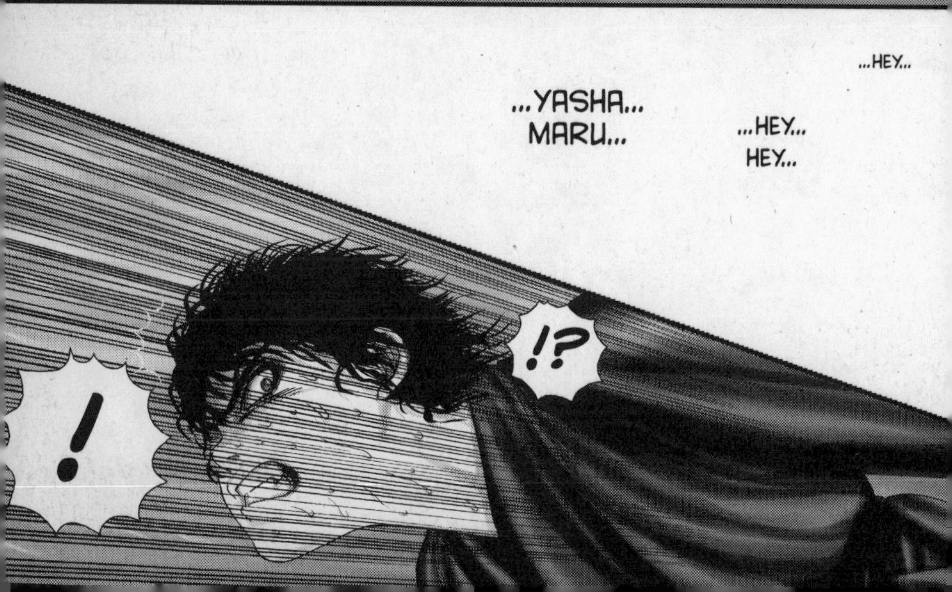
...HEY...
...HEY... HEY...
...YASHA... MARU...
!?
!

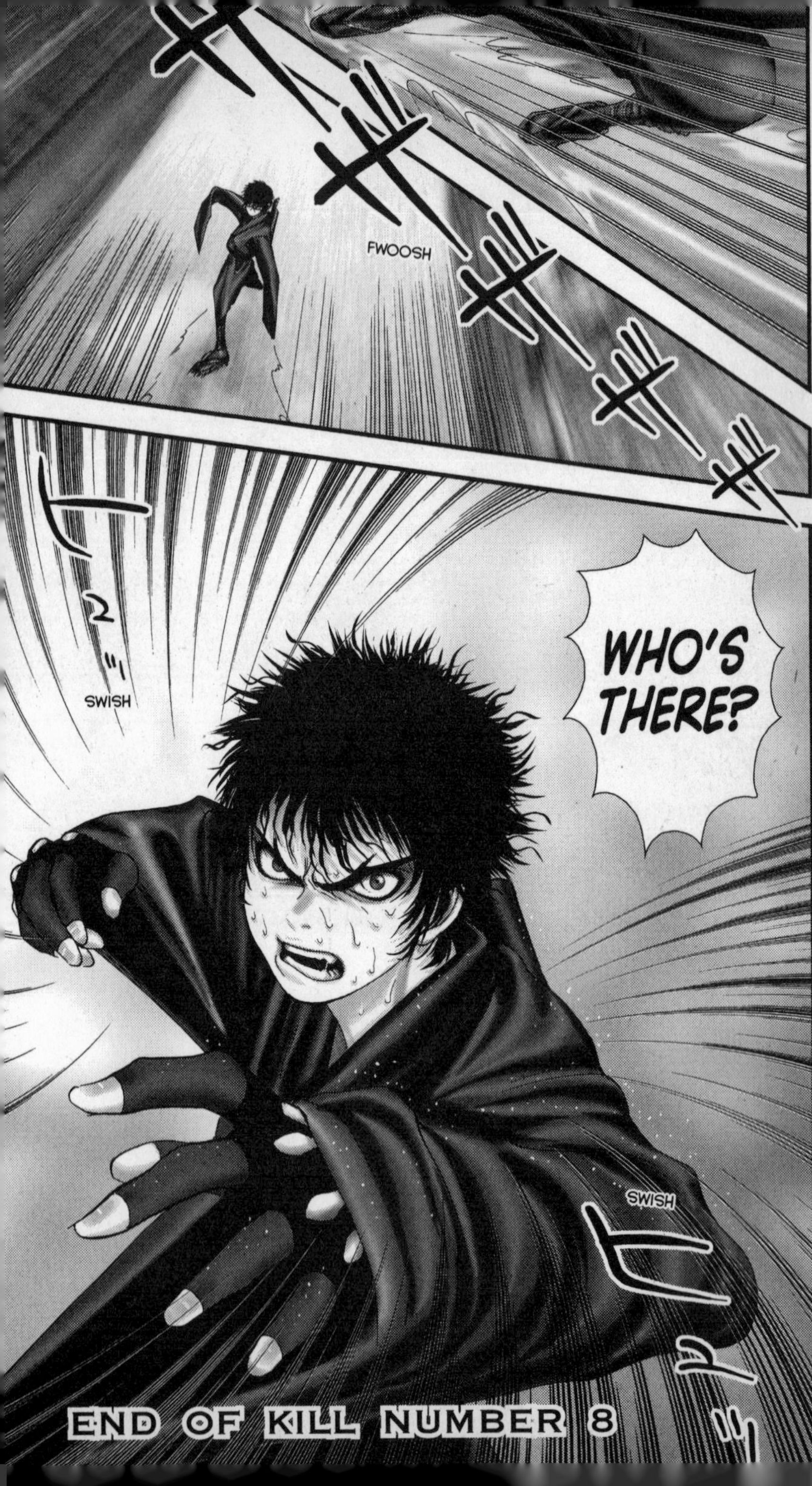
FWOOSH
WHO'S THERE?
SWISH
SWISH
END OF KILL NUMBER 8

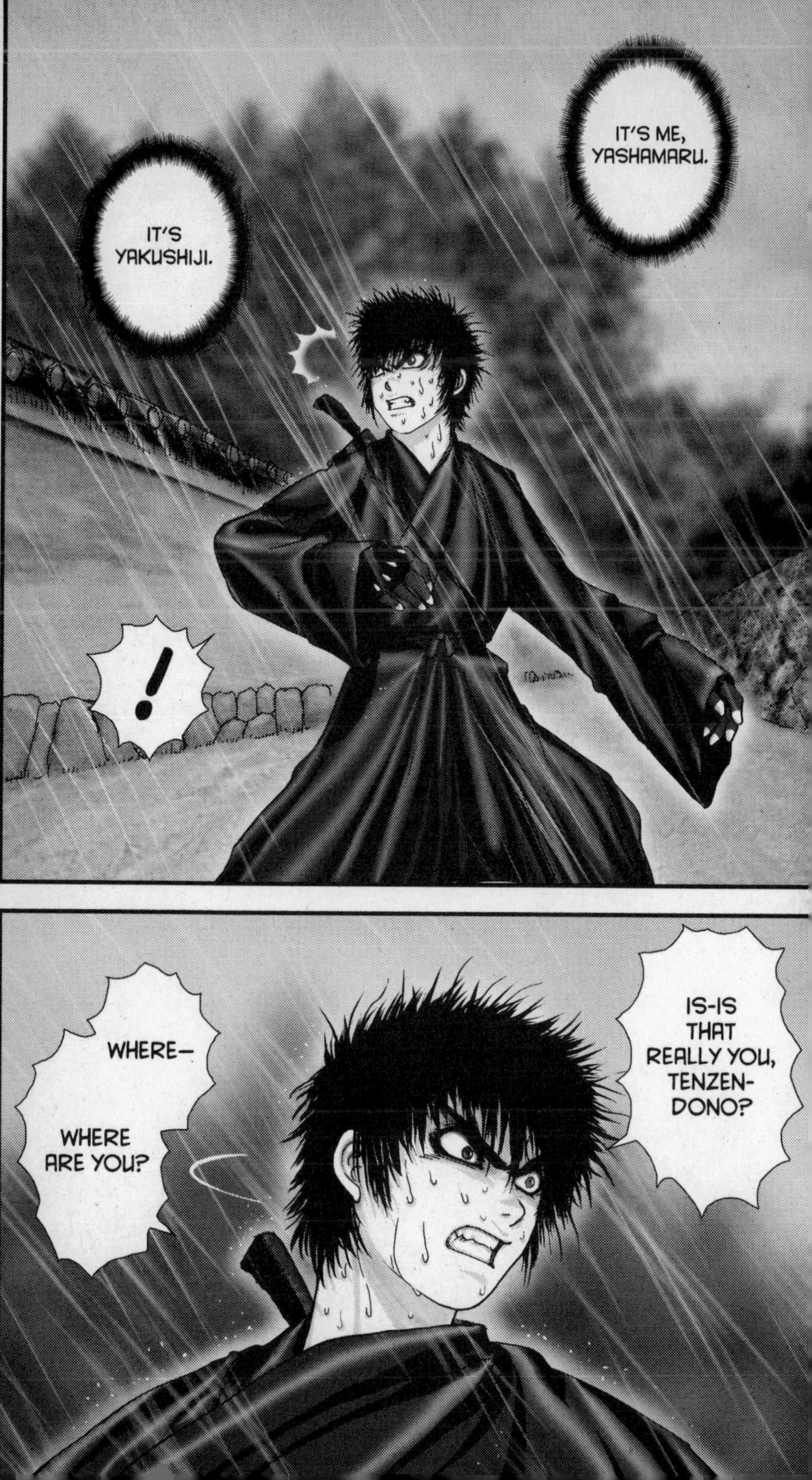
IT'S ME, YASHAMARU.
IT'S YAKUSHIJI.
!
IS-IS THAT REALLY YOU, TENZEN-DONO?
WHERE—
WHERE ARE YOU?

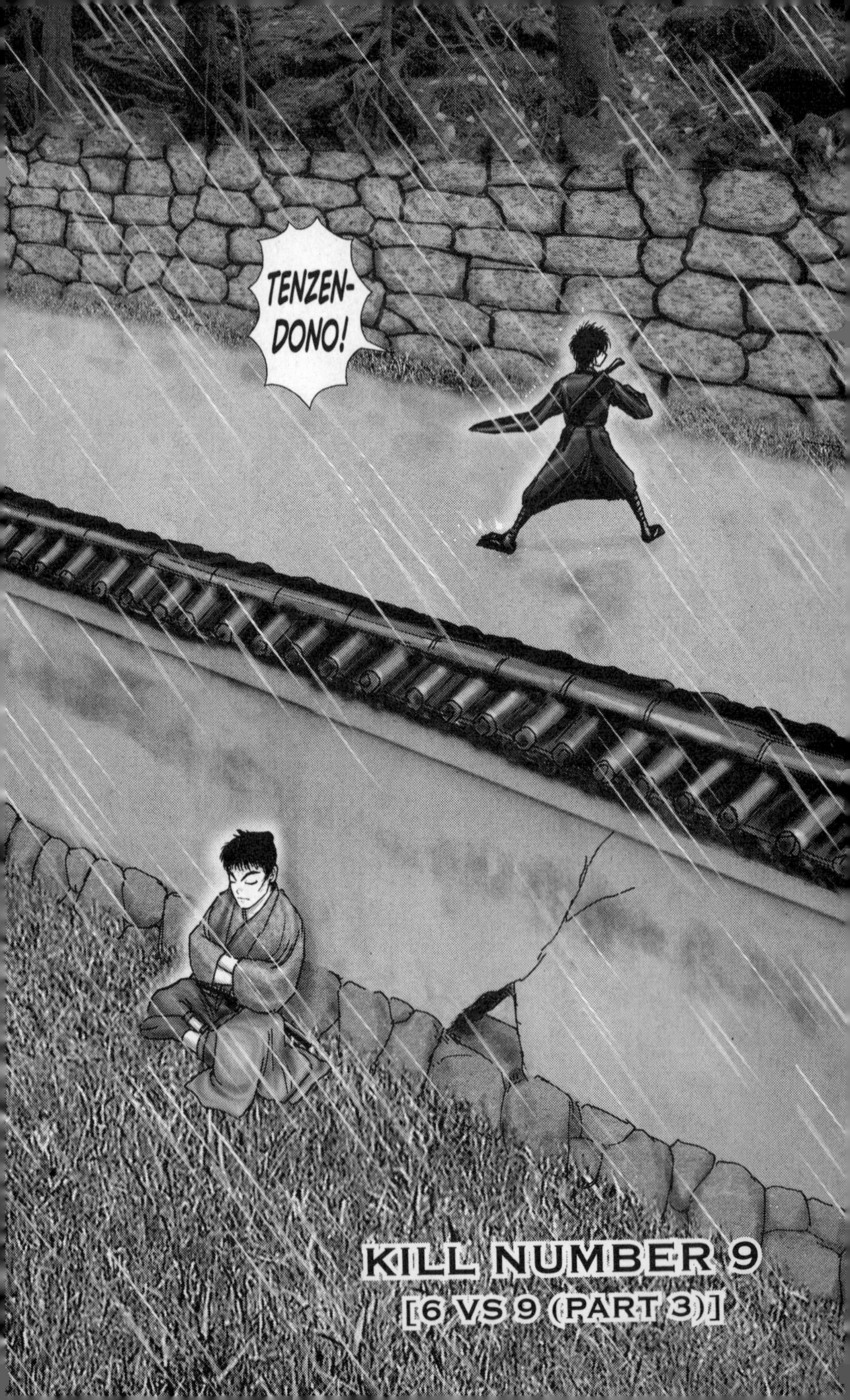
TENZEN-DONO!

KILL NUMBER 9

[6 VS 9 (PART 3)]

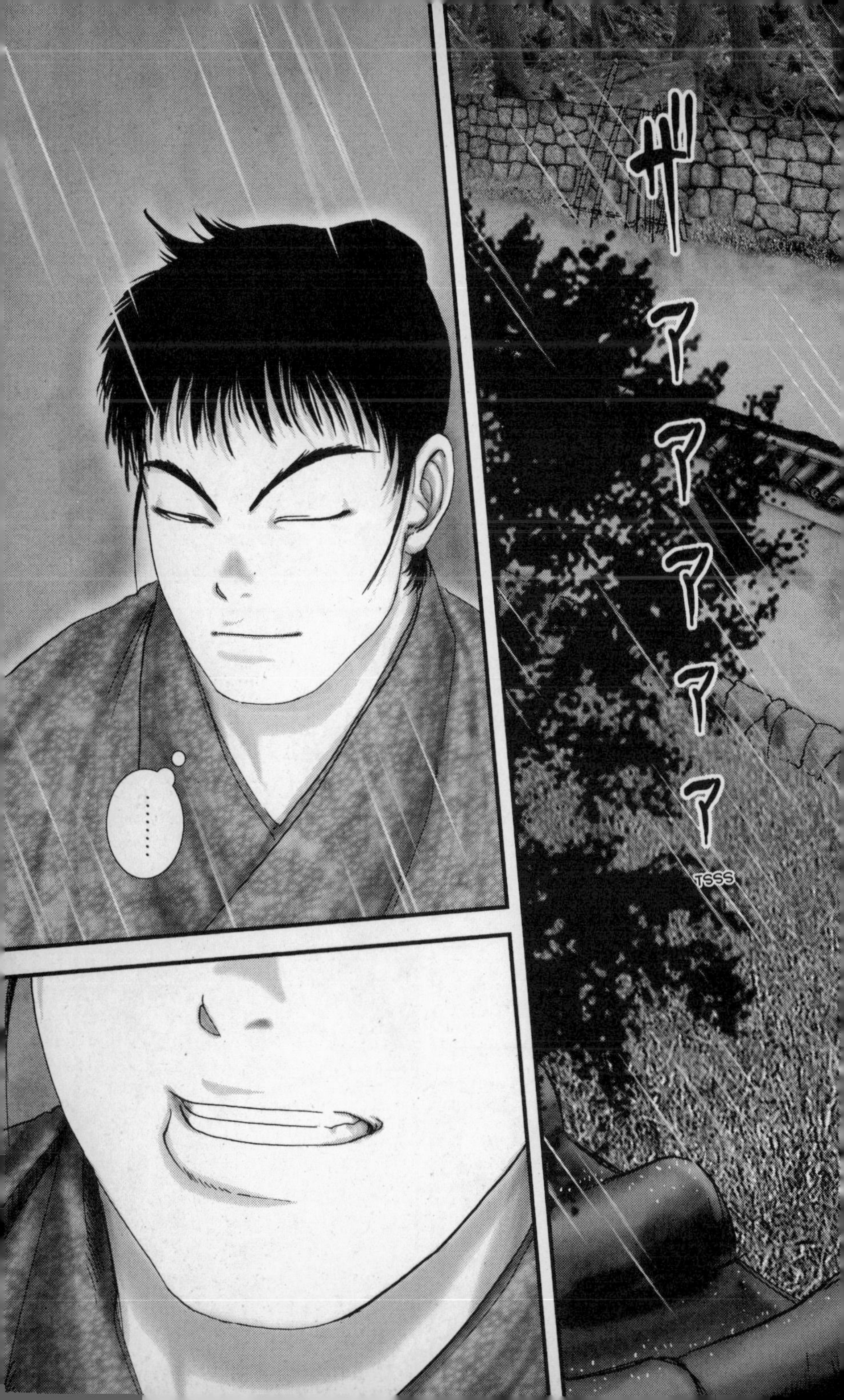

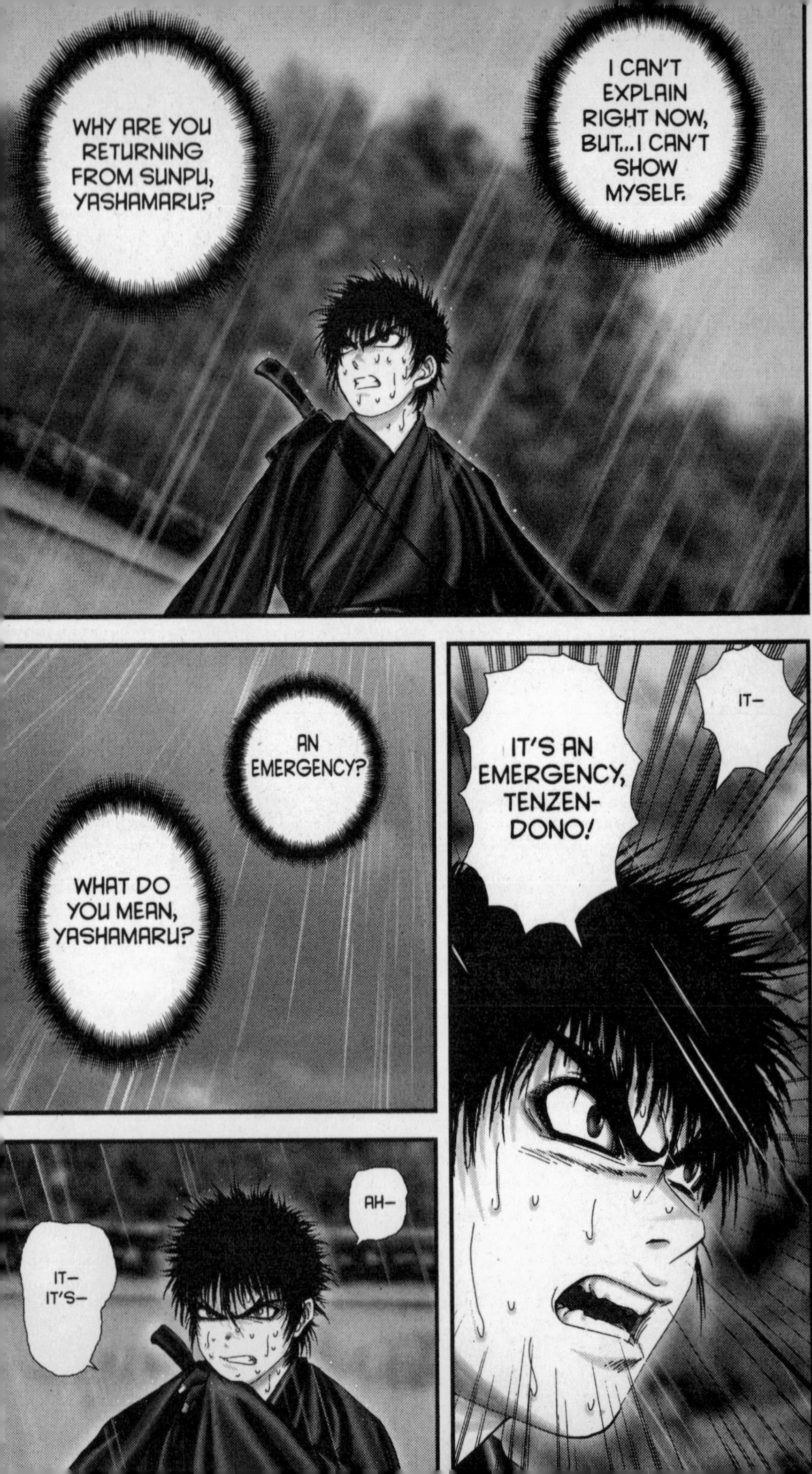
WHY ARE YOU RETURNING FROM SUNPU, YASHAMARU?
I CAN'T EXPLAIN RIGHT NOW, BUT...I CAN'T SHOW MYSELF.
AN EMERGENCY?
WHAT DO YOU MEAN, YASHAMARU?
AH—
IT— IT'S—
IT—
IT'S AN EMERGENCY, TENZEN-DONO!

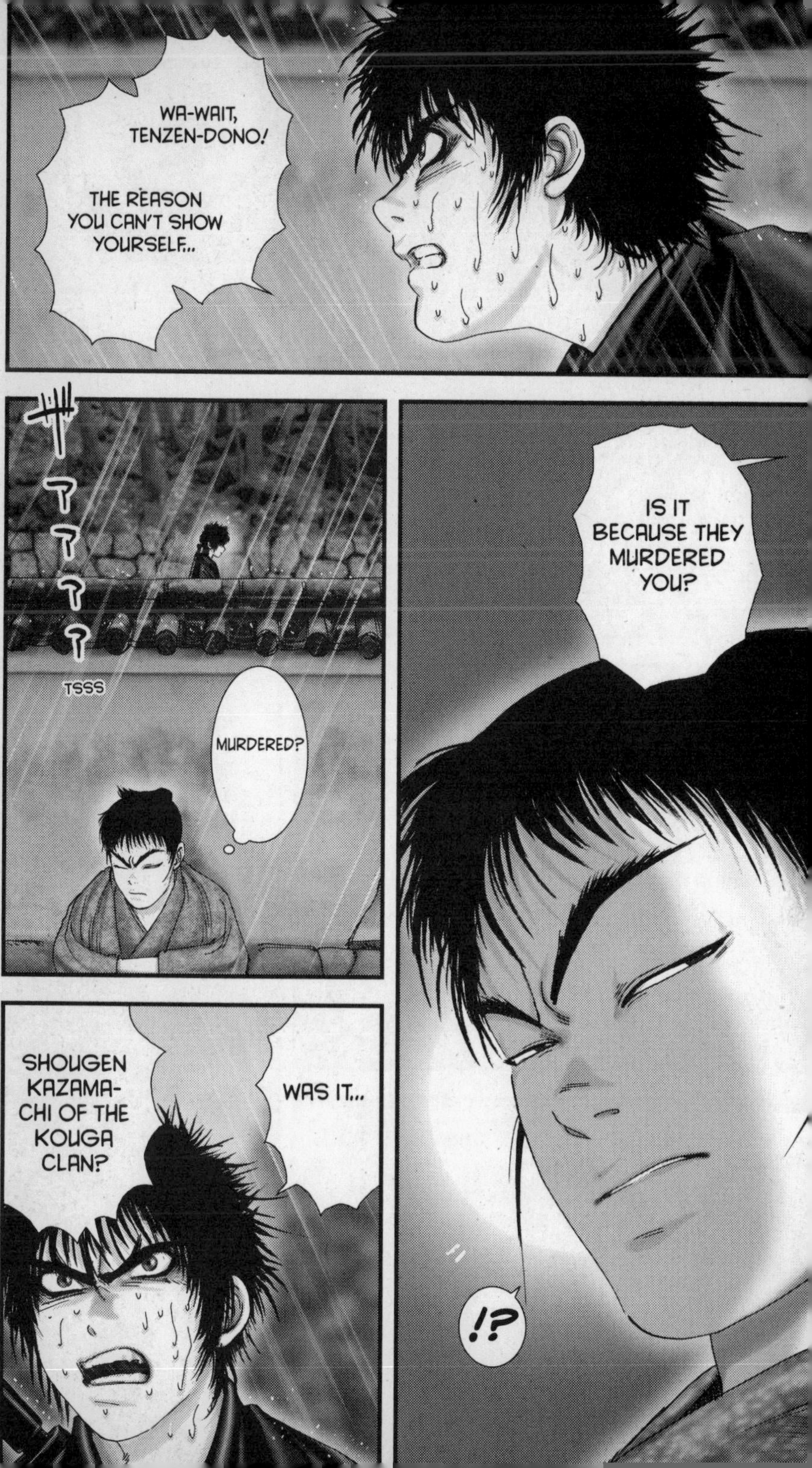
WA-WAIT, TENZEN-DONO!
THE REASON YOU CAN'T SHOW YOURSELF...
IS IT BECAUSE THEY MURDERED YOU?
!?
TSSS
MURDERED?
WAS IT...
SHOUGEN KAZAMA-CHI OF THE KOUGA CLAN?

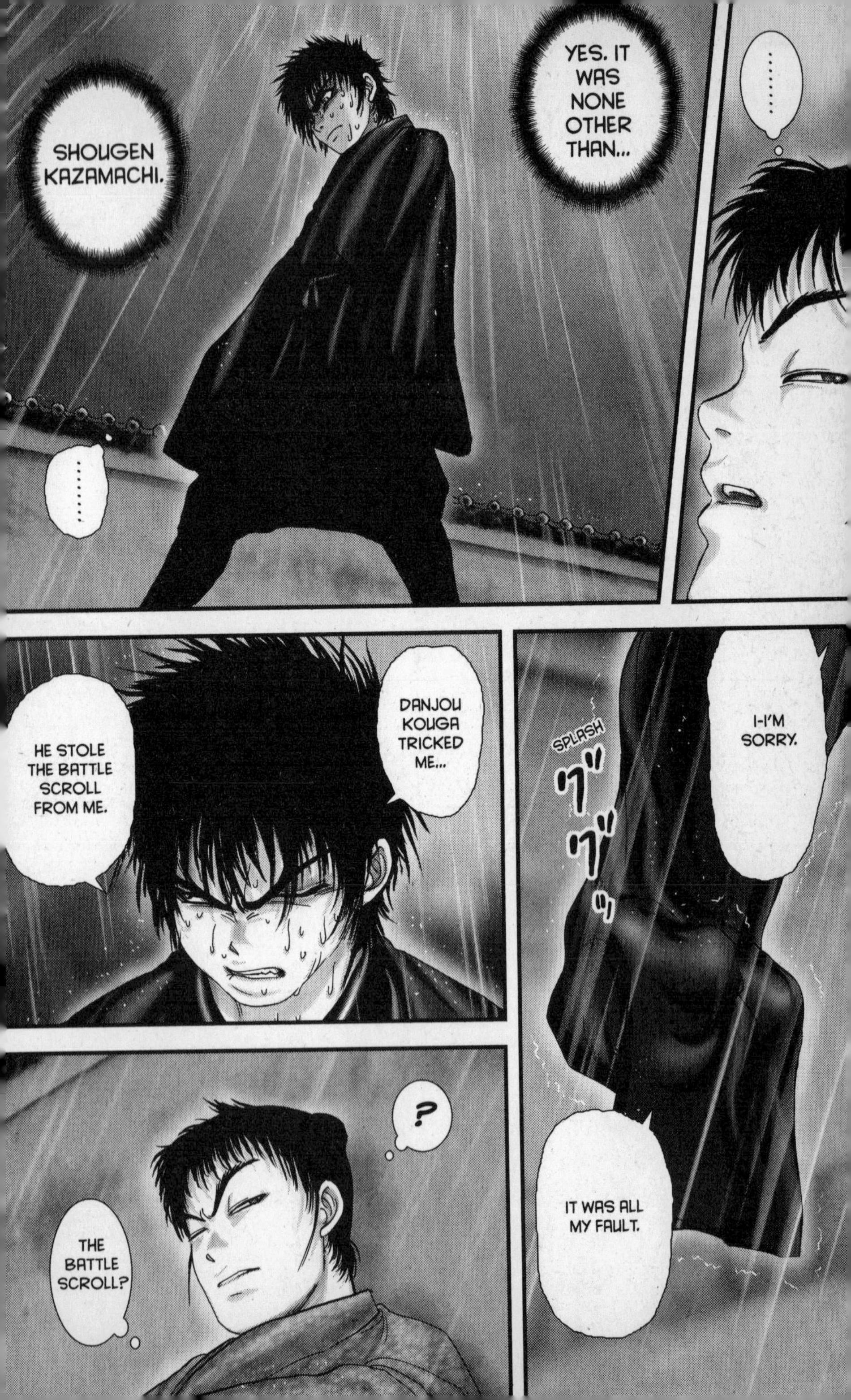

......
YES. IT WAS NONE OTHER THAN...
SHOUGEN KAZAMACHI.
......
I-I'M SORRY.
SPLASH
IT WAS ALL MY FAULT.
DANJOU KOUGA TRICKED ME...
HE STOLE THE BATTLE SCROLL FROM ME.
?
THE BATTLE SCROLL?

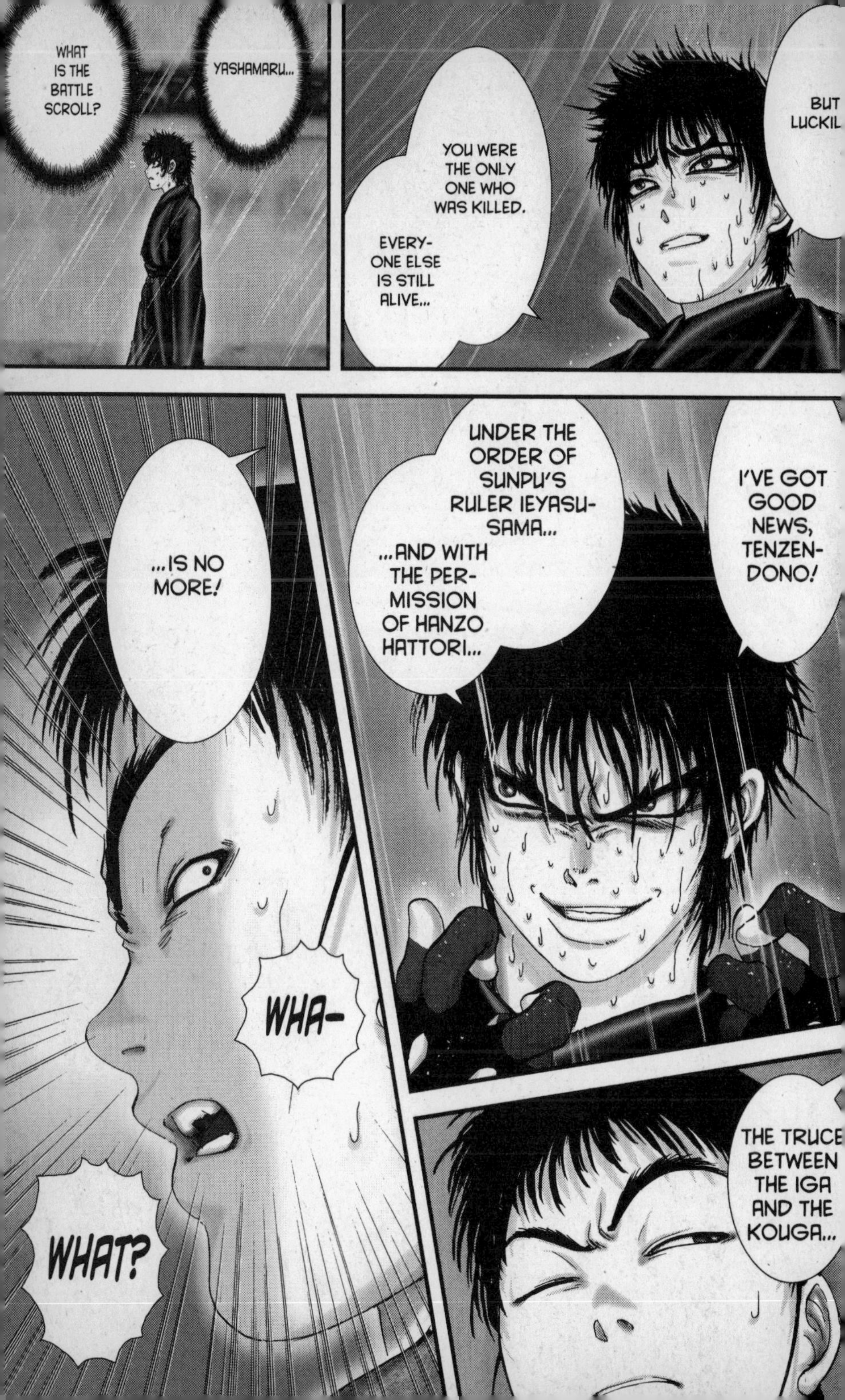
BUT LUCKIL
YOU WERE THE ONLY ONE WHO WAS KILLED.
EVERY-ONE ELSE IS STILL ALIVE...
YASHAMARU...
WHAT IS THE BATTLE SCROLL?
I'VE GOT GOOD NEWS, TENZEN-DONO!
UNDER THE ORDER OF SUNPU'S RULER IEYASU-SAMA...
...AND WITH THE PER-MISSION OF HANZO HATTORI...
THE TRUCE BETWEEN THE IGA AND THE KOUGA...
...IS NO MORE!
WHA-
WHAT?

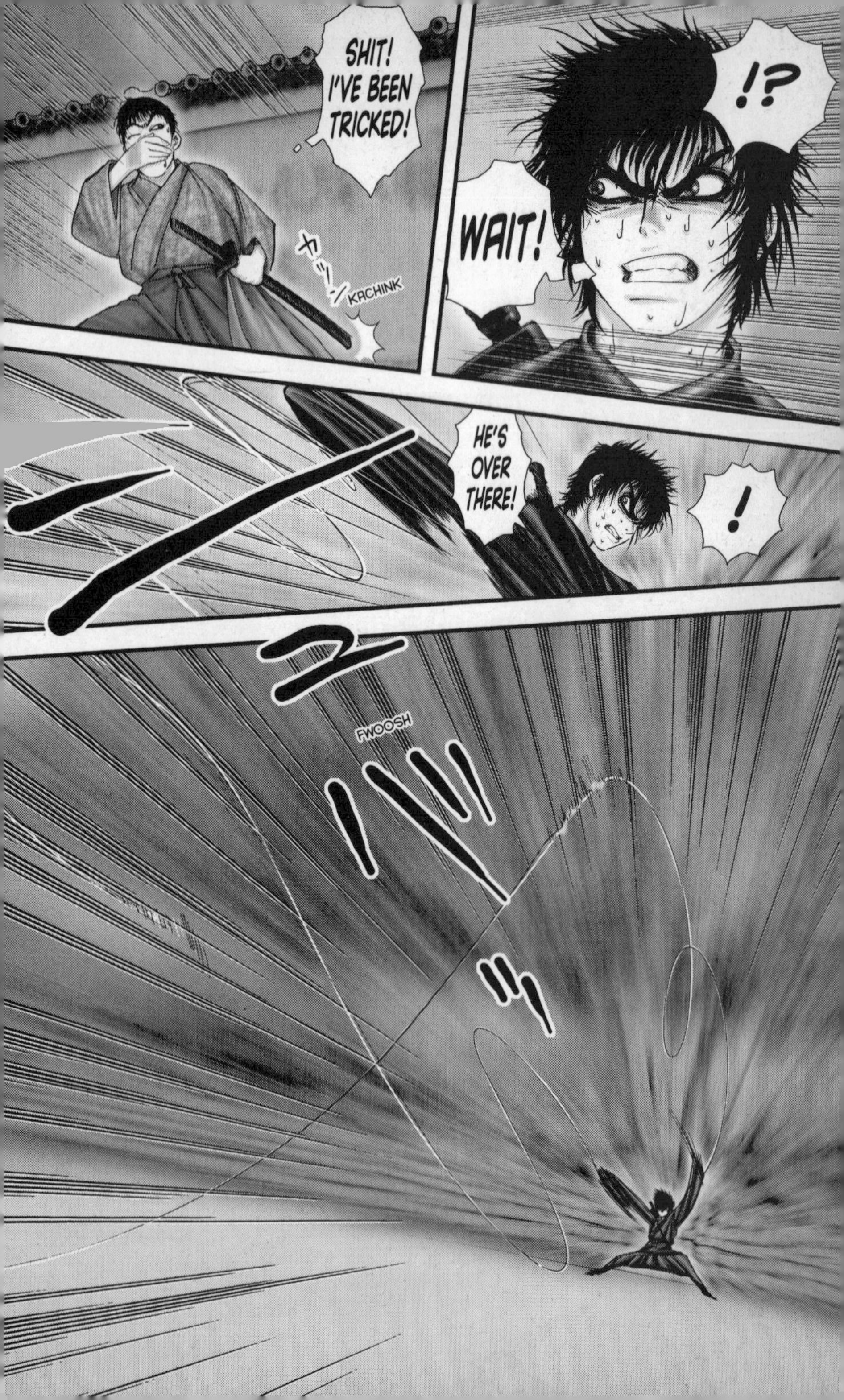
!?
WAIT!
SHIT! I'VE BEEN TRICKED!
KACHINK
HE'S OVER THERE!
!
FWOOSH

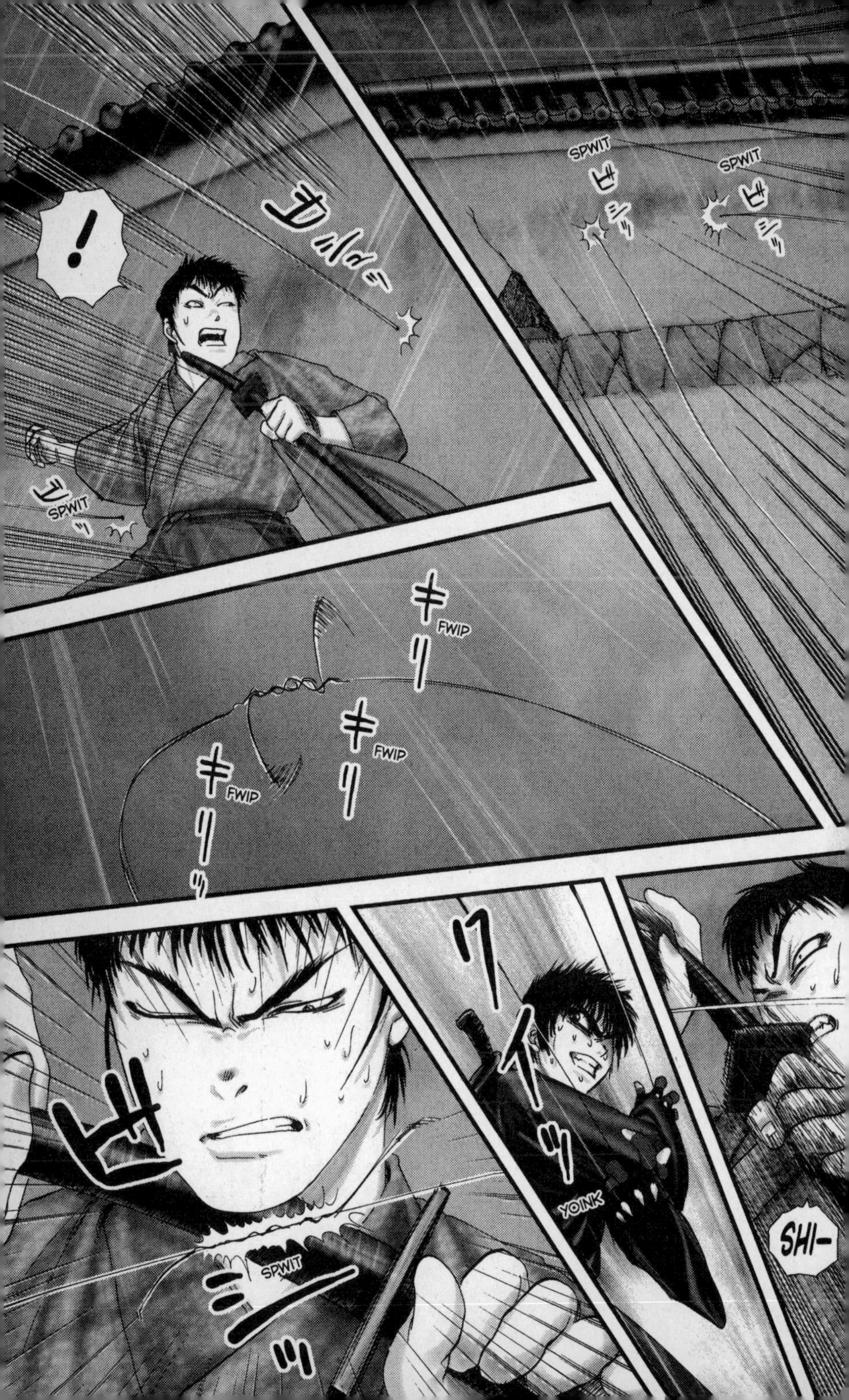
SPWIT
SPWIT
!
SPWIT
FWIP
FWIP
FWIP
SHI-
YOINK
SPWIT

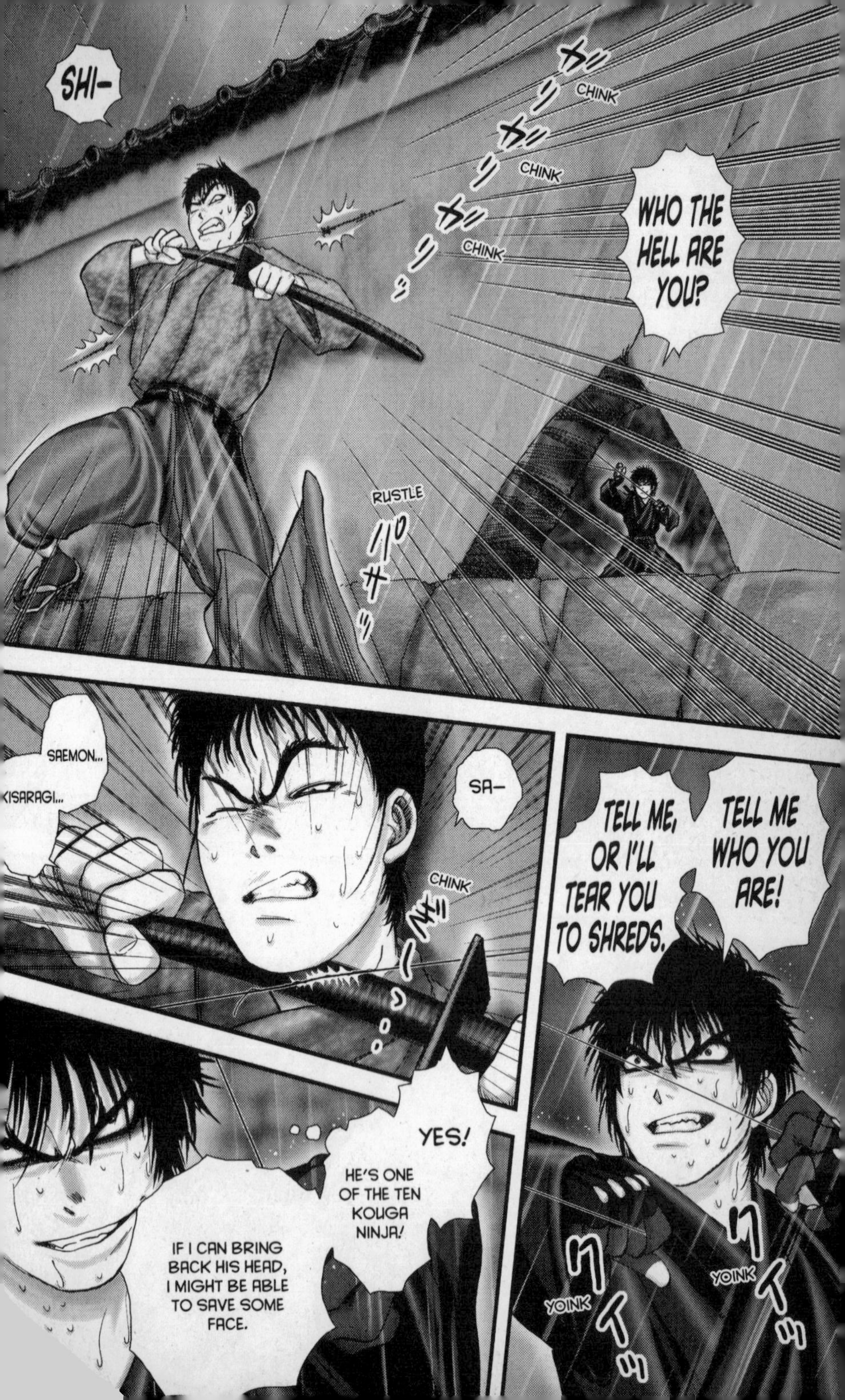
CHINK
CHINK
CHINK
WHO THE HELL ARE YOU?
SHI-
RUSTLE
TELL ME WHO YOU ARE!
TELL ME, OR I'LL TEAR YOU TO SHREDS.
YOINK
YOINK
SA-
CHINK
SAEMON...
KISARAGI...
YES!
...
HE'S ONE OF THE TEN KOUGA NINJA!
IF I CAN BRING BACK HIS HEAD, I MIGHT BE ABLE TO SAVE SOME FACE.

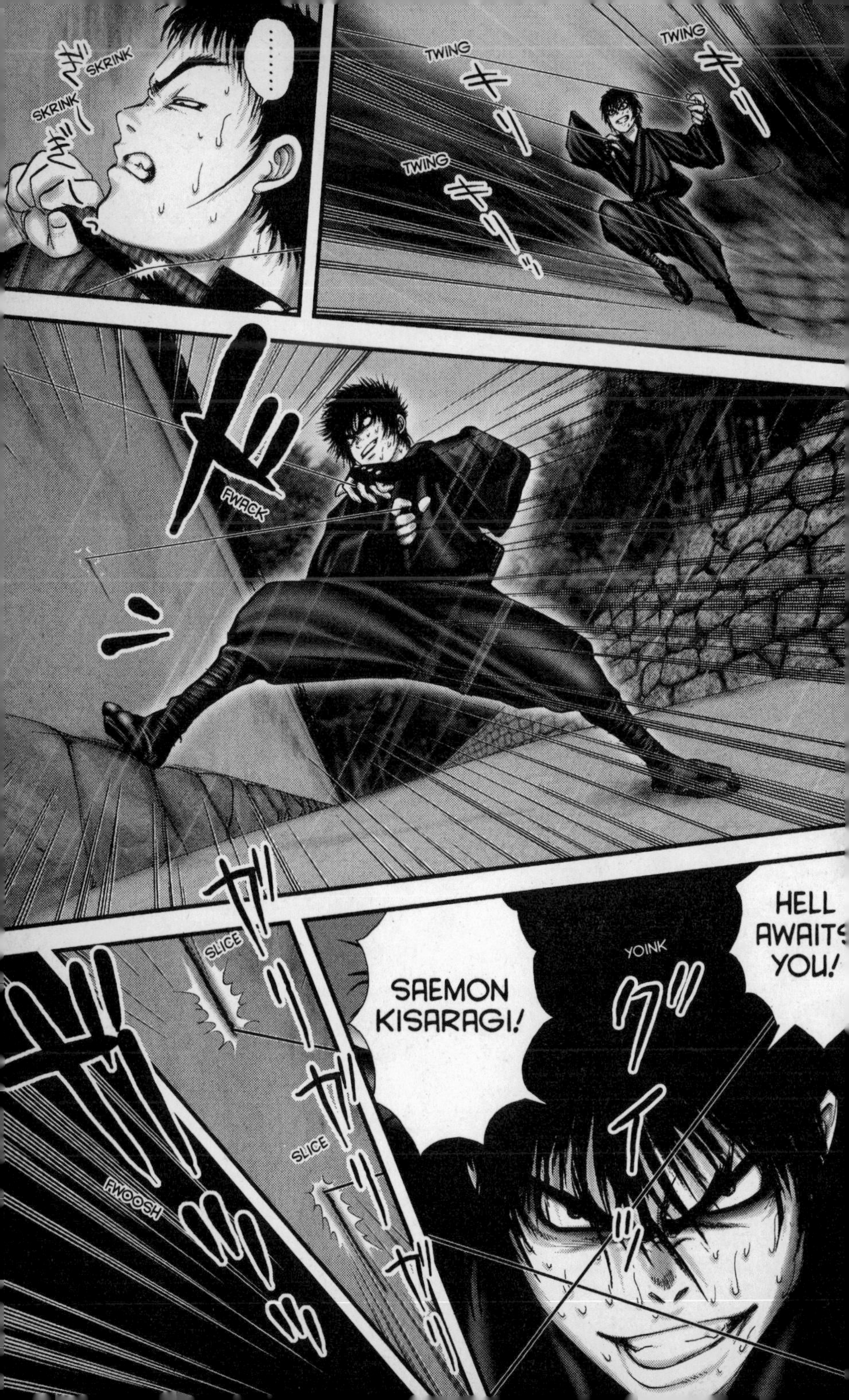
TWING
TWING
TWING
......
SKRINK
SKRINK
FWACK
HELL AWAITS YOU!
YOINK
SAEMON KISARAGI!
SLICE
SLICE
FWOOSH

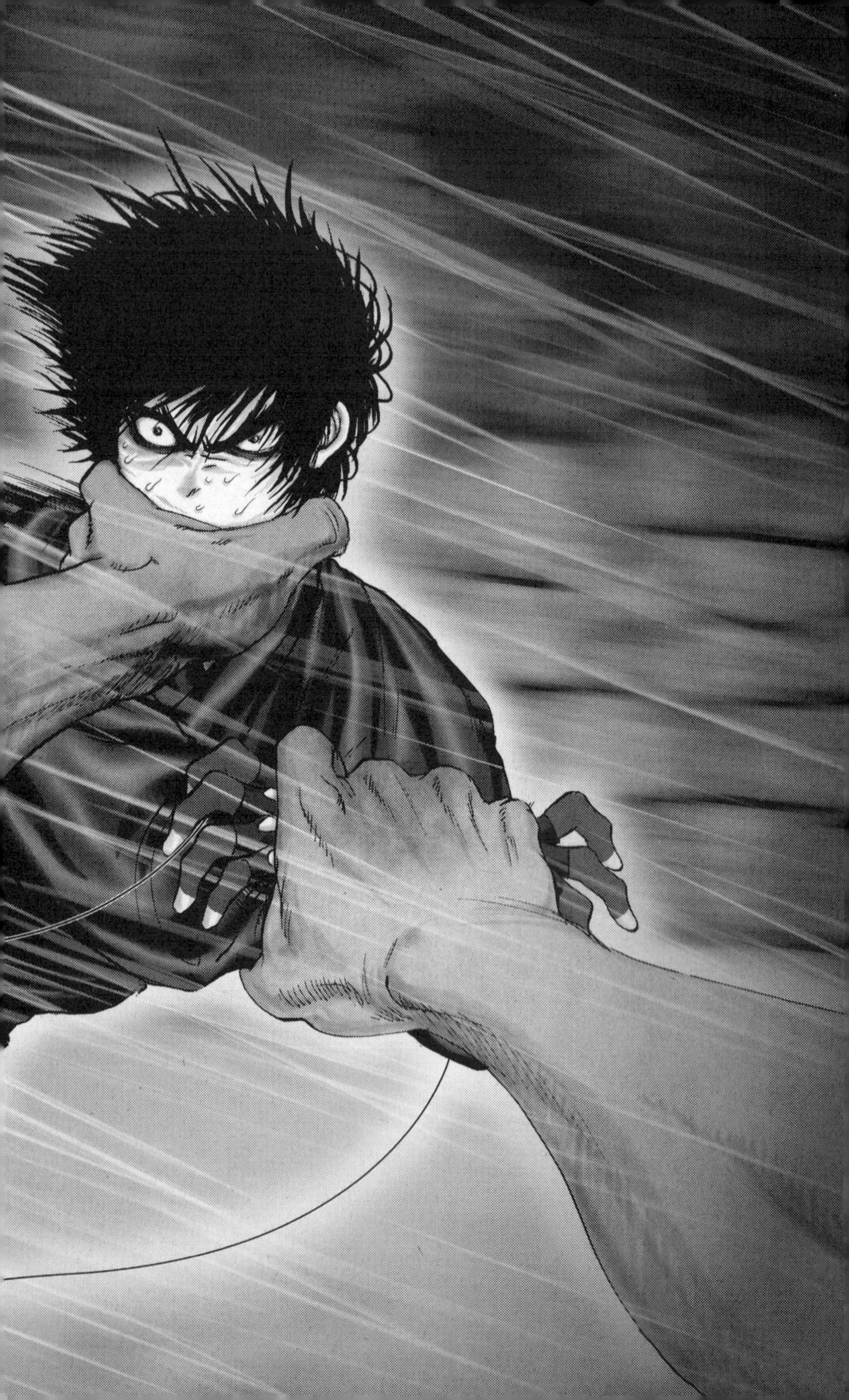

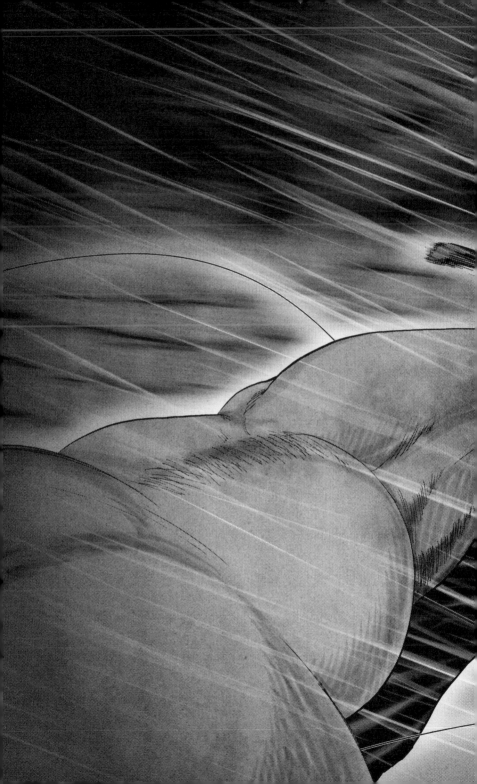

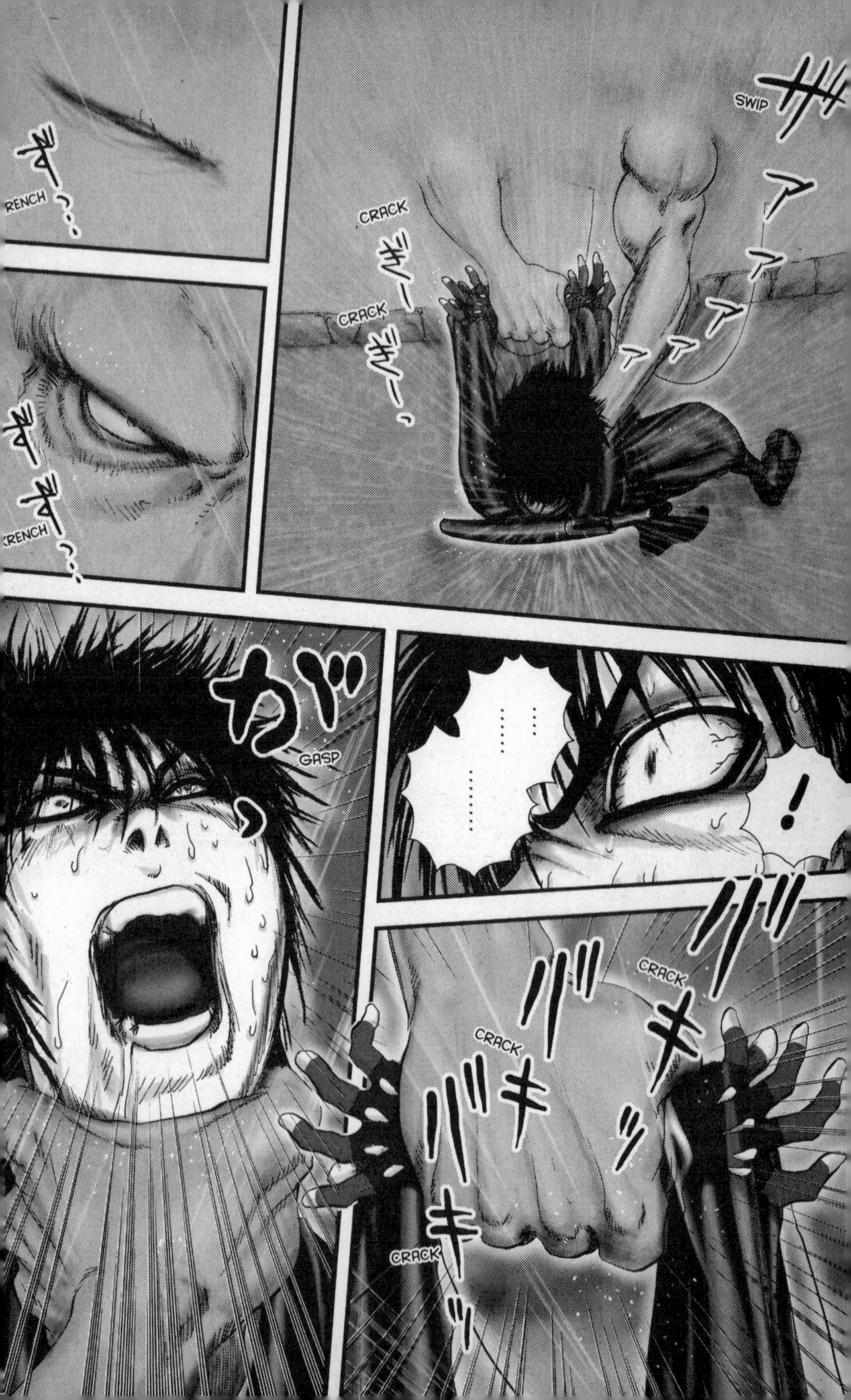

SWIP
CRACK
CRACK
RENCH
RENCH
……
!
CRACK
CRACK
CRACK
GASP

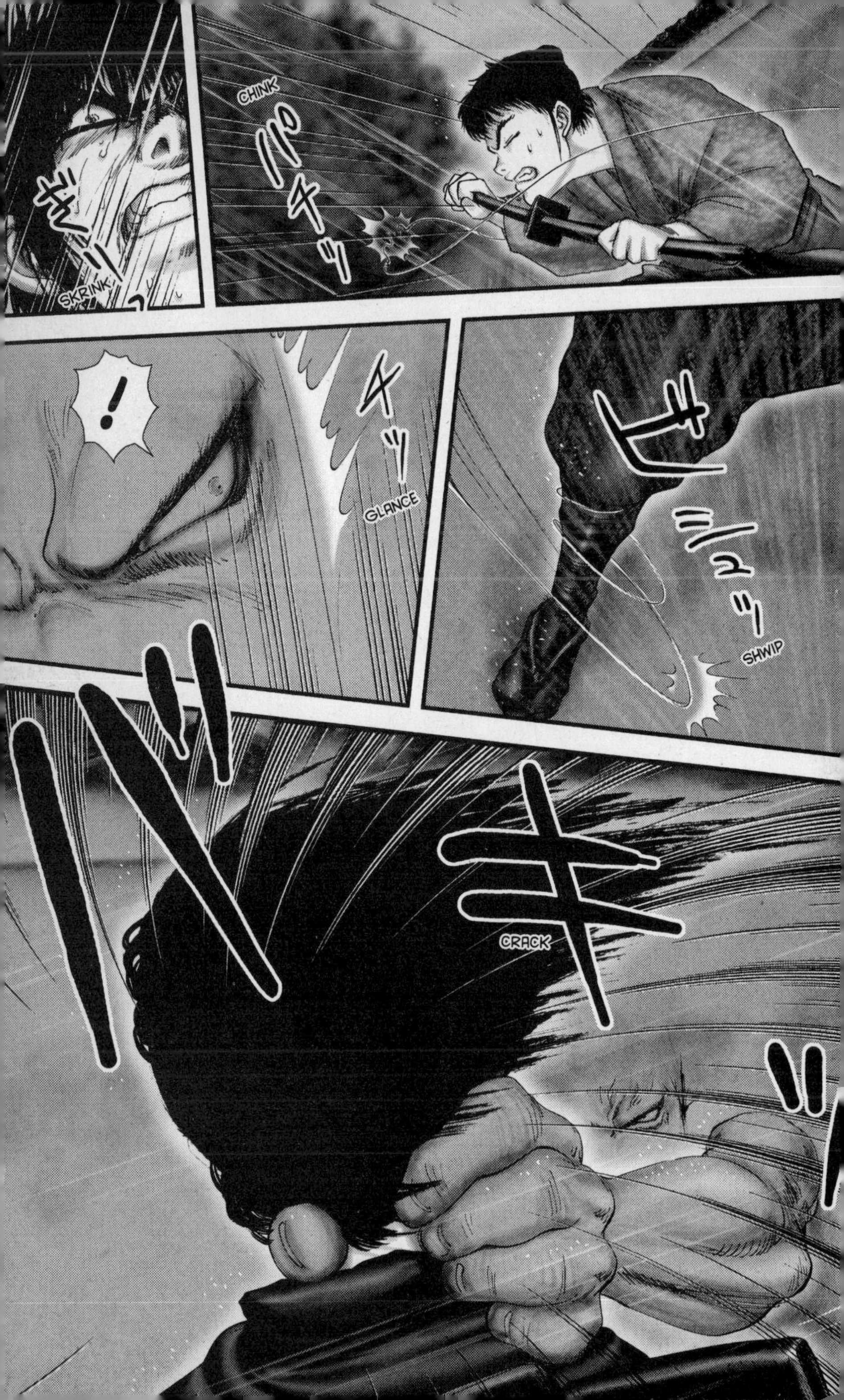

CHINK
SKRINK
SHWIP
!
GLANCE
CRACK

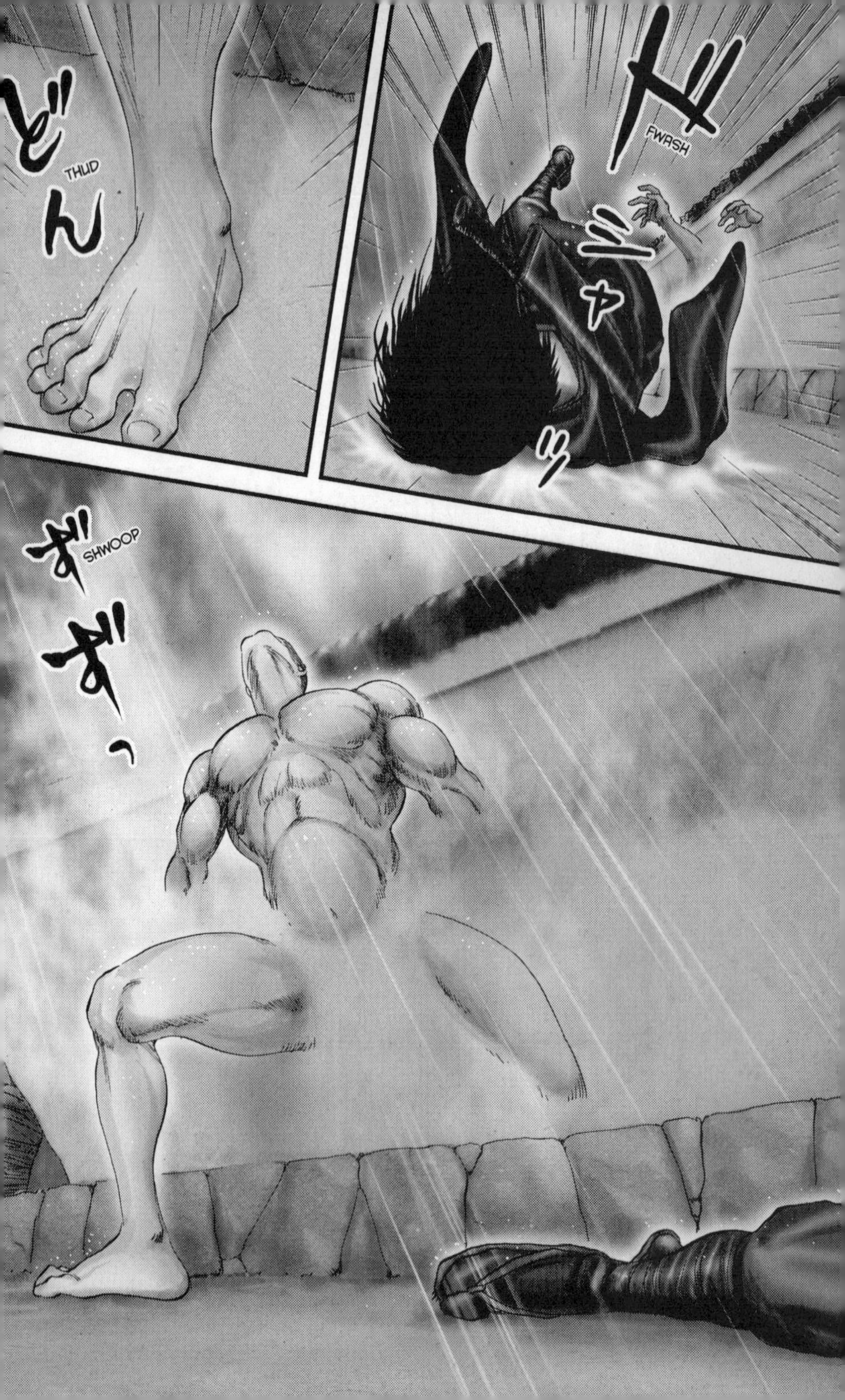
FWASH
どん
THUD
SHWOOP

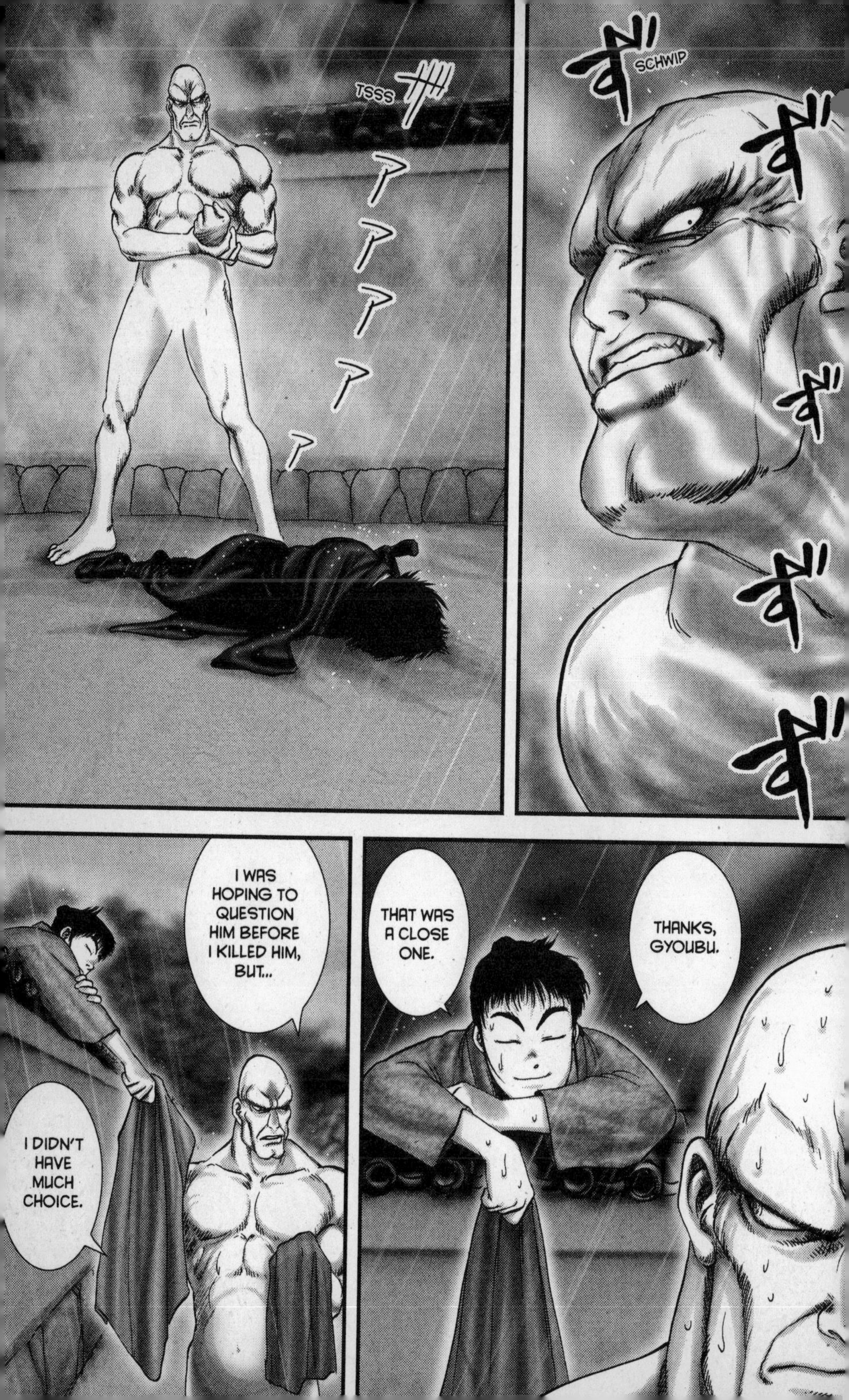
ず
SCHWIP
ず
ず
ず
ず
TSSS
アアアアア
THANKS, GYOUBU.
THAT WAS A CLOSE ONE.
I WAS HOPING TO QUESTION HIM BEFORE I KILLED HIM, BUT...
I DIDN'T HAVE MUCH CHOICE.

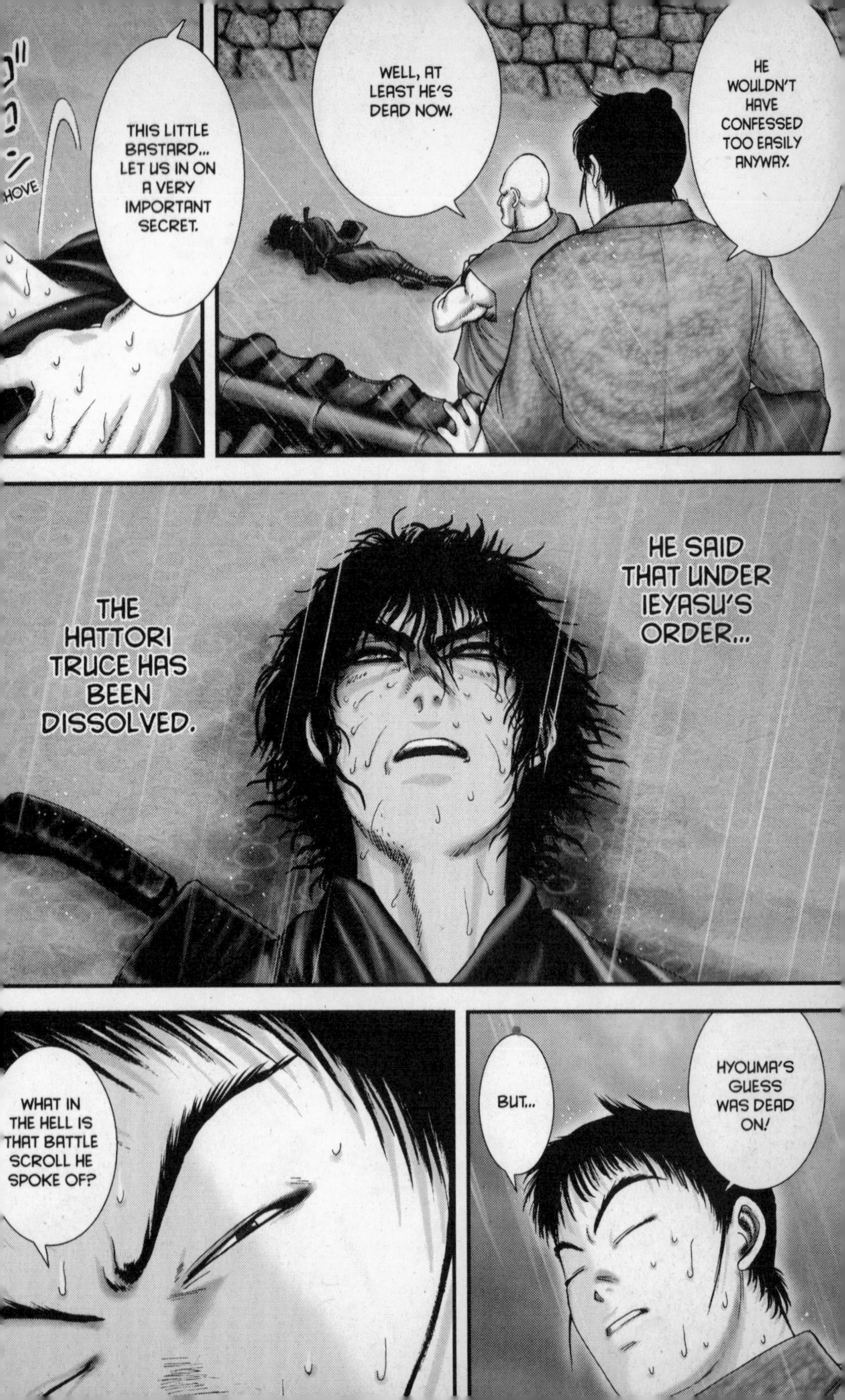
HE WOULDN'T HAVE CONFESSED TOO EASILY ANYWAY.
WELL, AT LEAST HE'S DEAD NOW.
THIS LITTLE BASTARD... LET US IN ON A VERY IMPORTANT SECRET.
SHOVE
HE SAID THAT UNDER IEYASU'S ORDER...
THE HATTORI TRUCE HAS BEEN DISSOLVED.
HYOUMA'S GUESS WAS DEAD ON!
BUT...
WHAT IN THE HELL IS THAT BATTLE SCROLL HE SPOKE OF?

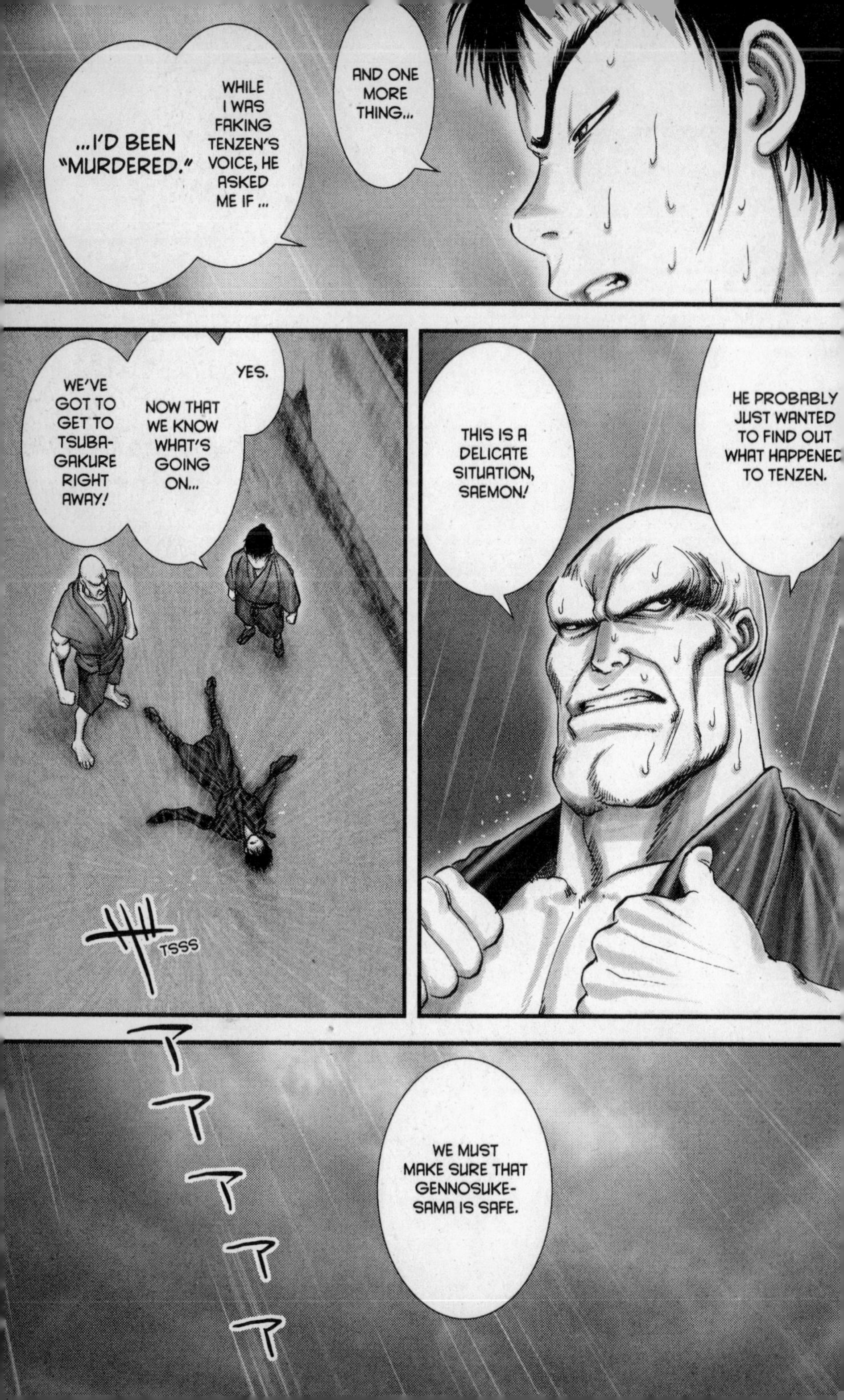
AND ONE MORE THING...
WHILE I WAS FAKING TENZEN'S VOICE, HE ASKED ME IF ...
...I'D BEEN "MURDERED."
HE PROBABLY JUST WANTED TO FIND OUT WHAT HAPPENED TO TENZEN.
THIS IS A DELICATE SITUATION, SAEMON!
YES.
NOW THAT WE KNOW WHAT'S GOING ON...
WE'VE GOT TO GET TO TSUBA-GAKURE RIGHT AWAY!
TSSS
WE MUST MAKE SURE THAT GENNOSUKE-SAMA IS SAFE.
アアアアアア

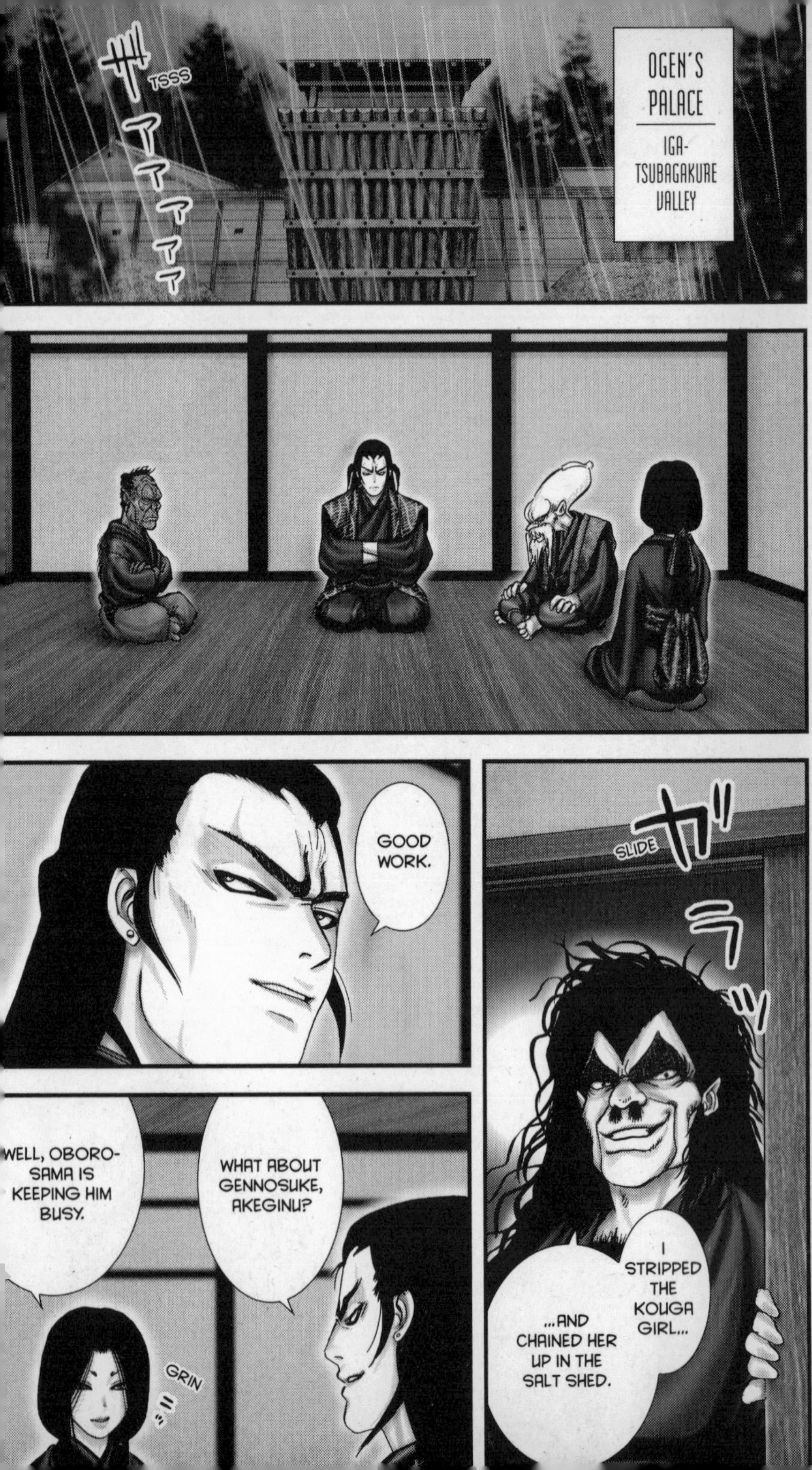
TSSS
OGEN'S PALACE
IGA-TSUBAGAKURE VALLEY
SLIDE
I STRIPPED THE KOUGA GIRL...
...AND CHAINED HER UP IN THE SALT SHED.
GOOD WORK.
WHAT ABOUT GENNOSUKE, AKEGINU?
WELL, OBORO-SAMA IS KEEPING HIM BUSY.
GRIN

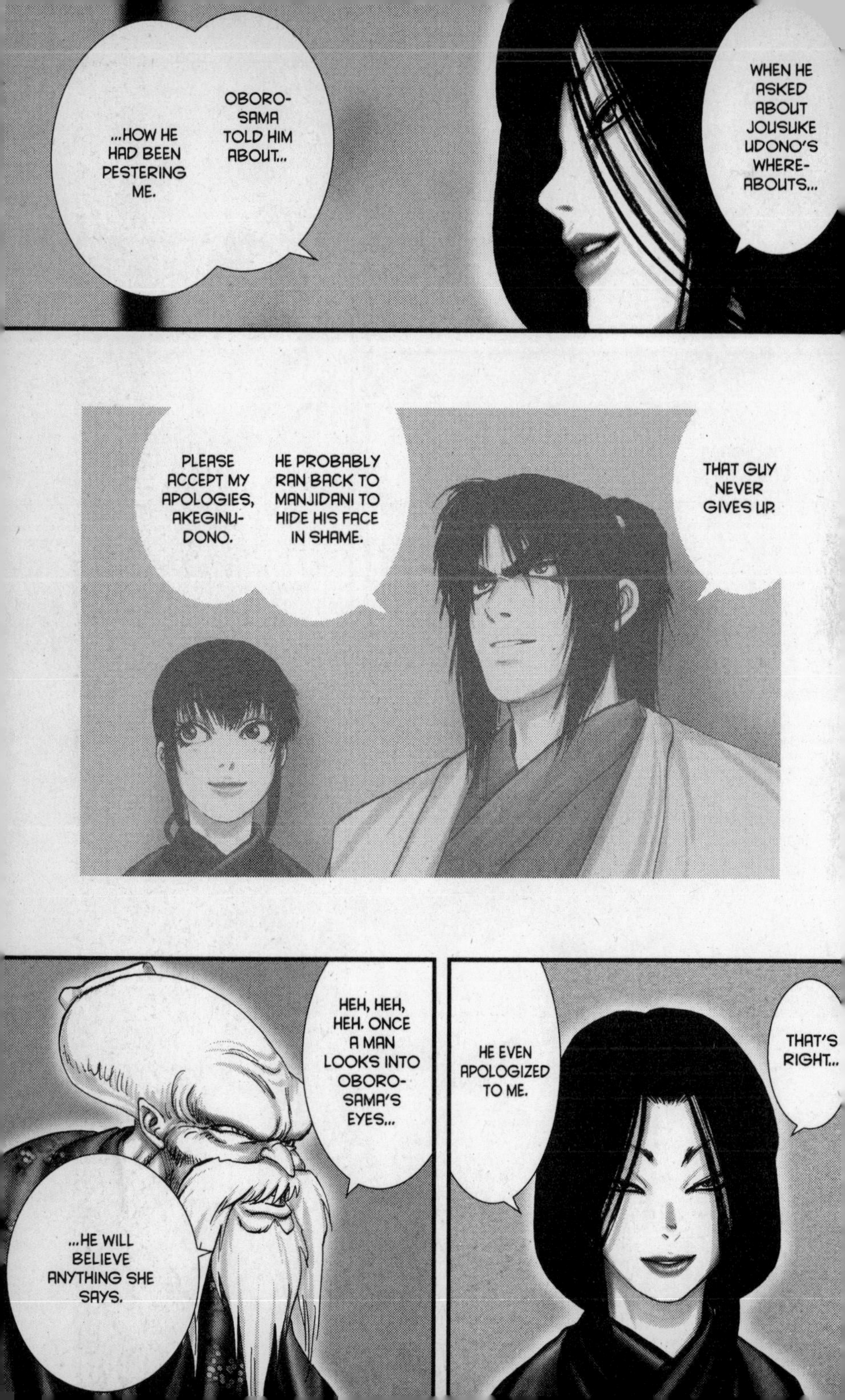
WHEN HE ASKED ABOUT JOUSUKE UDONO'S WHERE-ABOUTS...
OBORO-SAMA TOLD HIM ABOUT...
...HOW HE HAD BEEN PESTERING ME.
THAT GUY NEVER GIVES UP.
HE PROBABLY RAN BACK TO MANJIDANI TO HIDE HIS FACE IN SHAME.
PLEASE ACCEPT MY APOLOGIES, AKEGINU-DONO.
THAT'S RIGHT...
HE EVEN APOLOGIZED TO ME.
HEH, HEH, HEH. ONCE A MAN LOOKS INTO OBORO-SAMA'S EYES...
...HE WILL BELIEVE ANYTHING SHE SAYS.

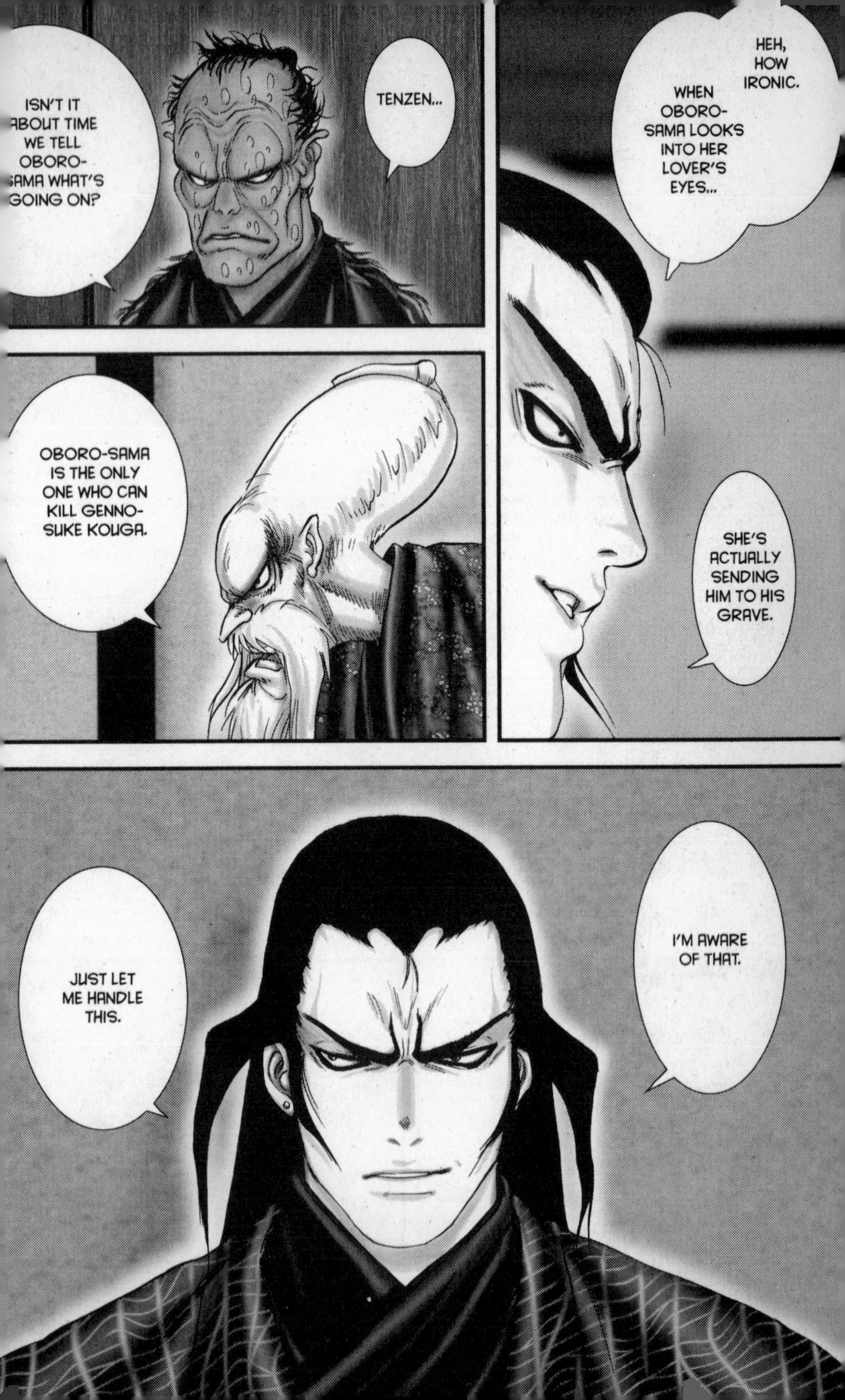
HEH, HOW IRONIC.
WHEN OBORO-SAMA LOOKS INTO HER LOVER'S EYES...
SHE'S ACTUALLY SENDING HIM TO HIS GRAVE.
TENZEN...
ISN'T IT ABOUT TIME WE TELL OBORO-SAMA WHAT'S GOING ON?
OBORO-SAMA IS THE ONLY ONE WHO CAN KILL GENNO-SUKE KOUGA.
I'M AWARE OF THAT.
JUST LET ME HANDLE THIS.

HMM... THIS MUD IS PERFECT.

THWICK

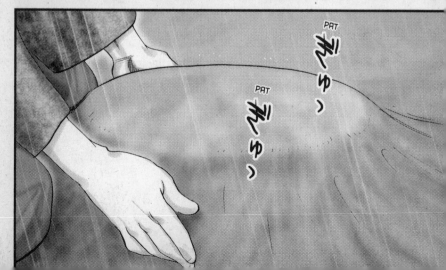

PAT

PAT

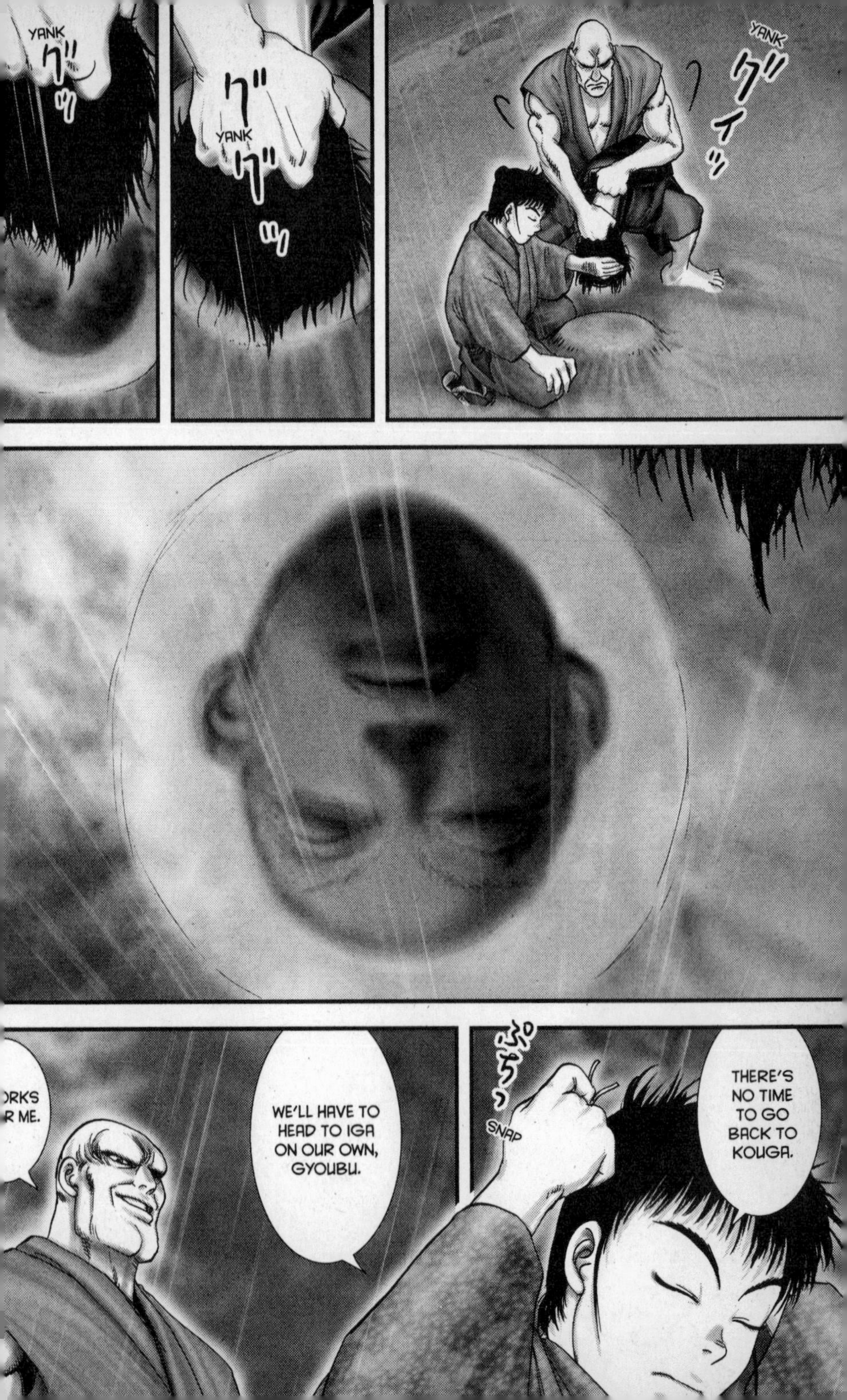
YANK
グイッ
YANK
グ
YANK
グッ
YANK
グッ
ぷちっ
SNAP
THERE'S NO TIME TO GO BACK TO KOUGA.
WE'LL HAVE TO HEAD TO IGA ON OUR OWN, GYOUBU.

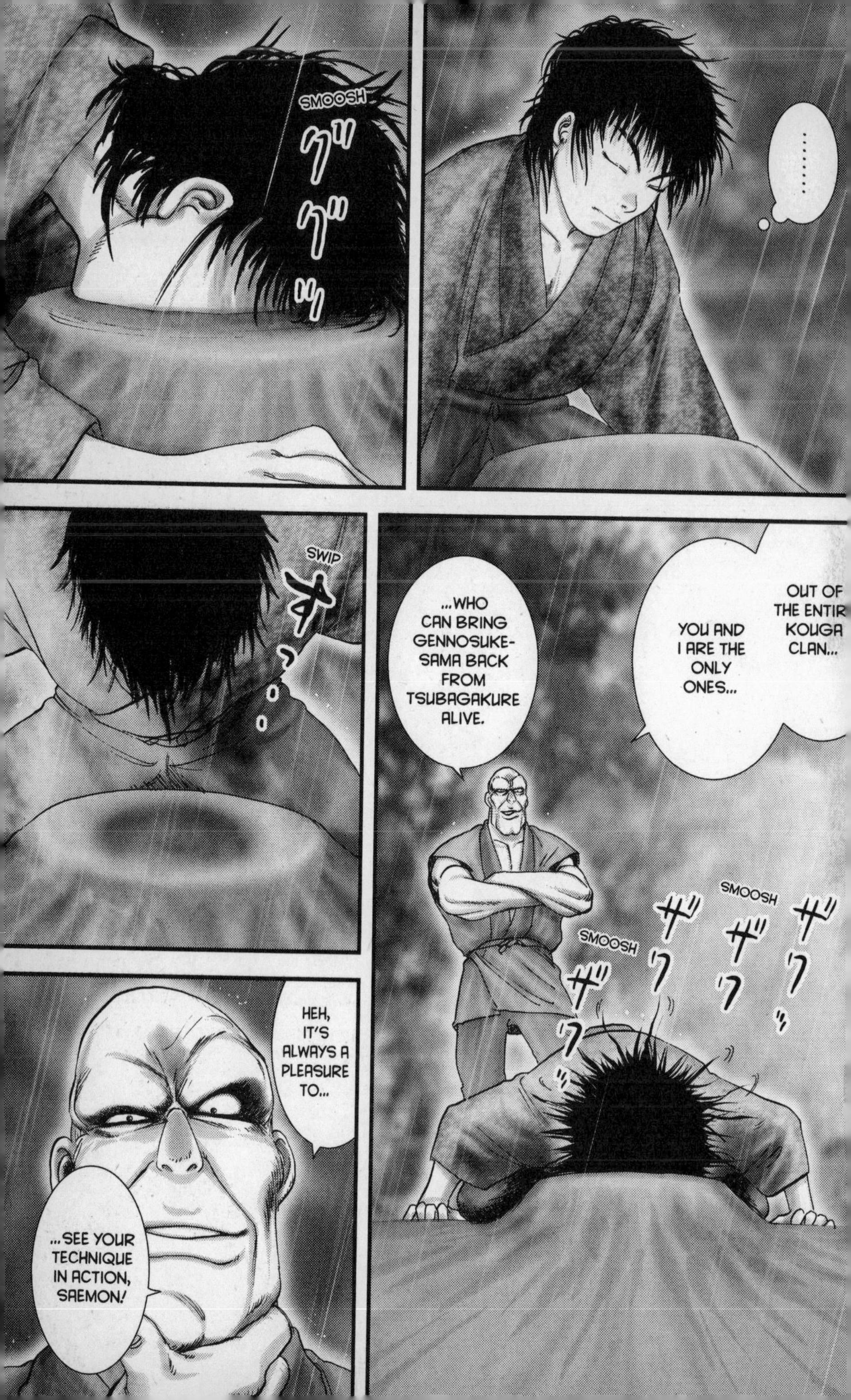

......
SMOOSH
OUT OF THE ENTIRE KOUGA CLAN...
YOU AND I ARE THE ONLY ONES...
...WHO CAN BRING GENNOSUKE-SAMA BACK FROM TSUBAGAKURE ALIVE.
SMOOSH
SMOOSH
SWIP
HEH, IT'S ALWAYS A PLEASURE TO...
...SEE YOUR TECHNIQUE IN ACTION, SAEMON!

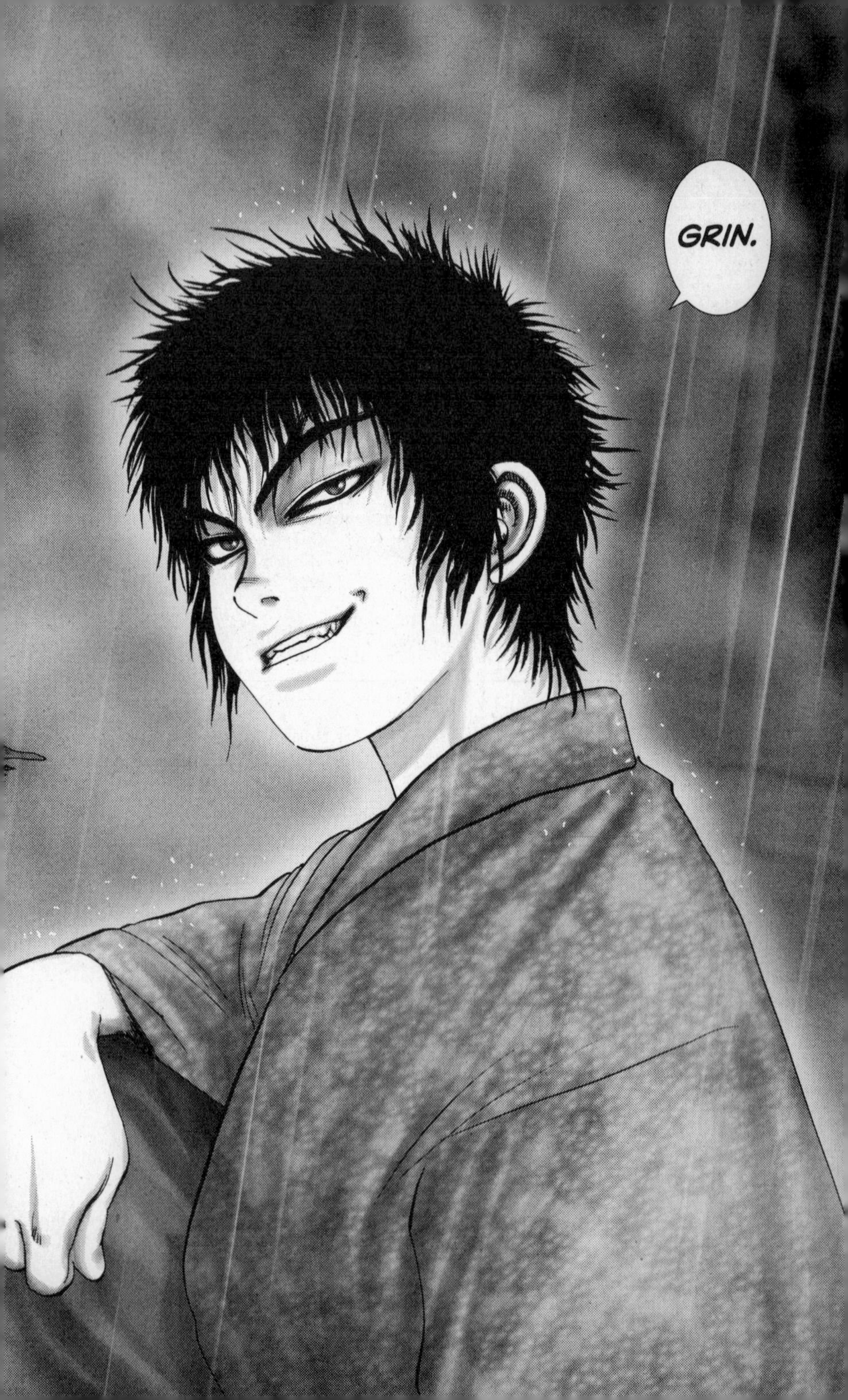
GRIN.

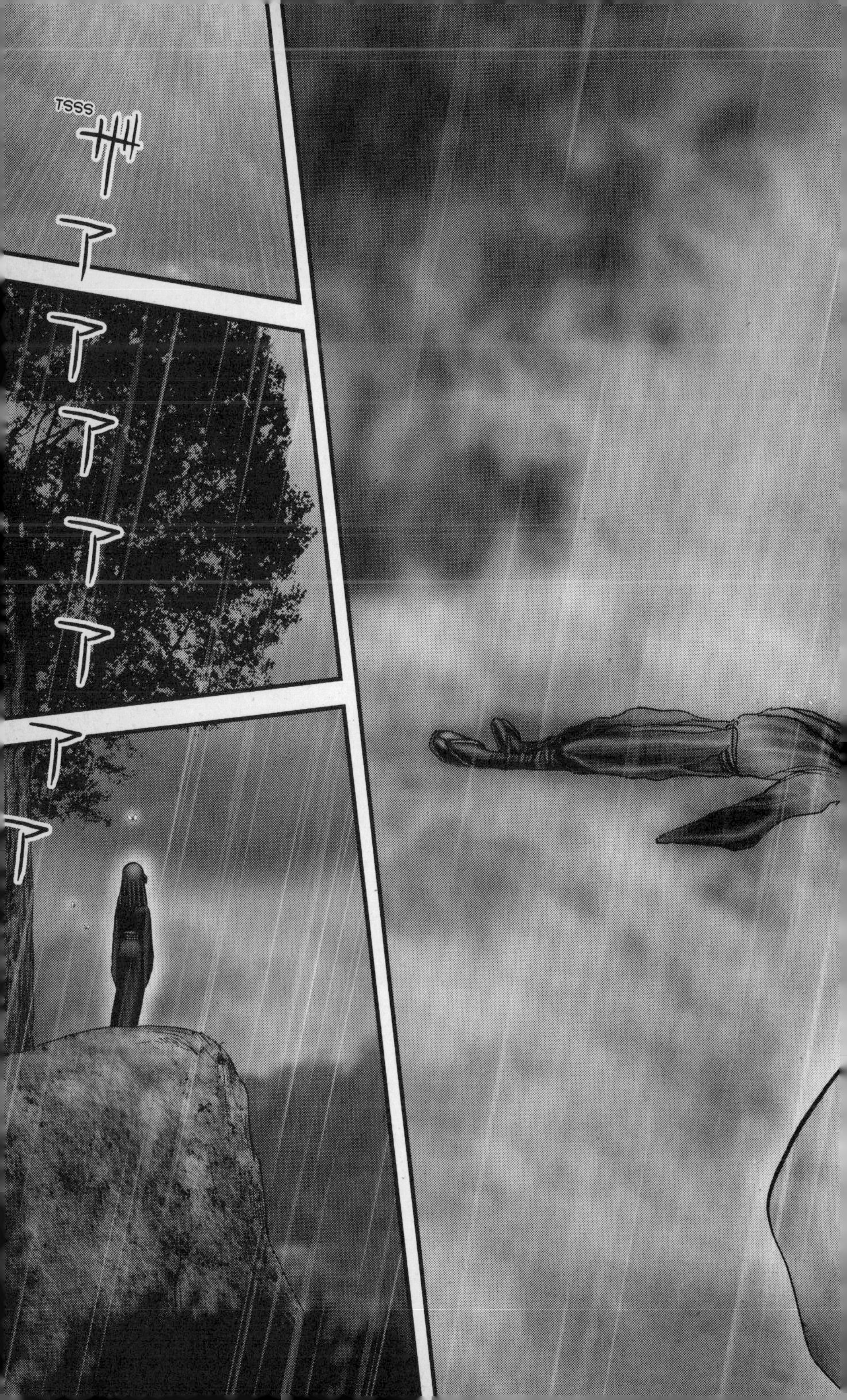
TSSS
ザアアアアアアア

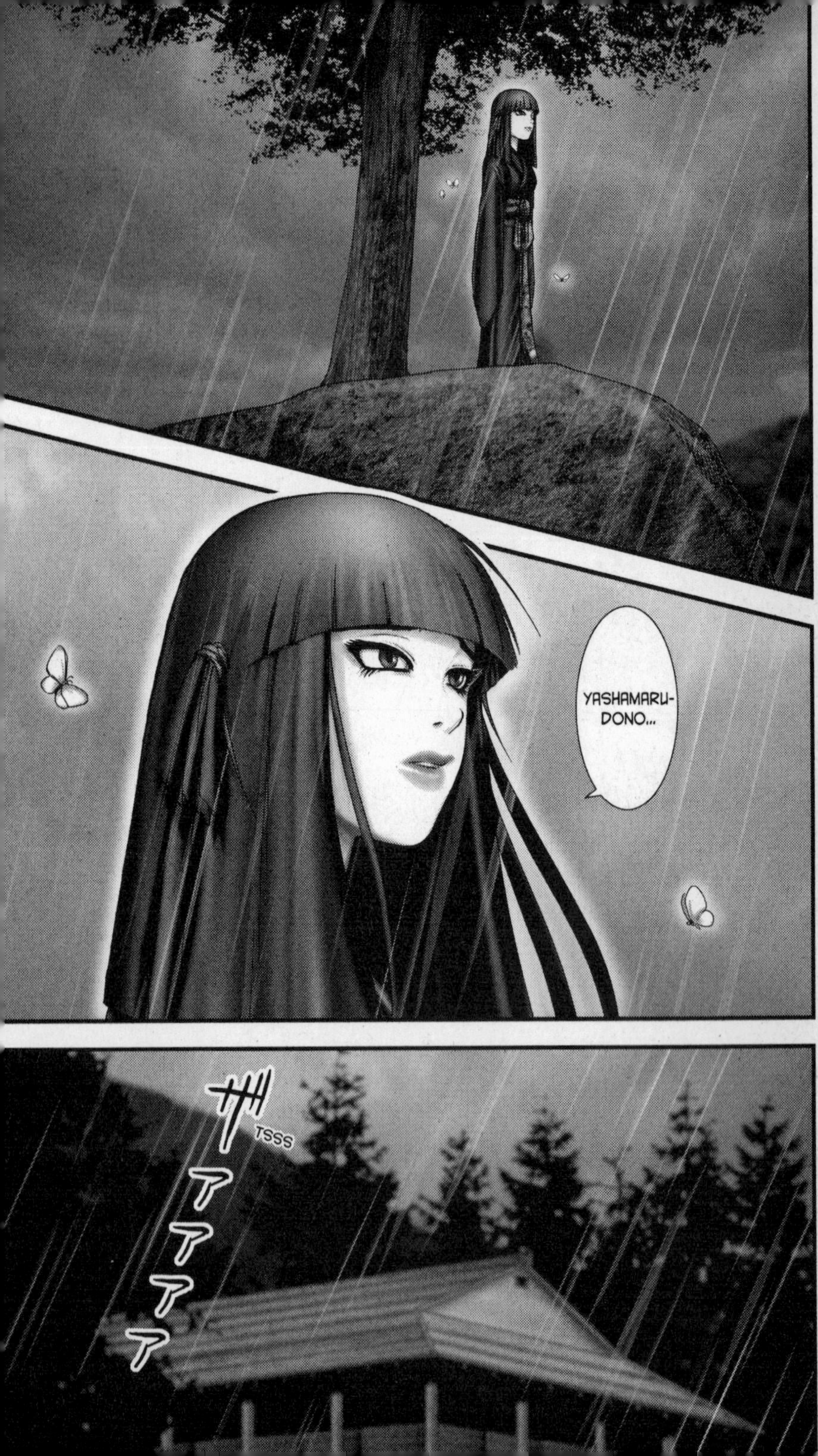
YASHAMARU-DONO...
ザァァァァ
TSSS

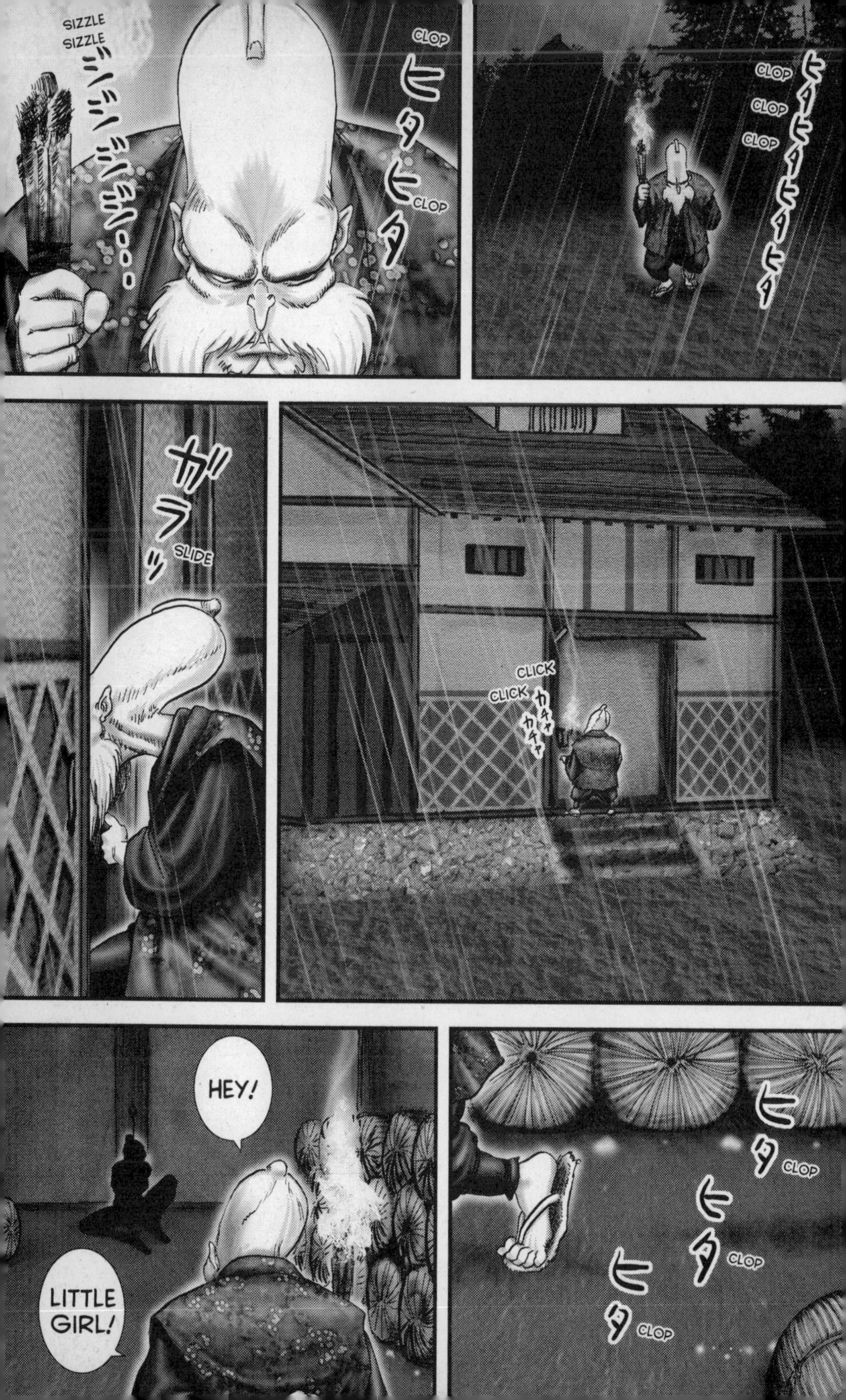

ヒタヒタヒタヒタ
CLOP
CLOP
CLOP
SIZZLE
SIZZLE
ジジジジジ…
ヒタ
CLOP
ヒタ
CLOP
カチャ
CLICK
カチャ
CLICK
ガラッ
SLIDE
ヒタ
CLOP
ヒタ
CLOP
ヒタ
CLOP
HEY!
LITTLE GIRL!

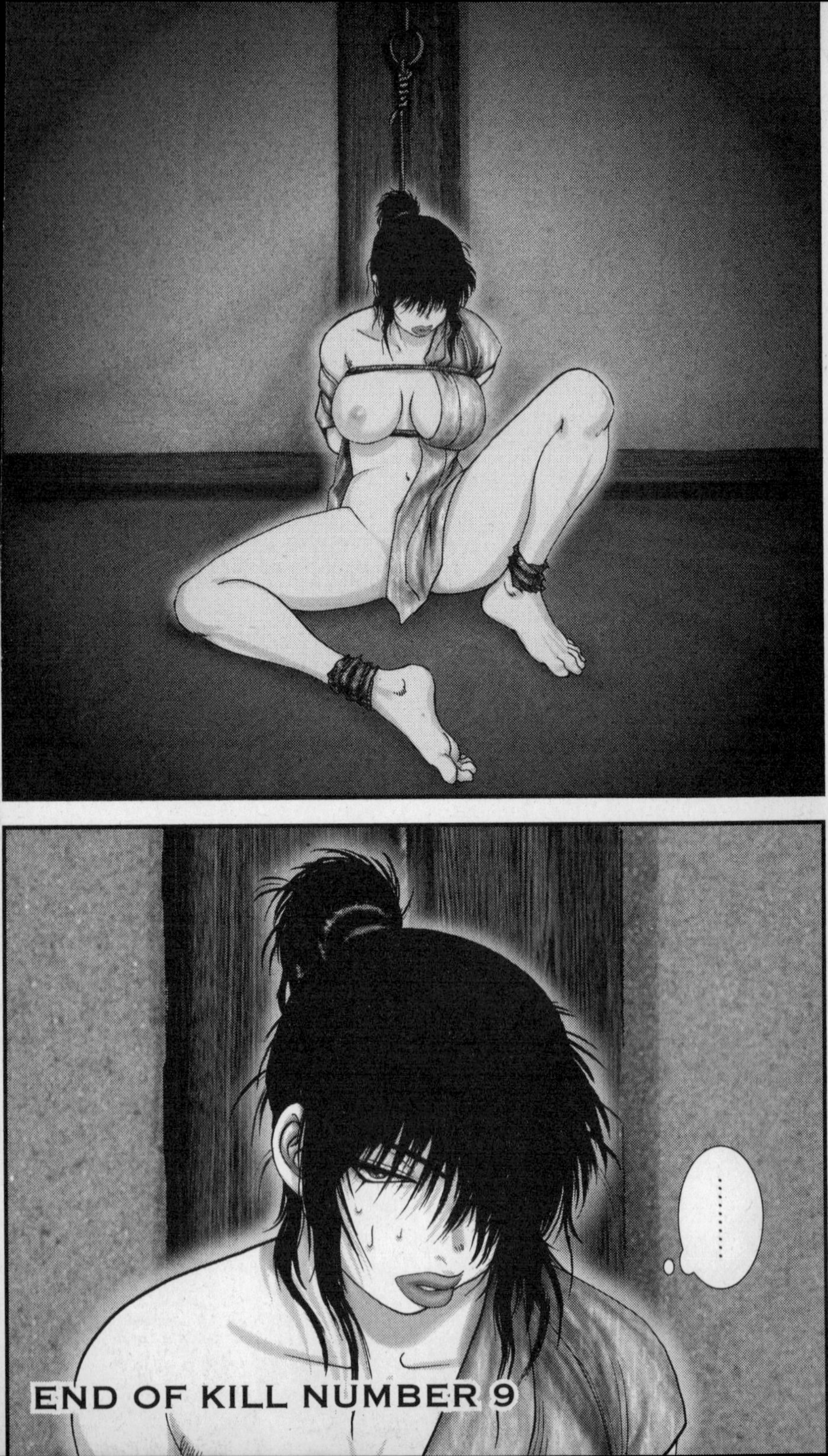
……
END OF KILL NUMBER 9

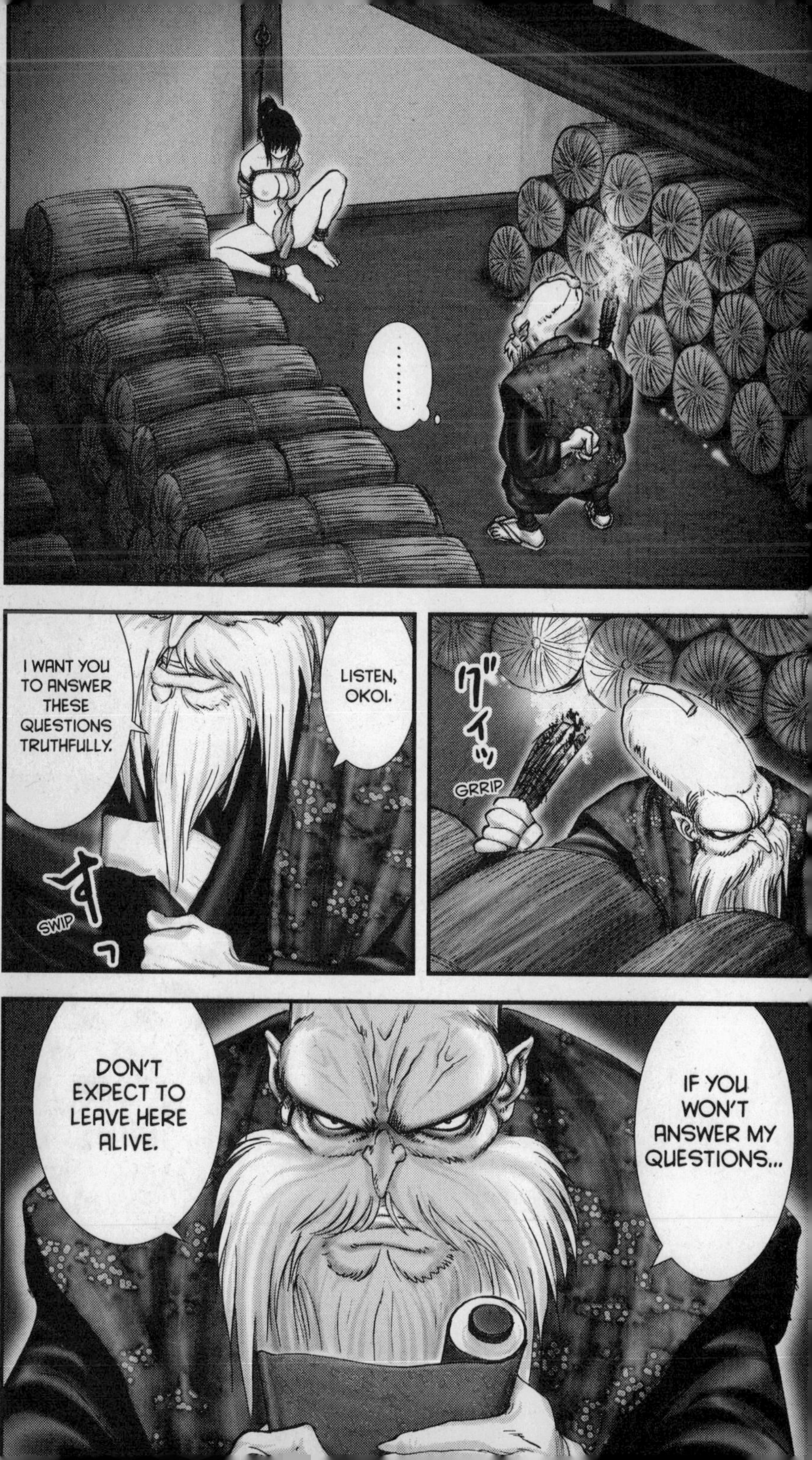
......
グイッ
GRRIP
LISTEN, OKOI.
I WANT YOU TO ANSWER THESE QUESTIONS TRUTHFULLY.
SWIP
IF YOU WON'T ANSWER MY QUESTIONS...
DON'T EXPECT TO LEAVE HERE ALIVE.

KILL NUMBER 10
[6 VS 8]

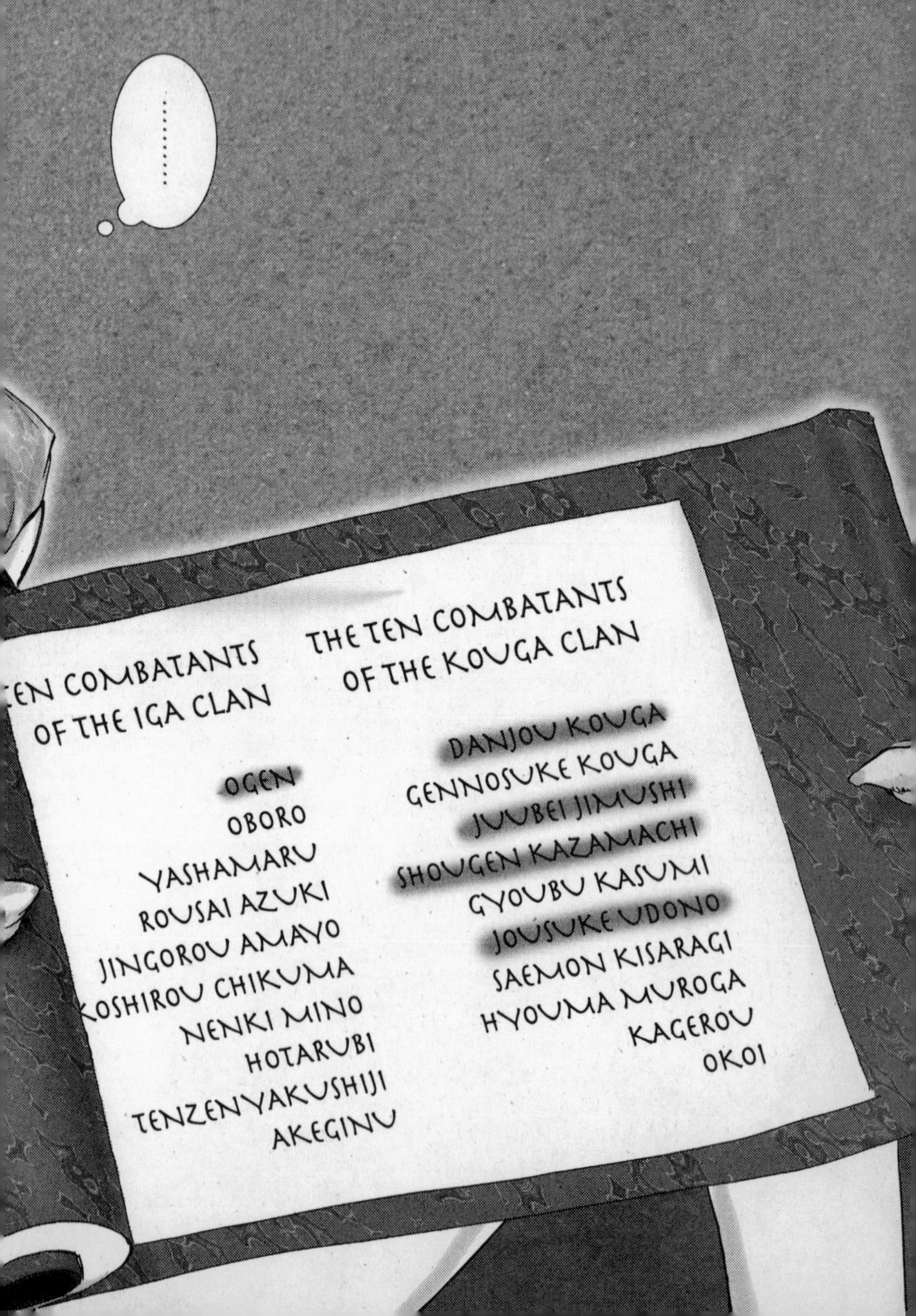
......
EN COMBATANTS
OF THE IGA CLAN
OGEN
OBORO
YASHAMARU
ROUSAI AZUKI
JINGOROU AMAYO
KOSHIROU CHIKUMA
NENKI MINO
HOTARUBI
TENZEN YAKUSHIJI
AKEGINU
THE TEN COMBATANTS
OF THE KOUGA CLAN
DANJOU KOUGA
GENNOSUKE KOUGA
JUUBEI JIMUSHI
SHOUGEN KAZAMACHI
GYOUBU KASUMI
JOUSUKE UDONO
SAEMON KISARAGI
HYOUMA MUROGA
KAGEROU
OKOI

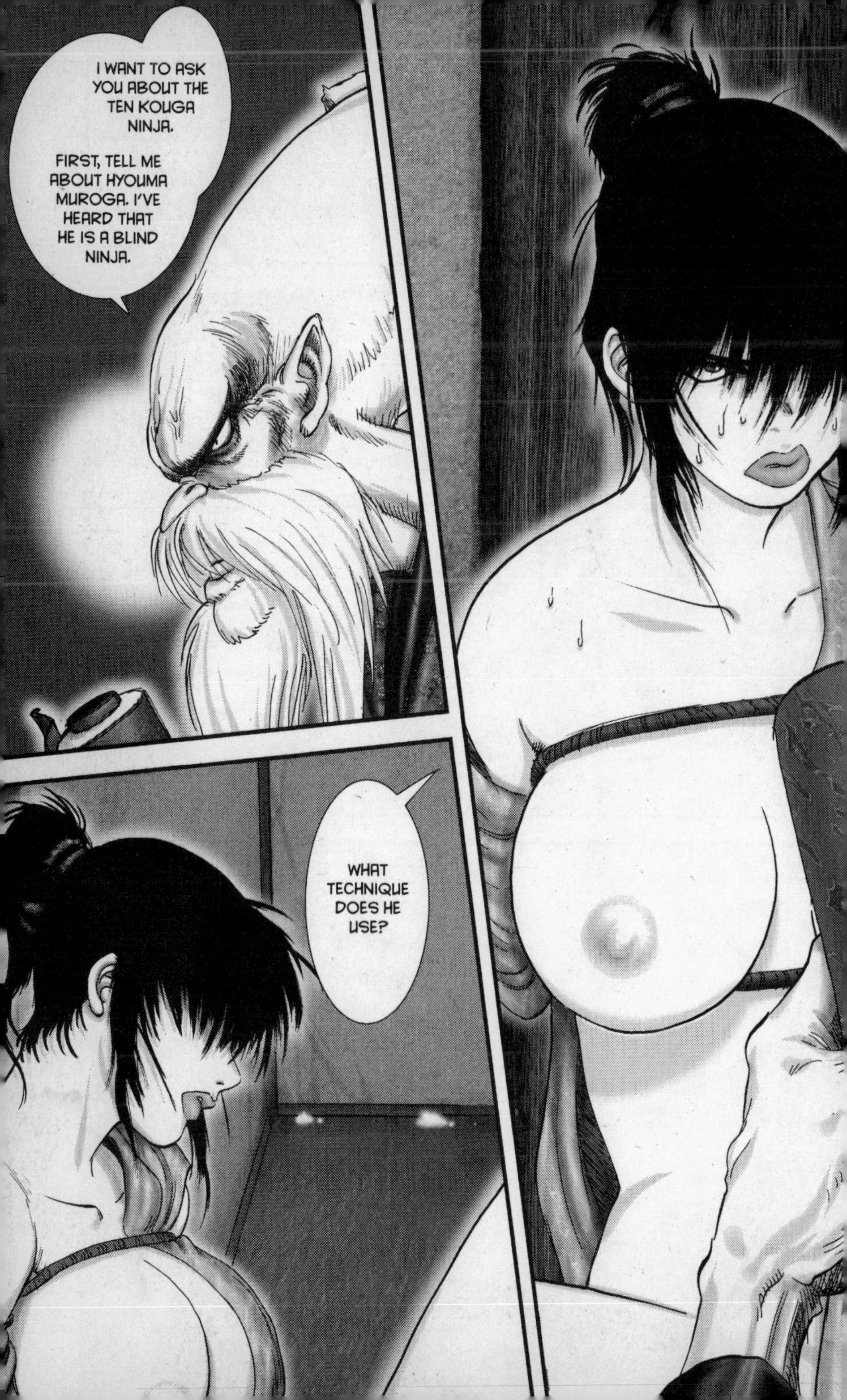
I WANT TO ASK YOU ABOUT THE TEN KOUGA NINJA.
FIRST, TELL ME ABOUT HYOUMA MUROGA. I'VE HEARD THAT HE IS A BLIND NINJA.
WHAT TECHNIQUE DOES HE USE?

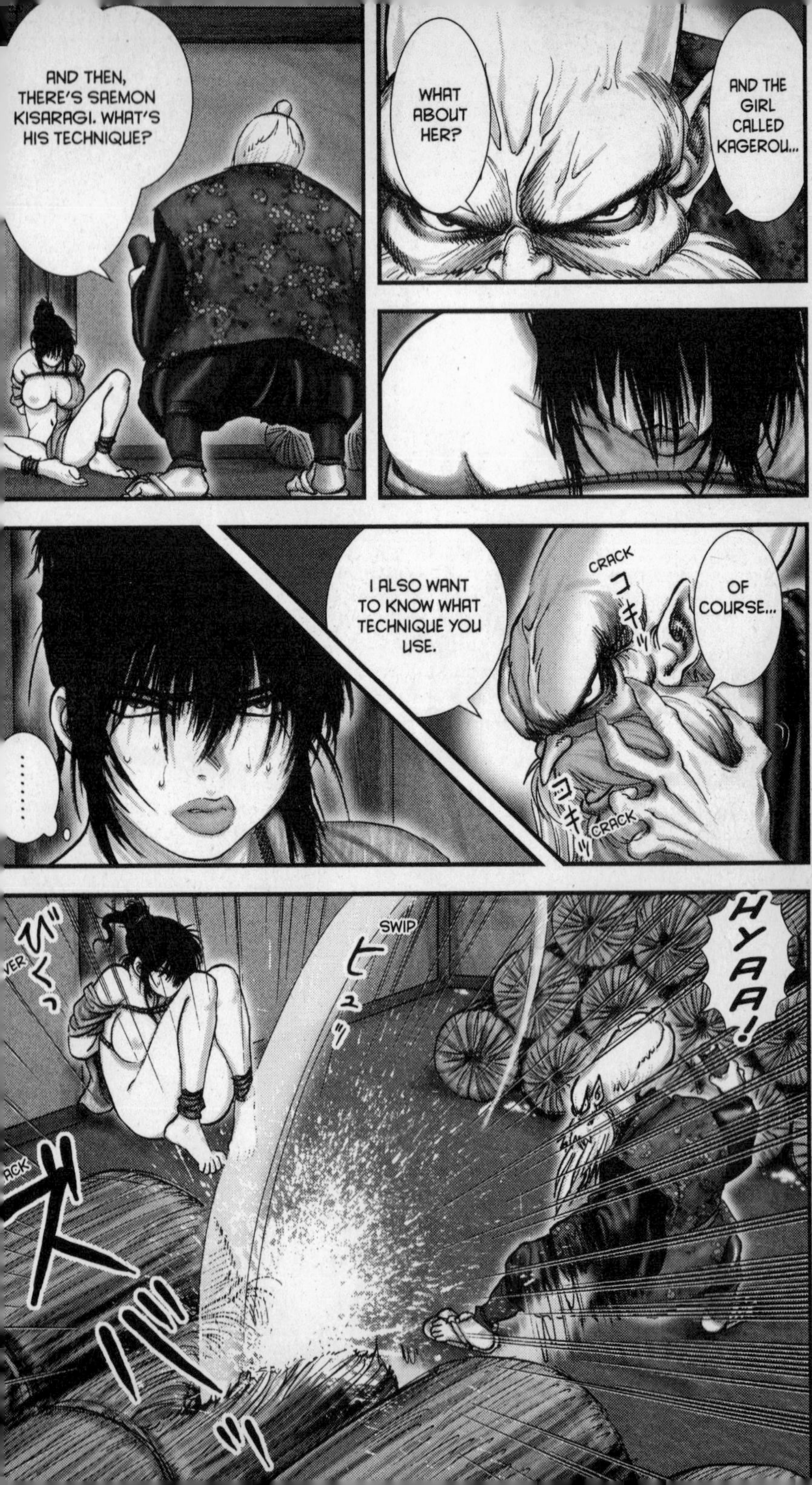
AND THE GIRL CALLED KAGEROU...
WHAT ABOUT HER?
AND THEN, THERE'S SAEMON KISARAGI. WHAT'S HIS TECHNIQUE?
CRACK
コキッ
OF COURSE...
I ALSO WANT TO KNOW WHAT TECHNIQUE YOU USE.
コキッ
CRACK
......
HYAA!
SWIP
ヒュッ
びくっ
VER
ACK
ズ

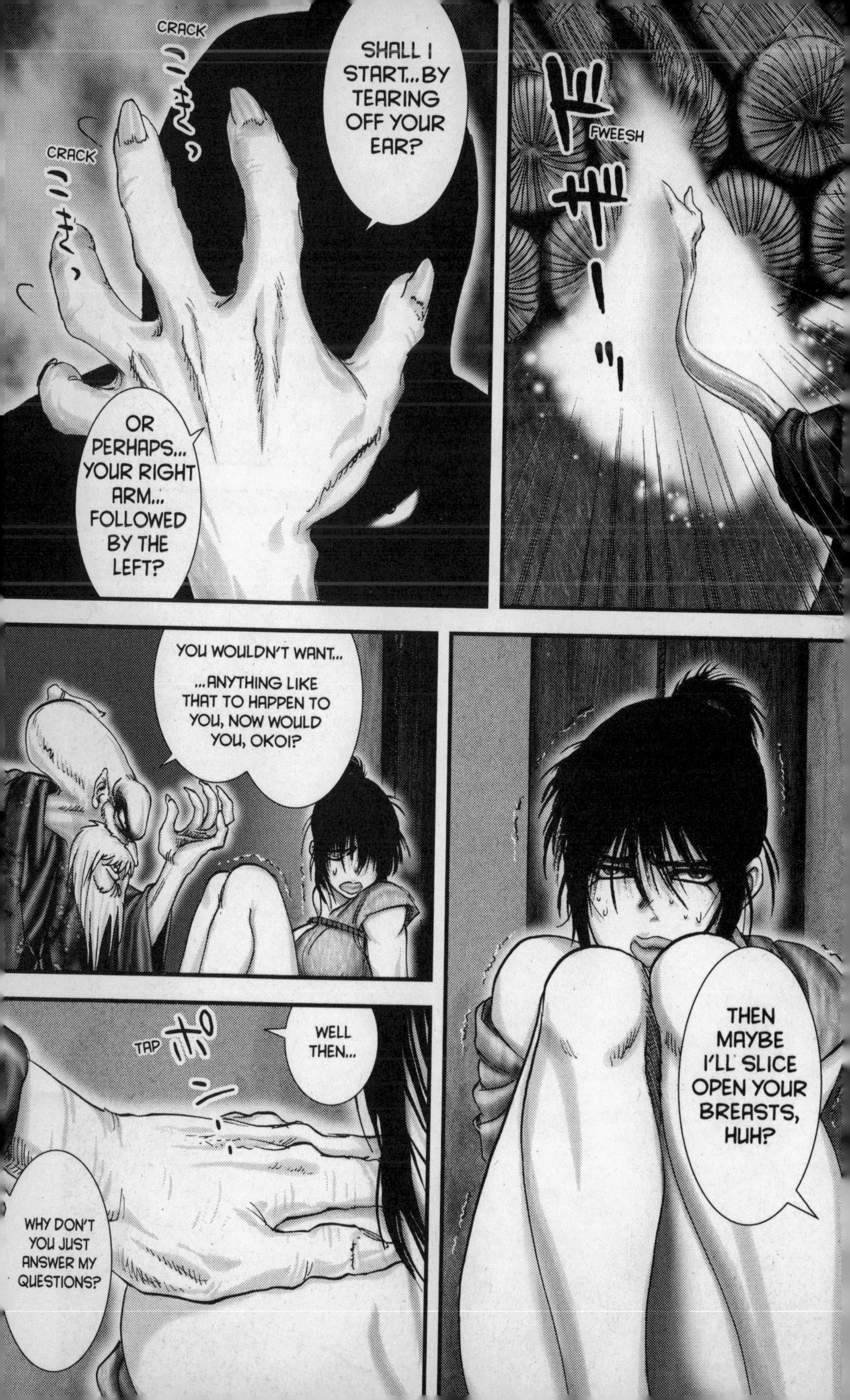
FWEESH
CRACK
CRACK
SHALL I START...BY TEARING OFF YOUR EAR?
OR PERHAPS... YOUR RIGHT ARM... FOLLOWED BY THE LEFT?
THEN MAYBE I'LL SLICE OPEN YOUR BREASTS, HUH?
YOU WOULDN'T WANT...
...ANYTHING LIKE THAT TO HAPPEN TO YOU, NOW WOULD YOU, OKOI?
WELL THEN...
TAP
WHY DON'T YOU JUST ANSWER MY QUESTIONS?

!

WHA–?

STICK

GRIN

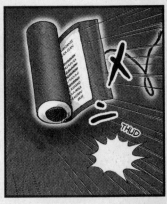

YANK

PAT

YOU
LITTLE–

THUD

MY-MY
HANDS
ARE
STUCK!

SUCK

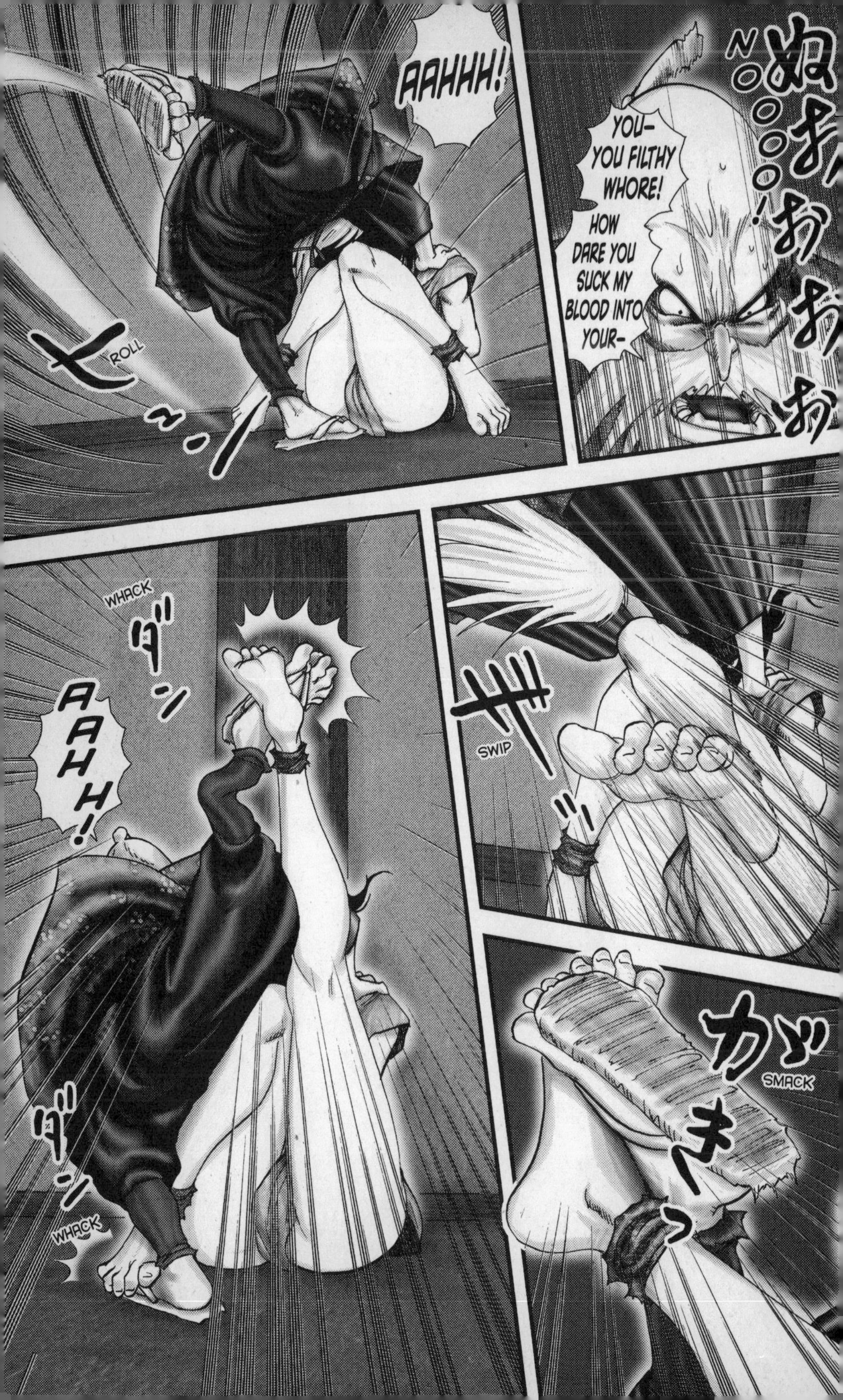
NOOOOOO!
YOU-
YOU FILTHY
WHORE!
HOW
DARE YOU
SUCK MY
BLOOD INTO
YOUR-
AAHHH!
ROLL
SWIP
SMACK
WHACK
AAHH!
WHACK

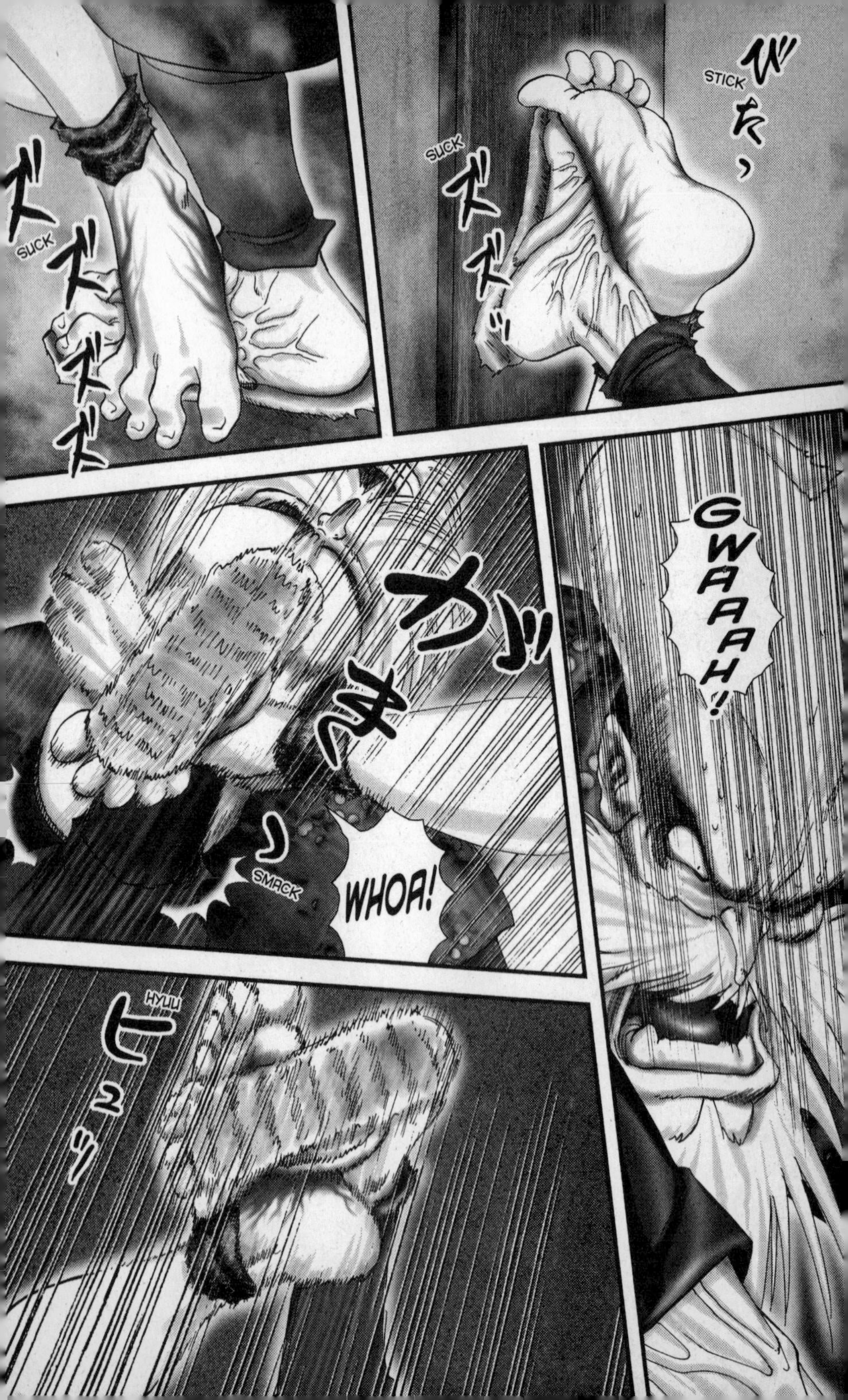

STICK
SUCK
SUCK
GWAAAAH!
SMACK
WHOA!
HYUU

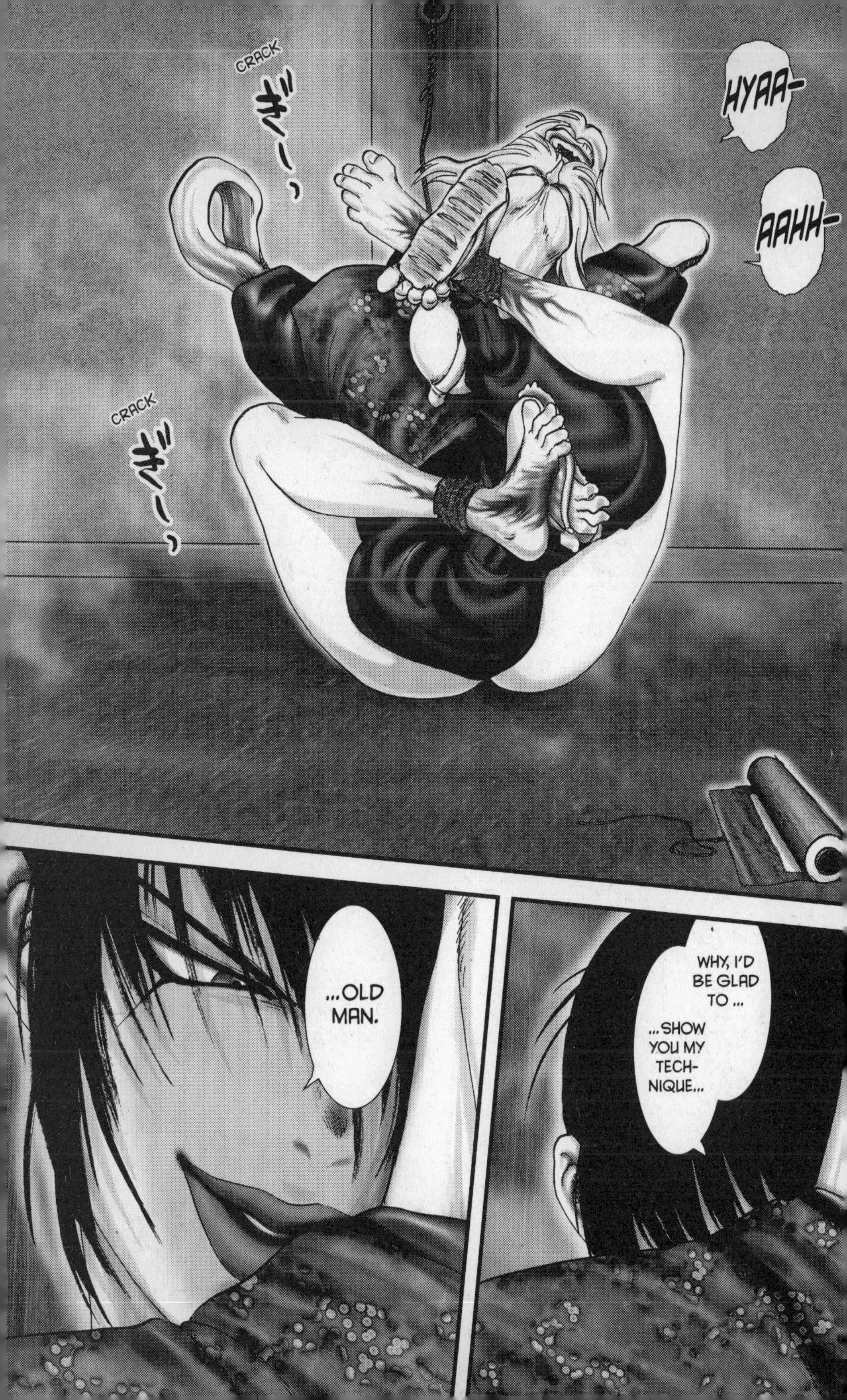
HYAA-
AAHH-
CRACK
CRACK
WHY, I'D BE GLAD TO ...
...SHOW YOU MY TECH-NIQUE...
...OLD MAN.

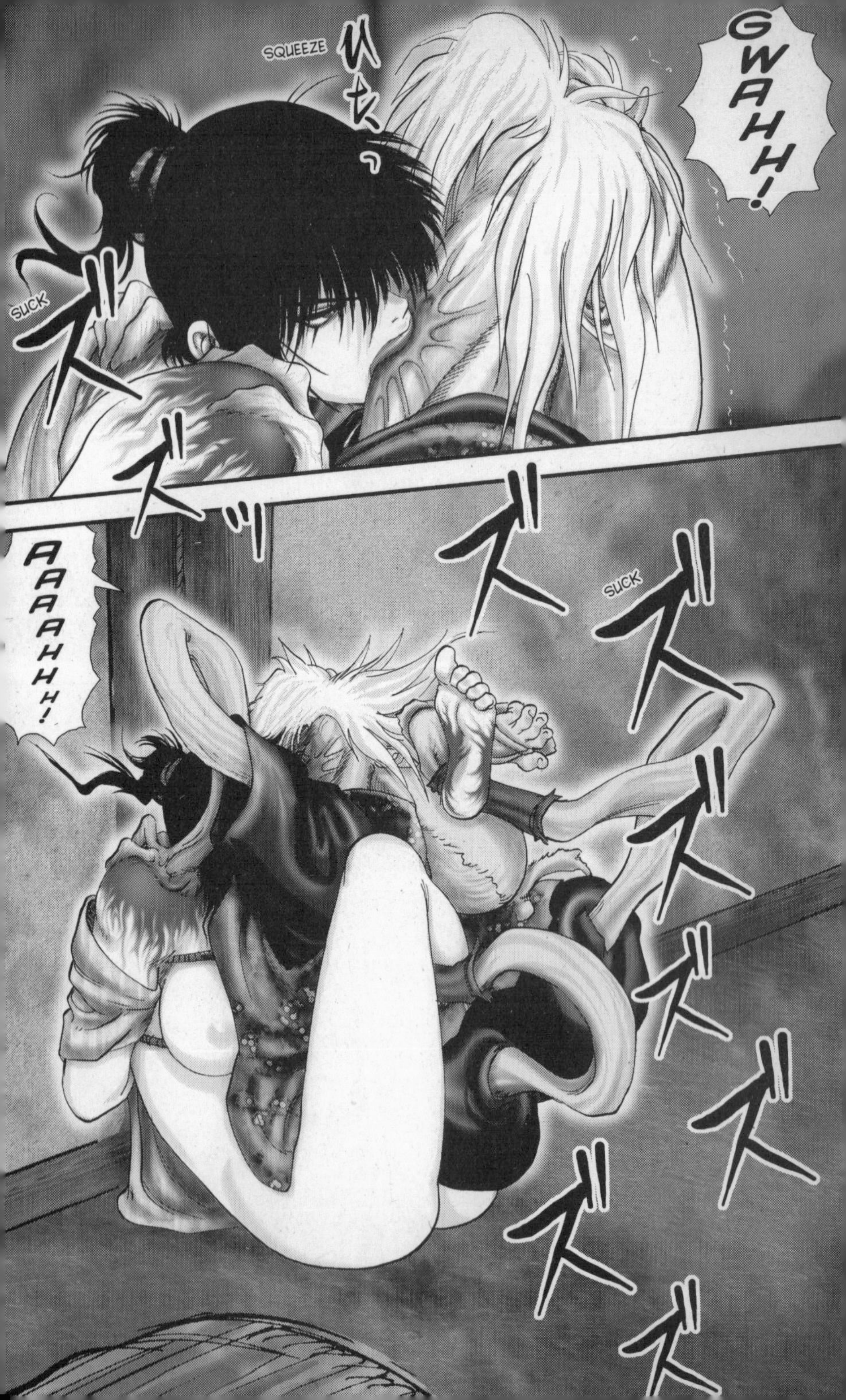
GWAHH!
SQUEEZE
SUCK
SUCK
AAAAAHHH!

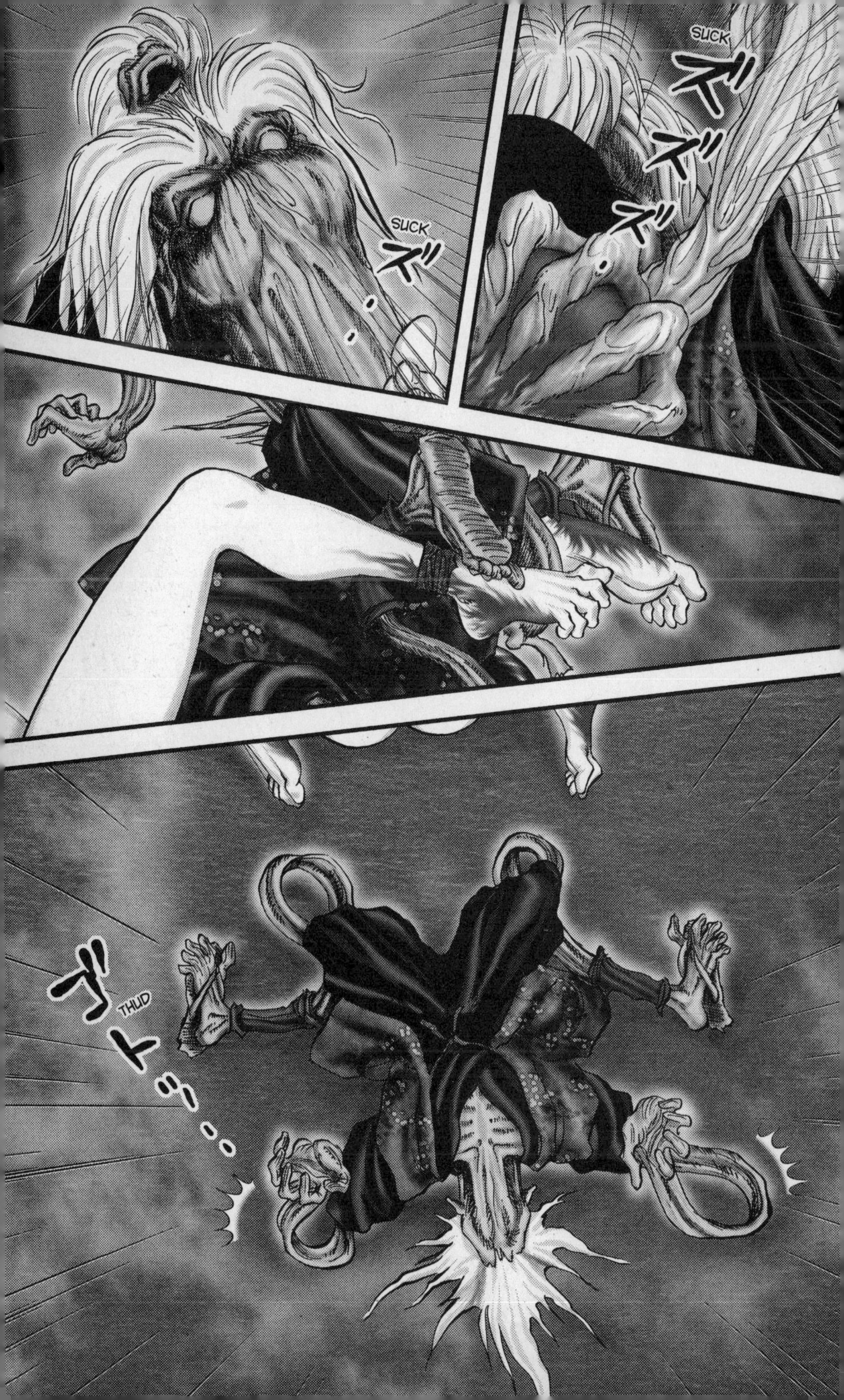
SUCK
ズズズ・・
SUCK
ズ・・
THUD
ゴトッ・・・

DID YOU FINALLY MAKE IT TO HEAVEN...

...OLD MAN?

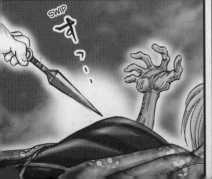

SWIP

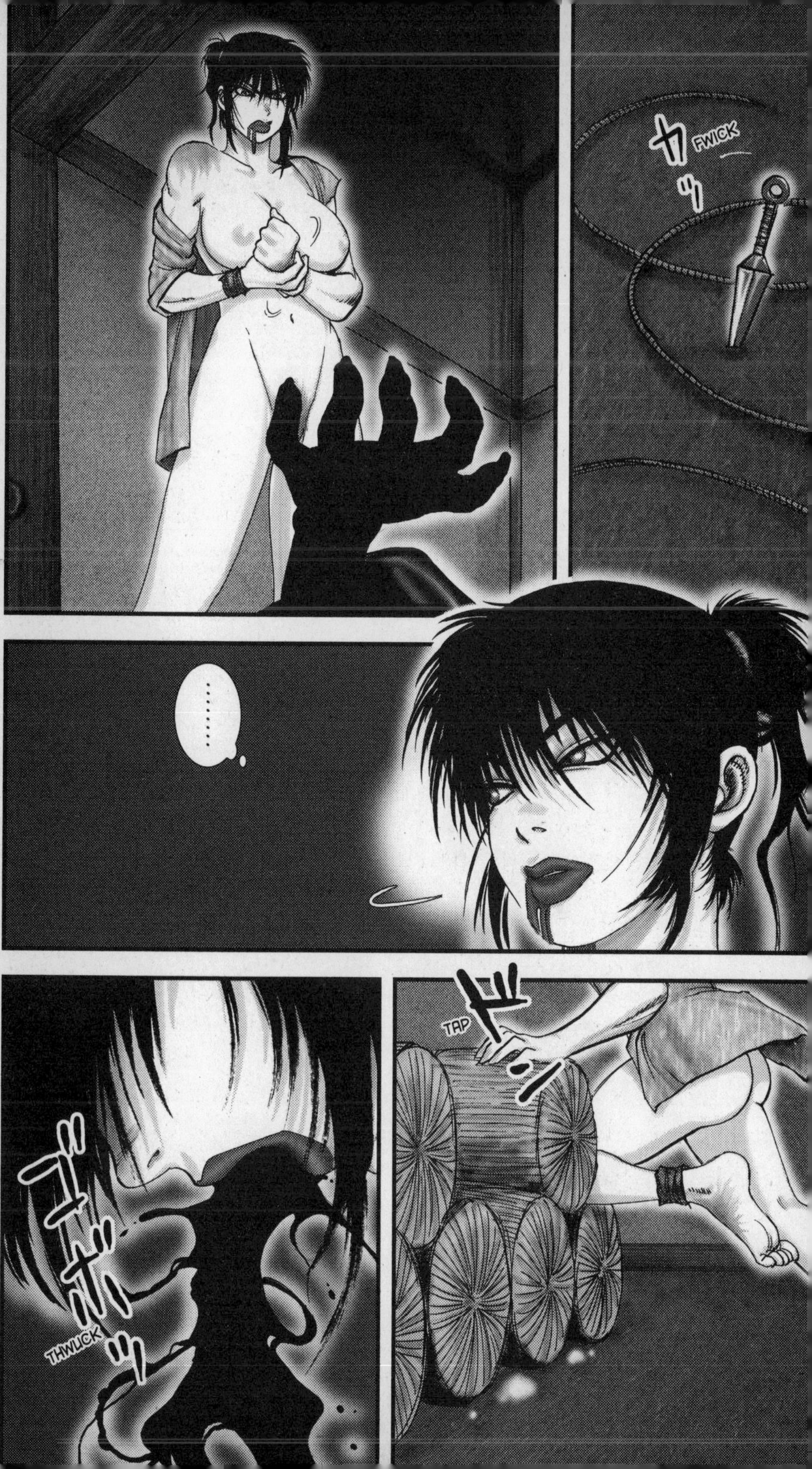
FWICK
......
TAP
THWUCK

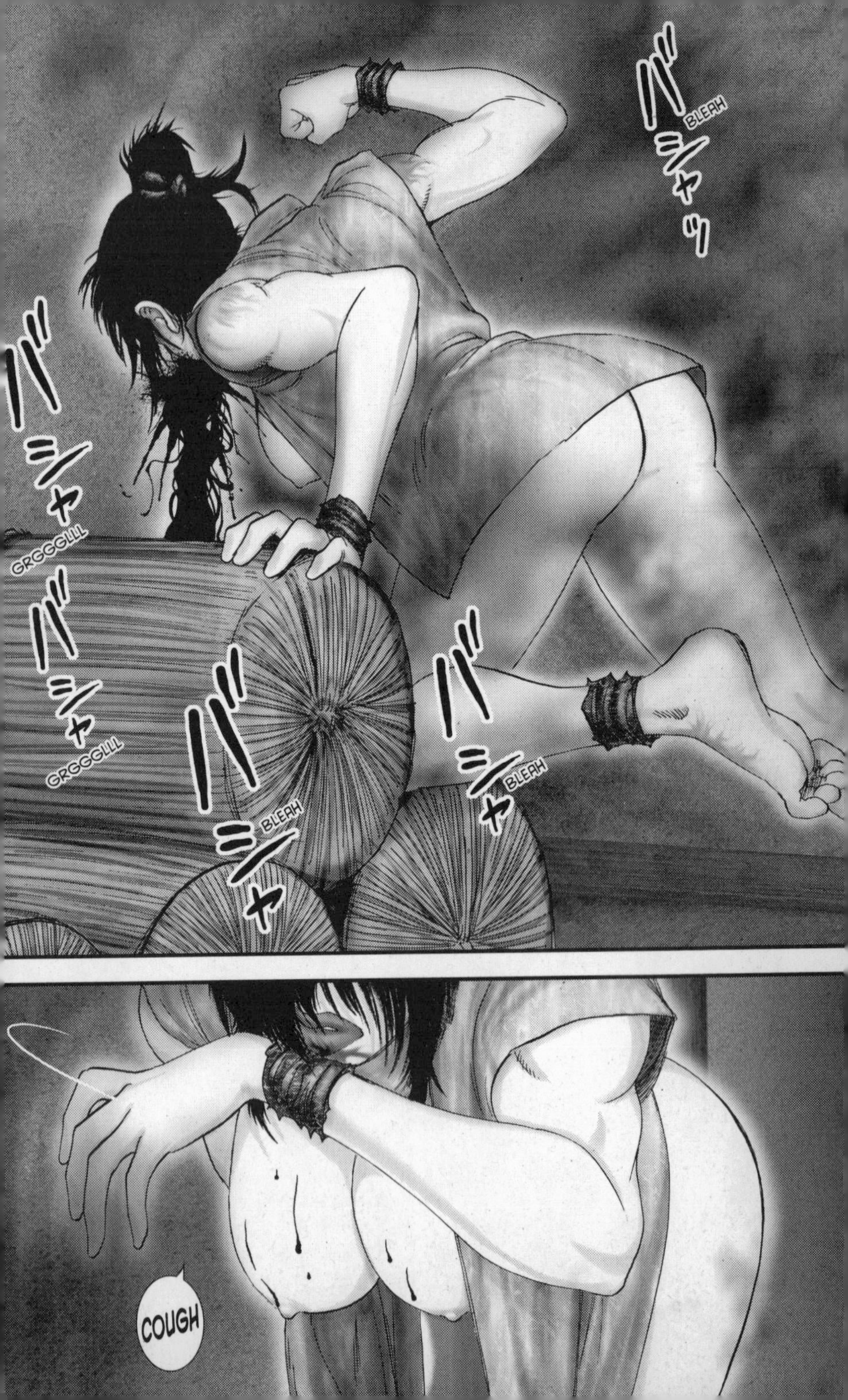
バシャッ
BLEAH
バシャ
BLEAH
バシャ
BLEAH
バシャ
GRGGGLLL
バシャ
GRGGGLLL
COUGH

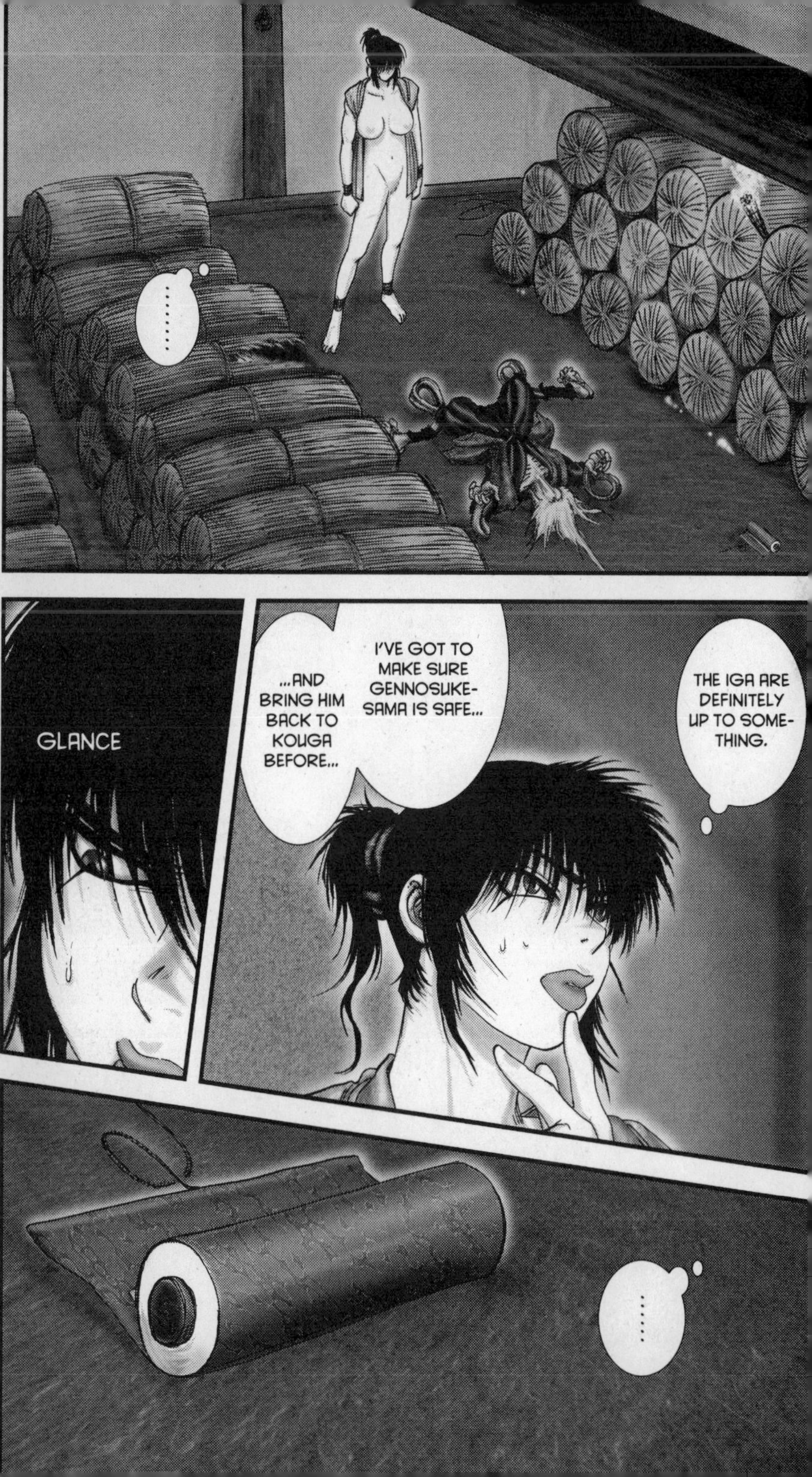
......
THE IGA ARE DEFINITELY UP TO SOMETHING.
I'VE GOT TO MAKE SURE GENNOSUKE-SAMA IS SAFE...
...AND BRING HIM BACK TO KOUGA BEFORE...
GLANCE
......

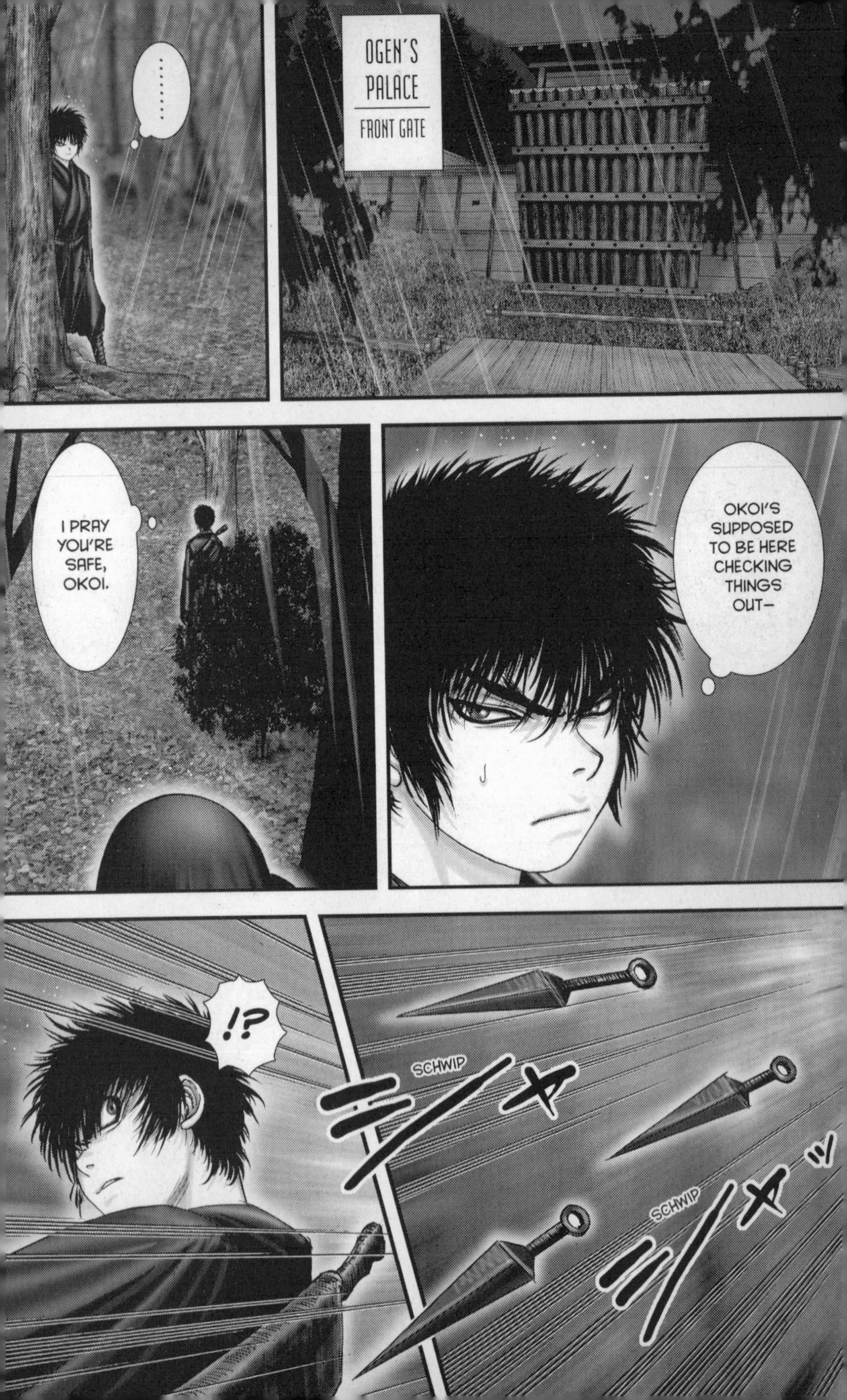
OGEN'S PALACE
FRONT GATE
......
OKOI'S SUPPOSED TO BE HERE CHECKING THINGS OUT—
I PRAY YOU'RE SAFE, OKOI.
SCHWIP
SCHWIP
!?

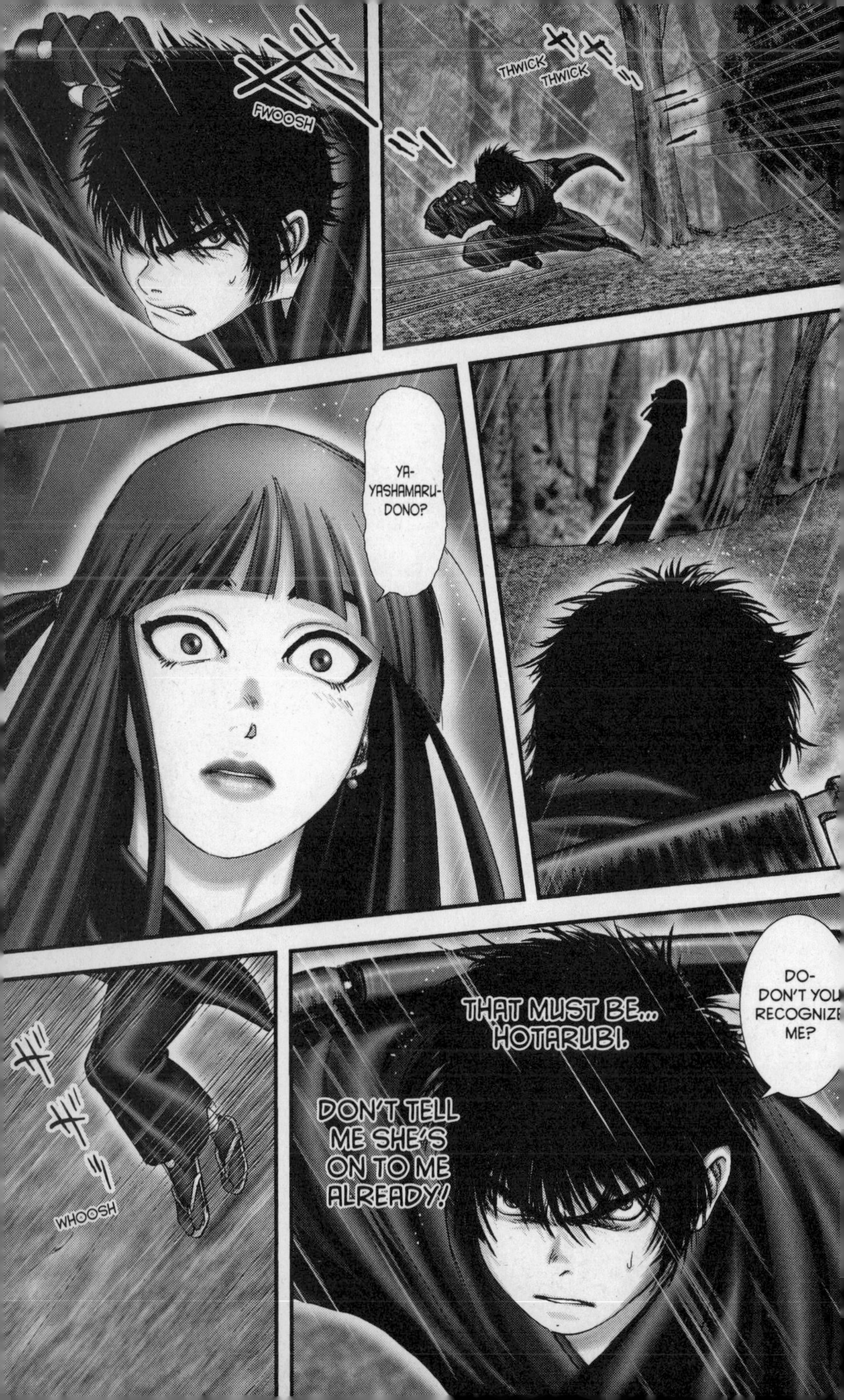
THWICK THWICK
FWOOSH
YA-YASHAMARU-DONO?
DO-DON'T YOU RECOGNIZE ME?
THAT MUST BE... HOTARUBI.
DON'T TELL ME SHE'S ON TO ME ALREADY!
WHOOSH

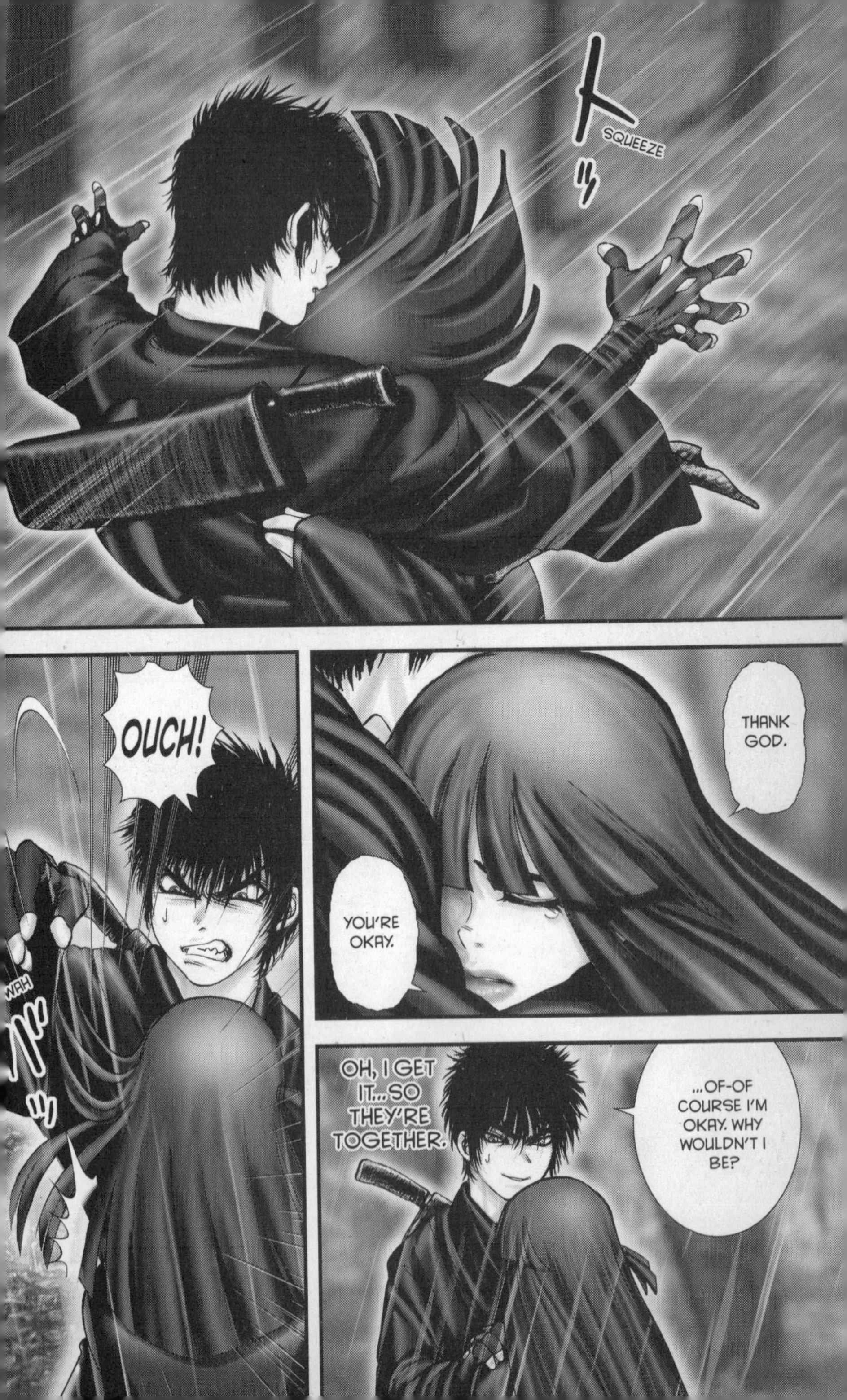
SQUEEZE
THANK GOD.
YOU'RE OKAY.
...OF-OF COURSE I'M OKAY. WHY WOULDN'T I BE?
OH, I GET IT... SO THEY'RE TOGETHER.
OUCH!
WAH

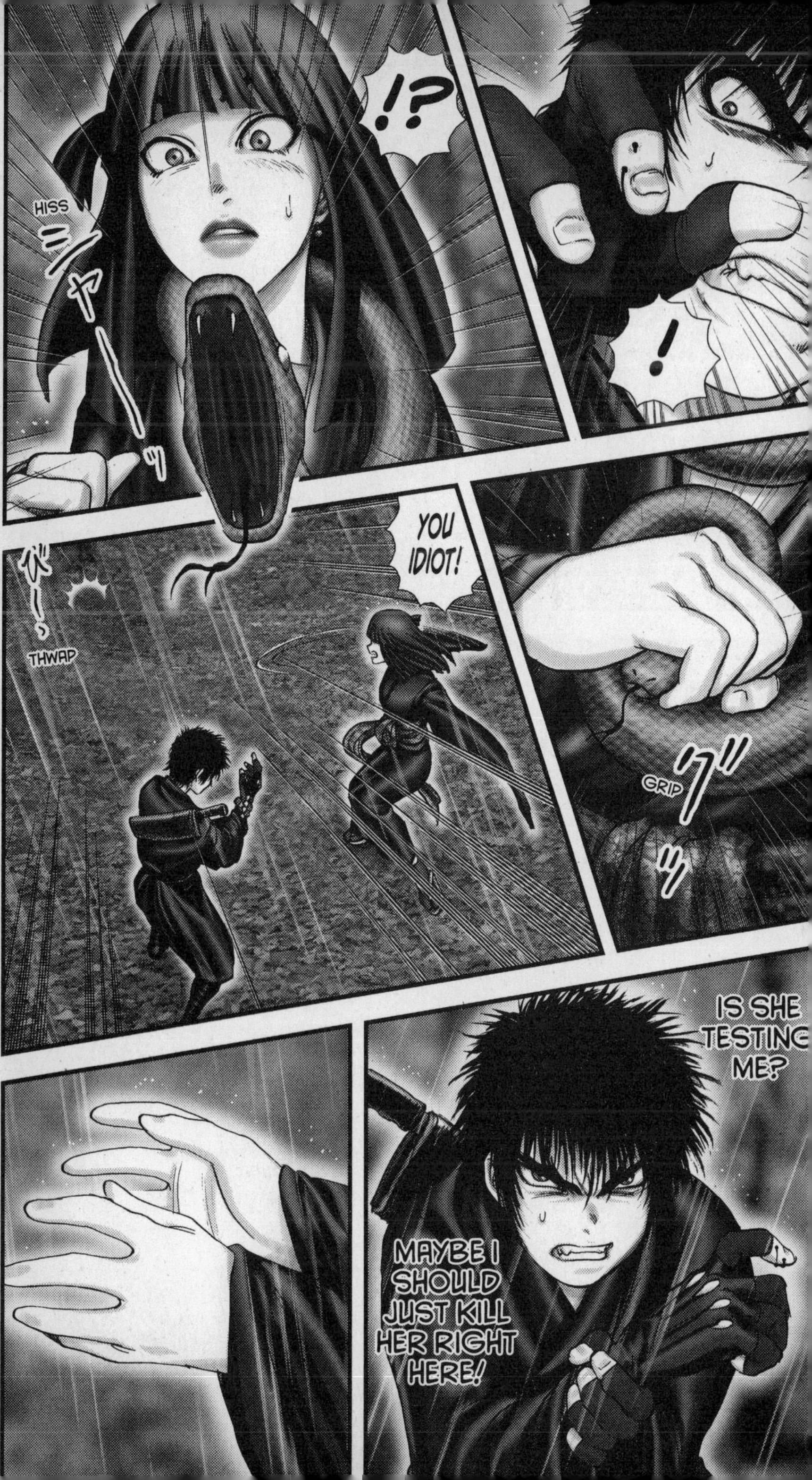
!
!?
HISS
シャーッ
GRIP
グッ
YOU IDIOT!
THWAP
IS SHE TESTING ME?
MAYBE I SHOULD JUST KILL HER RIGHT HERE!

I-I'M SORRY.

MAYBE I'M OVER-ANALYZING.

WHAT A WEIRD GIRL.

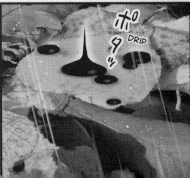

DRIP

I CAN'T BELIEVE YOU DOUBTED ME.

THE SNAKE IS ONE THING, BUT...

WELL, THAT WAS KIND OF A ROUGH WAY TO GREET ME, DON'T YOU THINK?

YOUR HAIR LOOKS TOTALLY DIFFERENT...

...THAN IT DID BEFORE YOU LEFT FOR SUNPU.

I-I'M SO SORRY. IT'S JUST THAT...

GRR
きっ

I BET THAT DANJOU KOUGA...

...OR SHOUGEN KAZAMACHI DID THAT TO YOU, DIDN'T THEY?

U-UM... YEAH... SOMETHING LIKE THAT.

I- I SHOULD LOOK EXACTLY LIKE HIM...

IT— IT DOES?

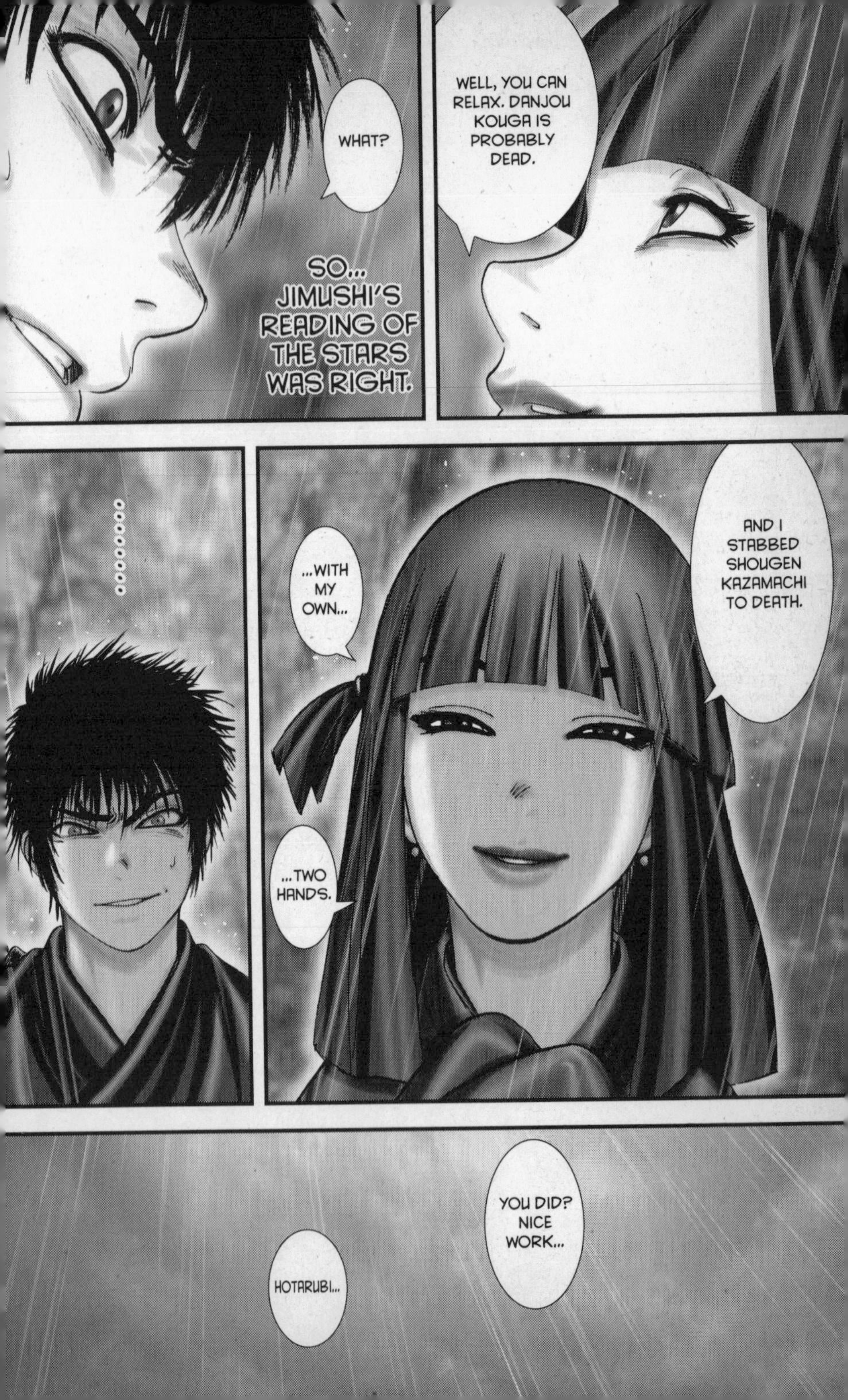
WELL, YOU CAN RELAX. DANJOU KOUGA IS PROBABLY DEAD.
WHAT?
SO... JIMUSHI'S READING OF THE STARS WAS RIGHT.
AND I STABBED SHOUGEN KAZAMACHI TO DEATH.
...WITH MY OWN...
...TWO HANDS.
....
YOU DID? NICE WORK...
HOTARUBI...

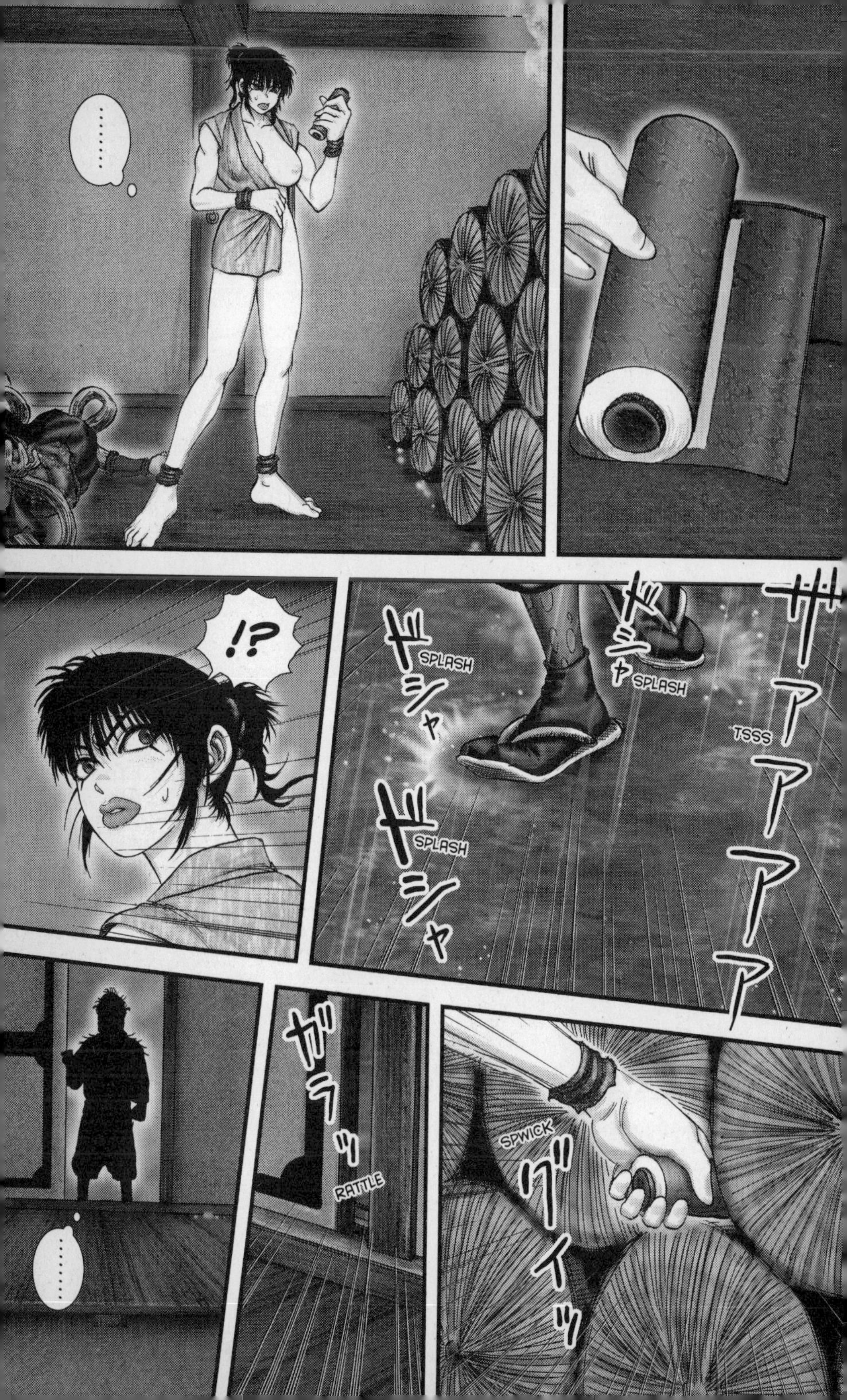

......
ザァァアアア
TSSS
ザシャ
SPLASH
ザシャ
SPLASH
ザシャ
SPLASH
!?
ヅイッ
SPWICK
ガラッ
RATTLE
......

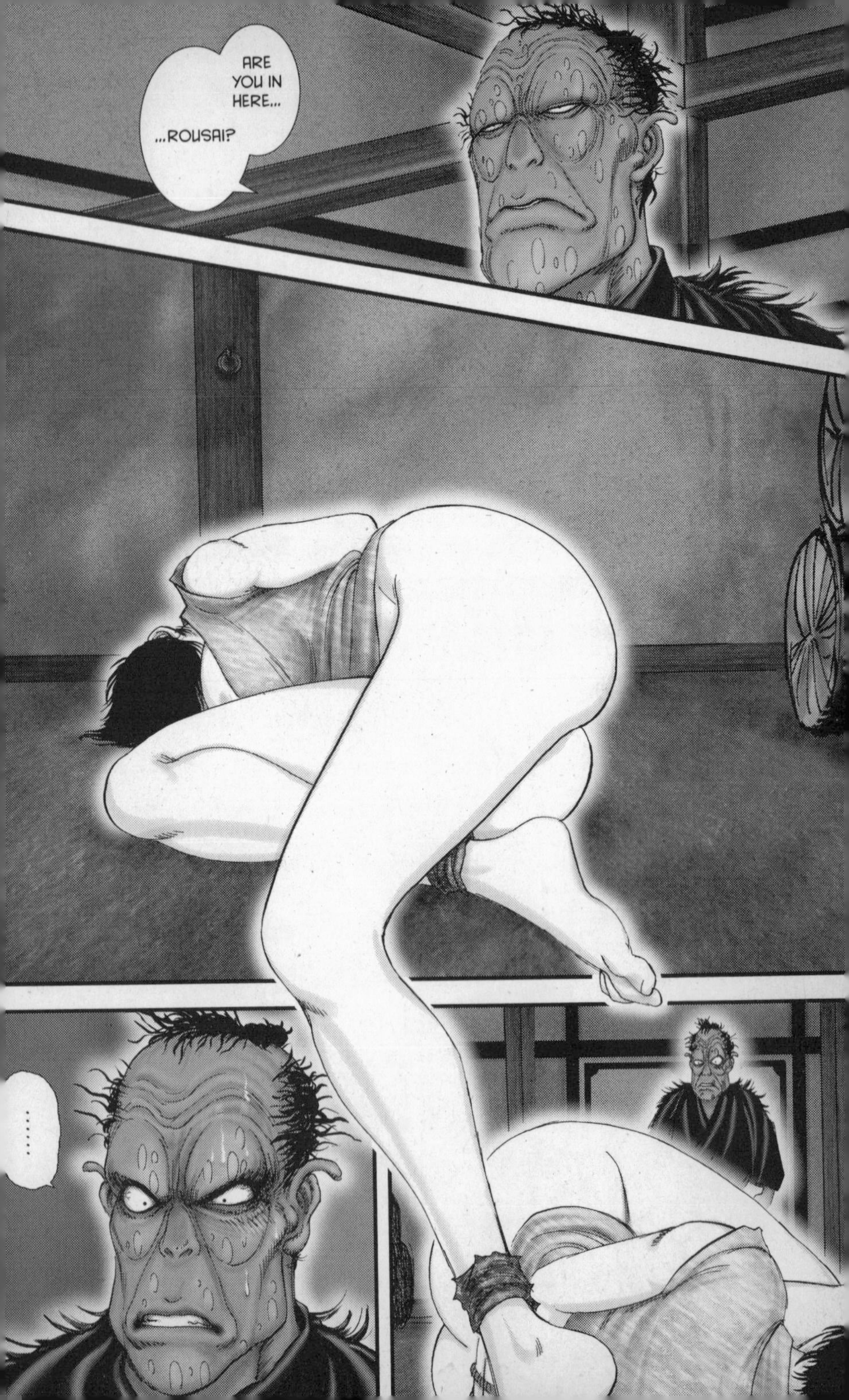
ARE YOU IN HERE...
...ROUSAI?
......

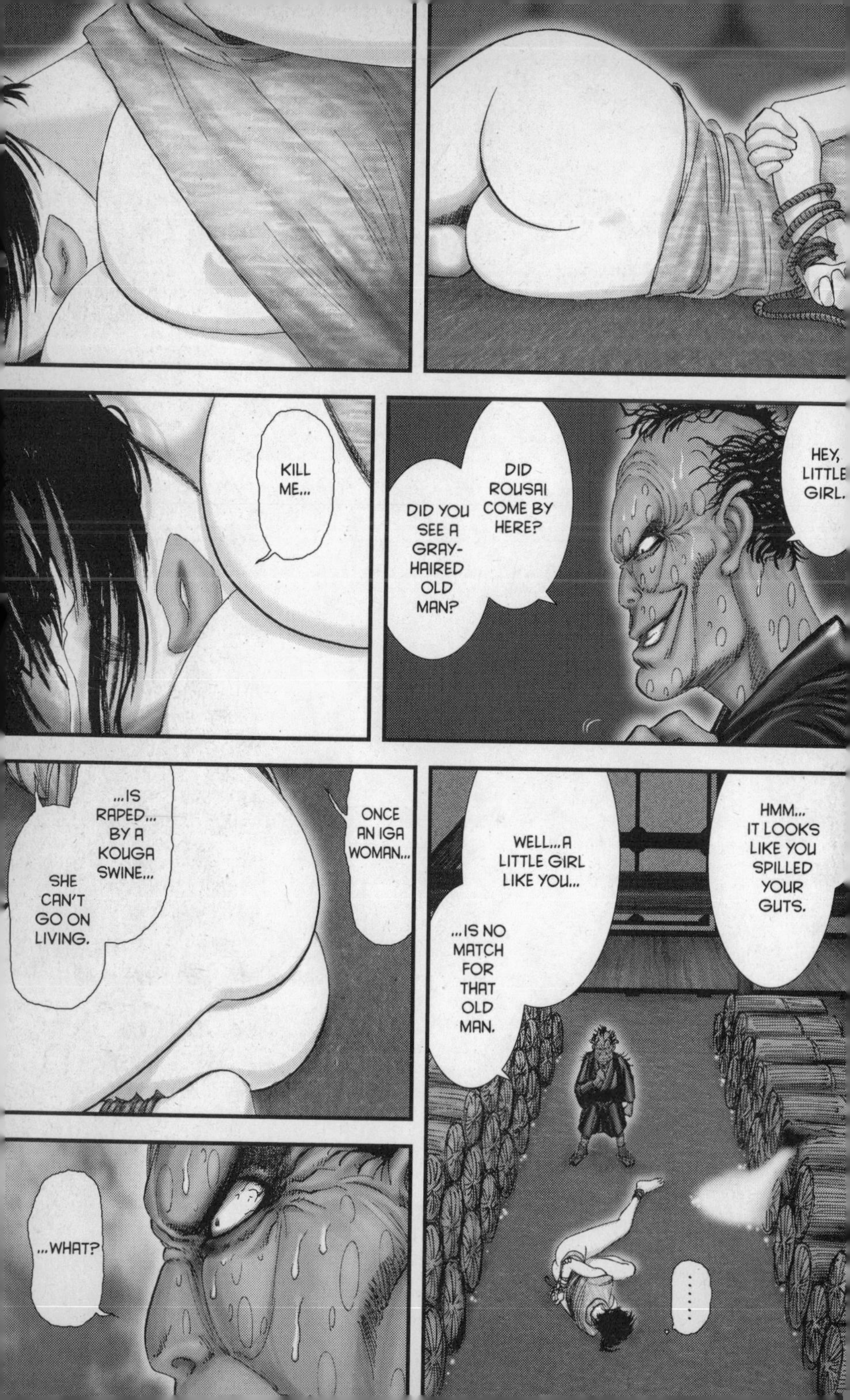
HEY, LITTLE GIRL.
DID ROUSAI COME BY HERE?
DID YOU SEE A GRAY-HAIRED OLD MAN?
KILL ME...
HMM... IT LOOKS LIKE YOU SPILLED YOUR GUTS.
WELL...A LITTLE GIRL LIKE YOU...
...IS NO MATCH FOR THAT OLD MAN.
......
ONCE AN IGA WOMAN...
...IS RAPED... BY A KOUGA SWINE...
SHE CAN'T GO ON LIVING.
...WHAT?

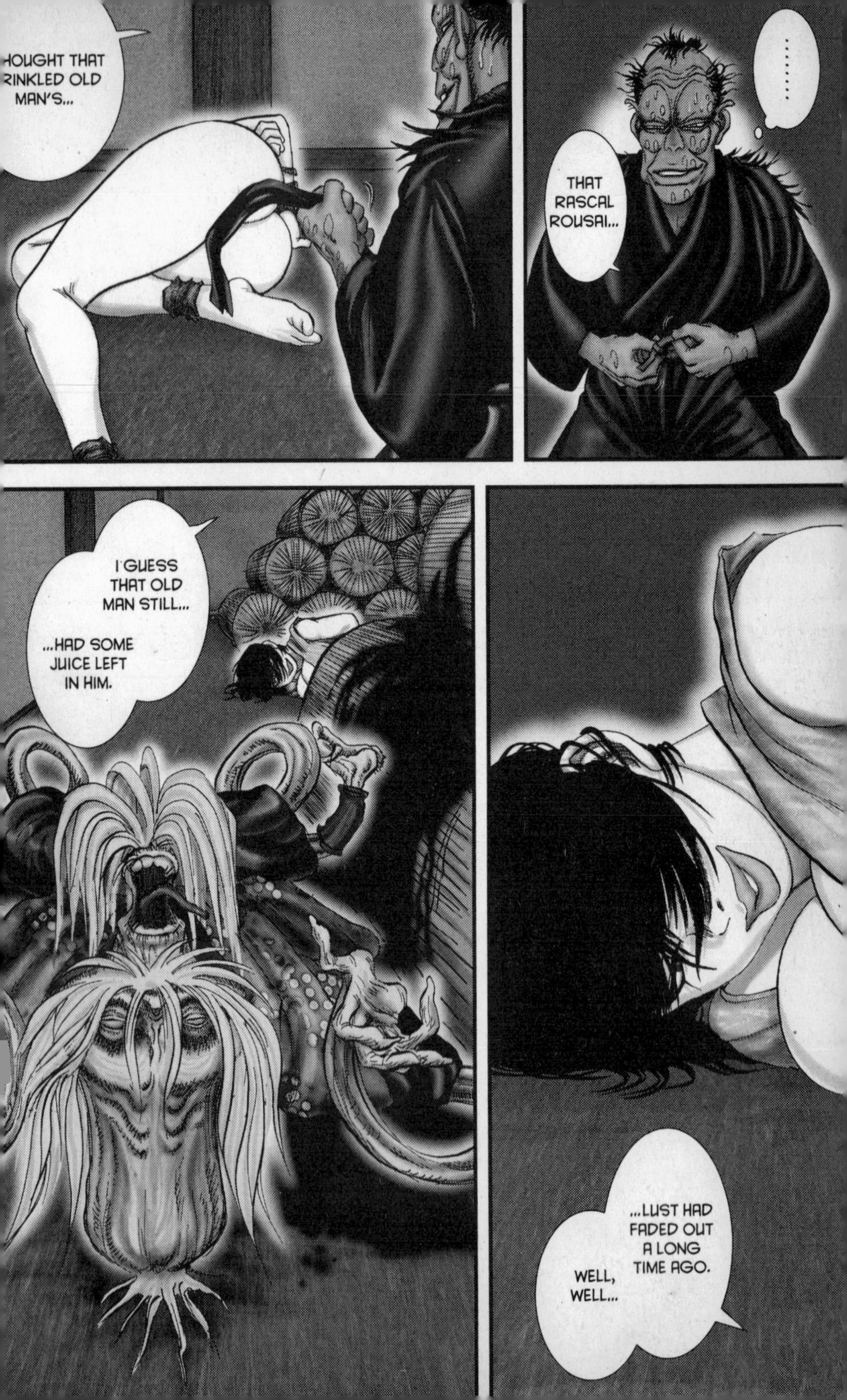
......
THAT RASCAL ROUSAI...
HOUGHT THAT RINKLED OLD MAN'S...
...LUST HAD FADED OUT A LONG TIME AGO.
WELL, WELL...
I GUESS THAT OLD MAN STILL...
...HAD SOME JUICE LEFT IN HIM.

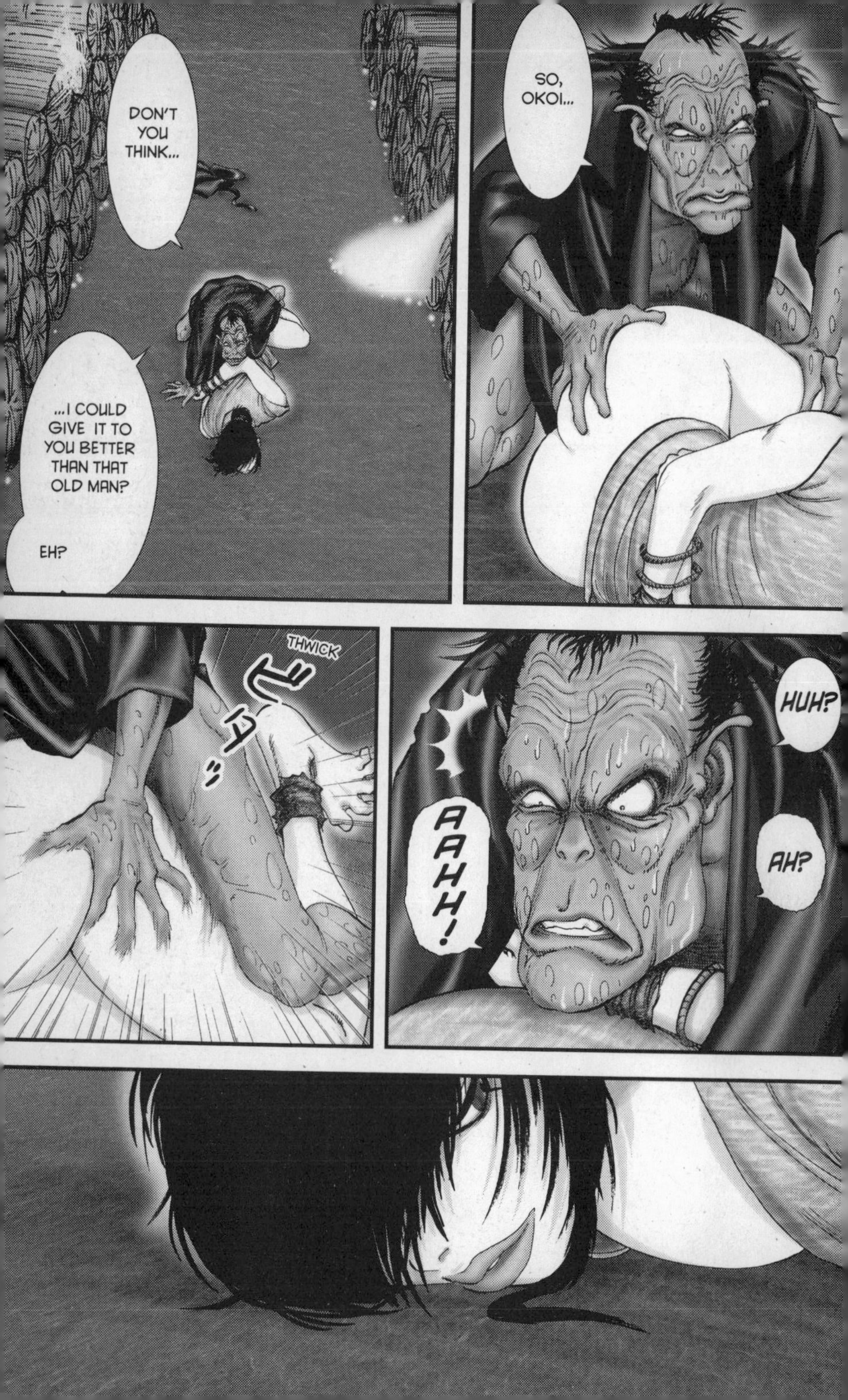
SO, OKOI...
DON'T YOU THINK...
...I COULD GIVE IT TO YOU BETTER THAN THAT OLD MAN?
EH?
HUH?
AH?
AAHH!
THWICK

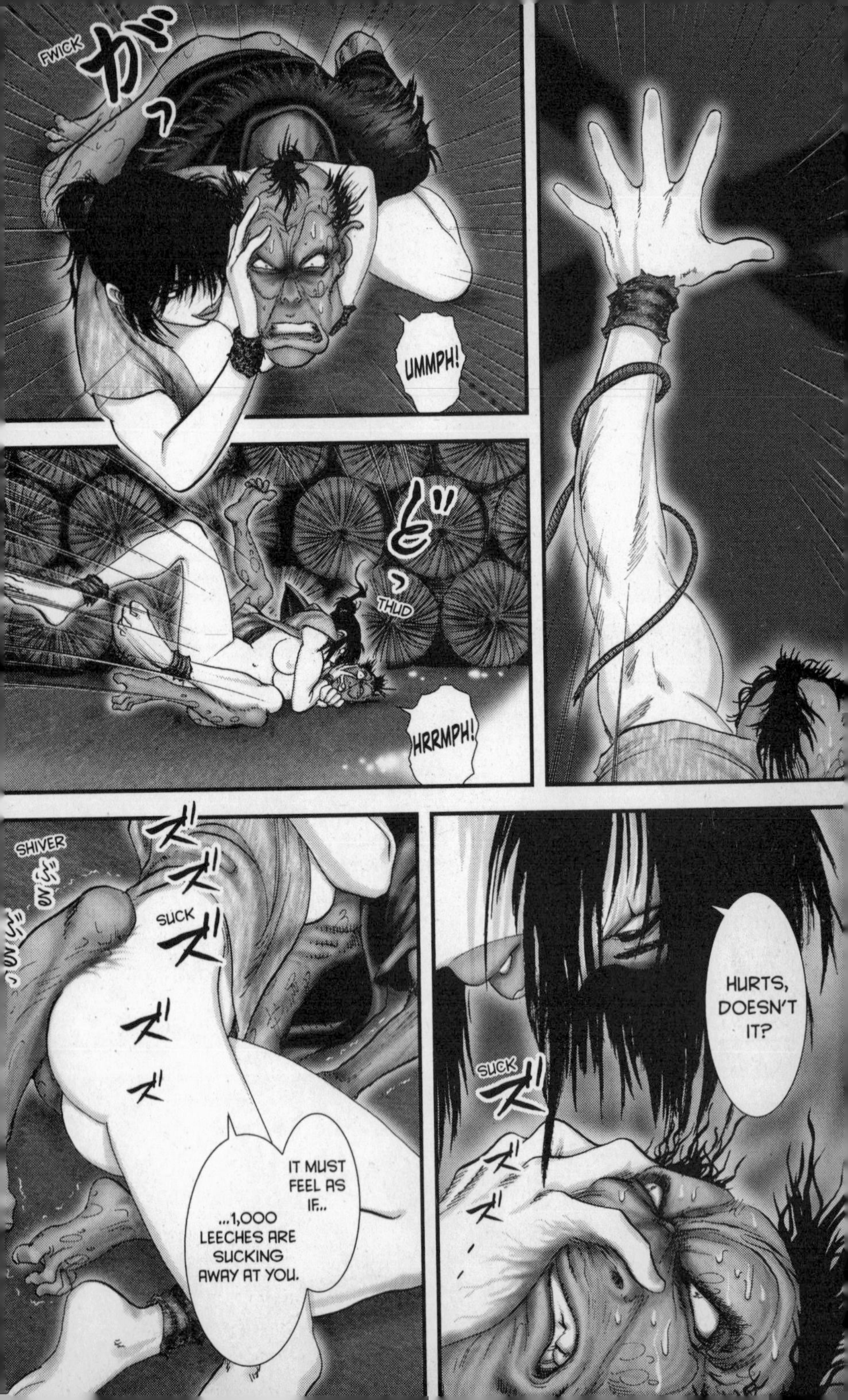
FWICK
ガッ
UMMPH!
ドッ
THUD
HRRMPH!
HURTS, DOESN'T IT?
SUCK
ズ
ズ
ズ
SHIVER
ぶるぶる
ズ
ズ
SUCK
ズ
ズ
ズ
IT MUST FEEL AS IF...
...1,000 LEECHES ARE SUCKING AWAY AT YOU.

I'M GONNA SUCK UP...

...EVERY LAST DROP OF YOUR BLOOD.

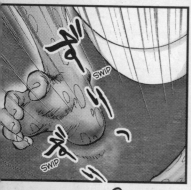

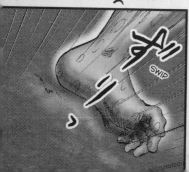

AAAHHH!

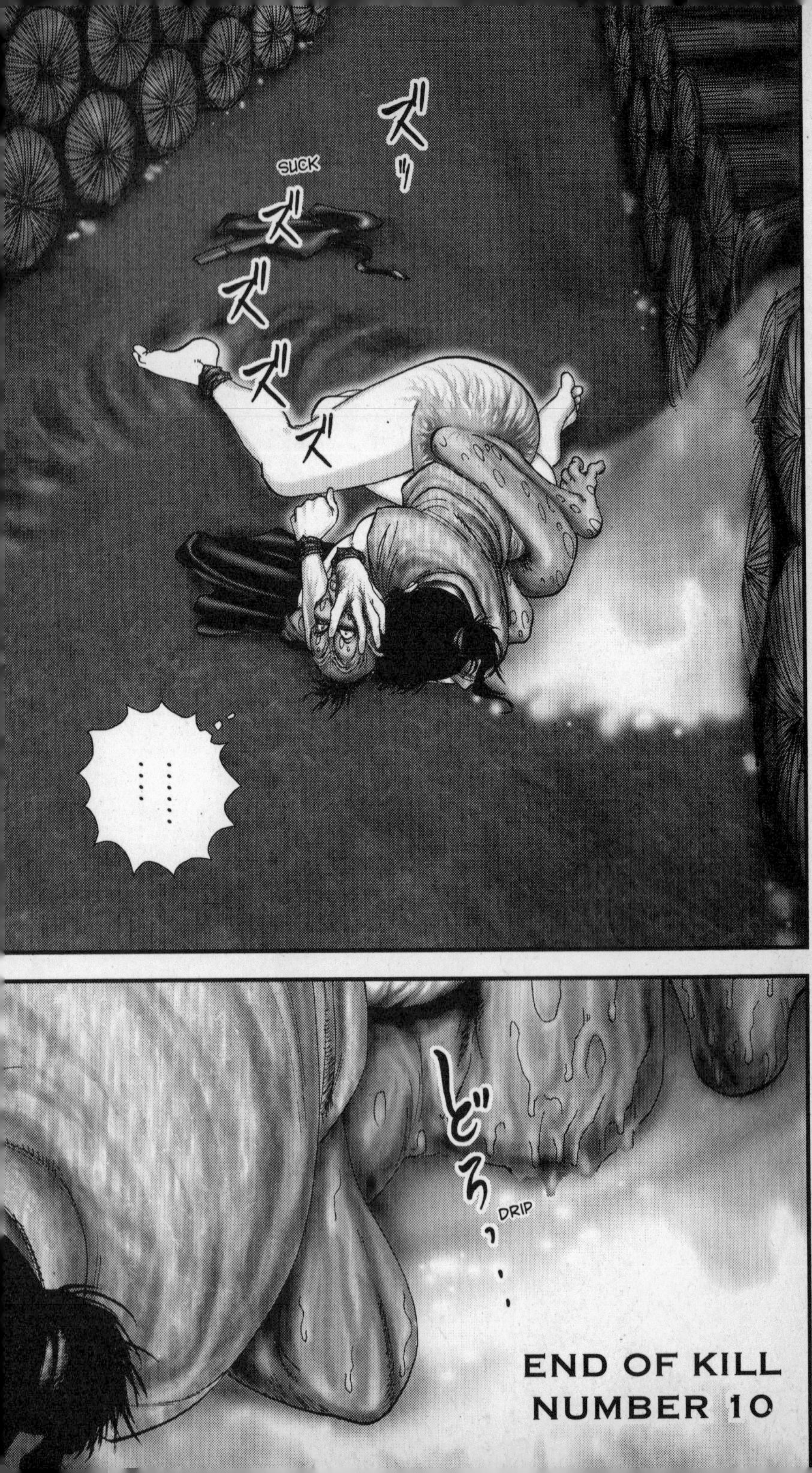
ズッ
SUCK
ズズズズ
......
どろっ...
DRIP
END OF KILL NUMBER 10

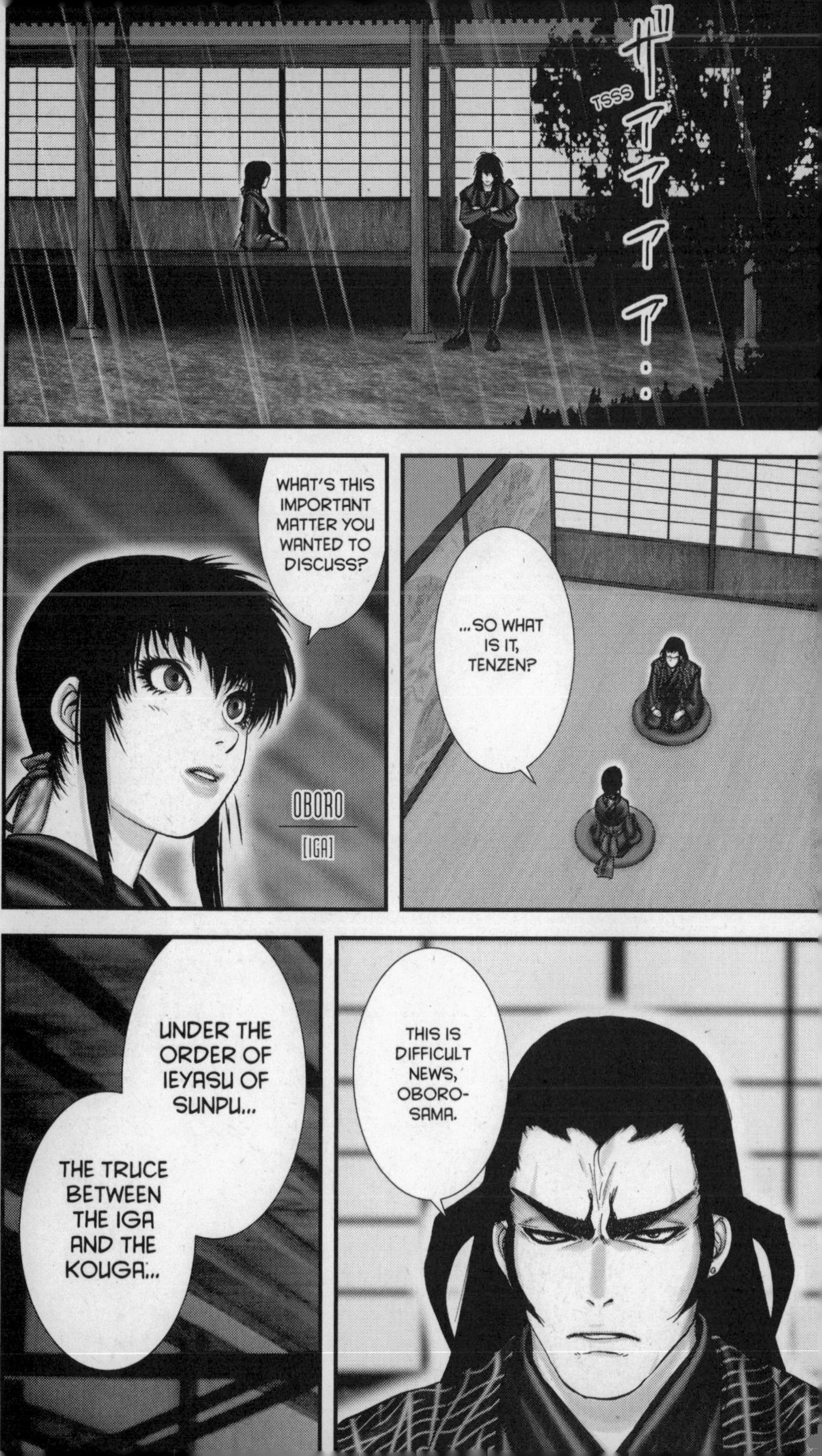
TSSS
...SO WHAT IS IT, TENZEN?
WHAT'S THIS IMPORTANT MATTER YOU WANTED TO DISCUSS?
OBORO
[IGA]
THIS IS DIFFICULT NEWS, OBORO-SAMA.
UNDER THE ORDER OF IEYASU OF SUNPU...
THE TRUCE BETWEEN THE IGA AND THE KOUGA...

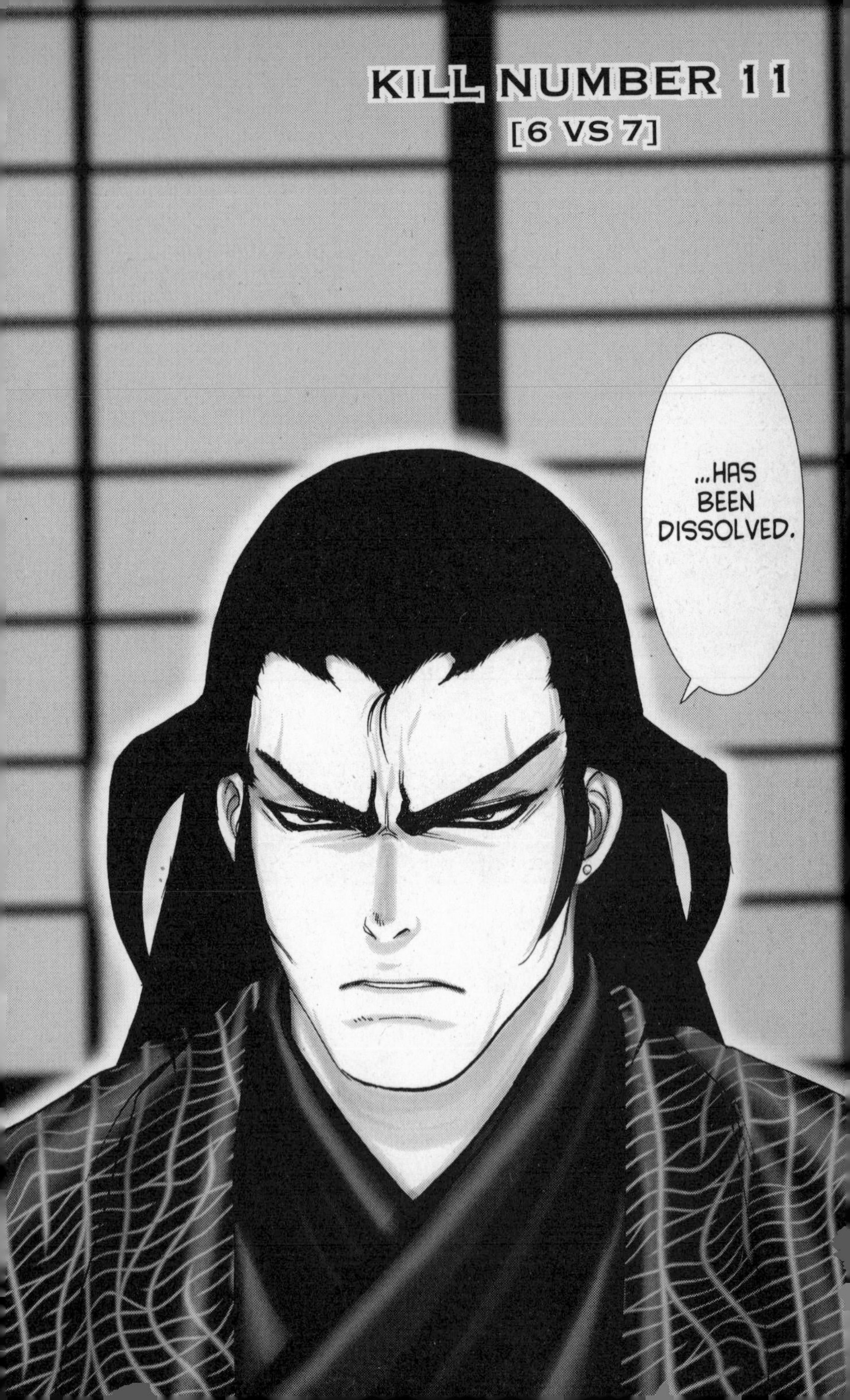
KILL NUMBER 11
[6 VS 7]
...HAS BEEN DISSOLVED.

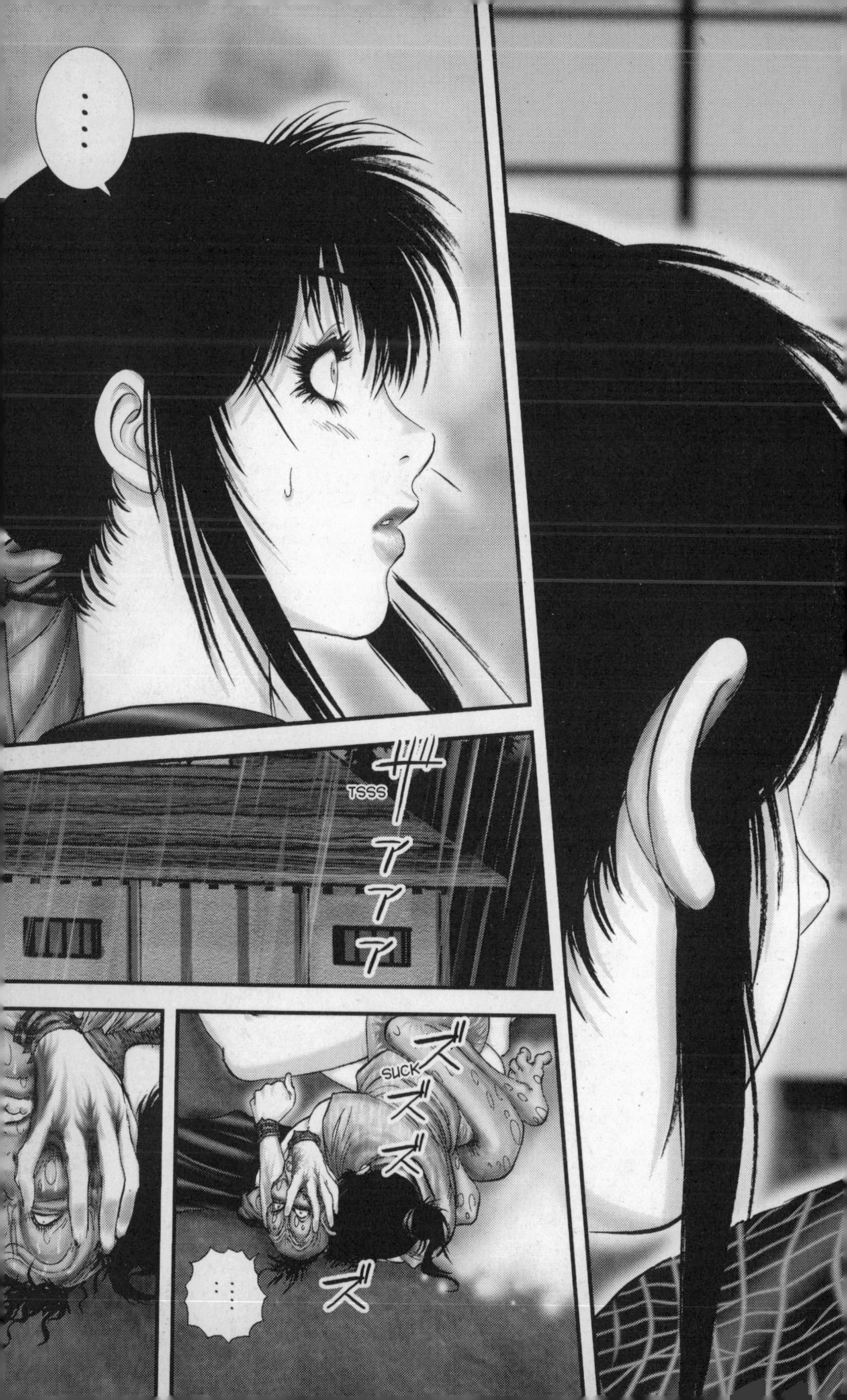
......
TSSS
ザァァァ
SUCK
ズズズズズ
......

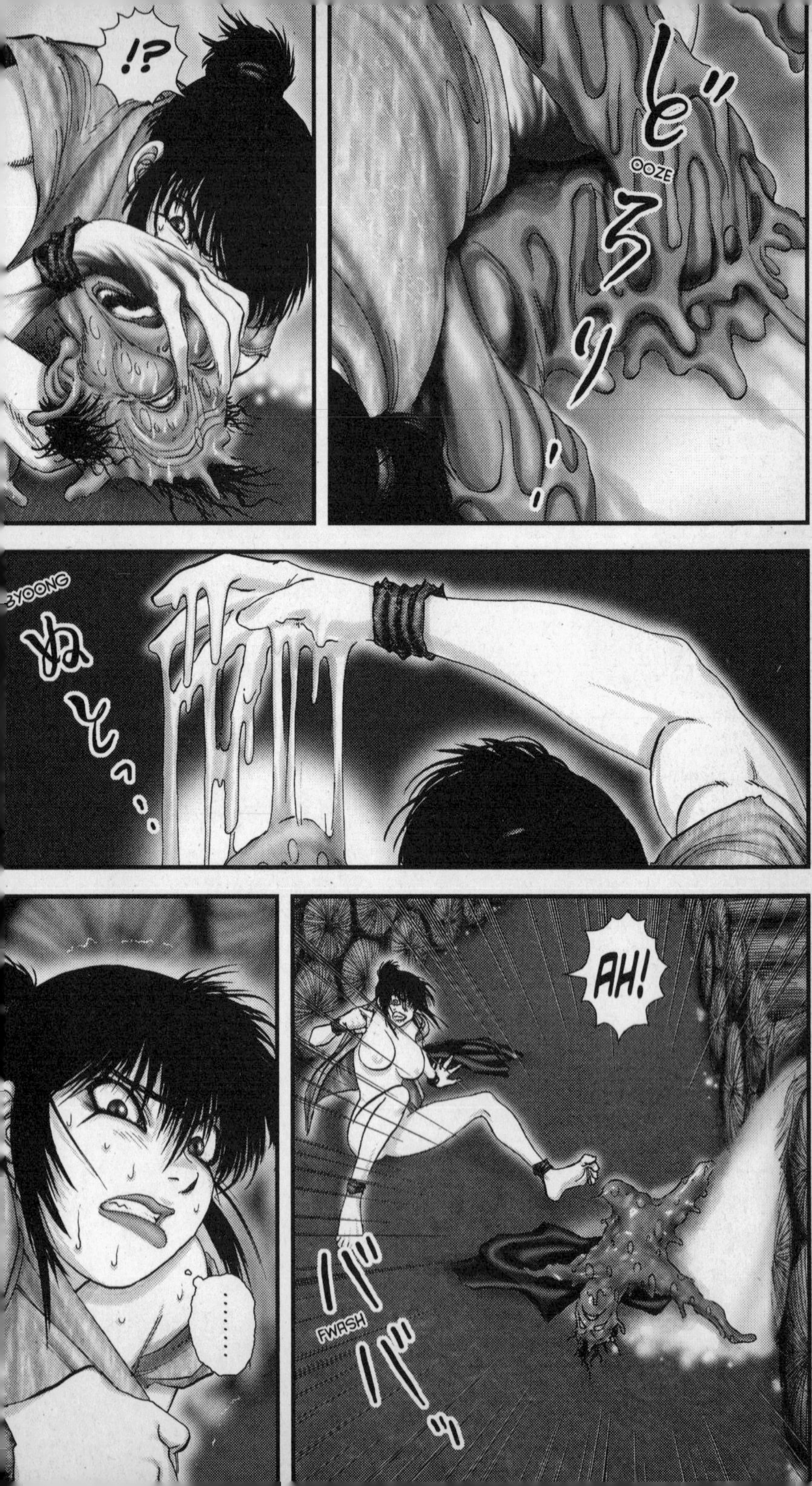
どろり
OOZE
!?
BYOONG
ぬとぉ…
AH!
ババッ
FWASH
……

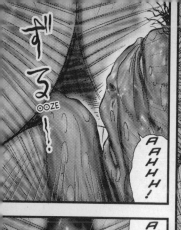

ずる！
OOZE

AAHH!

WAAHH!

AAHH!

AAHH!

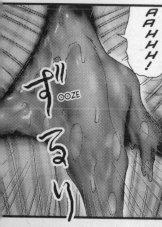

ずるり
OOZE

ズラ
SLIDE

SCHWICK
ガシ

！

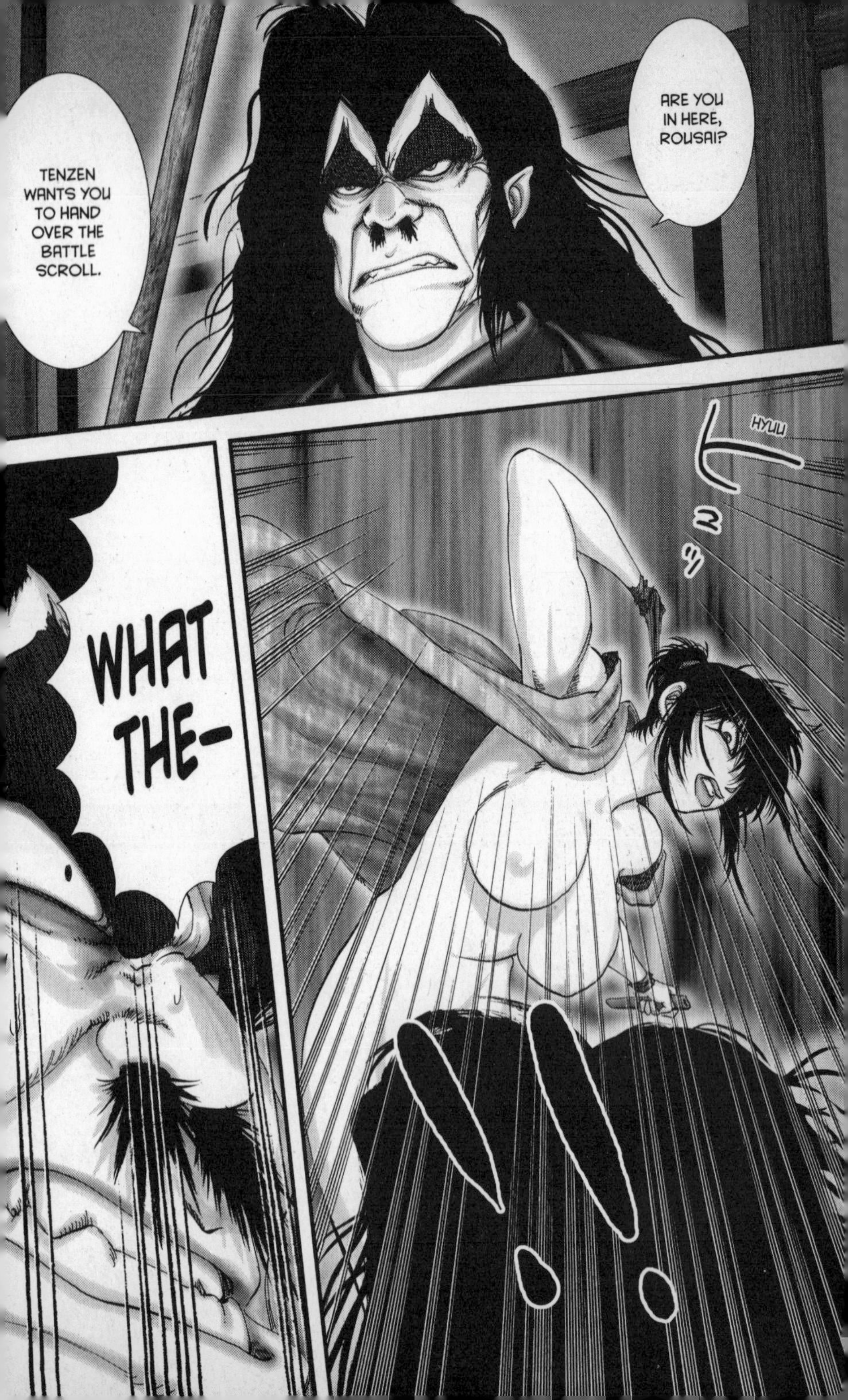
ARE YOU IN HERE, ROUSAI?
TENZEN WANTS YOU TO HAND OVER THE BATTLE SCROLL.
HYUU
WHAT THE-

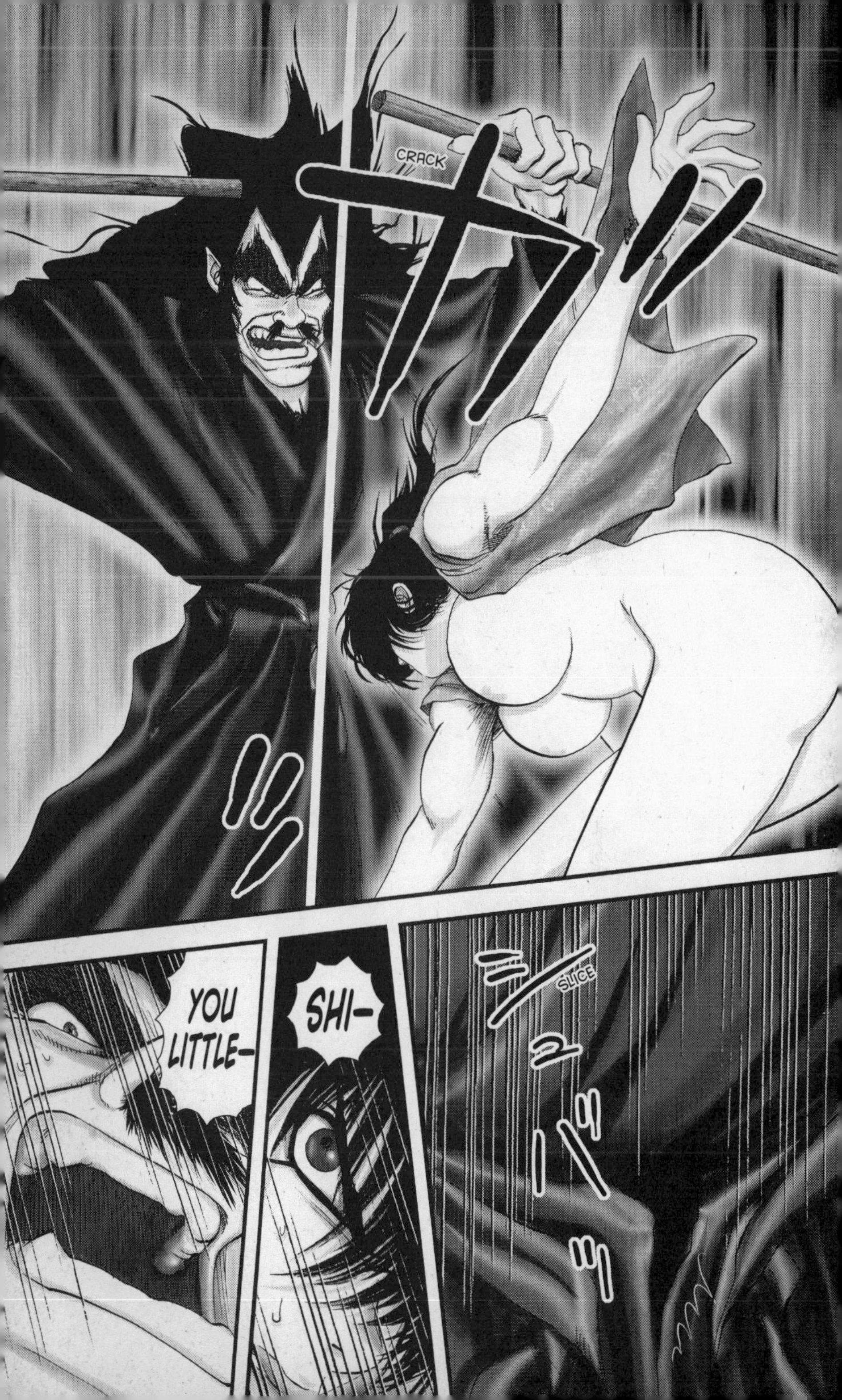
CRACK
SLICE
SHI-
YOU LITTLE-

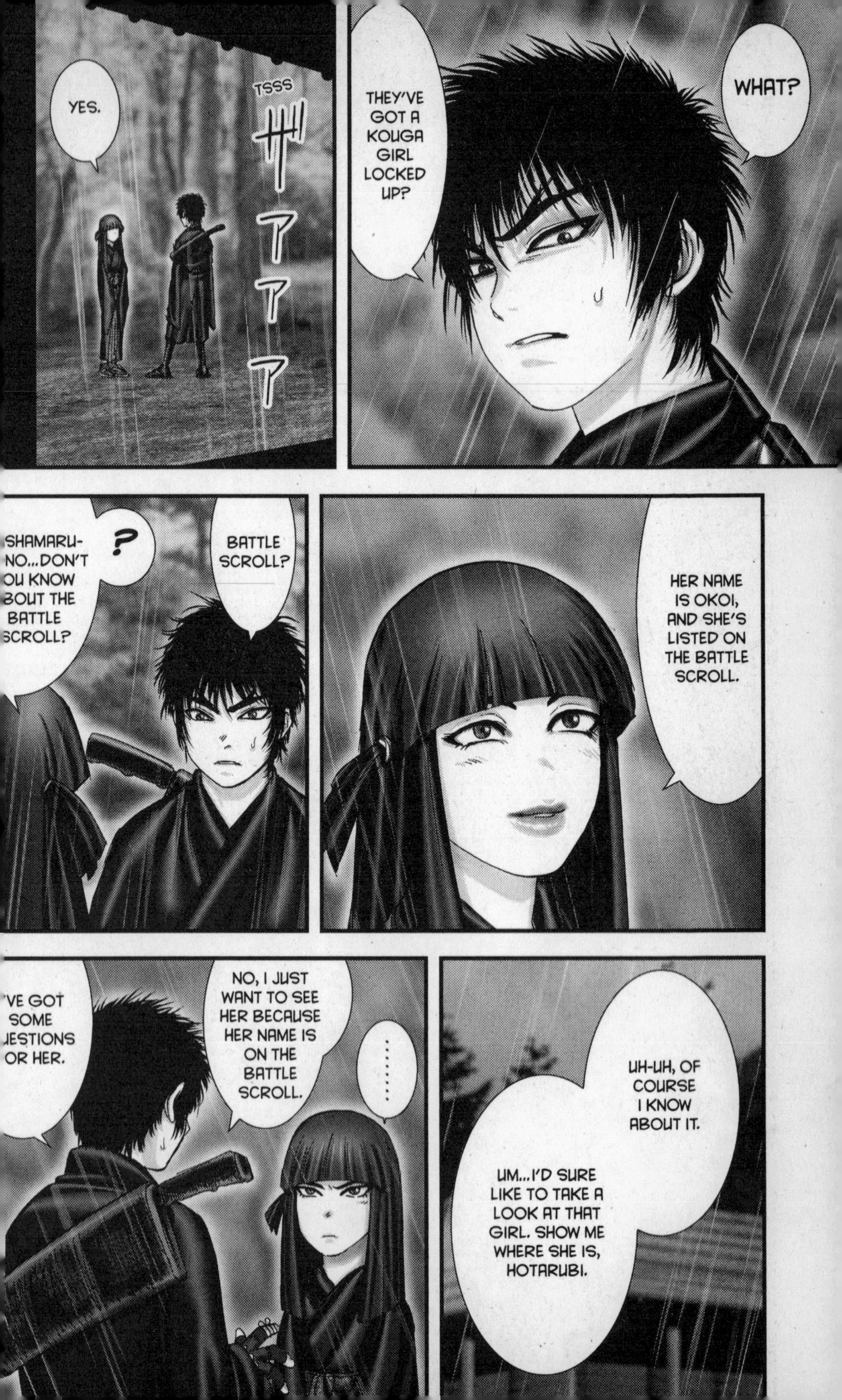
WHAT?
THEY'VE GOT A KOUGA GIRL LOCKED UP?
TSSS
YES.
HER NAME IS OKOI, AND SHE'S LISTED ON THE BATTLE SCROLL.
BATTLE SCROLL?
?
SHAMARU-NO...DON'T OU KNOW BOUT THE BATTLE SCROLL?
UH-UH, OF COURSE I KNOW ABOUT IT.
UM...I'D SURE LIKE TO TAKE A LOOK AT THAT GIRL. SHOW ME WHERE SHE IS, HOTARUBI.
......
NO, I JUST WANT TO SEE HER BECAUSE HER NAME IS ON THE BATTLE SCROLL.
'VE GOT SOME ESTIONS OR HER.

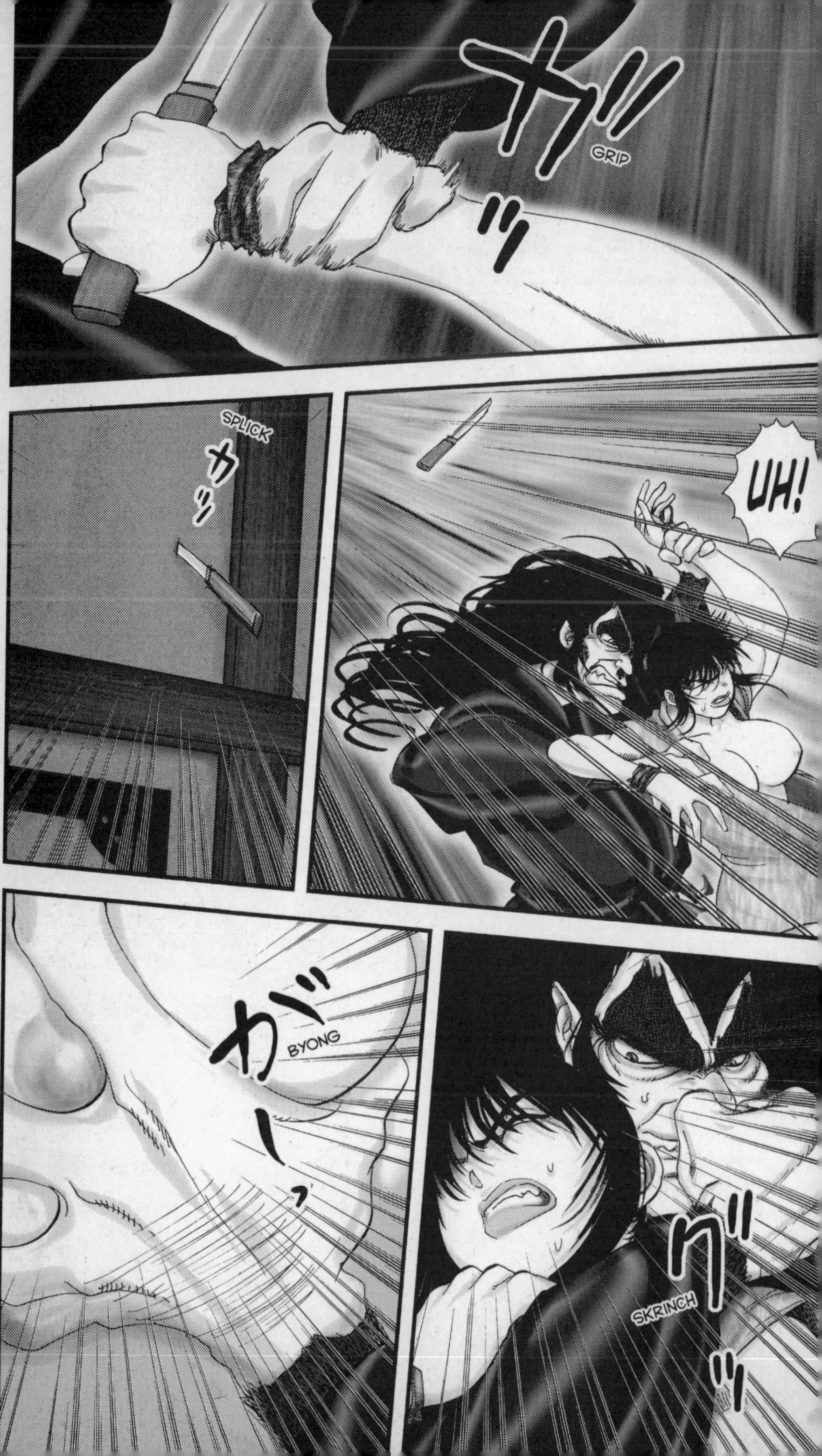

GRIP
UH!
SPLICK
SKRINCH
BYONG

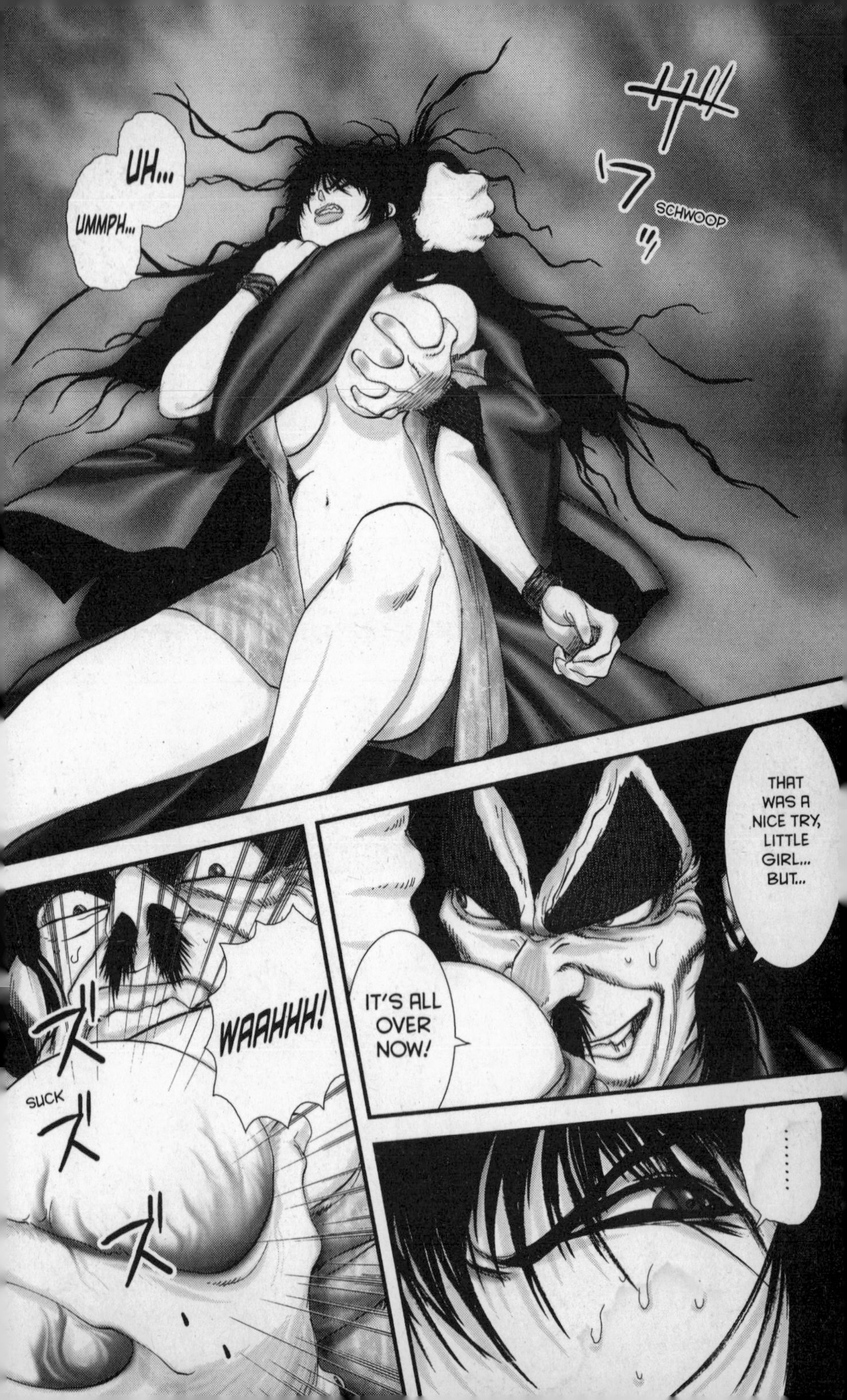
SCHWOOP
UH... UMMPH...
THAT WAS A NICE TRY, LITTLE GIRL... BUT...
IT'S ALL OVER NOW!
......
WAAHHH!
SUCK
ズズズ

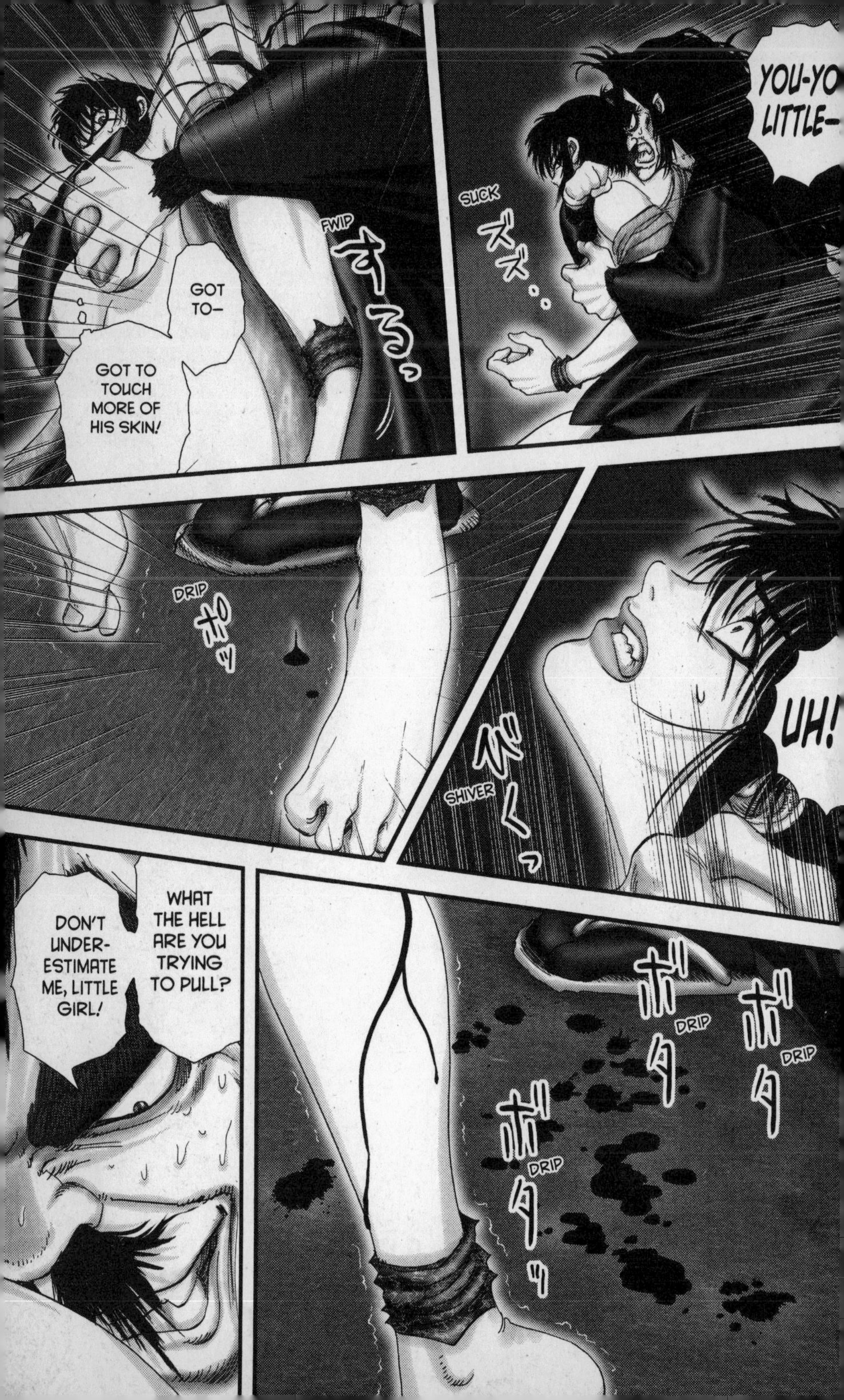
YOU-YO LITTLE–
SUCK
ズズ・・・
FWIP
するっ
GOT TO–
GOT TO TOUCH MORE OF HIS SKIN!
UH!
SHIVER
ビクッ
DRIP
ポッ
DRIP
ボタ
DRIP
ボタ
DRIP
ボタッ
WHAT THE HELL ARE YOU TRYING TO PULL?
DON'T UNDER-ESTIMATE ME, LITTLE GIRL!

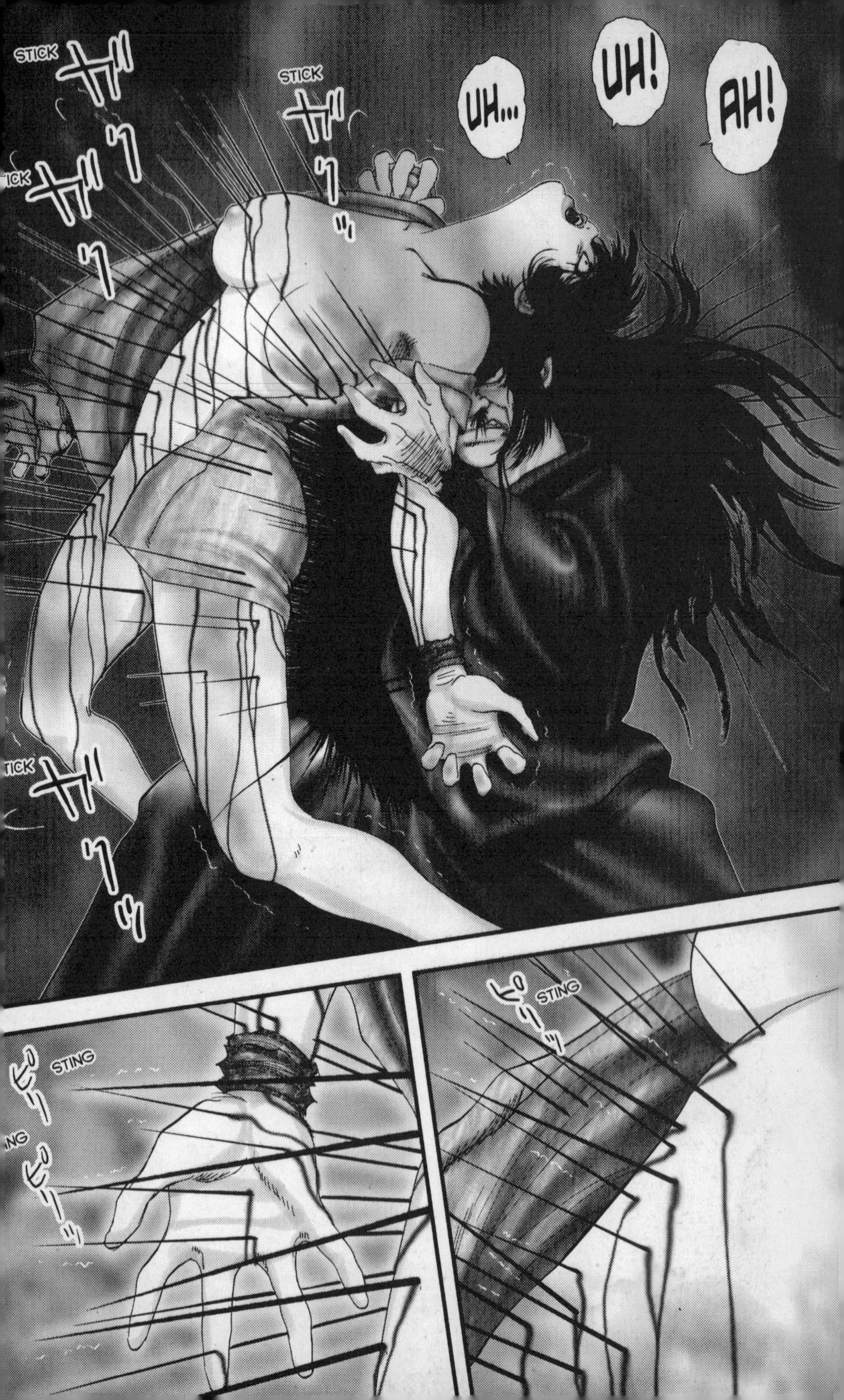
AH!
UH!
UH...
STICK
STICK
TICK
TICK
STING
STING
NG

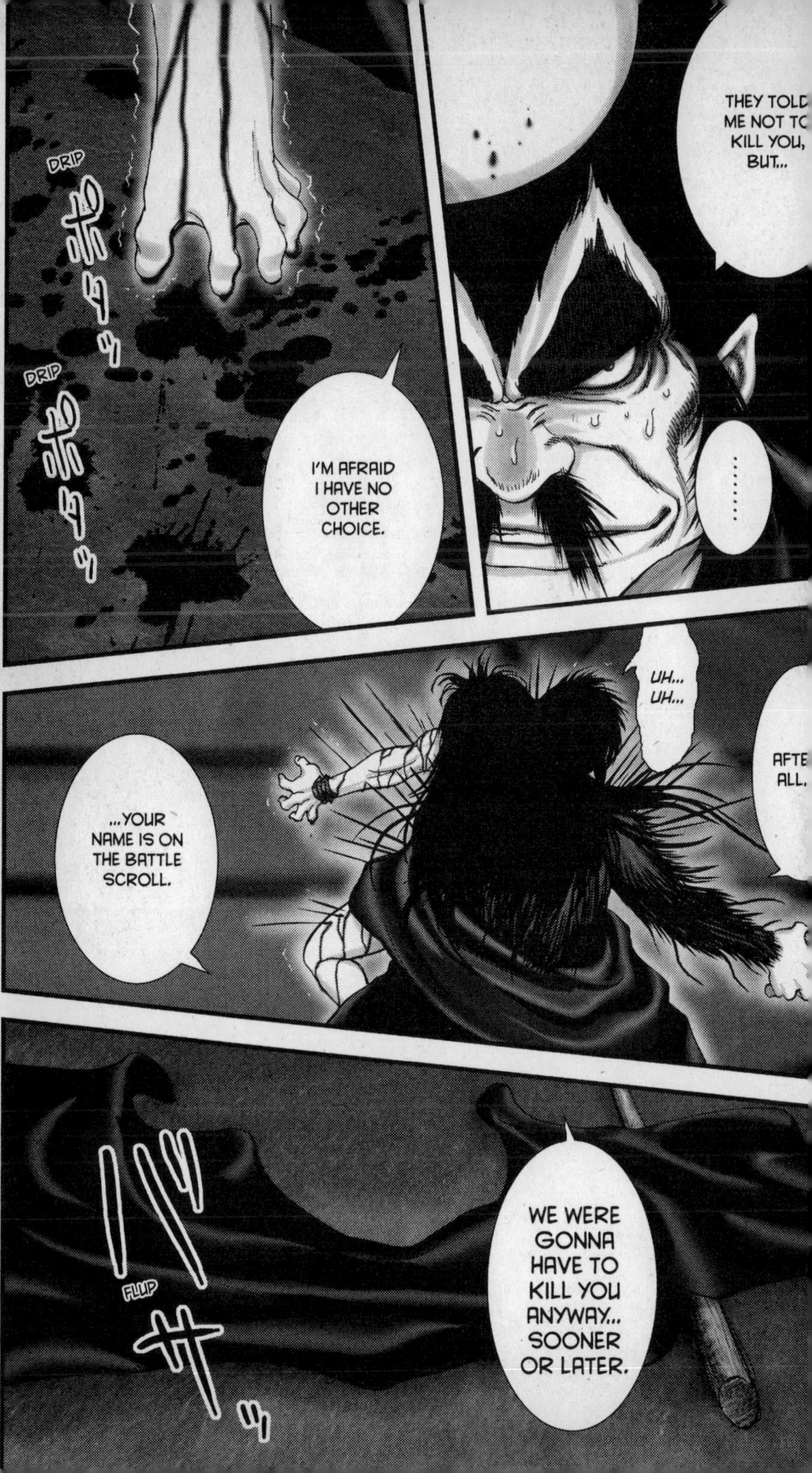
THEY TOLD ME NOT TO KILL YOU, BUT...
......
I'M AFRAID I HAVE NO OTHER CHOICE.
DRIP
DRIP
AFTER ALL,
UH... UH...
...YOUR NAME IS ON THE BATTLE SCROLL.
WE WERE GONNA HAVE TO KILL YOU ANYWAY... SOONER OR LATER.
FLUP

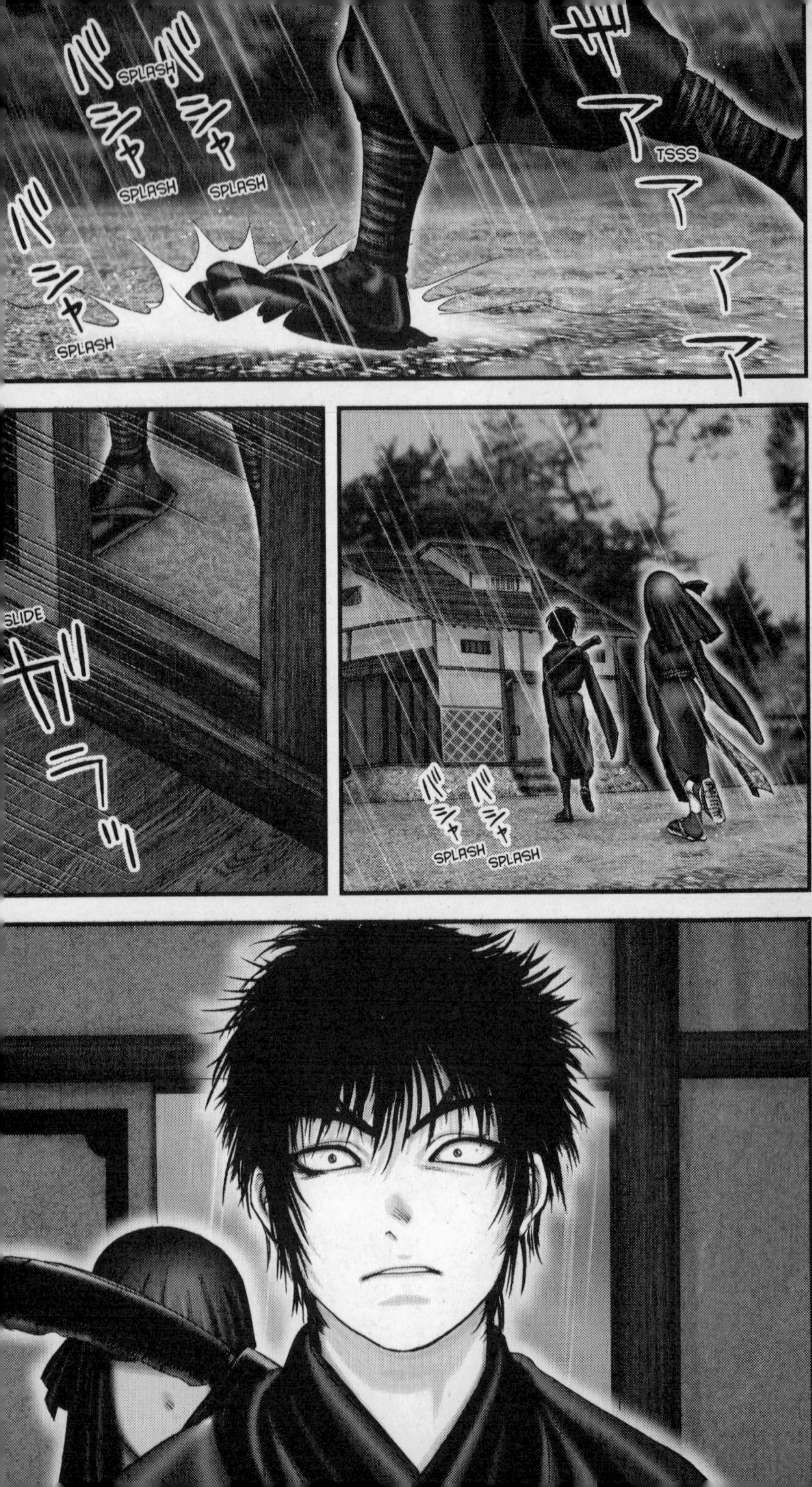
ザァァァァ
TSSS
バシャ
SPLASH
バシャ
SPLASH
バシャ
SPLASH
SPLASH
バシャ
SPLASH
バシャ
SPLASH
SLIDE
ガラッ

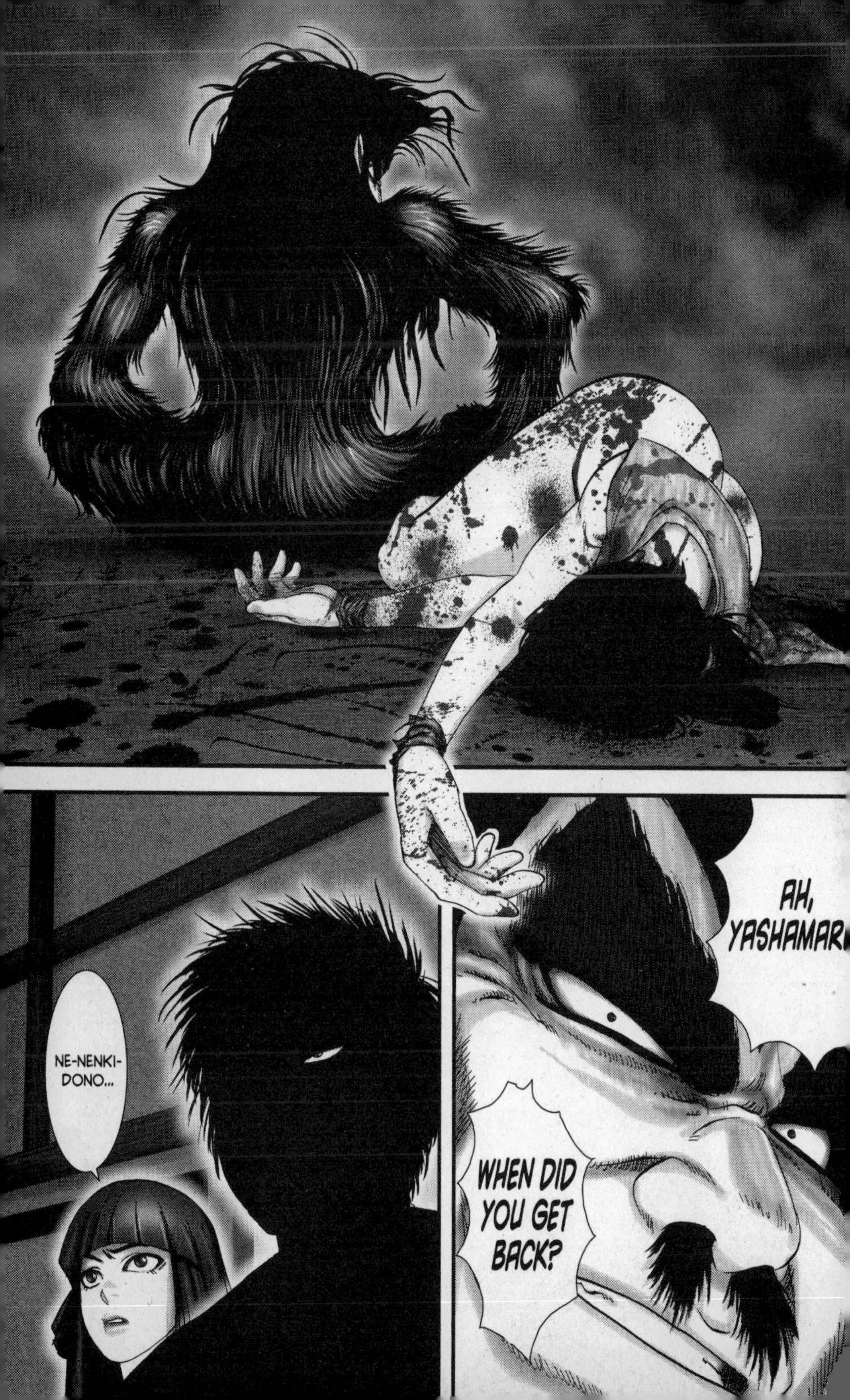
AH, YASHAMAR
WHEN DID YOU GET BACK?
NE-NENKI-DONO...

HEY, ASHAMARU.

SWIP

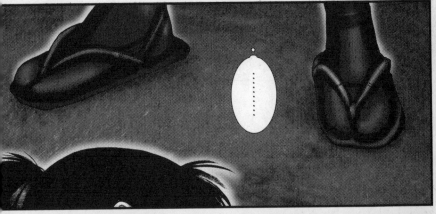

....

UH...

I JUST GOT BACK.

JUST...

...NOW.

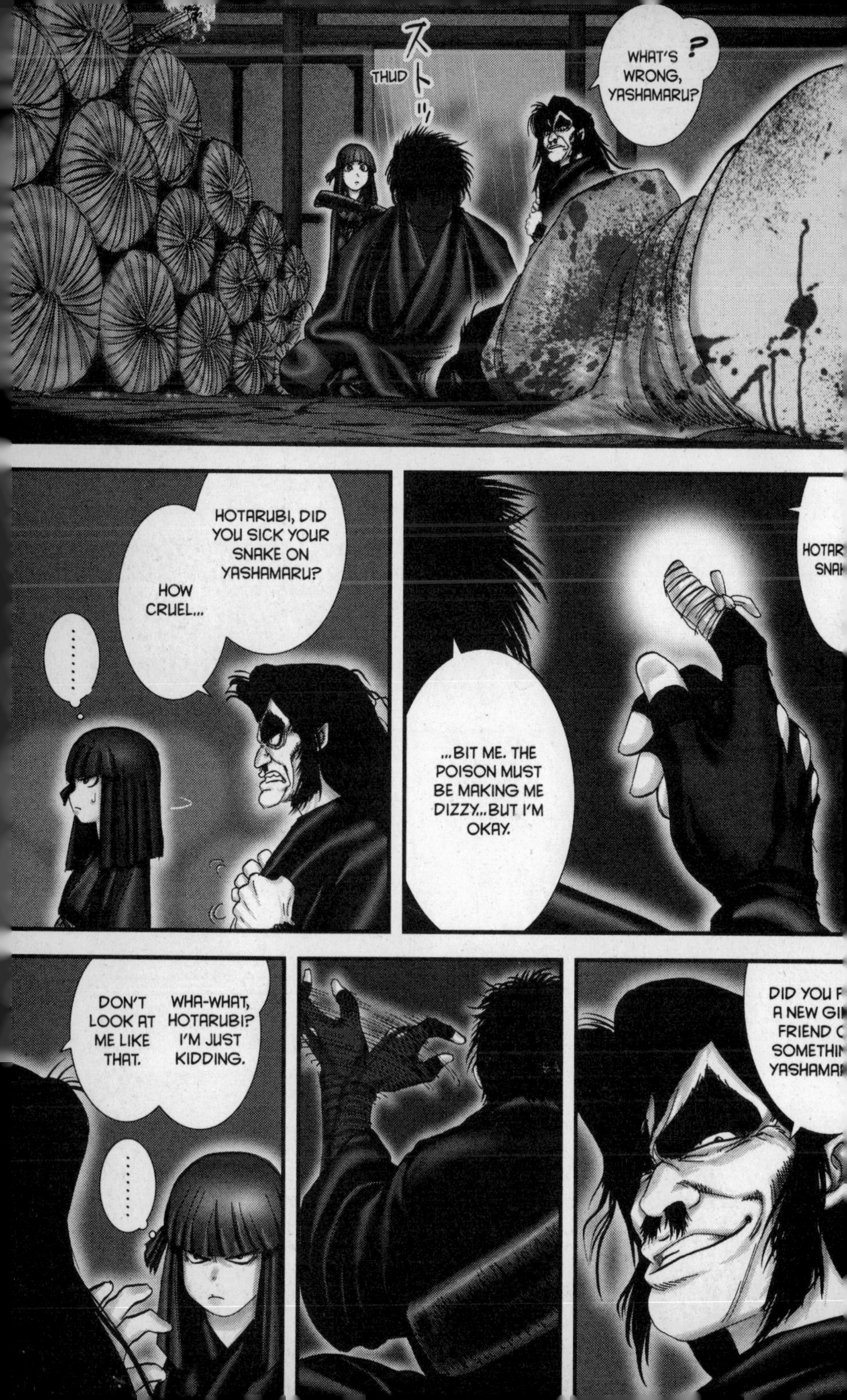
ストッ
THUD
?
WHAT'S WRONG, YASHAMARU?
...BIT ME. THE POISON MUST BE MAKING ME DIZZY...BUT I'M OKAY.
HOTARUBI, DID YOU SICK YOUR SNAKE ON YASHAMARU?
HOW CRUEL...
......
WHA-WHAT, HOTARUBI? I'M JUST KIDDING.
DON'T LOOK AT ME LIKE THAT.
......

OKOI...

OKOI...

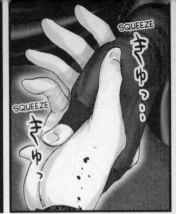

SQUEEZE

き ゅっ...

SQUEEZE

き ゅっ

・・・・

ビ クッ

SHIVER

I'M SORRY...
OKOI...

I'M...
TOO
LATE...

SQUEEZE

ぎゅっ

ぎゅうっ

SQUEEZE

SA...E...MO...N...

I KILLED...

...THE OLD MAN...ALL BY MYSELF.

SA...E...MO...N...

SA...E...MO...N...

SQUEEZE

○○○○○○

○ ○

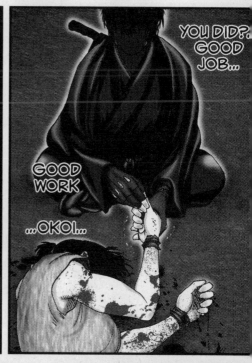

YOU DID? GOOD JOB...

GOOD WORK

...OKOI...

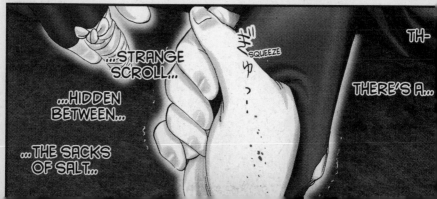

...STRANGE SCROLL...

...HIDDEN BETWEEN...

...THE SACKS OF SALT...

SQUEEZE

TH-

THERE'S A...

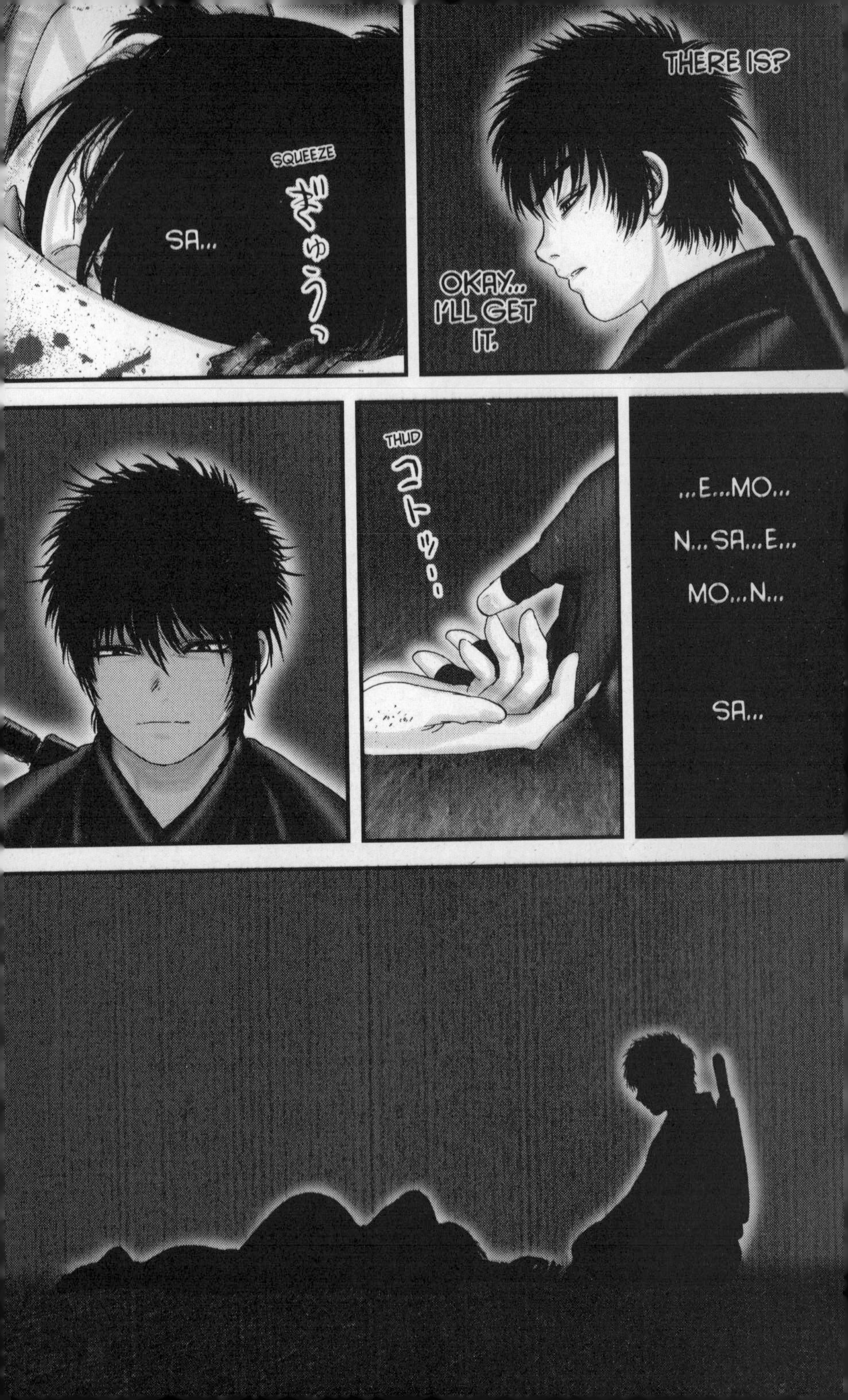
THERE IS?
OKAY... I'LL GET IT.
SQUEEZE
ぎゅう、
SA...
...E...MO... N...SA...E... MO...N...
SA...
THUD
コトッ..

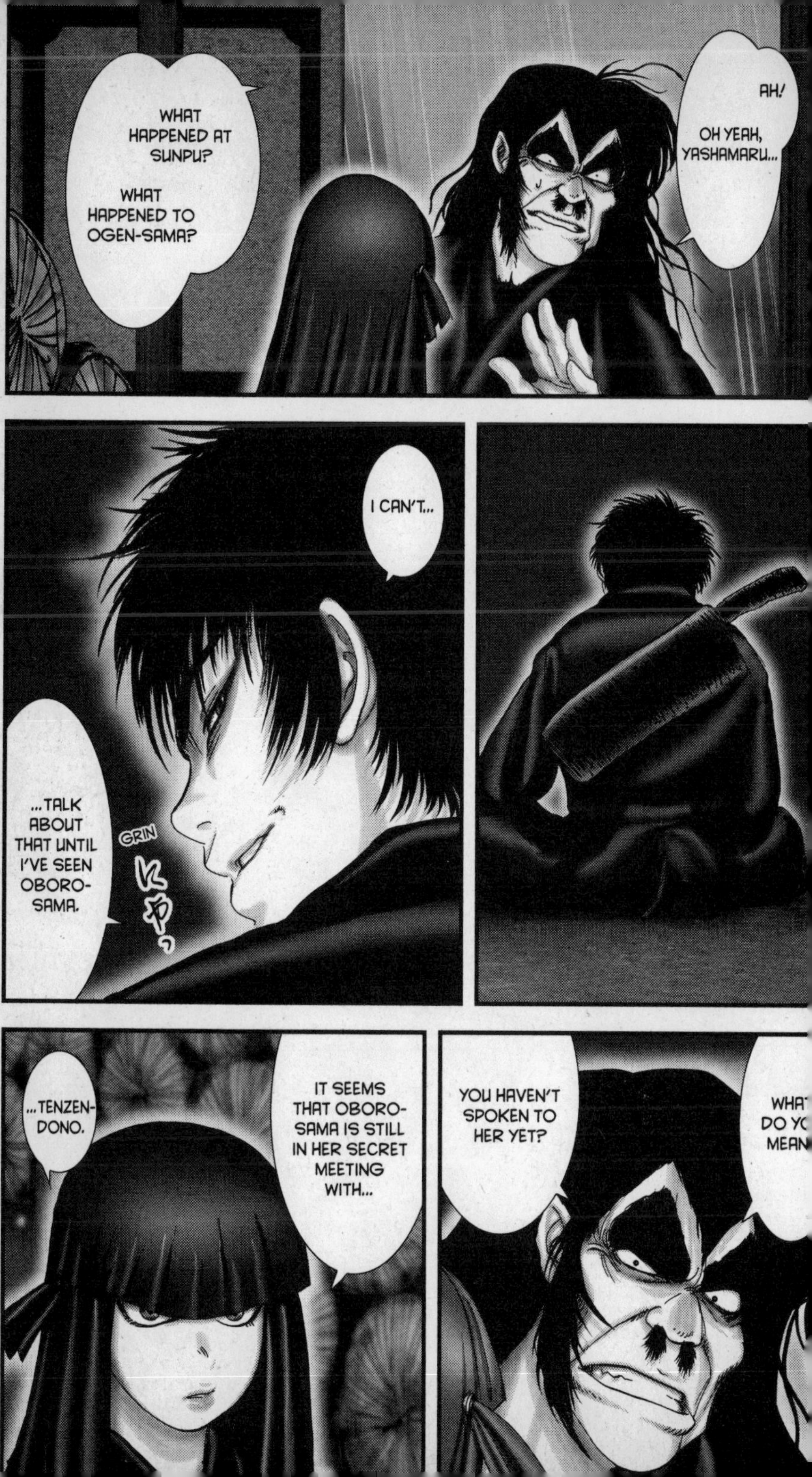
AH!
OH YEAH, YASHAMARU...
WHAT HAPPENED AT SUNPU?
WHAT HAPPENED TO OGEN-SAMA?
I CAN'T...
...TALK ABOUT THAT UNTIL I'VE SEEN OBORO-SAMA.
GRIN
にやっ
WHAT DO YO MEAN
YOU HAVEN'T SPOKEN TO HER YET?
IT SEEMS THAT OBORO-SAMA IS STILL IN HER SECRET MEETING WITH...
...TENZEN-DONO.

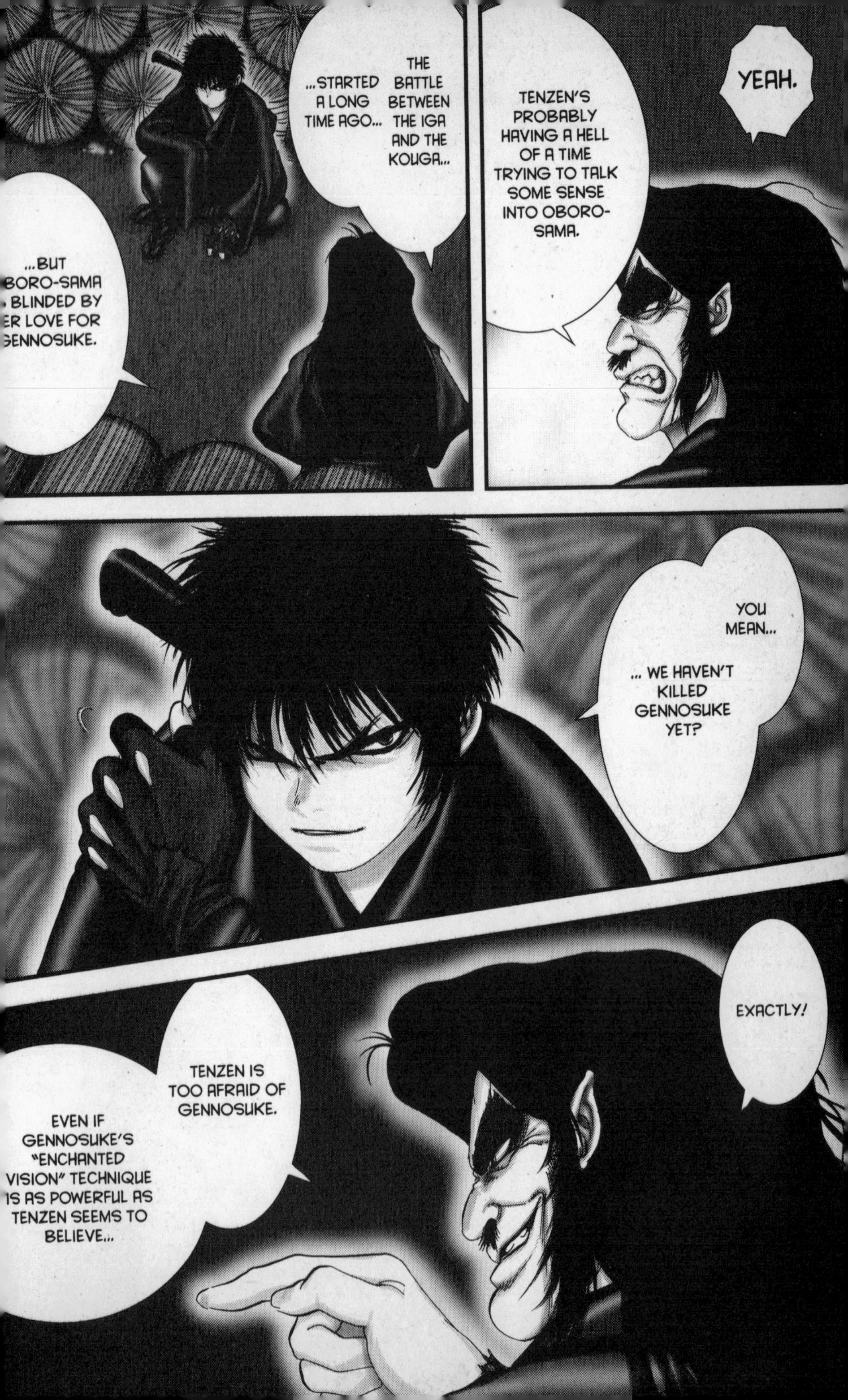
YEAH.
TENZEN'S PROBABLY HAVING A HELL OF A TIME TRYING TO TALK SOME SENSE INTO OBORO-SAMA.
THE BATTLE BETWEEN THE IGA AND THE KOUGA...
...STARTED A LONG TIME AGO...
...BUT BORO-SAMA BLINDED BY ER LOVE FOR GENNOSUKE.
YOU MEAN...
... WE HAVEN'T KILLED GENNOSUKE YET?
EXACTLY!
TENZEN IS TOO AFRAID OF GENNOSUKE.
EVEN IF GENNOSUKE'S "ENCHANTED VISION" TECHNIQUE IS AS POWERFUL AS TENZEN SEEMS TO BELIEVE...

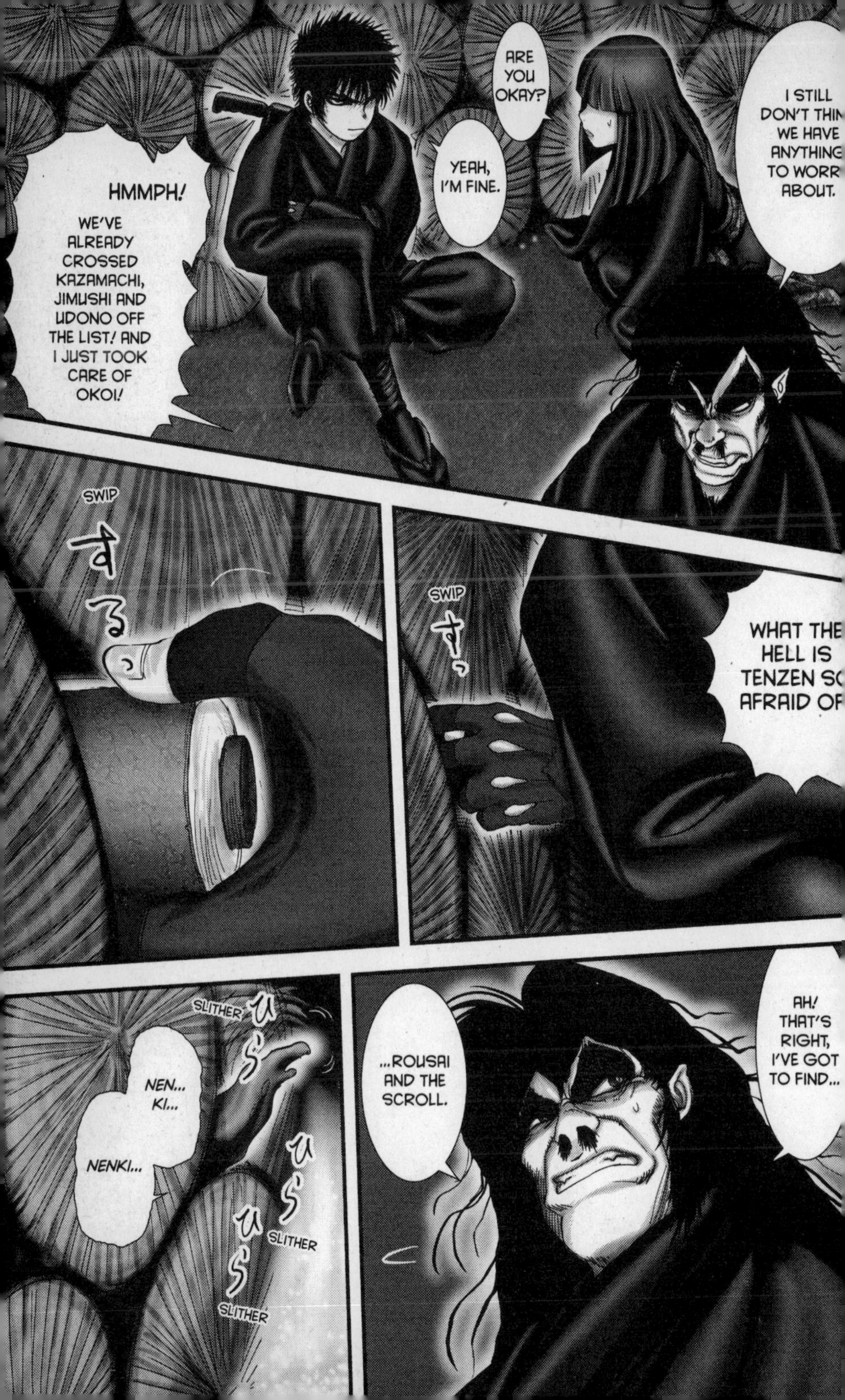
I STILL DON'T THIN WE HAVE ANYTHING TO WORR ABOUT.
ARE YOU OKAY?
YEAH, I'M FINE.
HMMPH!
WE'VE ALREADY CROSSED KAZAMACHI, JIMUSHI AND UDONO OFF THE LIST! AND I JUST TOOK CARE OF OKOI!
WHAT THE HELL IS TENZEN SC AFRAID OF
SWIP
すっ
SWIP
する
AH! THAT'S RIGHT, I'VE GOT TO FIND...
...ROUSAI AND THE SCROLL.
SLITHER
NEN... KI...
NENKI...
SLITHER
SLITHER

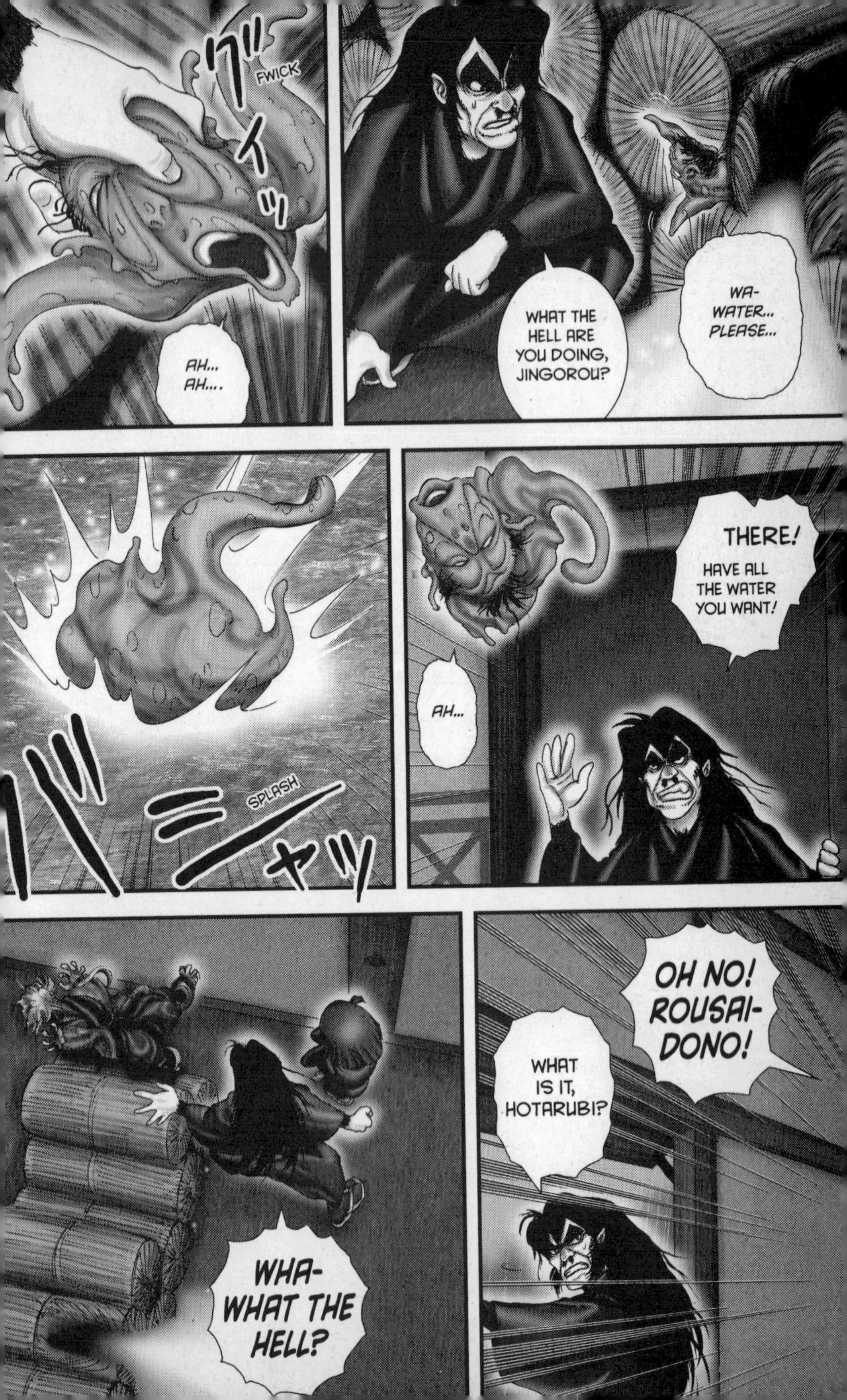
WA-
WATER...
PLEASE...
WHAT THE HELL ARE YOU DOING, JINGOROU?
FWICK
AH... AH....
THERE!
HAVE ALL THE WATER YOU WANT!
AH...
SPLASH
OH NO! ROUSAI-DONO!
WHAT IS IT, HOTARUBI?
WHA-WHAT THE HELL?

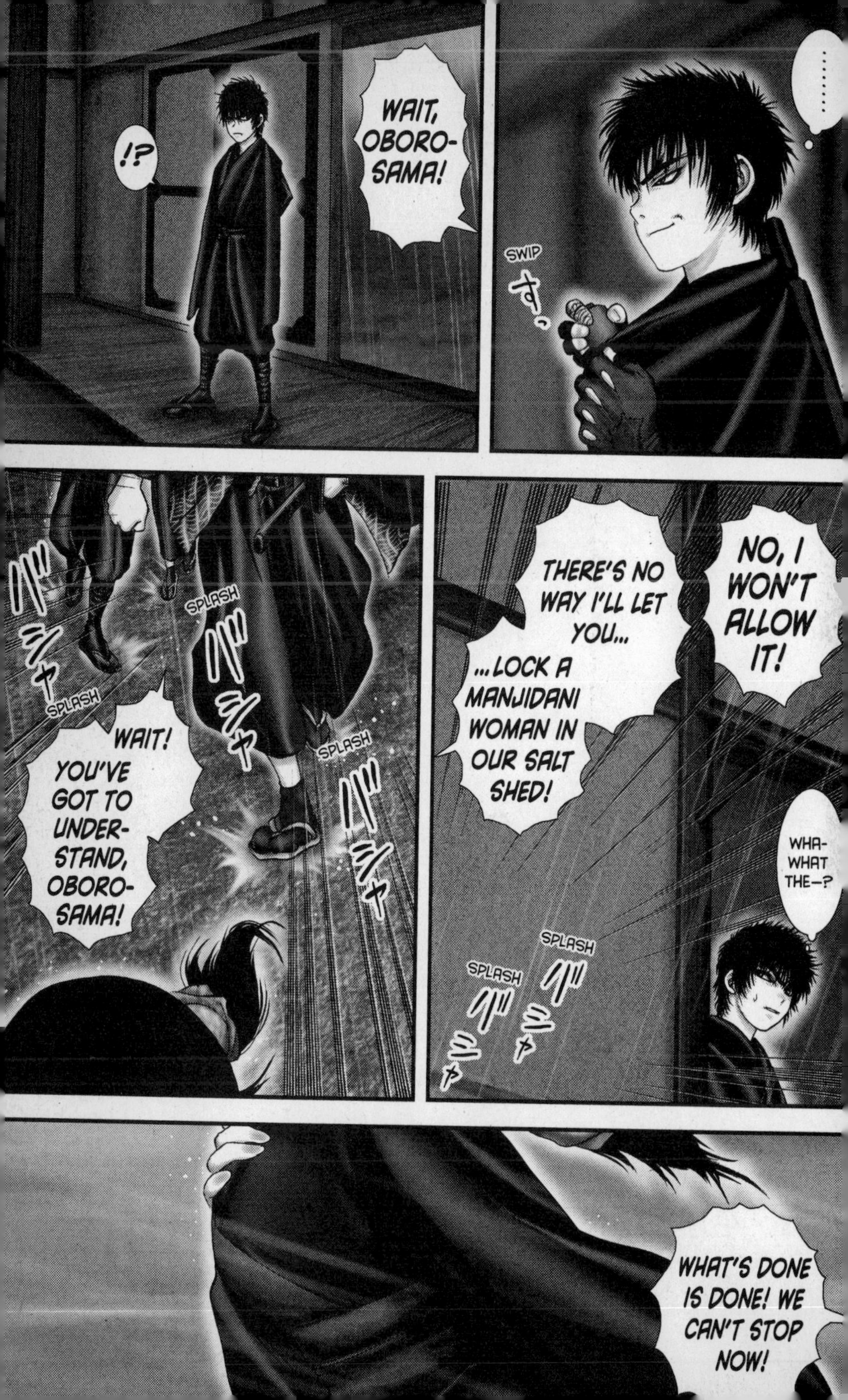
......
SWIP
WAIT, OBORO-SAMA!
!?
NO, I WON'T ALLOW IT!
THERE'S NO WAY I'LL LET YOU...
...LOCK A MANJIDANI WOMAN IN OUR SALT SHED!
WHA- WHAT THE—?
SPLASH
SPLASH
SPLASH
SPLASH
SPLASH
WAIT! YOU'VE GOT TO UNDERSTAND, OBORO-SAMA!
WHAT'S DONE IS DONE! WE CAN'T STOP NOW!

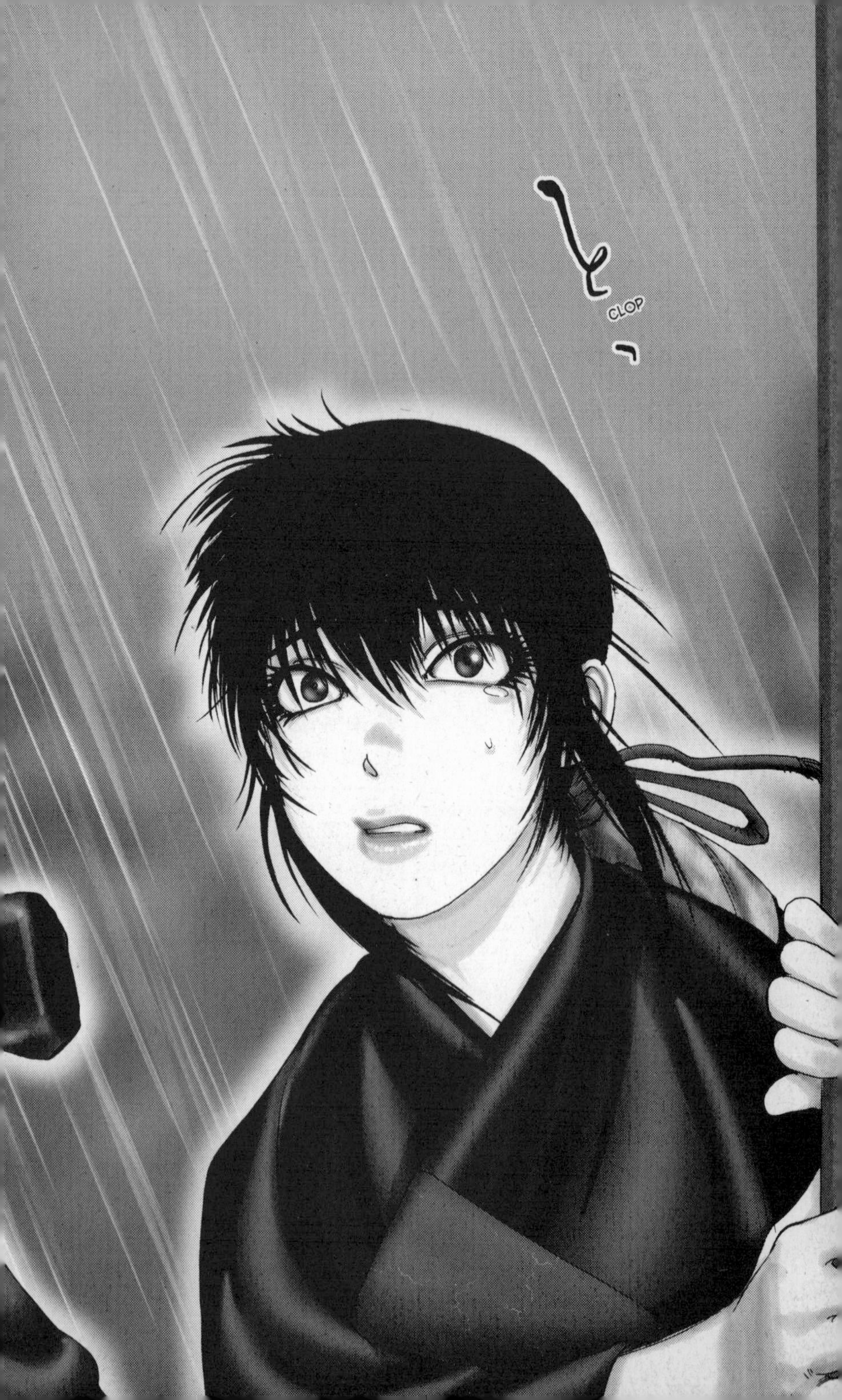
CLOP

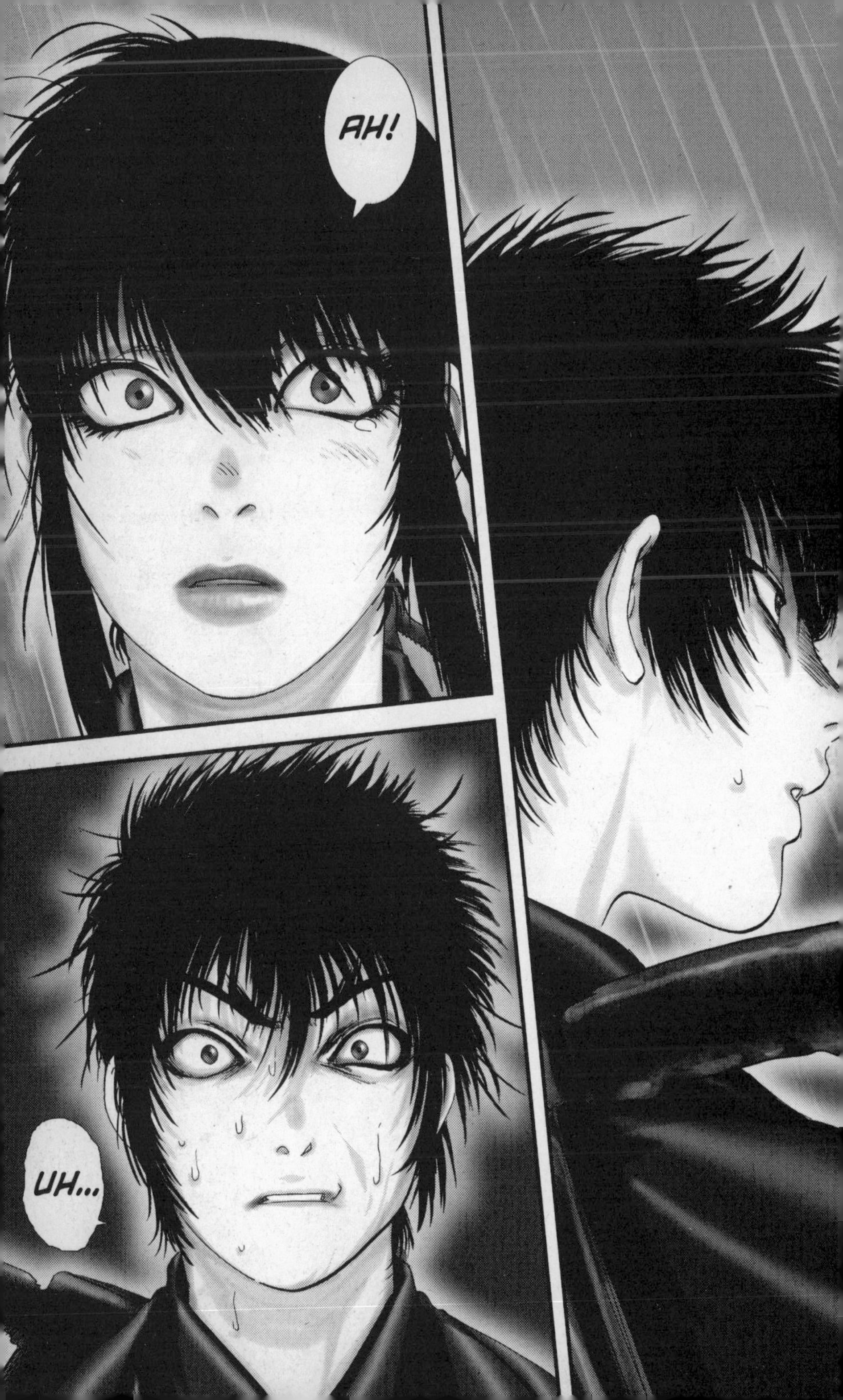
AH!
UH...

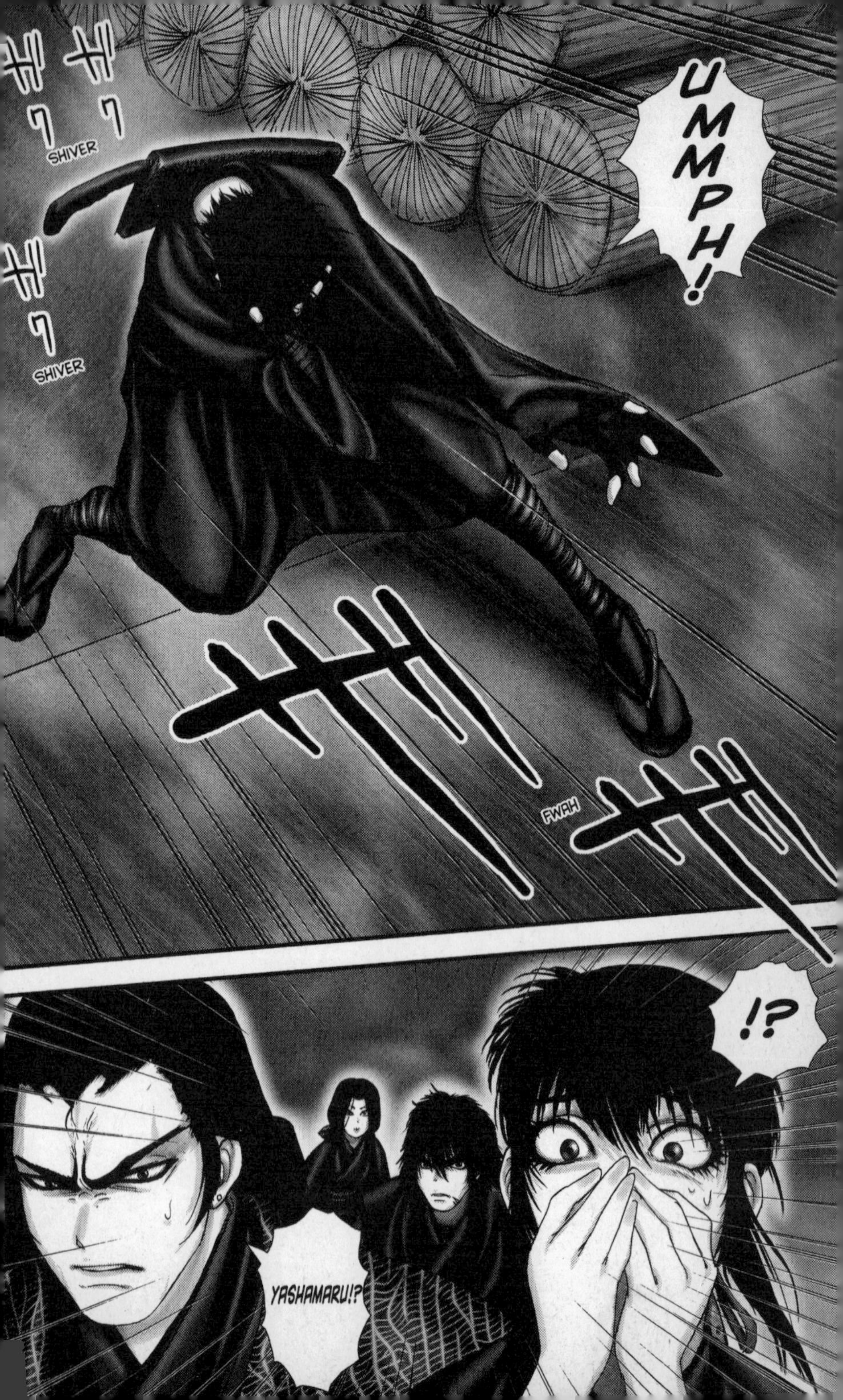

UMMPH!
SHIVER
SHIVER
FWAH
!?
YASHAMARU!?

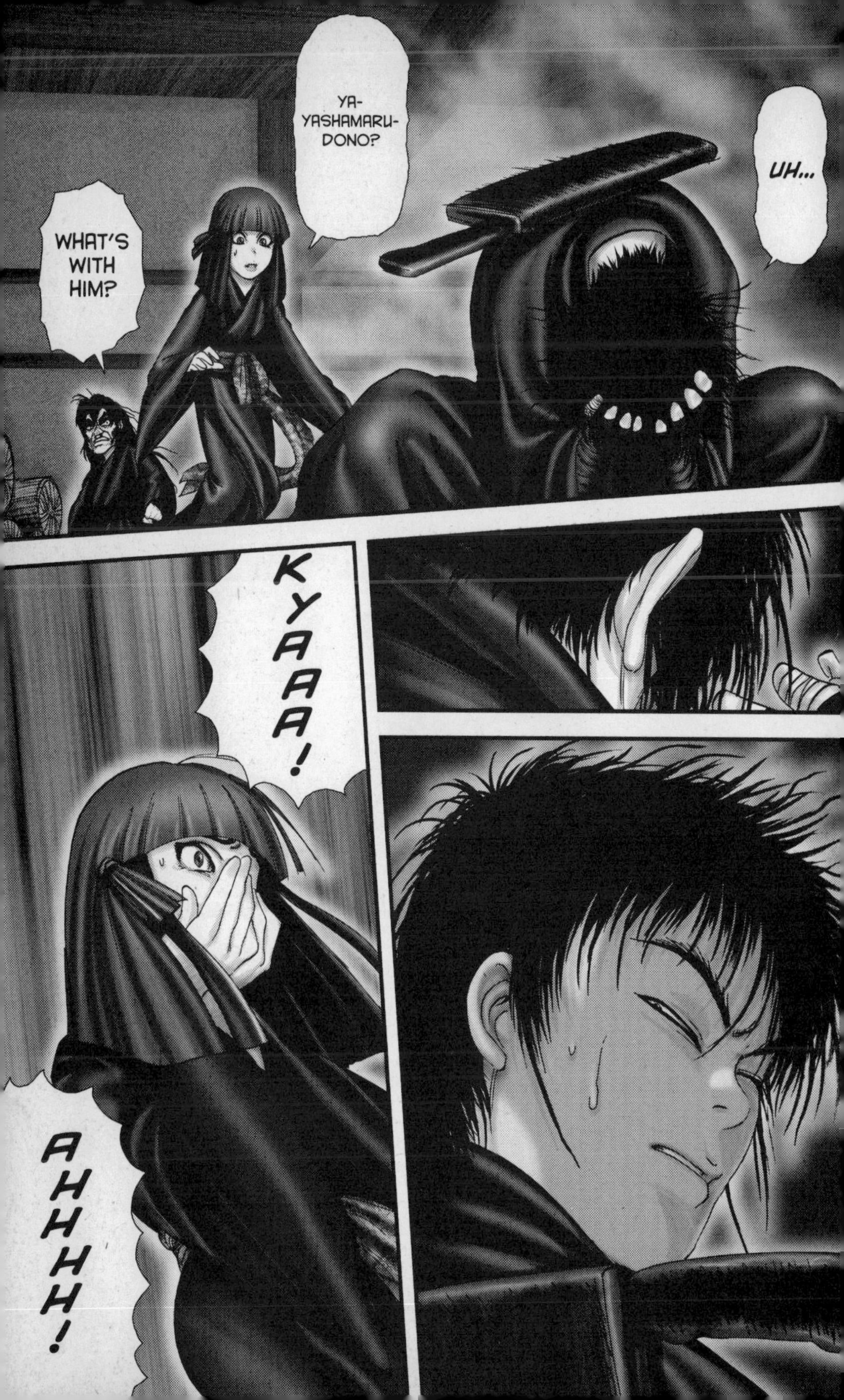
UH...
YA-YASHAMARU-DONO?
WHAT'S WITH HIM?
KYAAAA!
AHHHH!

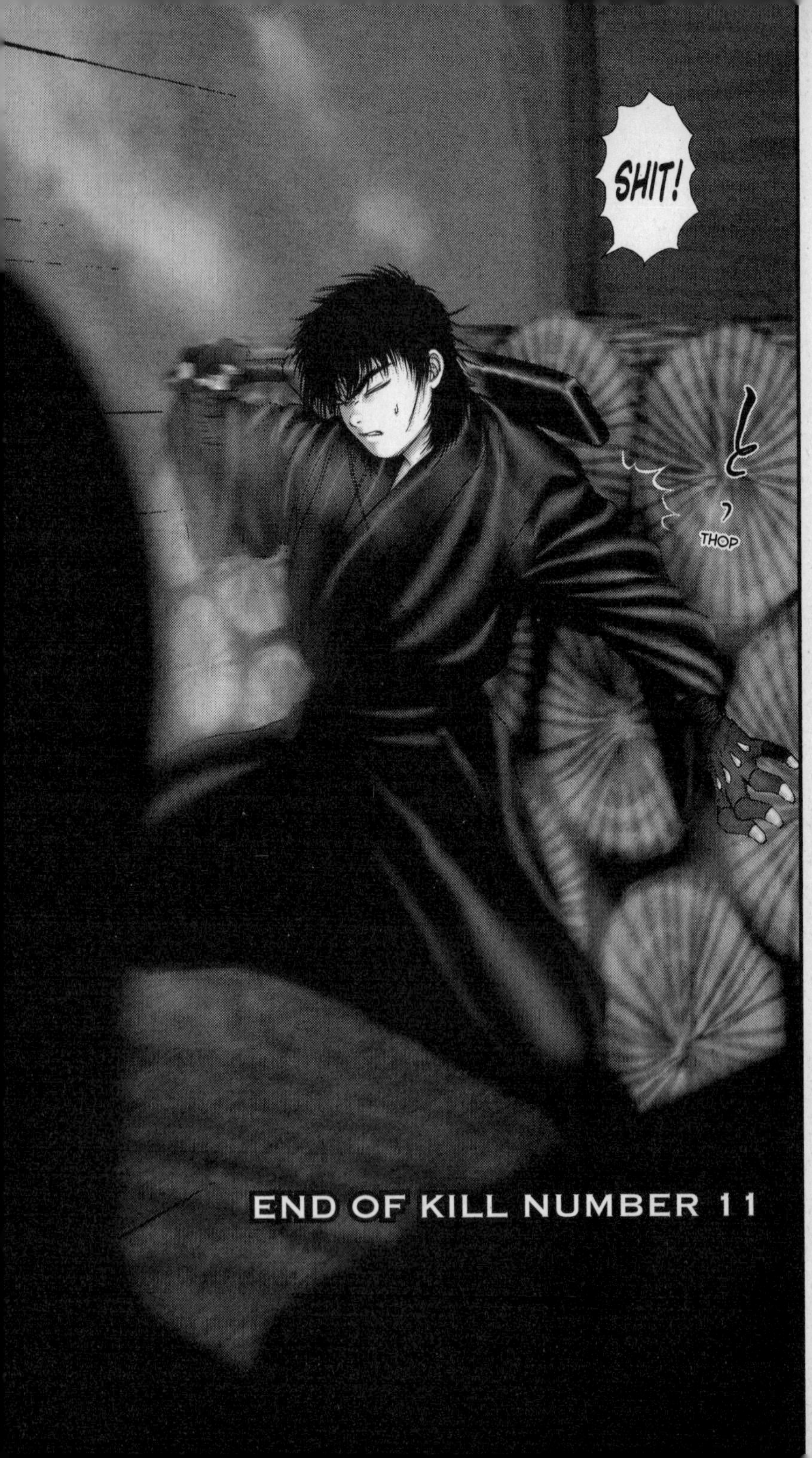
SHIT!
THOP
END OF KILL NUMBER 11

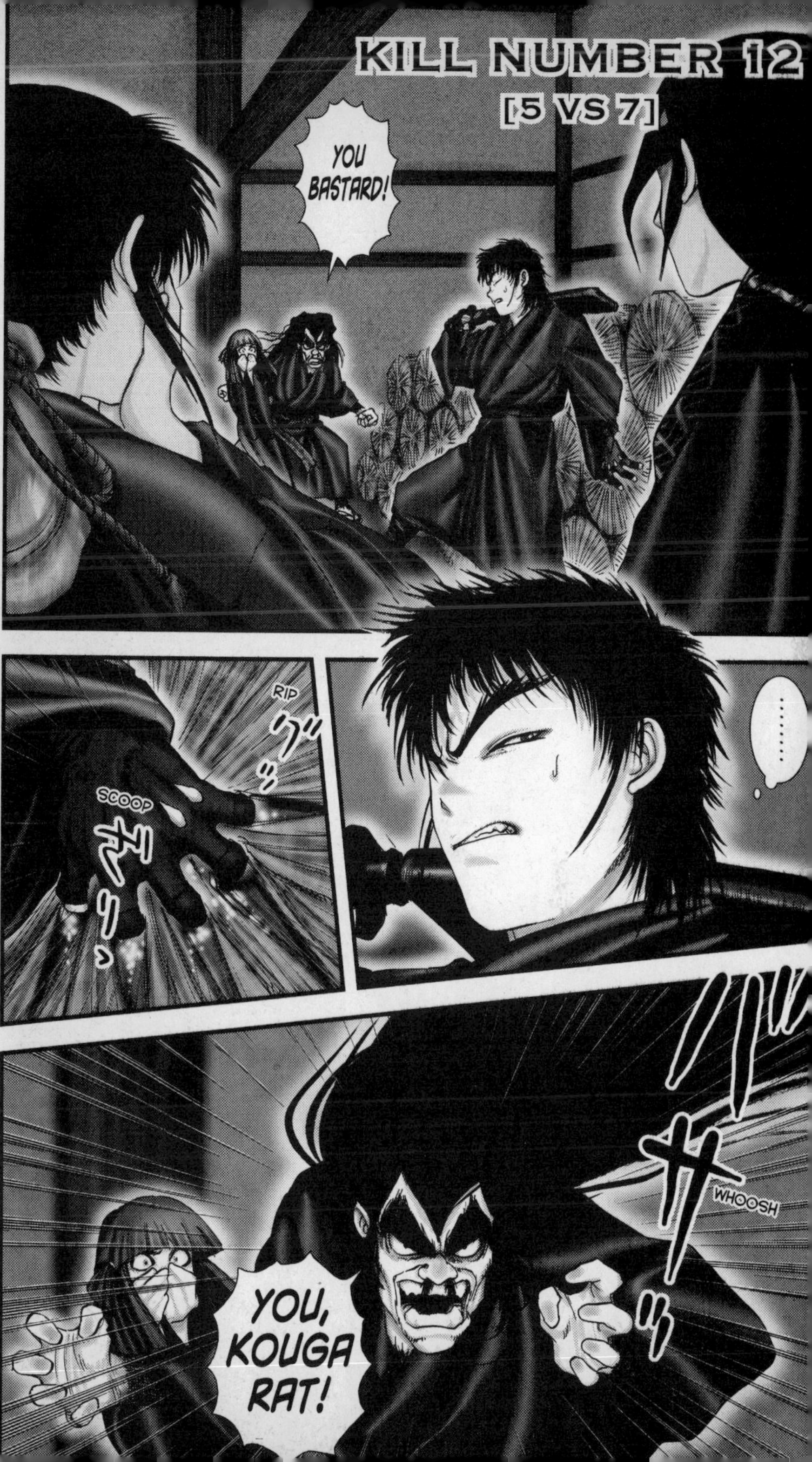
KILL NUMBER 12
[5 VS 7]
YOU BASTARD!
......
RIP
SCOOP
WHOOSH
YOU, KOUGA RAT!

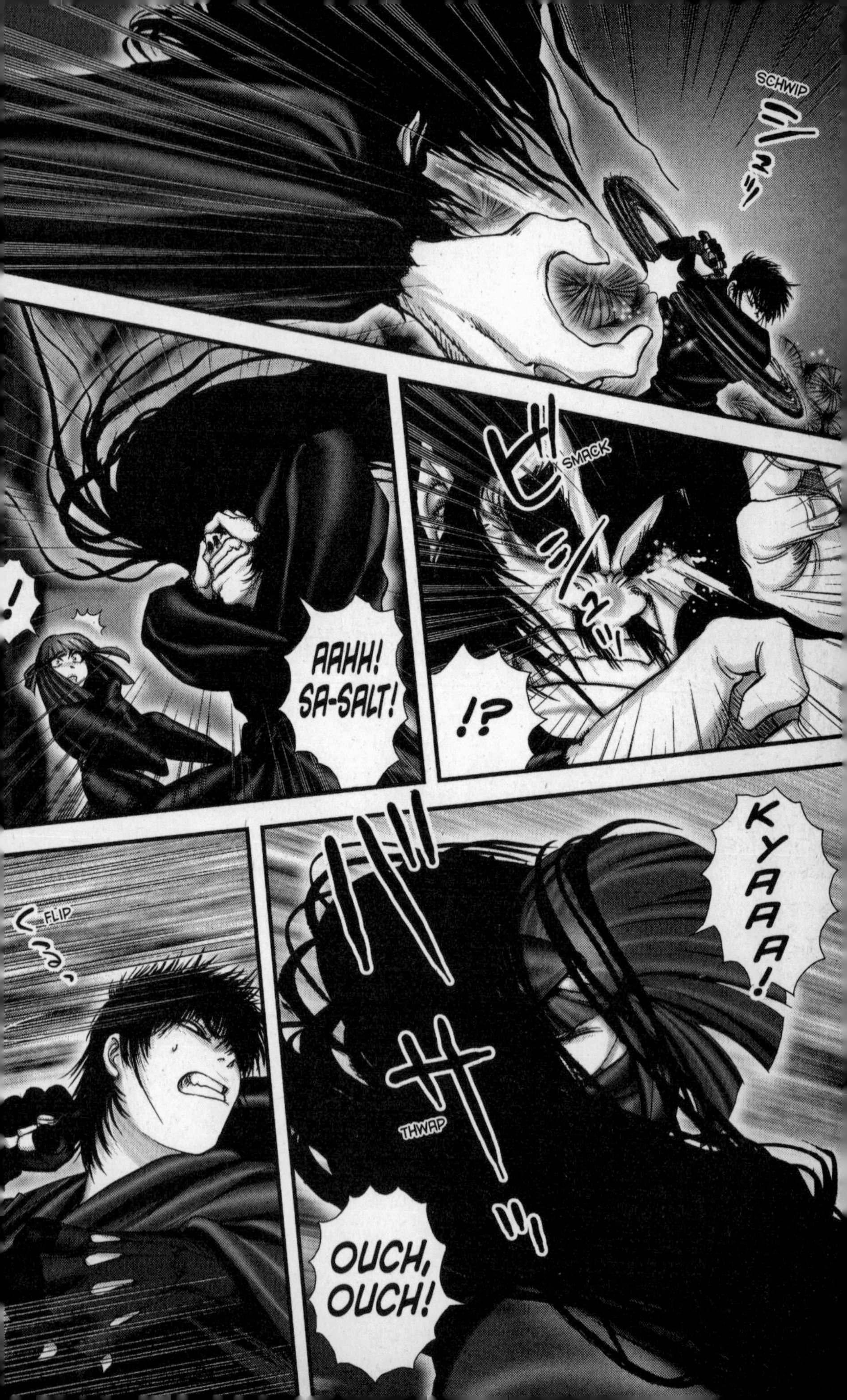
SCHWIP
SMACK
!?
AAHH!
SA-SALT!
!
KYAAAA!
THWAP
OUCH,
OUCH!
FLIP

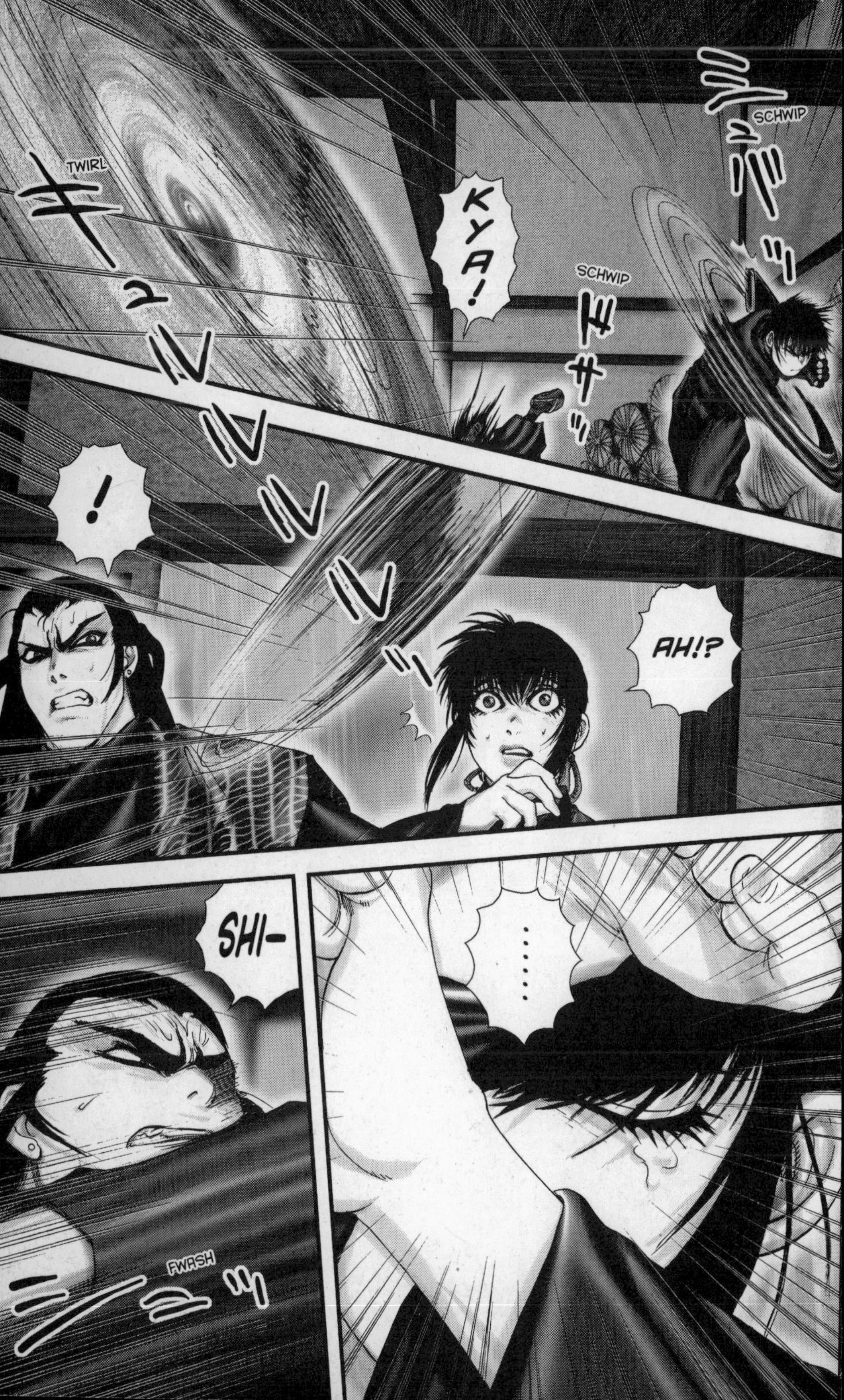
SCHWIP
KYA!
SCHWIP
TWIRL
AH!?
!
......
SHI-
FWASH

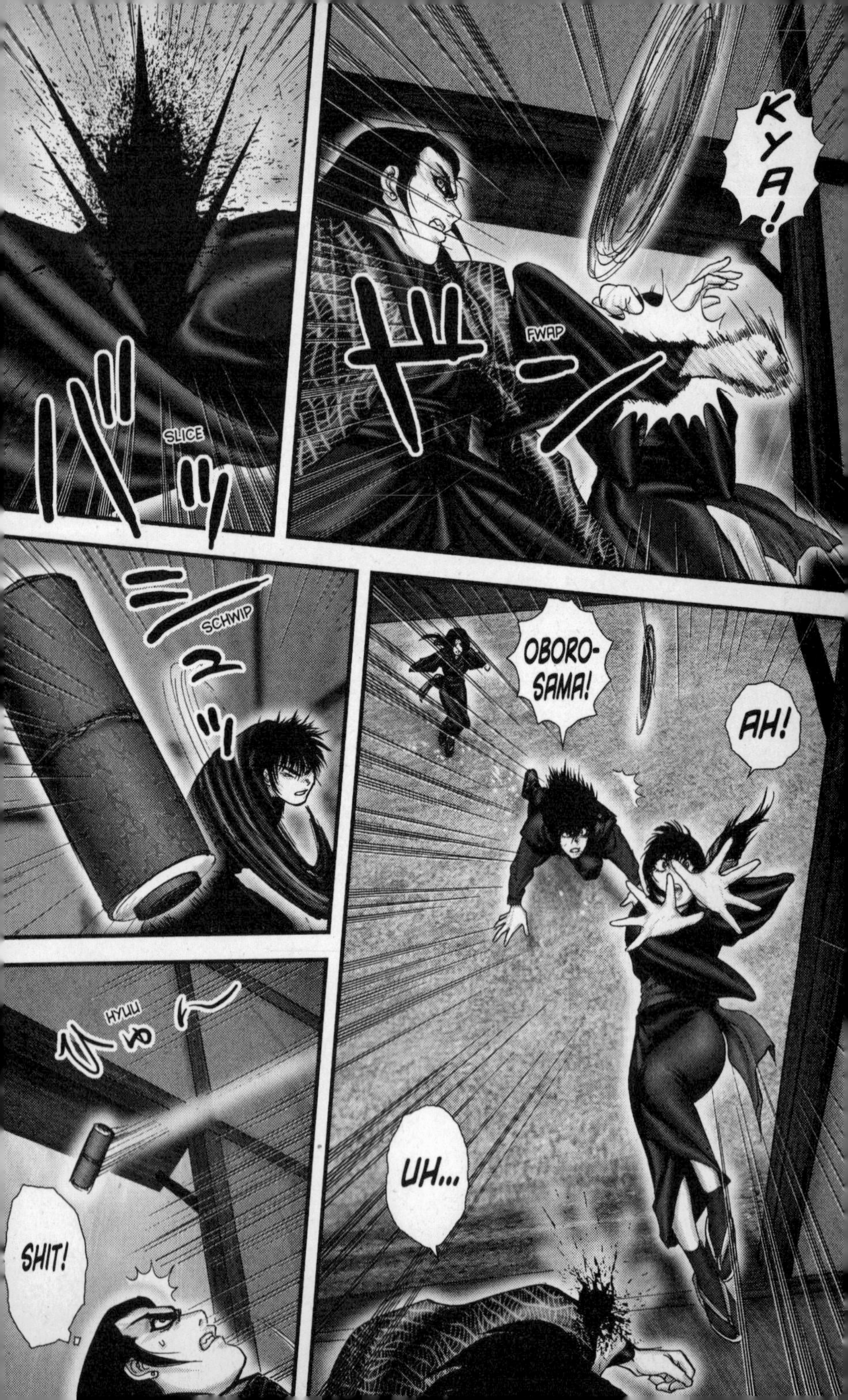
KYA!
FWAP
SLICE
OBORO-SAMA!
AH!
UH...
SCHWIP
HYUU
SHIT!

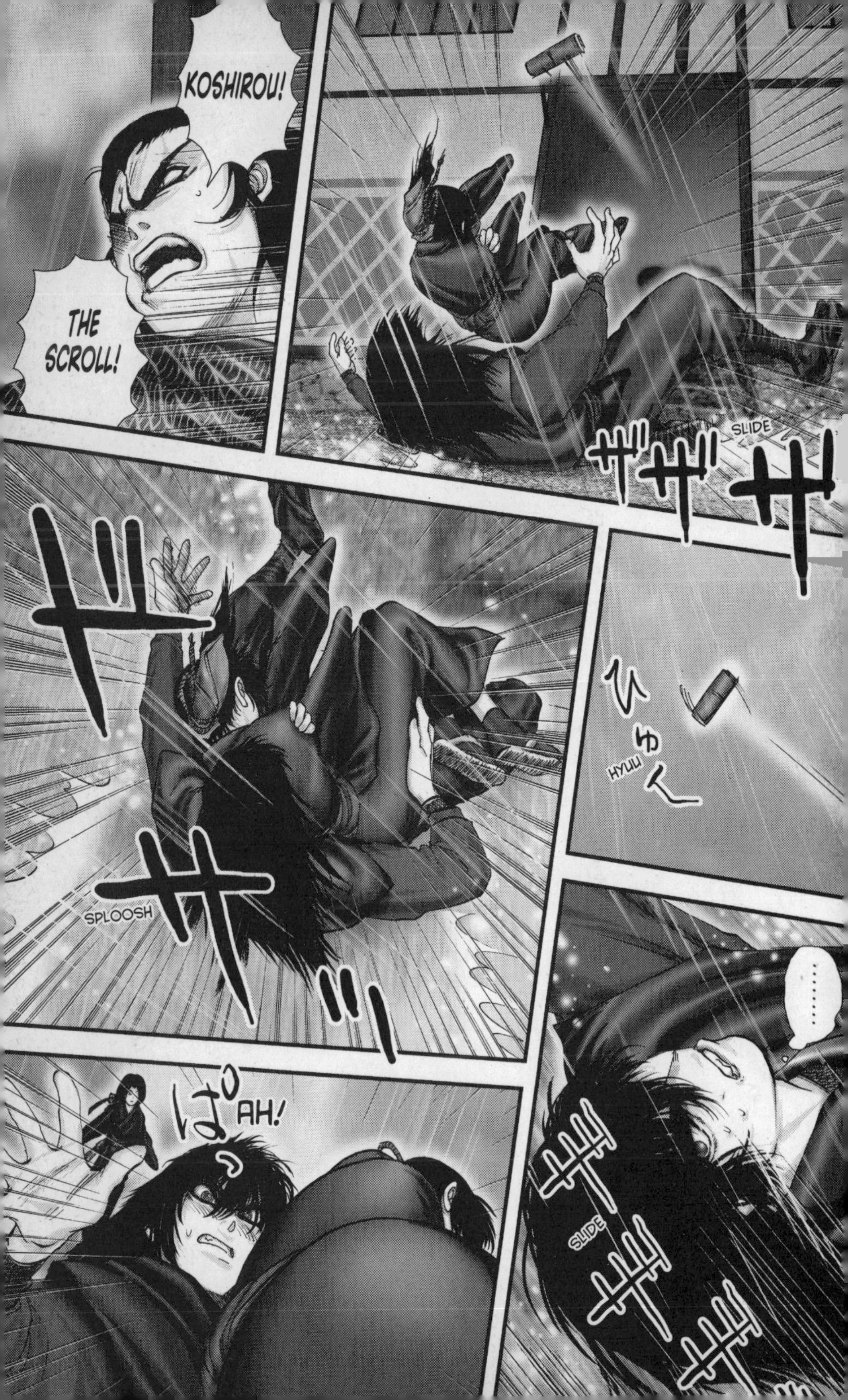

SLIDE
KOSHIROU!
THE SCROLL!
HYUU
SPLOOSH
......
SLIDE
AH!

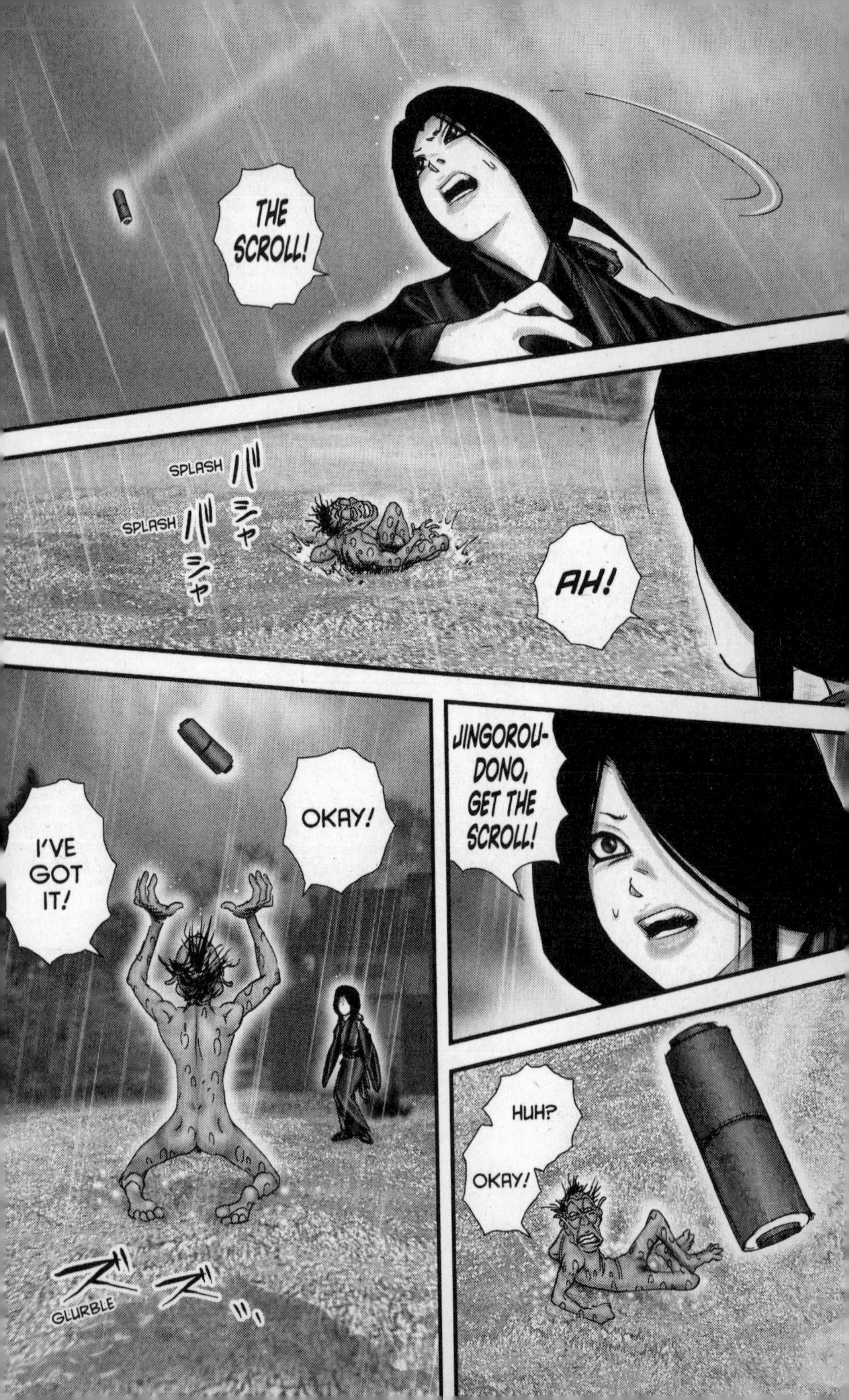
THE SCROLL!
SPLASH
バシャ
SPLASH
バシャ
AH!
JINGOROU-DONO, GET THE SCROLL!
HUH?
OKAY!
OKAY!
I'VE GOT IT!
ズズ
GLURBLE

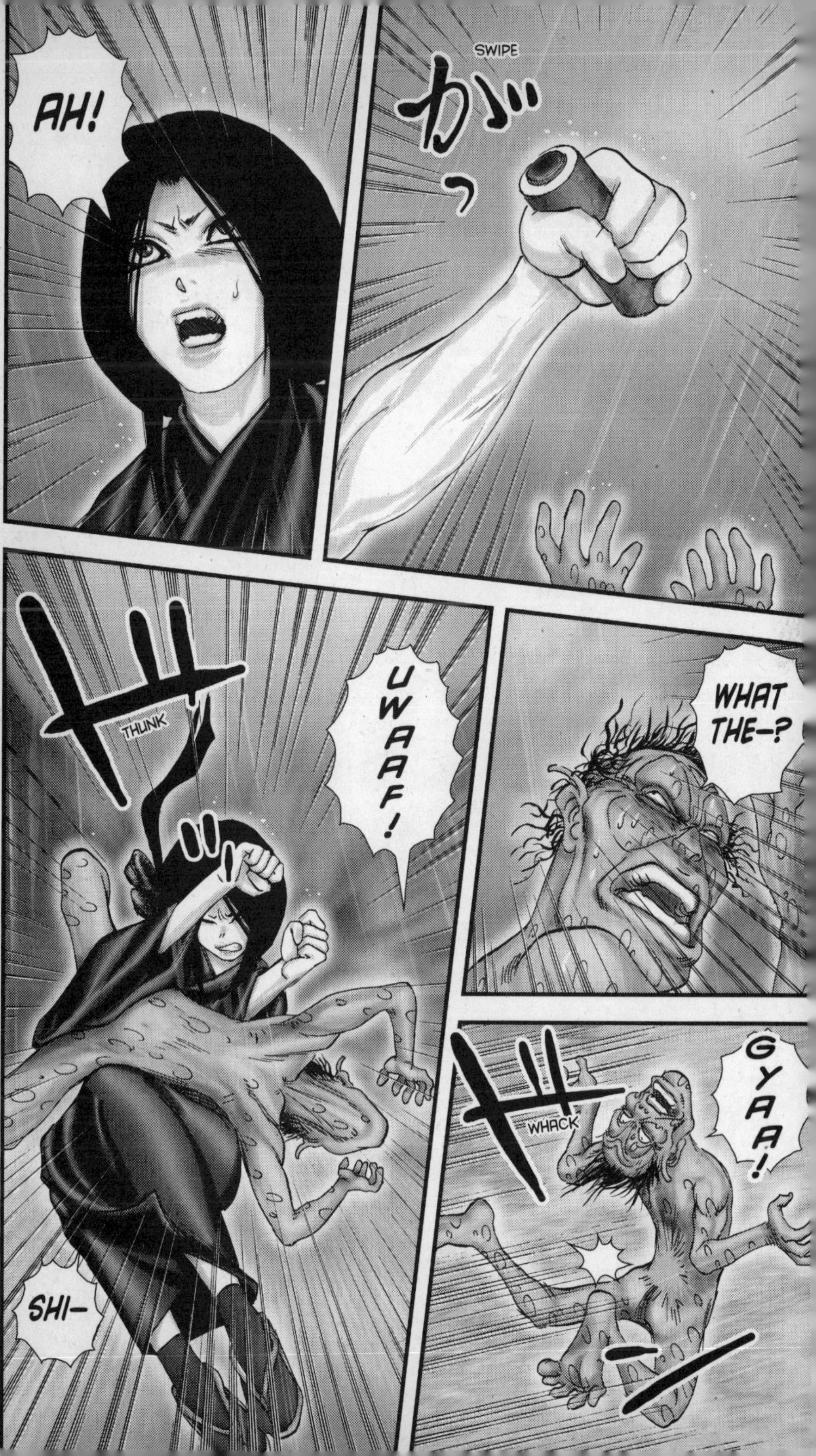
SWIPE
AH!
WHAT THE-?
WHACK
GYAA!
THUNK
UWAAF!
SHI-

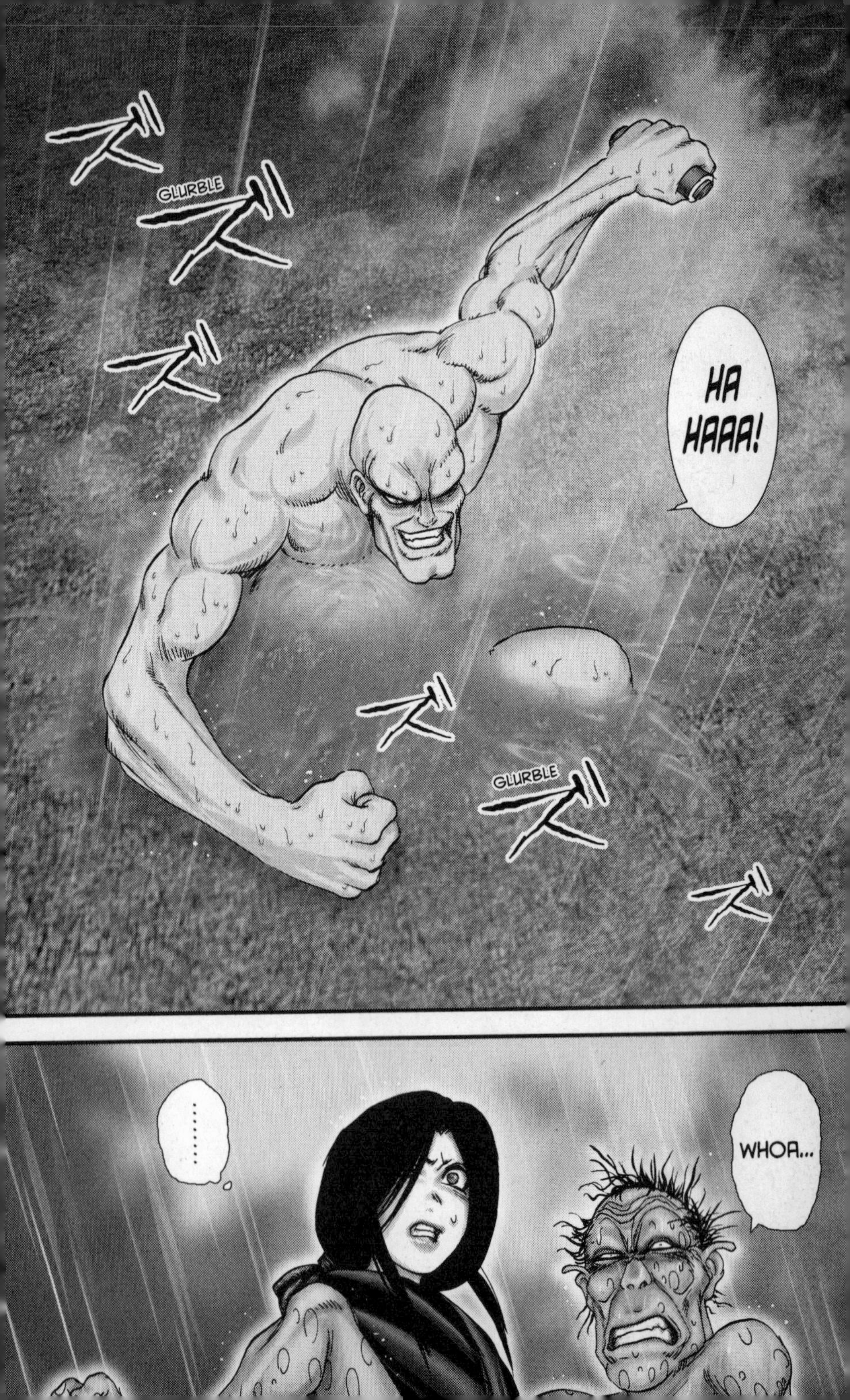
HA HAAA!
GLURBLE
GLURBLE
WHOA...
......

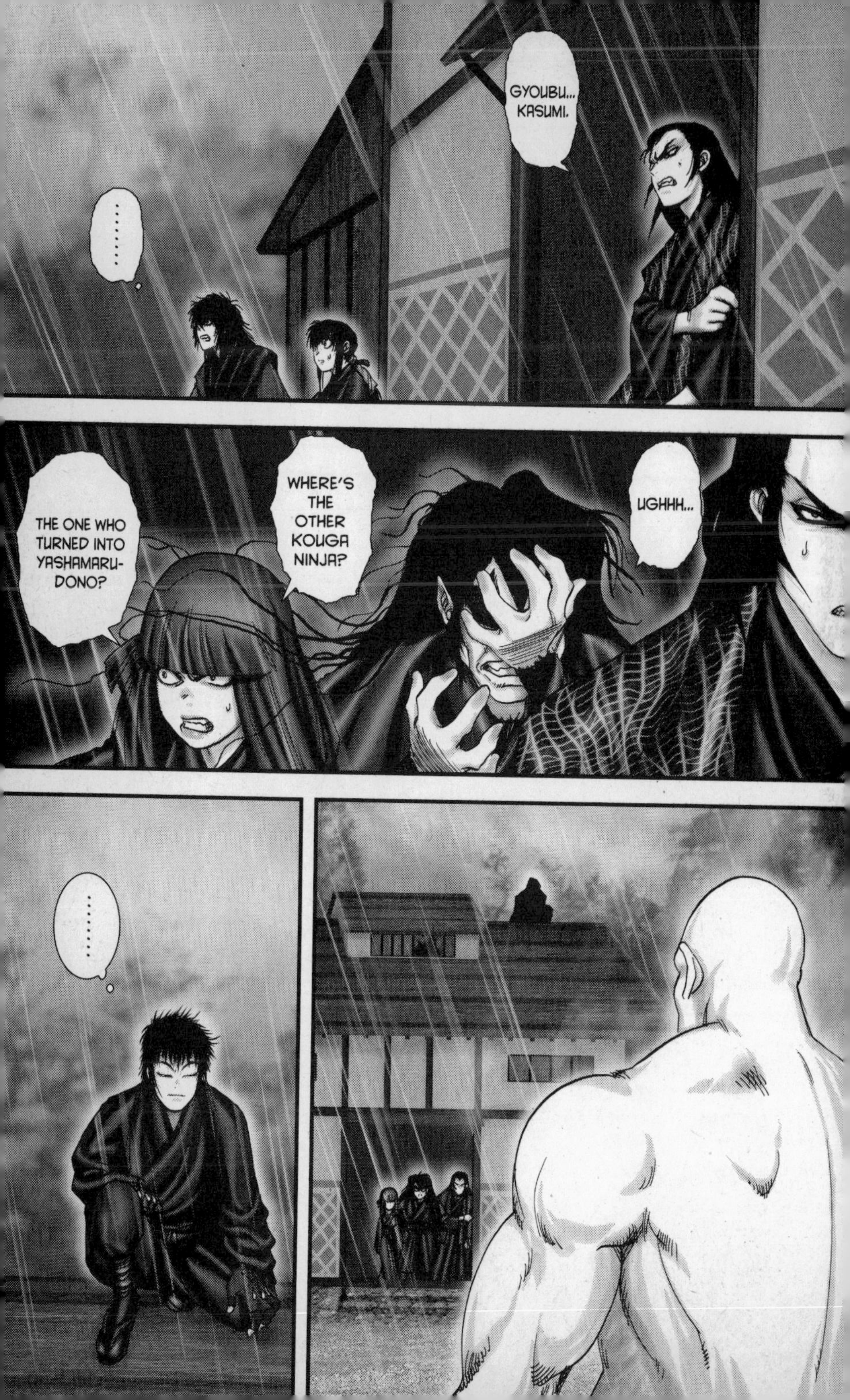
GYOUBU... KASUMI.
....
UGHHH...
WHERE'S THE OTHER KOUGA NINJA?
THE ONE WHO TURNED INTO YASHAMARU-DONO?
....

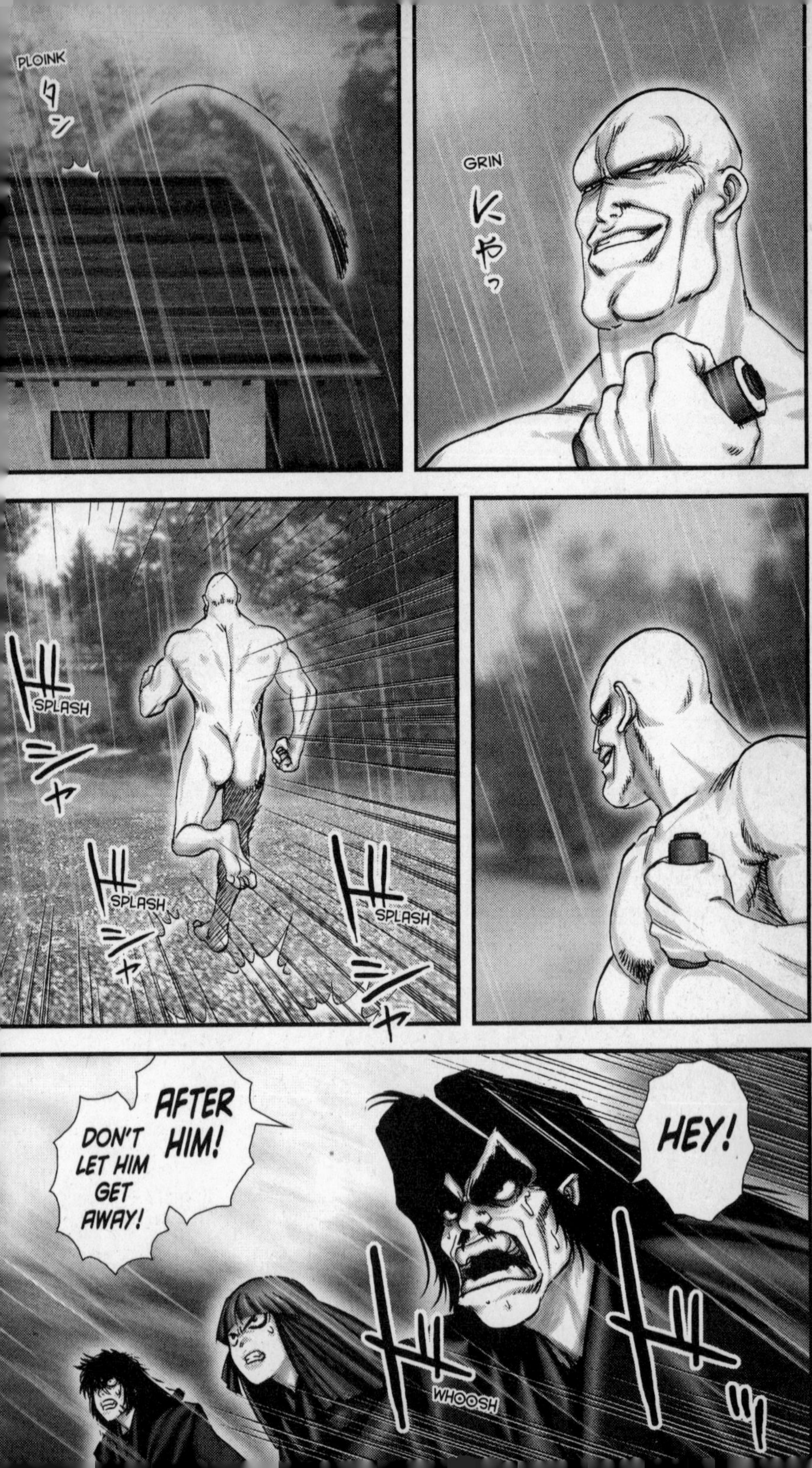
GRIN
にやっ
PLOINK
SPLASH
SPLASH
SPLASH
HEY!
AFTER HIM!
DON'T LET HIM GET AWAY!
WHOOSH

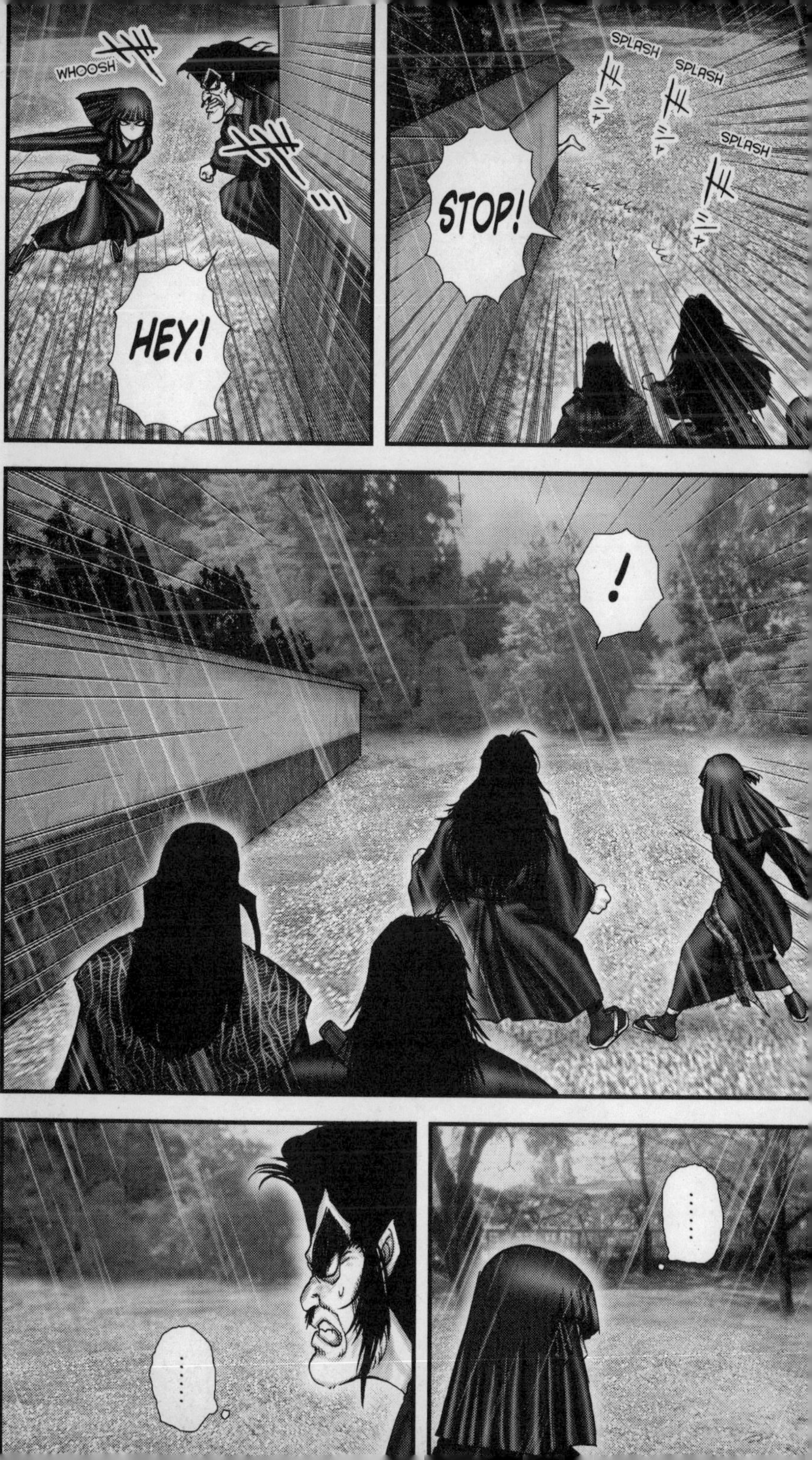
SPLASH
SPLASH
SPLASH
STOP!
WHOOSH
HEY!
!
......
......

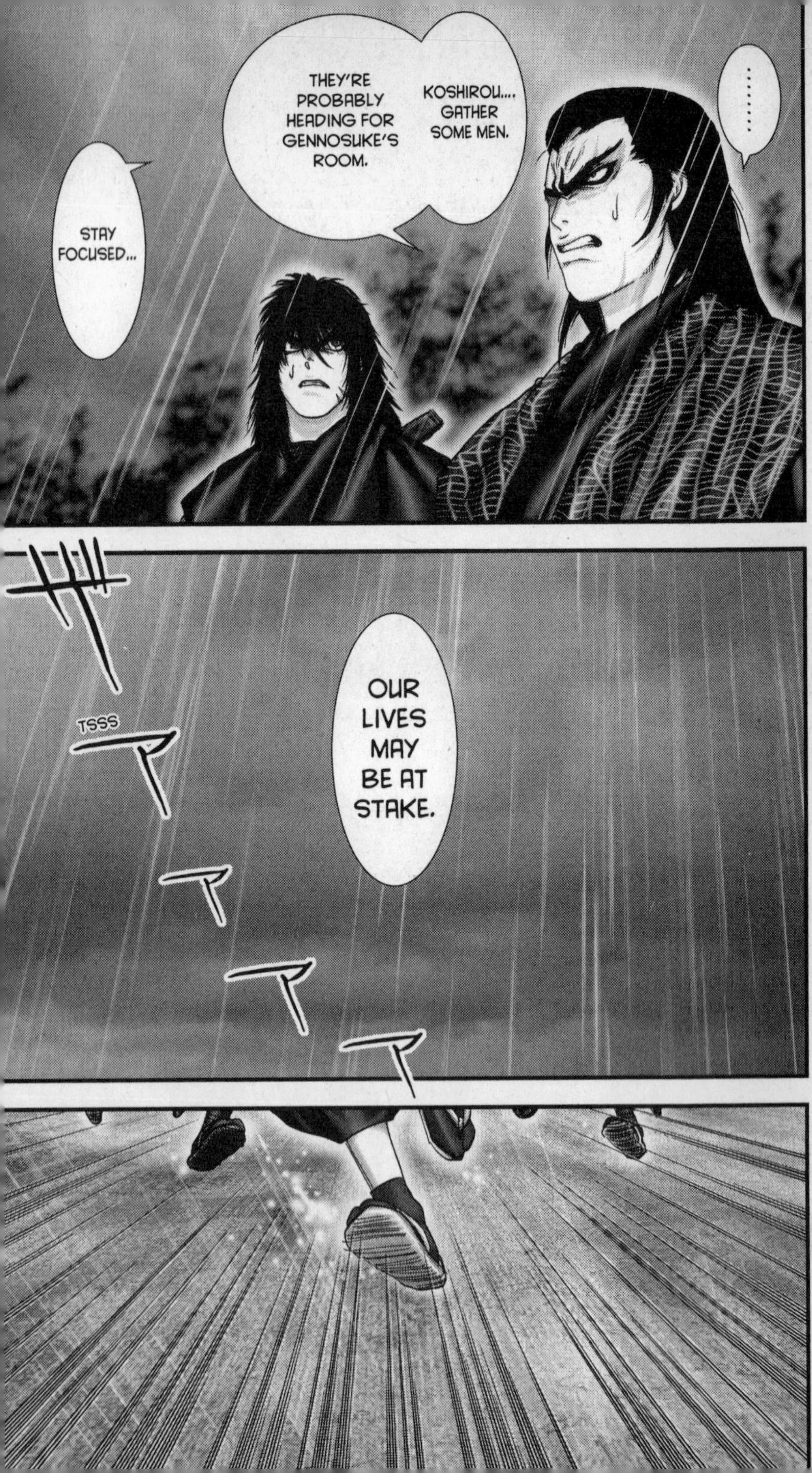
......
KOSHIROU.... GATHER SOME MEN.
THEY'RE PROBABLY HEADING FOR GENNOSUKE'S ROOM.
STAY FOCUSED...
OUR LIVES MAY BE AT STAKE.
TSSS

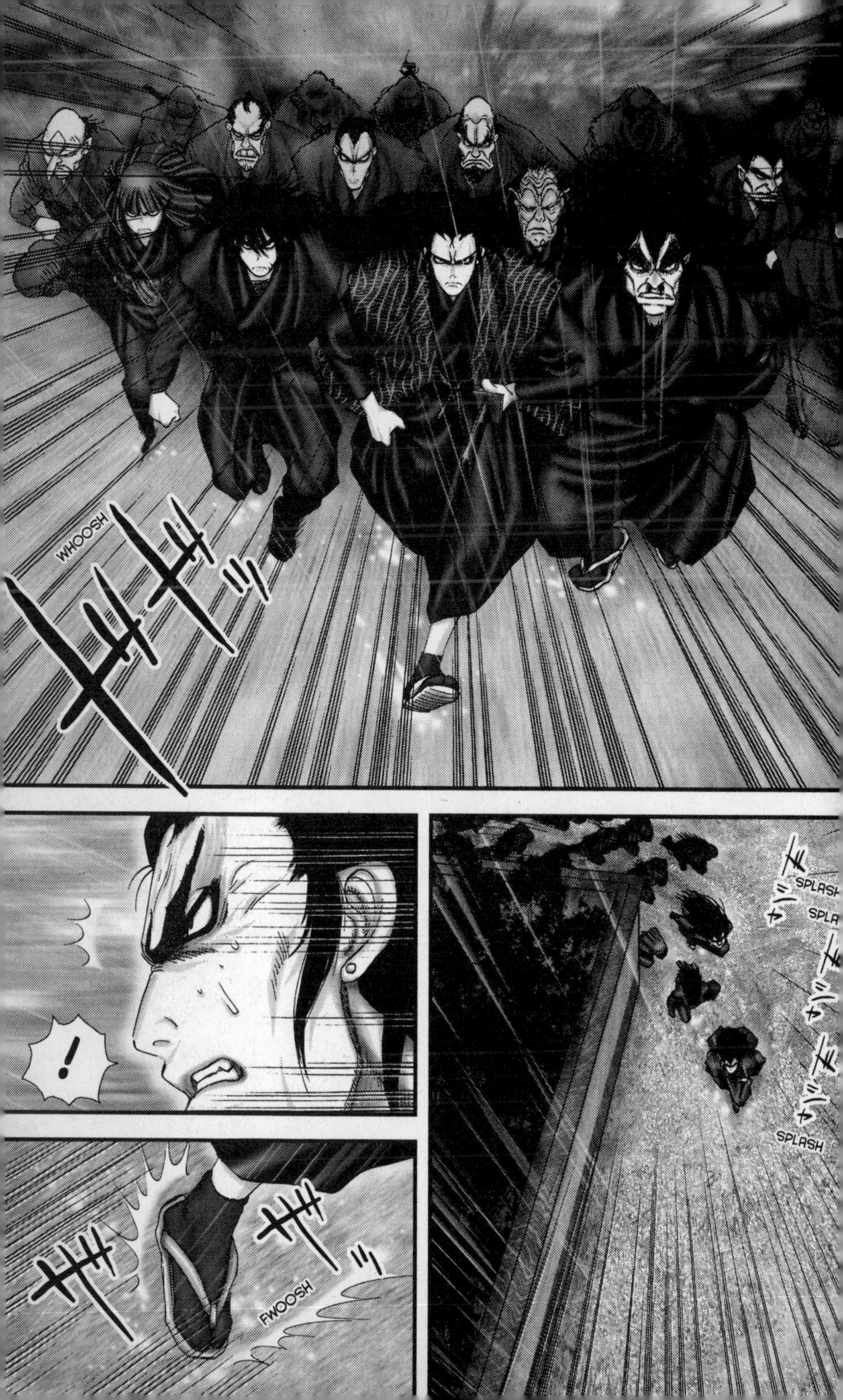
WHOOSH
SPLASH
SPLA
SPLASH
!
FWOOSH

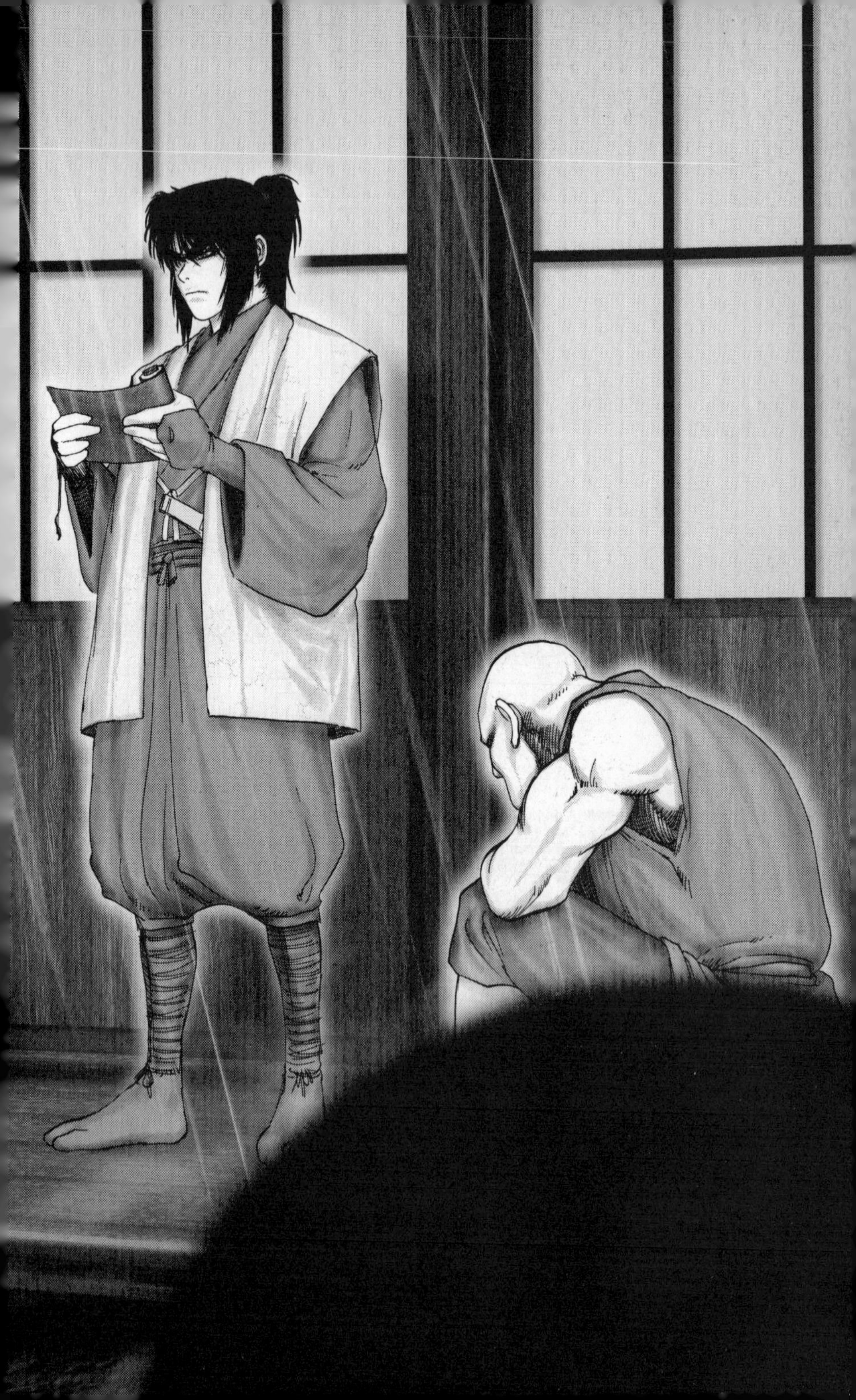

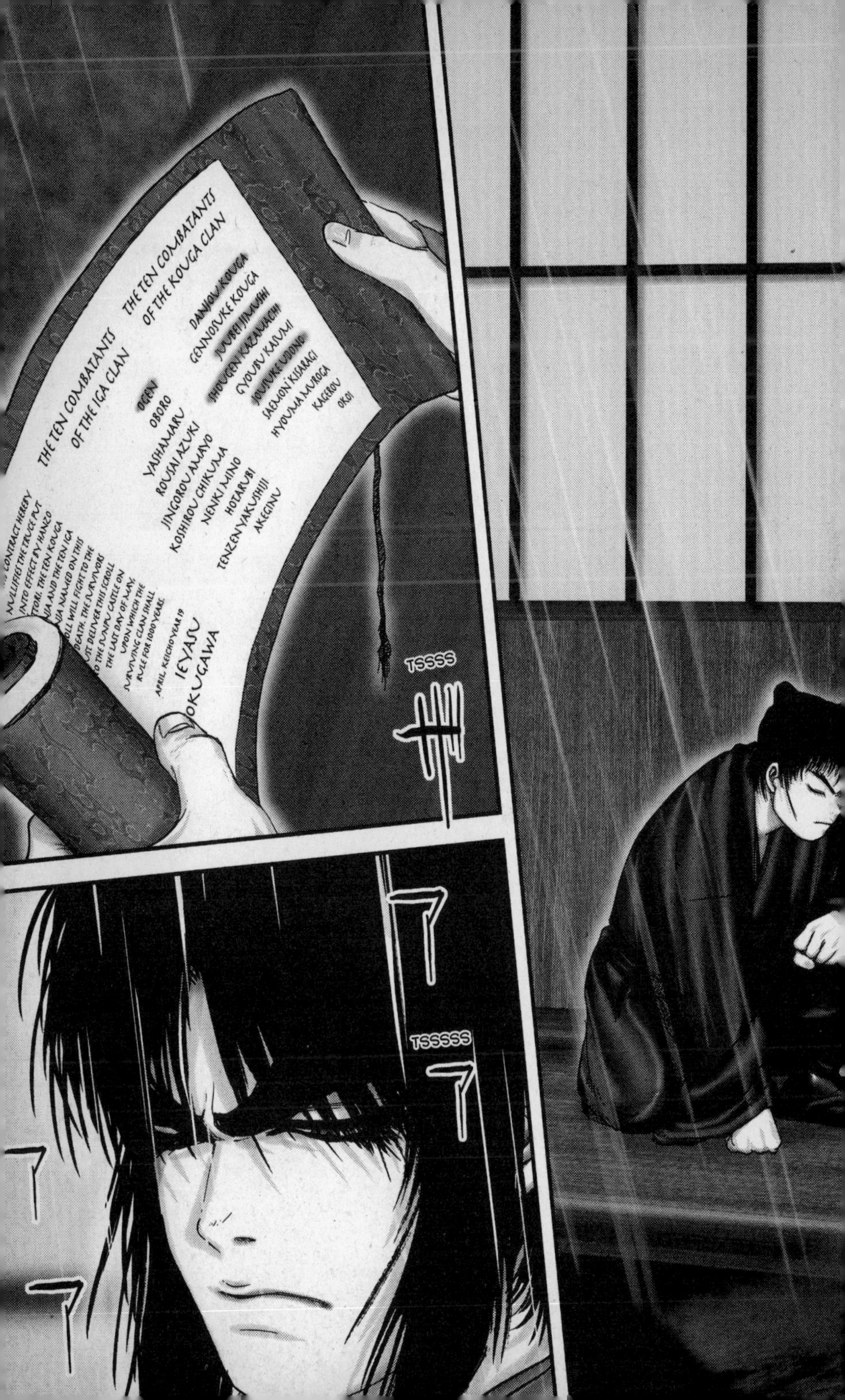
THE TEN COMBATANTS OF THE IGA CLAN
OGEN
OBORO
YASHAMARU
ROUSAI AZUKI
JINGOROU AMAYO
KOSHIROU CHIKUMA
NENKI MINO
HOTARUBI
TENZEN YAKUSHIJI
AKEGINU
THE TEN COMBATANTS OF THE KOUGA CLAN
DANJOU KOUGA
GENNOSUKE KOUGA
JUUBEI JIMUSHI
SHOUGEN KAZAMACHI
GYOUBU KASUMI
JOUSUKE UDONO
SAEMON KISARAGI
HYOUMA MUROGA
KAGEROU
OKOI
CONTRACT HEREBY NULLIFIES THE TRUCE PUT INTO EFFECT BY HANZO TTORI. THE TEN KOUGA JA AND THE TEN IGA JA NAMED ON THIS OLL WILL FIGHT TO THE DEATH. THE SURVIVORS ST DELIVER THIS SCROLL O THE SUNPU CASTLE ON THE LAST DAY OF MAY, UPON WHICH THE SURVIVING CLAN SHALL RULE FOR 1000 YEARS.
APRIL, KEICHO YEAR 19
IEYASU OKUGAWA
TSSSS
TSSSSS

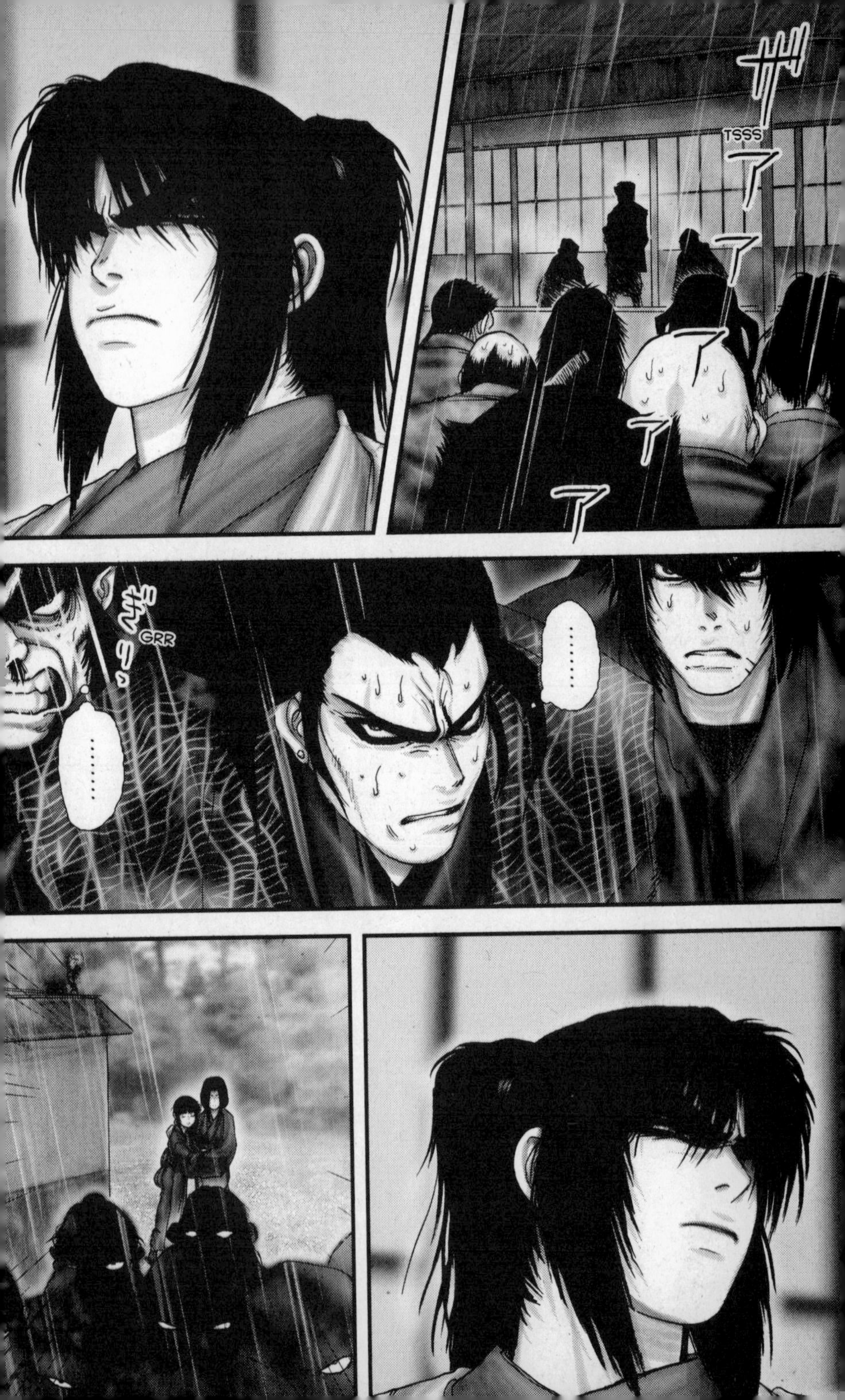
ザァァァァァァ
TSSS
ギリッ
GRR
......
......

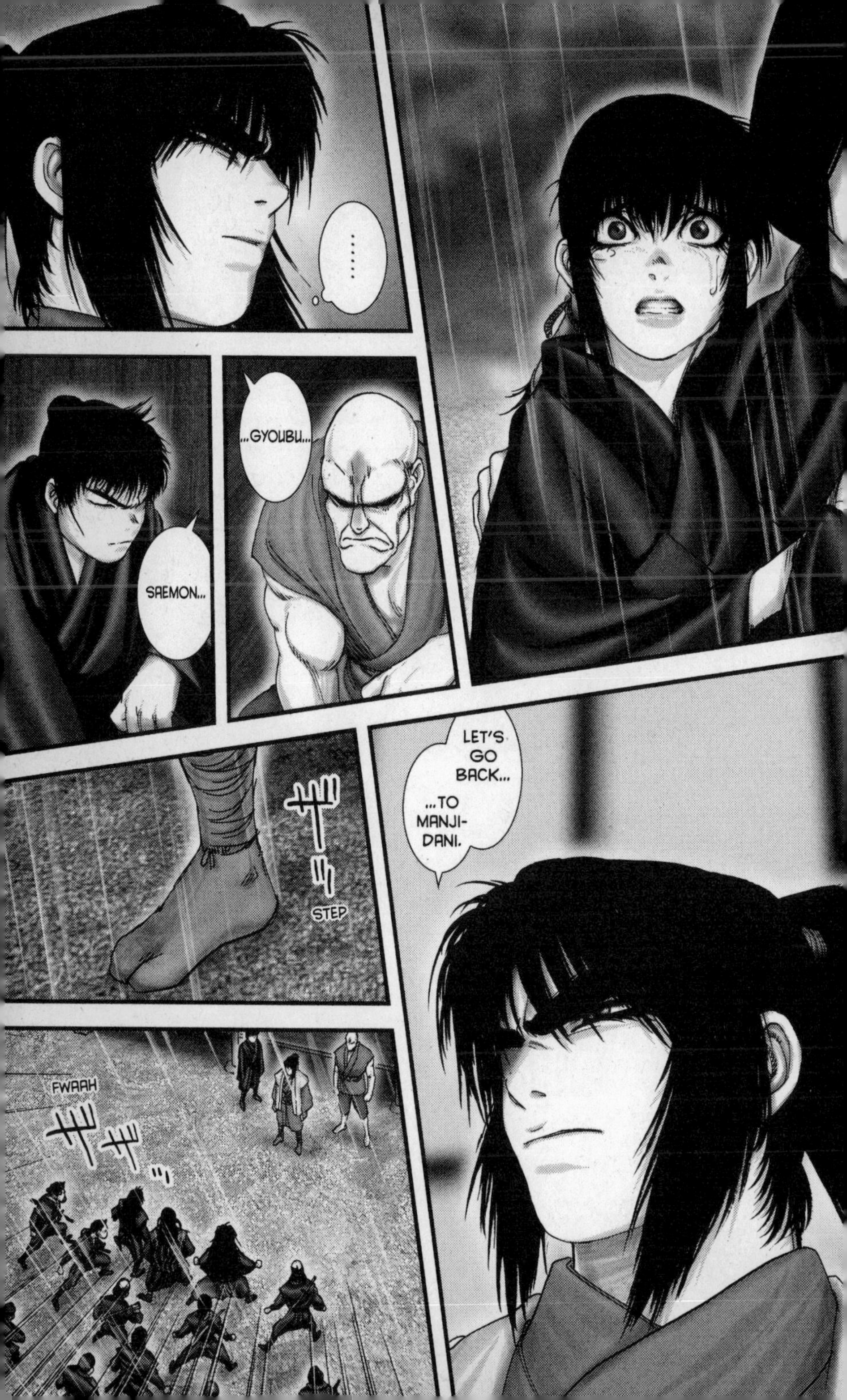
......
...GYOUBU...
SAEMON...
LET'S GO BACK...
...TO MANJI-DANI.
STEP
FWAAH

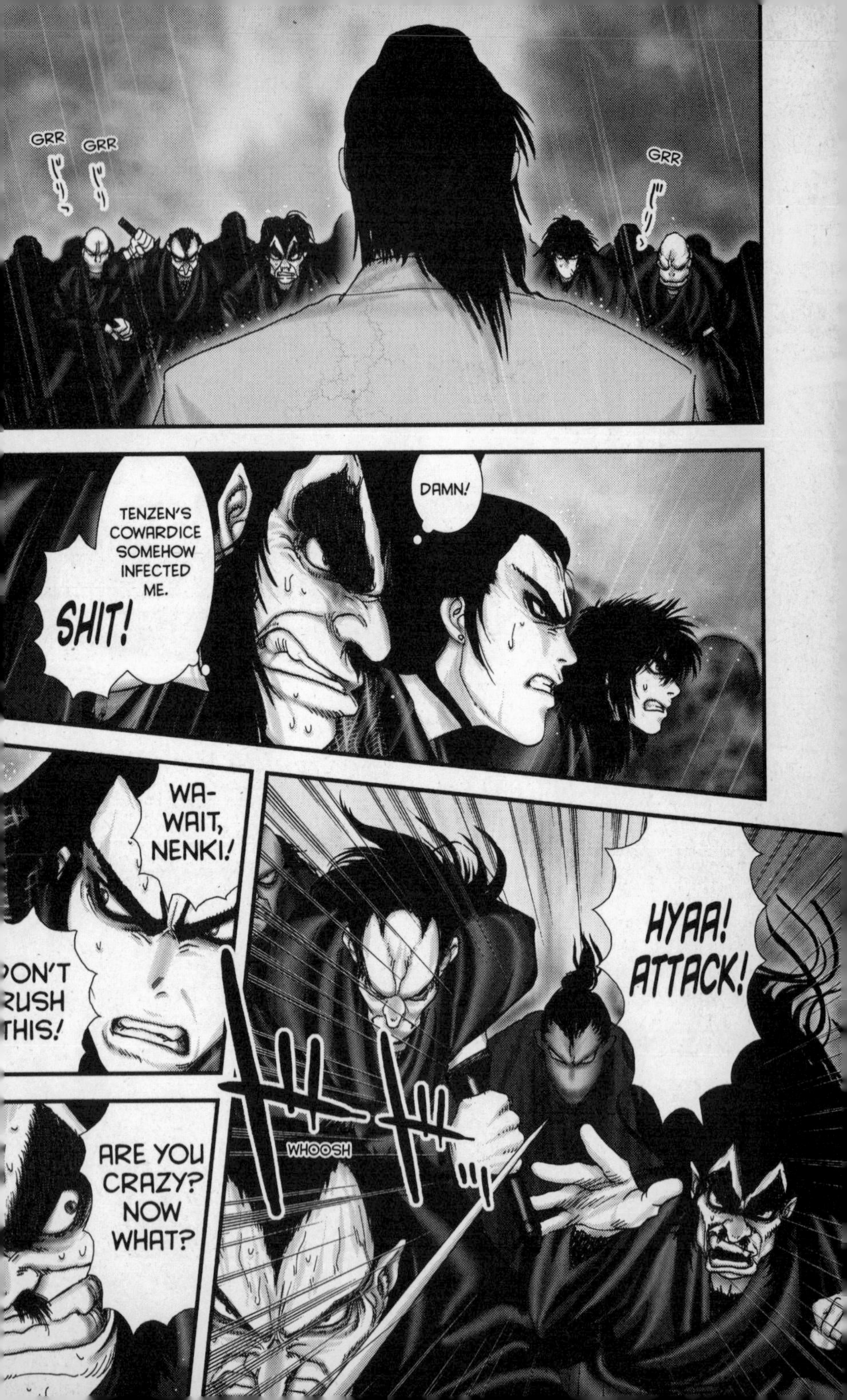
GRR
GRR
GRR
DAMN!
TENZEN'S COWARDICE SOMEHOW INFECTED ME.
SHIT!
HYAA! ATTACK!
WHOOSH
WA-WAIT, NENKI!
ON'T RUSH THIS!
ARE YOU CRAZY? NOW WHAT?

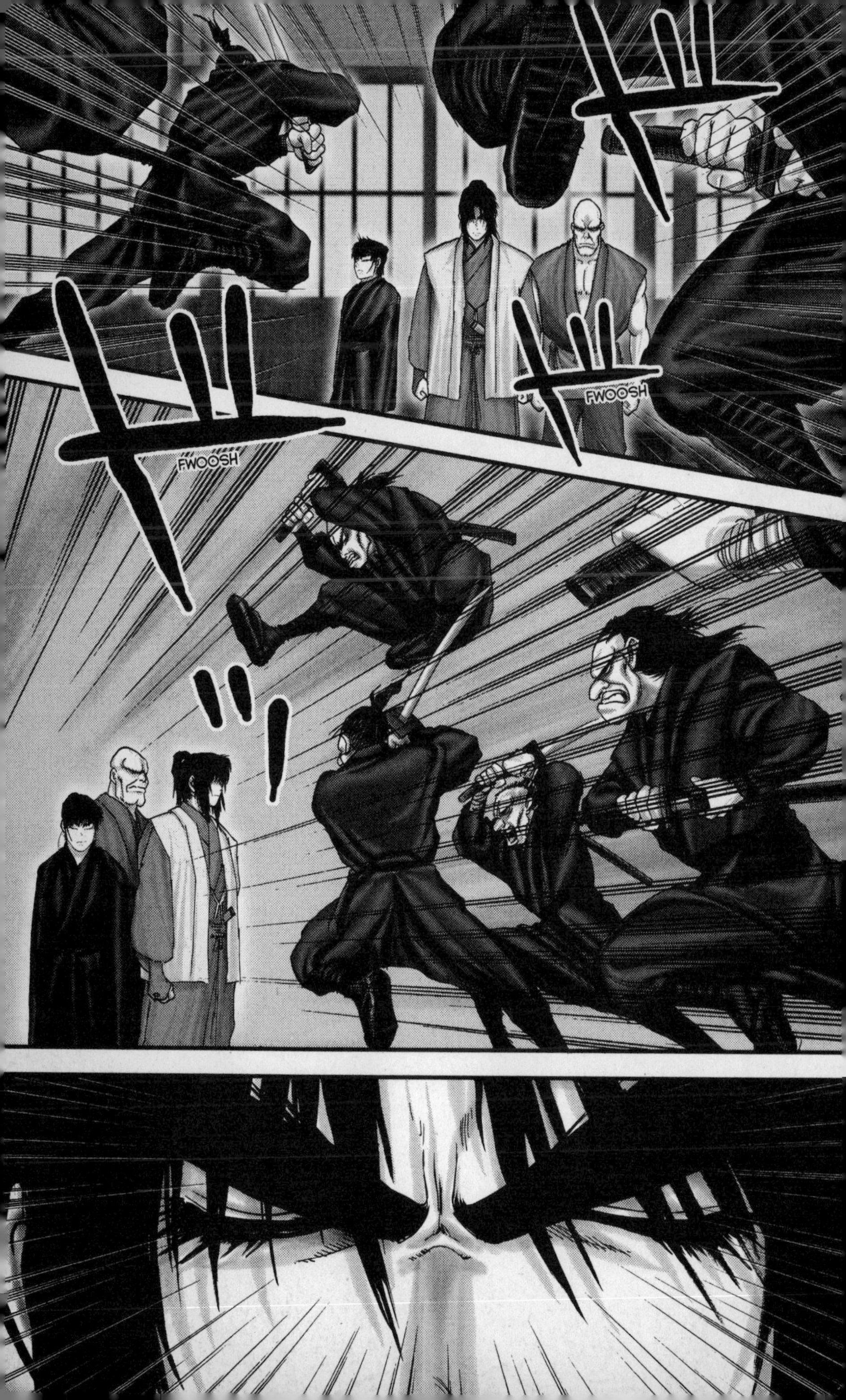
FWOOSH
FWOOSH

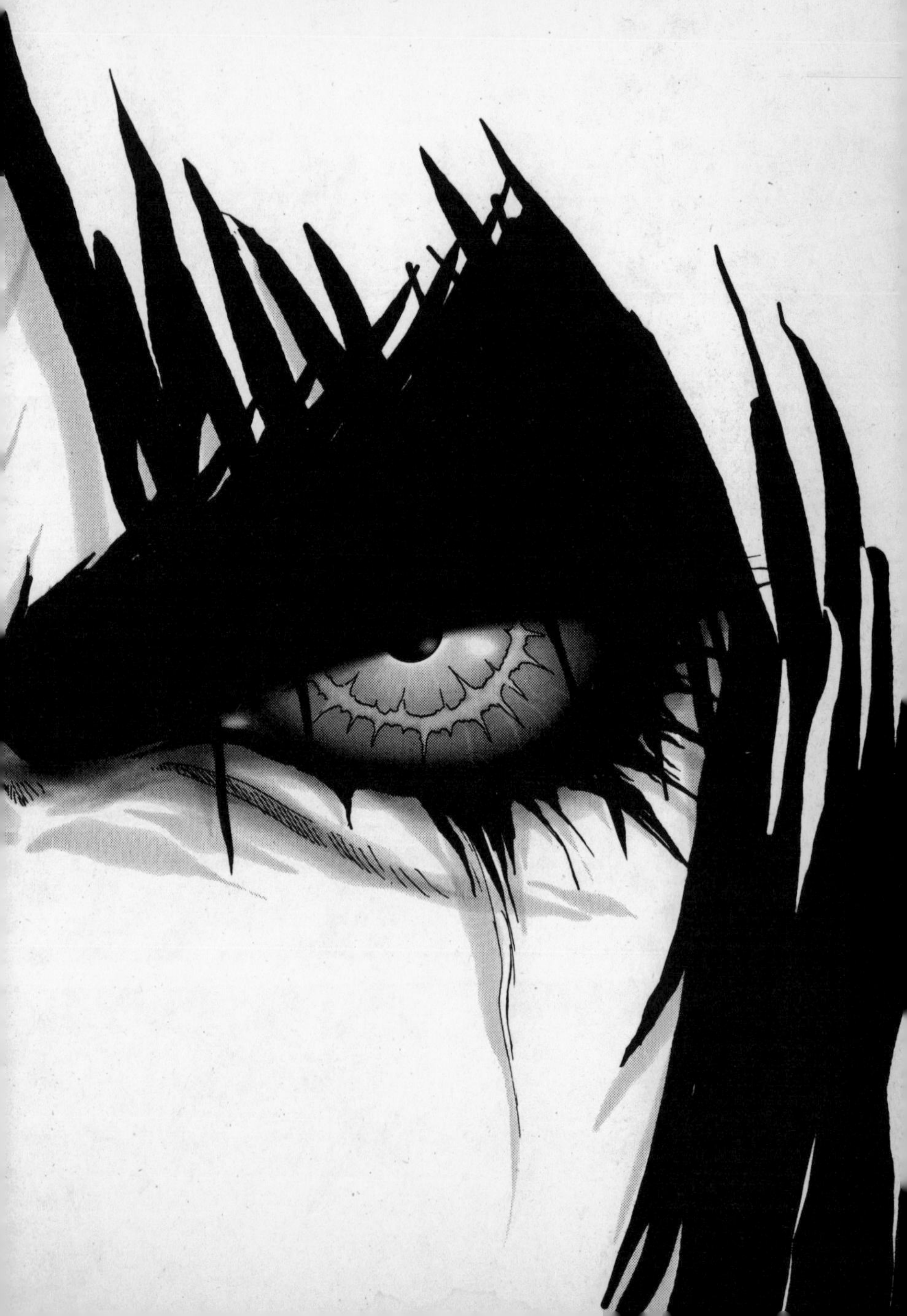

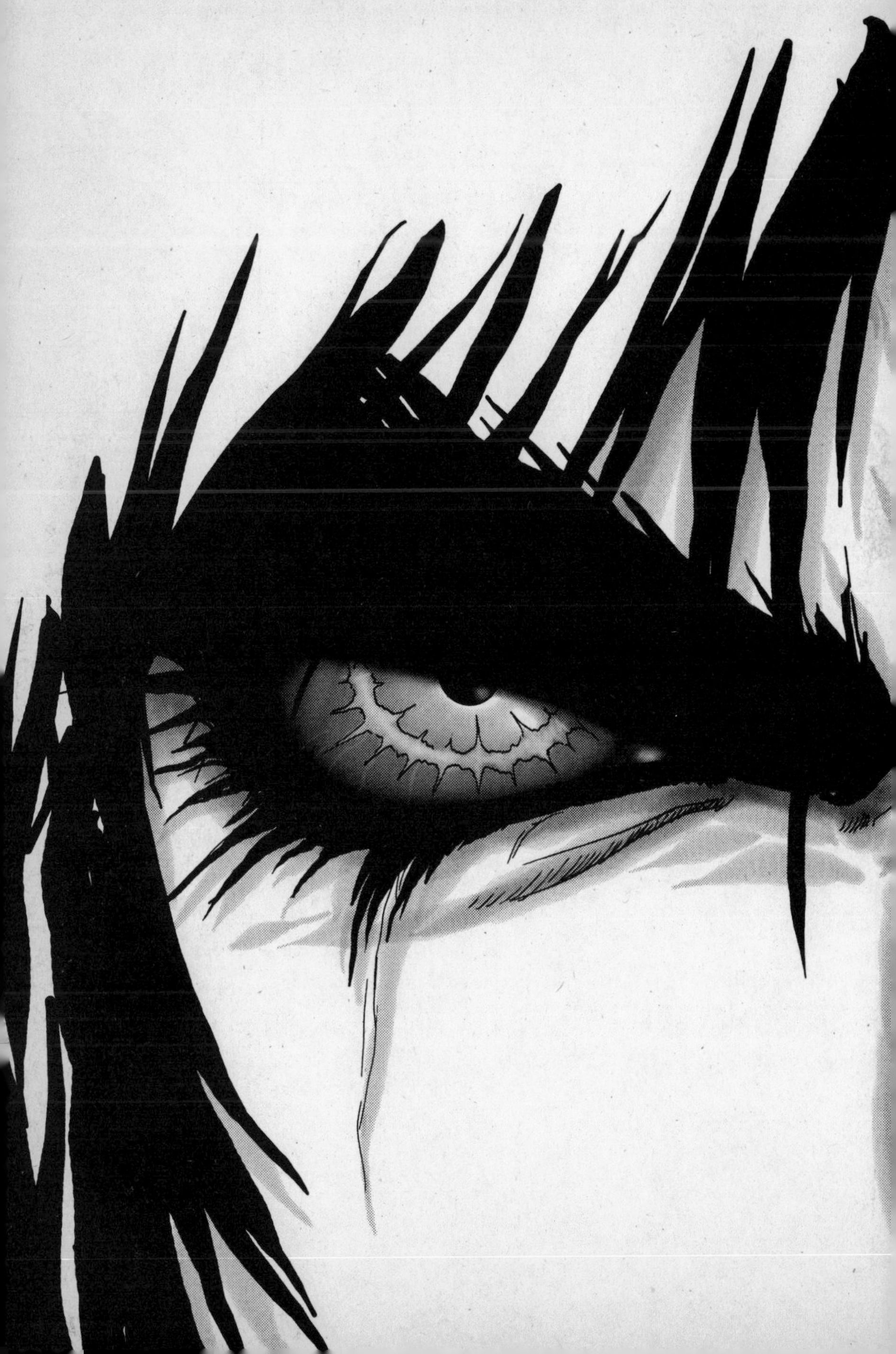

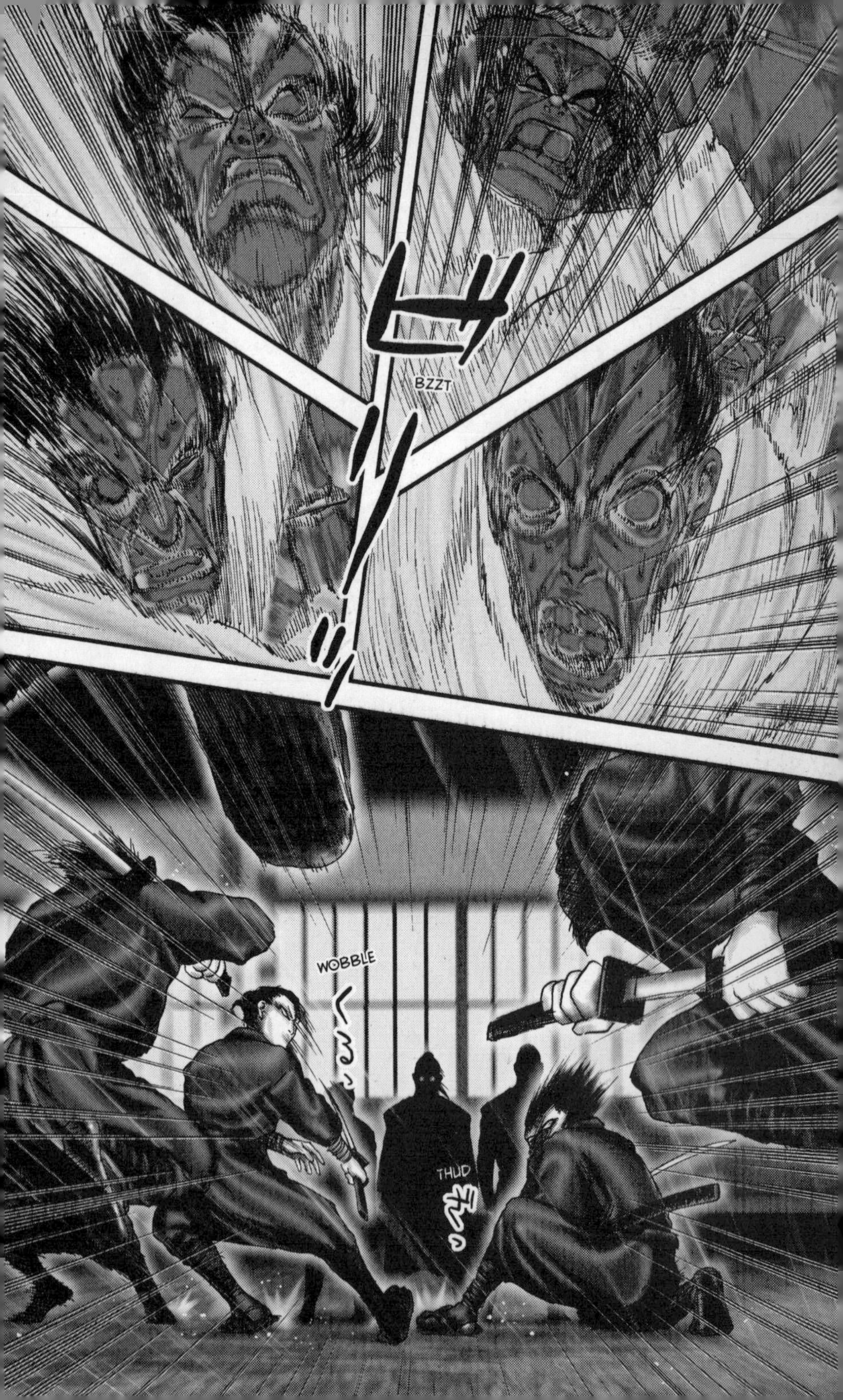
BZZT
WOBBLE
THUD

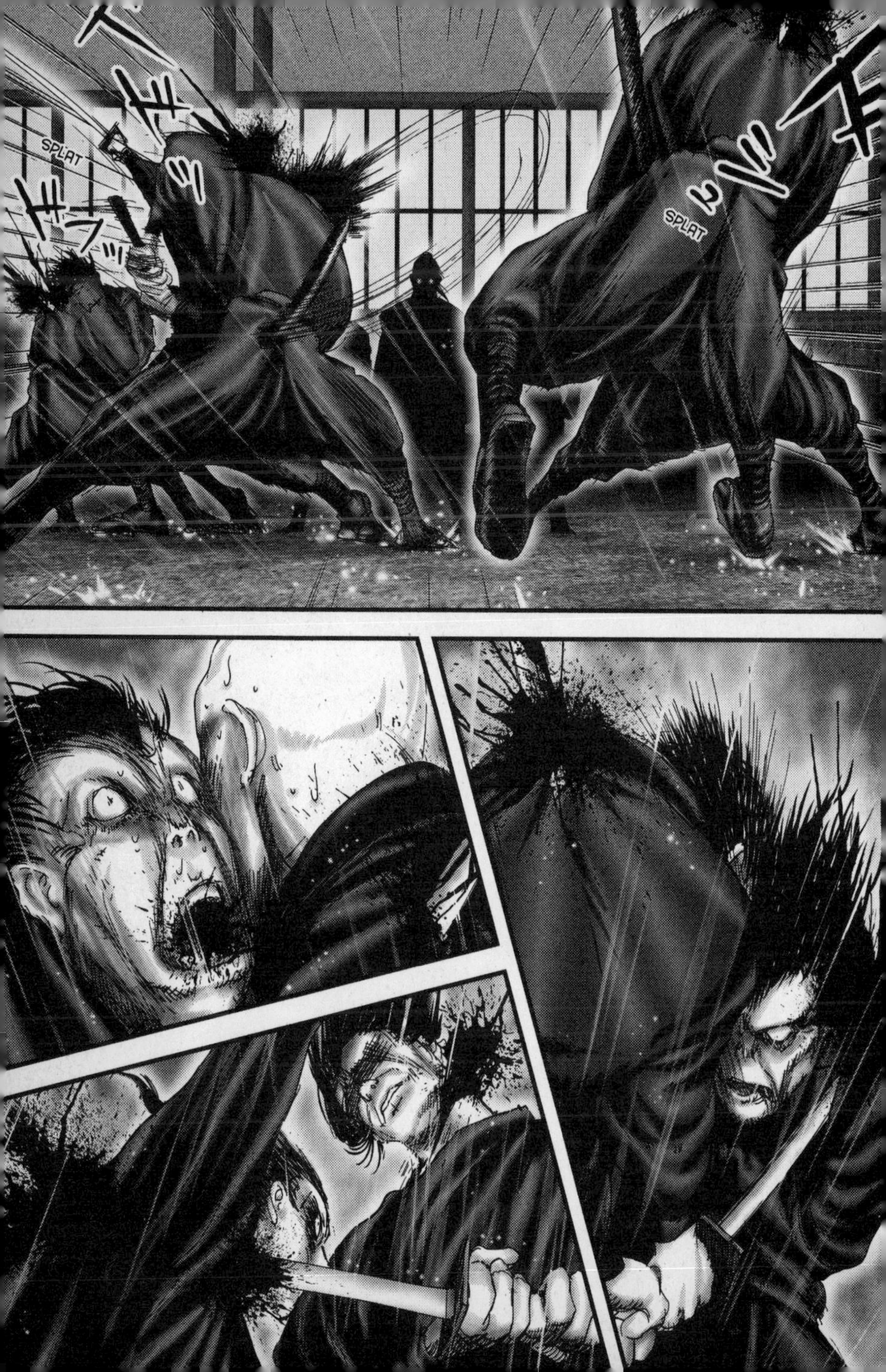
SPLAT
SPLAT

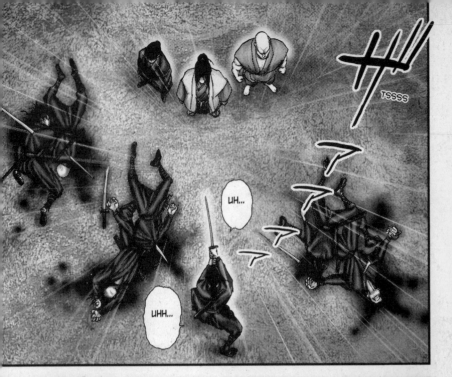

TSSSS

UH...

UHH...

SHIVER

UNNGGG...

SHUDDER
SHUDDER

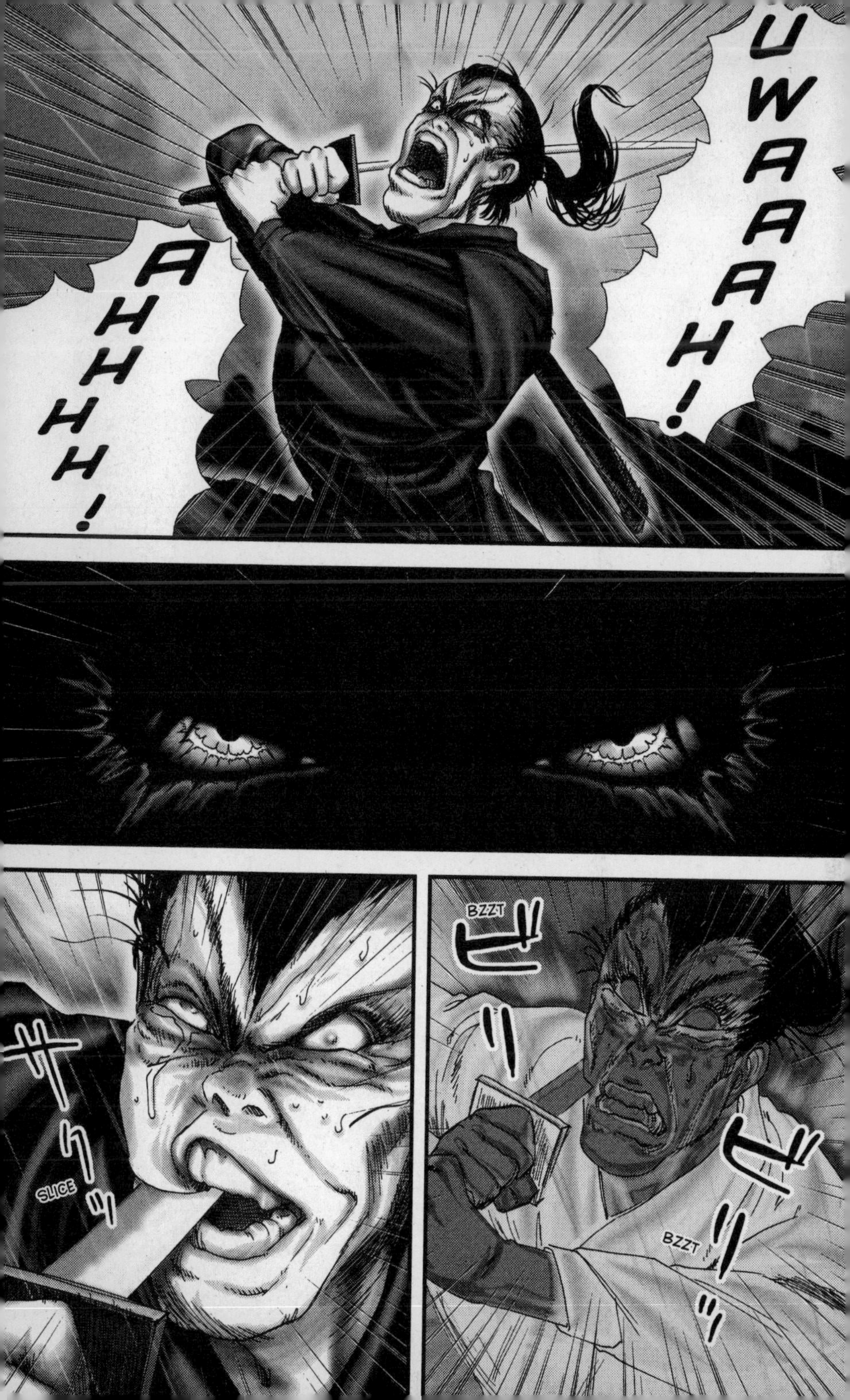
UWAAAAH!
AHHHHH!
BZZT
BZZT
SLICE

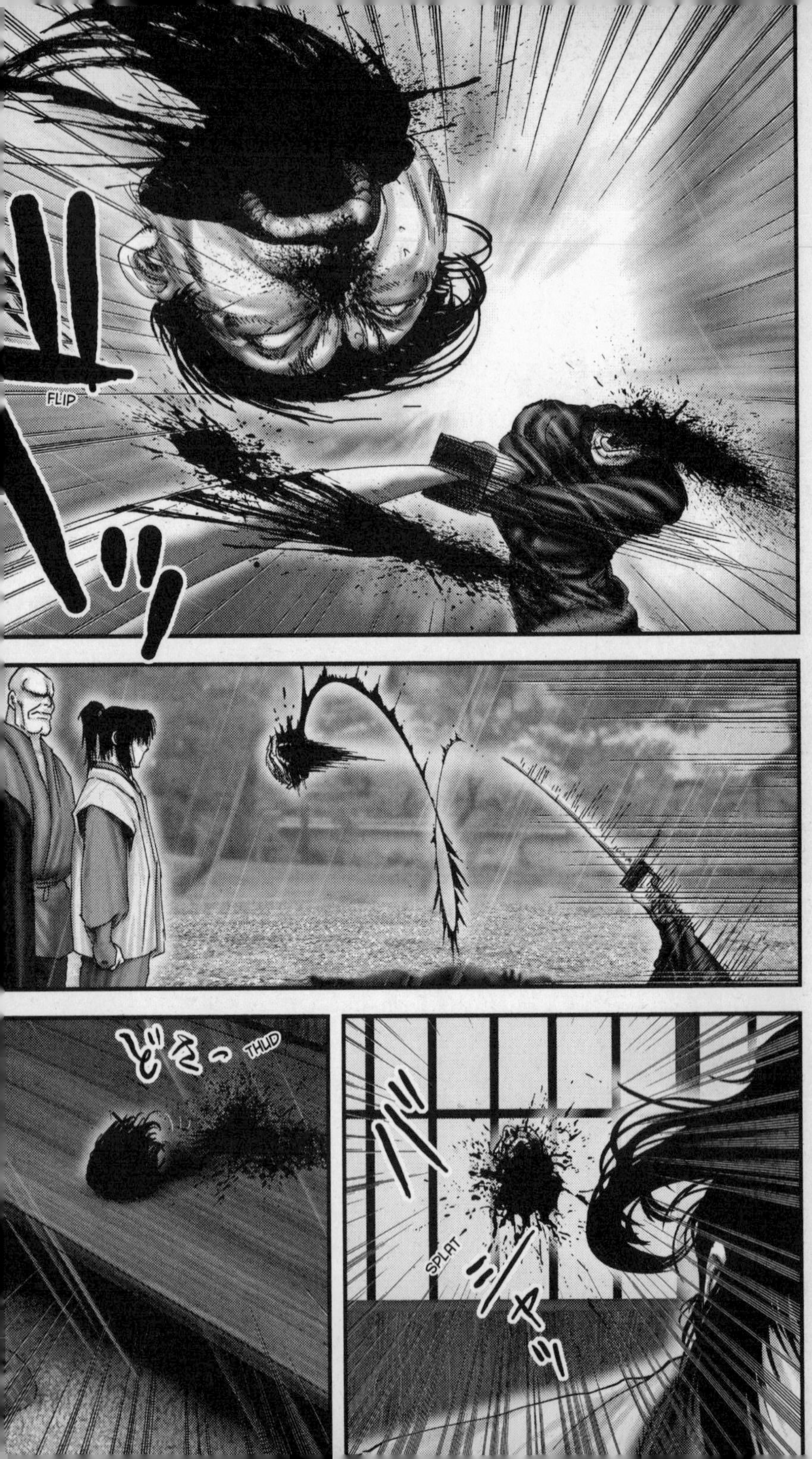
FLIP
SPLAT
THUD

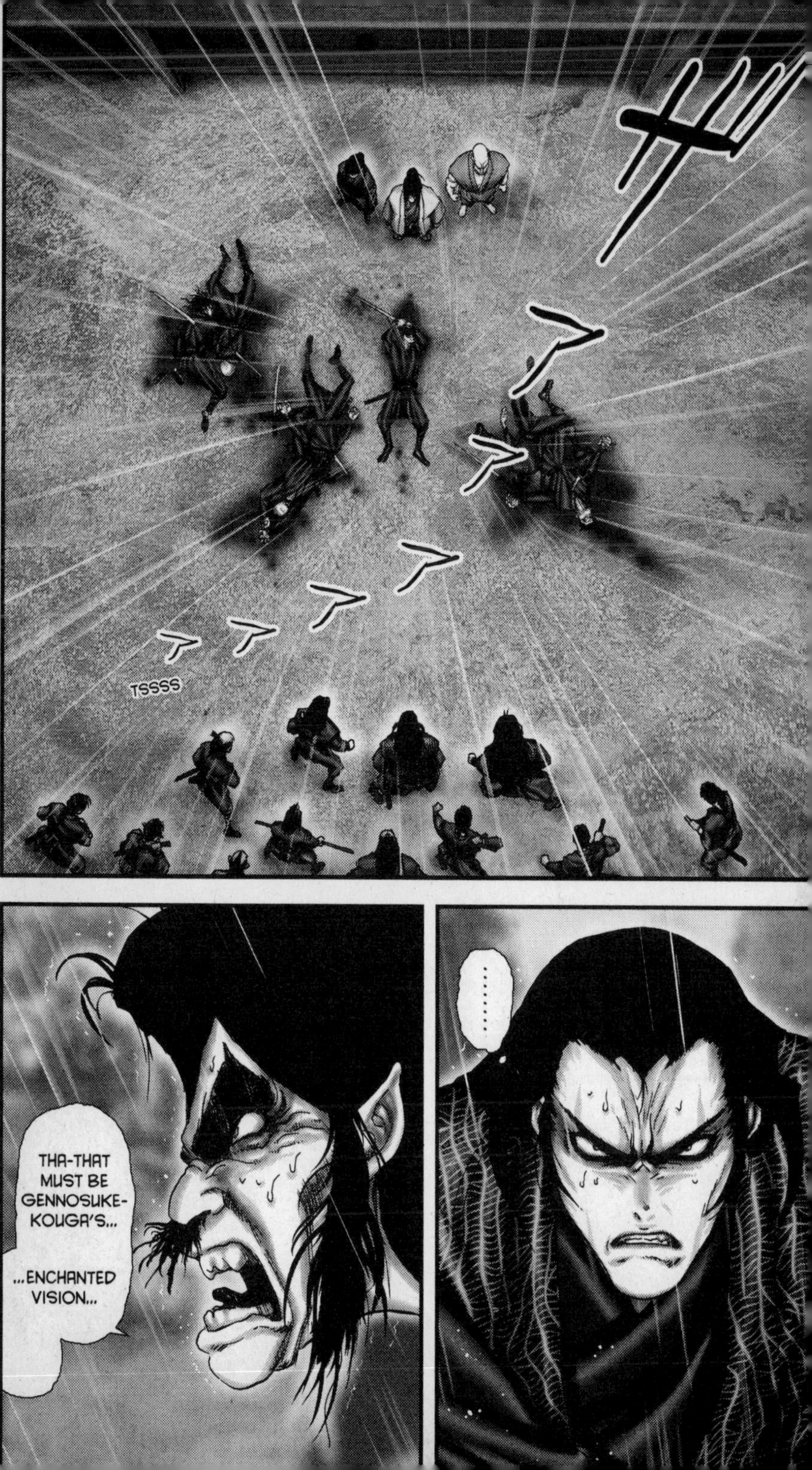
ザアアアアアア
TSSSS
......
THA-THAT MUST BE GENNOSUKE-KOUGA'S...
...ENCHANTED VISION...

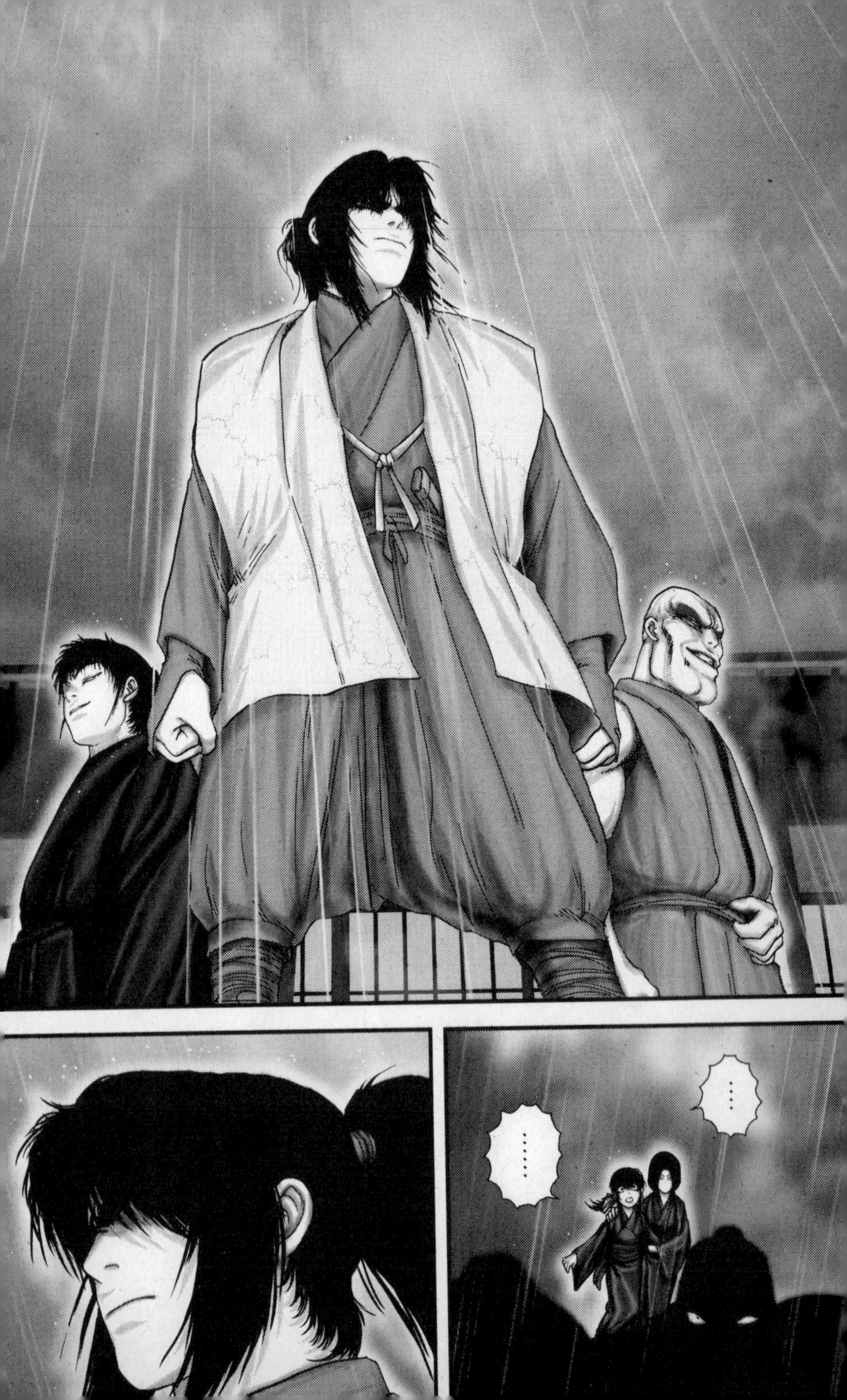
......
......

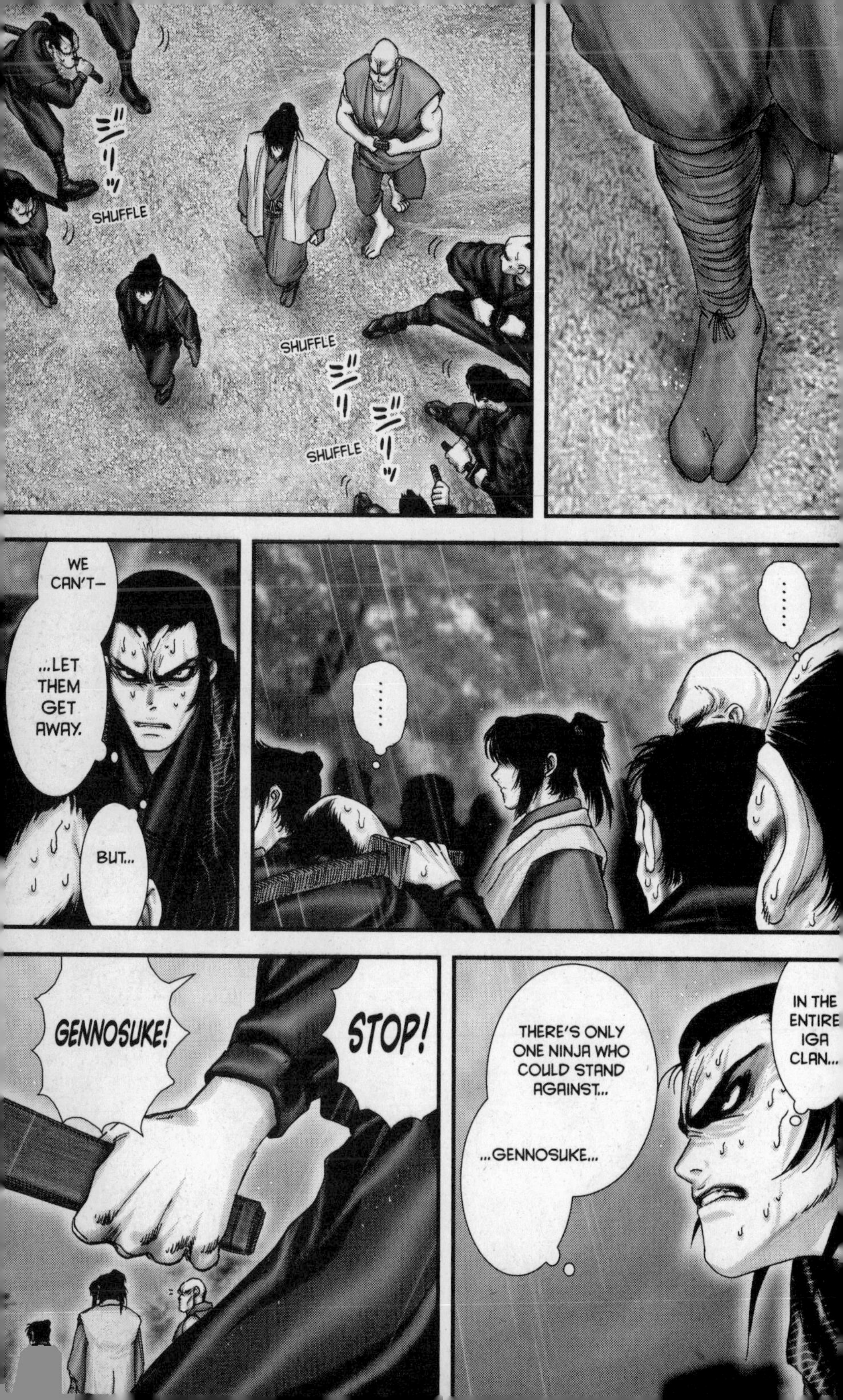
SHUFFLE
SHUFFLE
SHUFFLE
......
......
WE CAN'T—
...LET THEM GET AWAY.
BUT...
IN THE ENTIRE IGA CLAN...
THERE'S ONLY ONE NINJA WHO COULD STAND AGAINST...
...GENNOSUKE...
STOP!
GENNOSUKE!

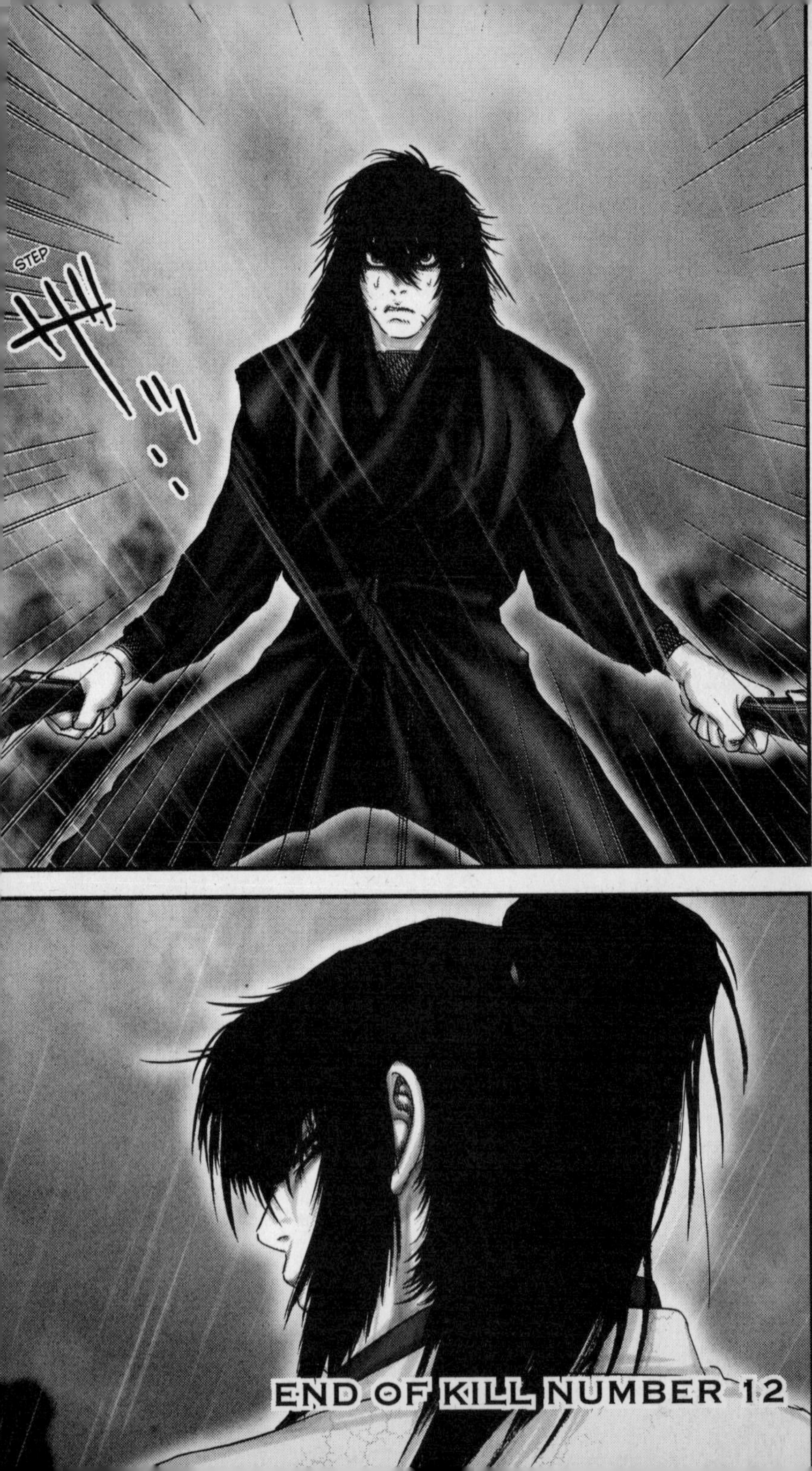
STEP
END OF KILL NUMBER 12

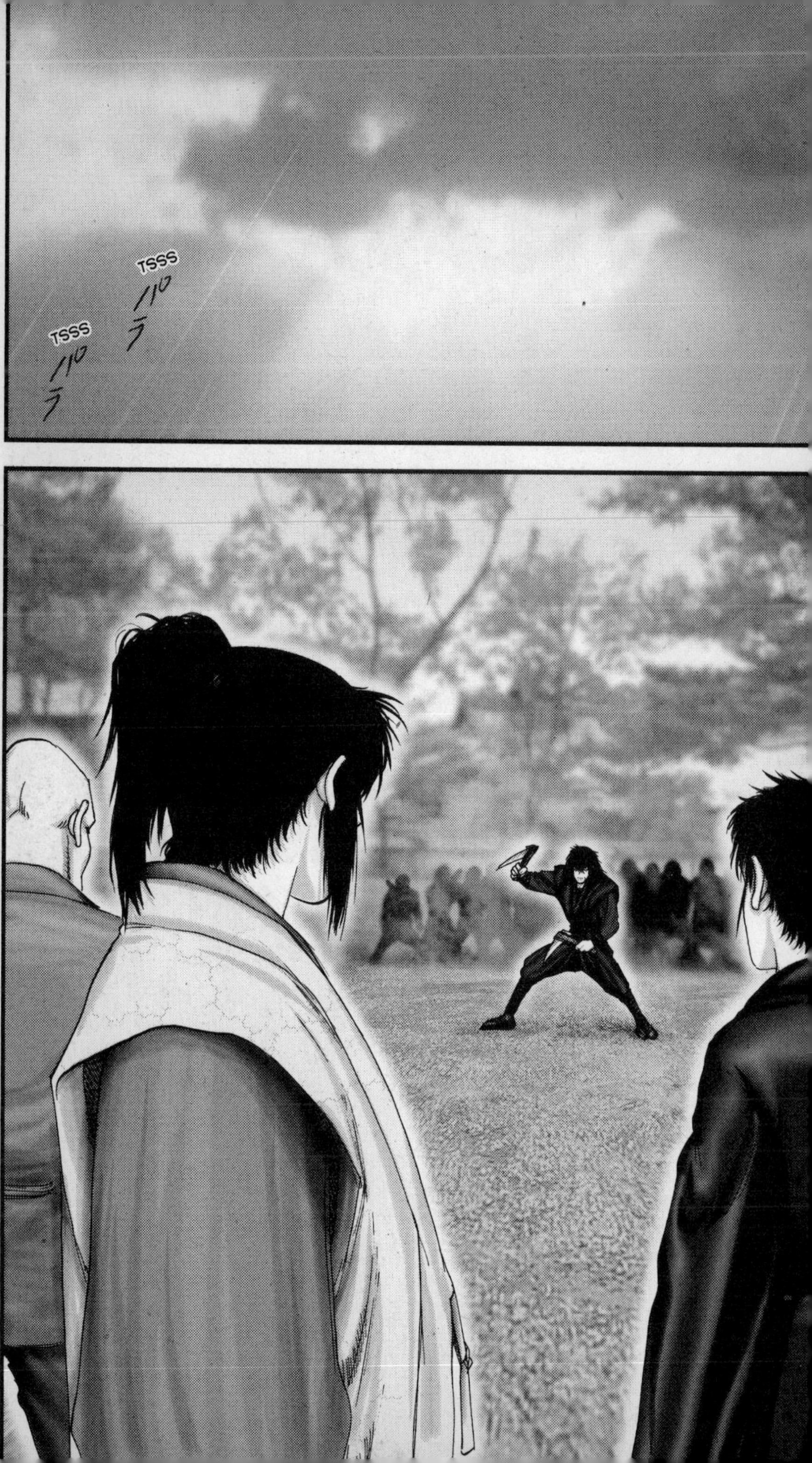
TSSS
パラ
TSSS
パラ

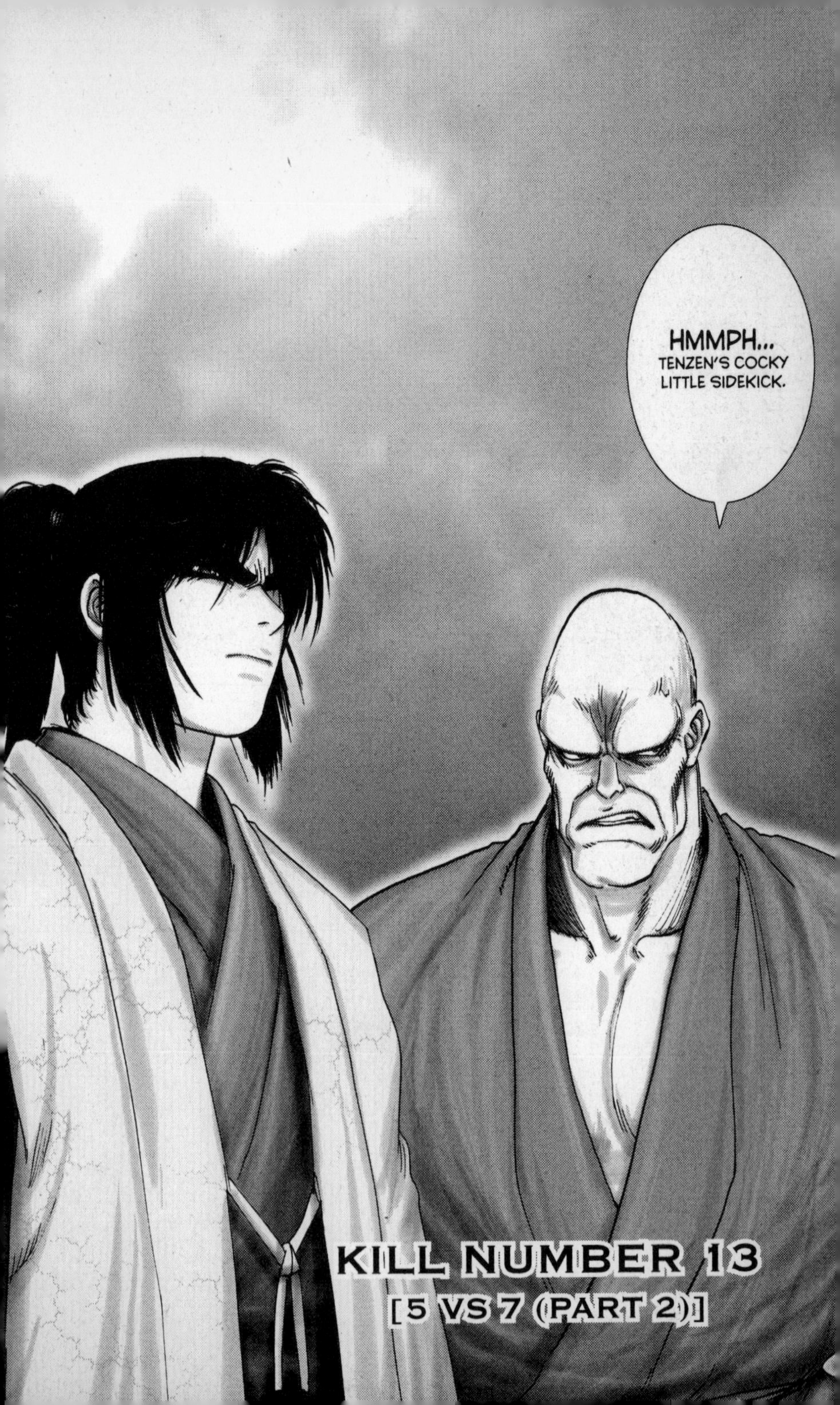
HMMPH... TENZEN'S COCKY LITTLE SIDEKICK.
KILL NUMBER 13
[5 VS 7 (PART 2)]

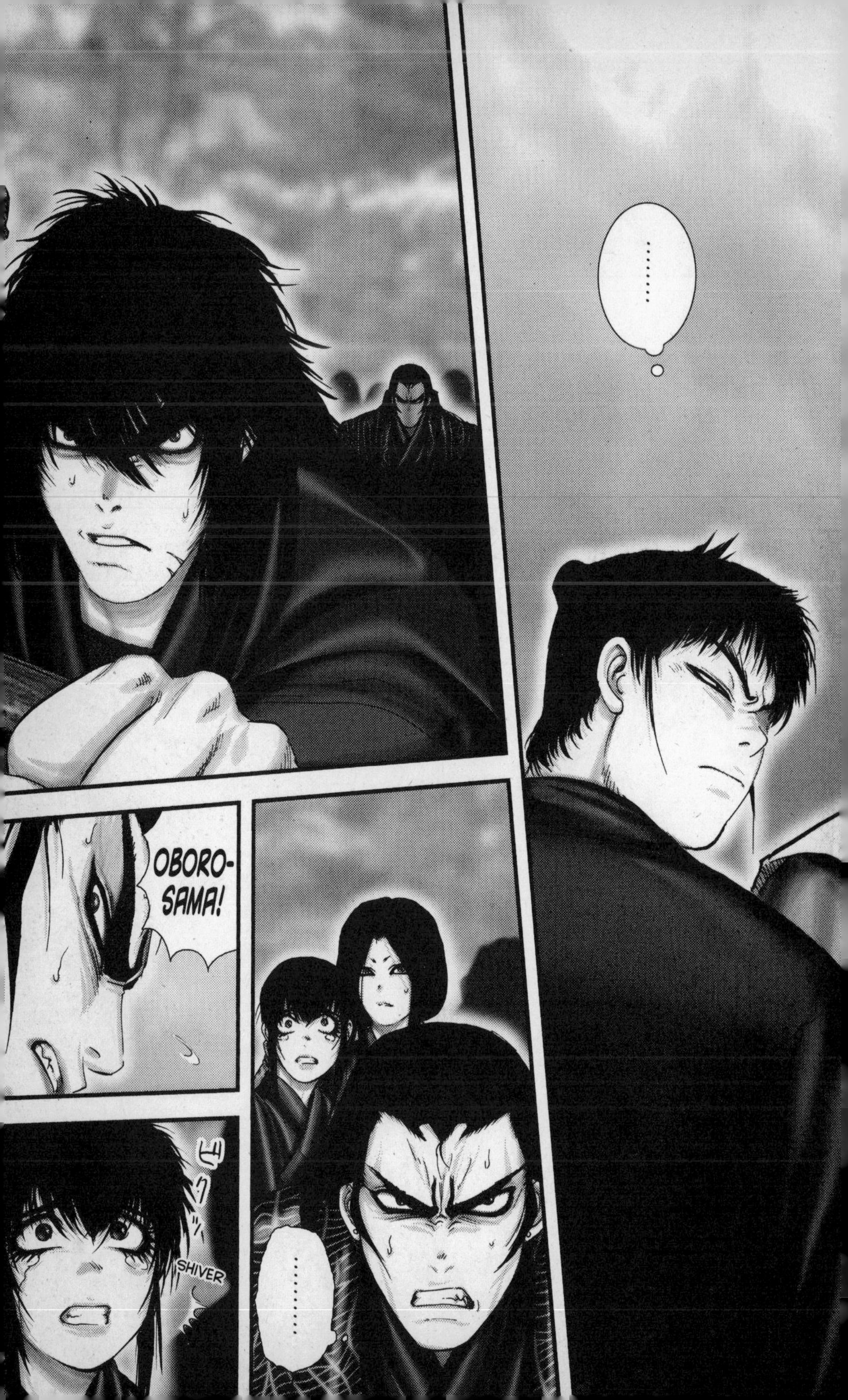
......
......
OBORO-SAMA!
SHIVER

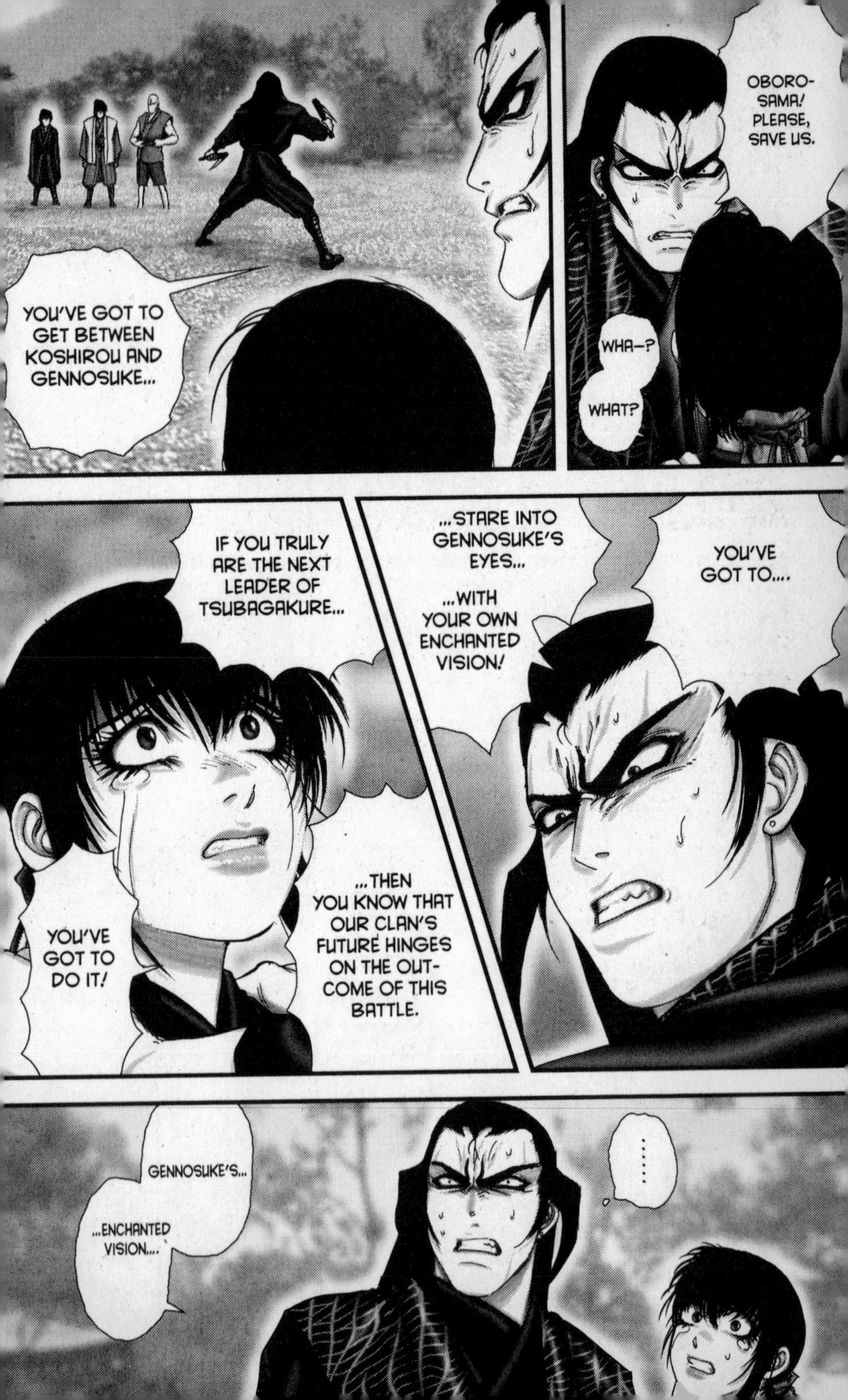
OBORO-SAMA! PLEASE, SAVE US.
WHA-?
WHAT?
YOU'VE GOT TO GET BETWEEN KOSHIROU AND GENNOSUKE...
YOU'VE GOT TO....
...STARE INTO GENNOSUKE'S EYES...
...WITH YOUR OWN ENCHANTED VISION!
IF YOU TRULY ARE THE NEXT LEADER OF TSUBAGAKURE...
...THEN YOU KNOW THAT OUR CLAN'S FUTURE HINGES ON THE OUT-COME OF THIS BATTLE.
YOU'VE GOT TO DO IT!
......
GENNOSUKE'S...
...ENCHANTED VISION....

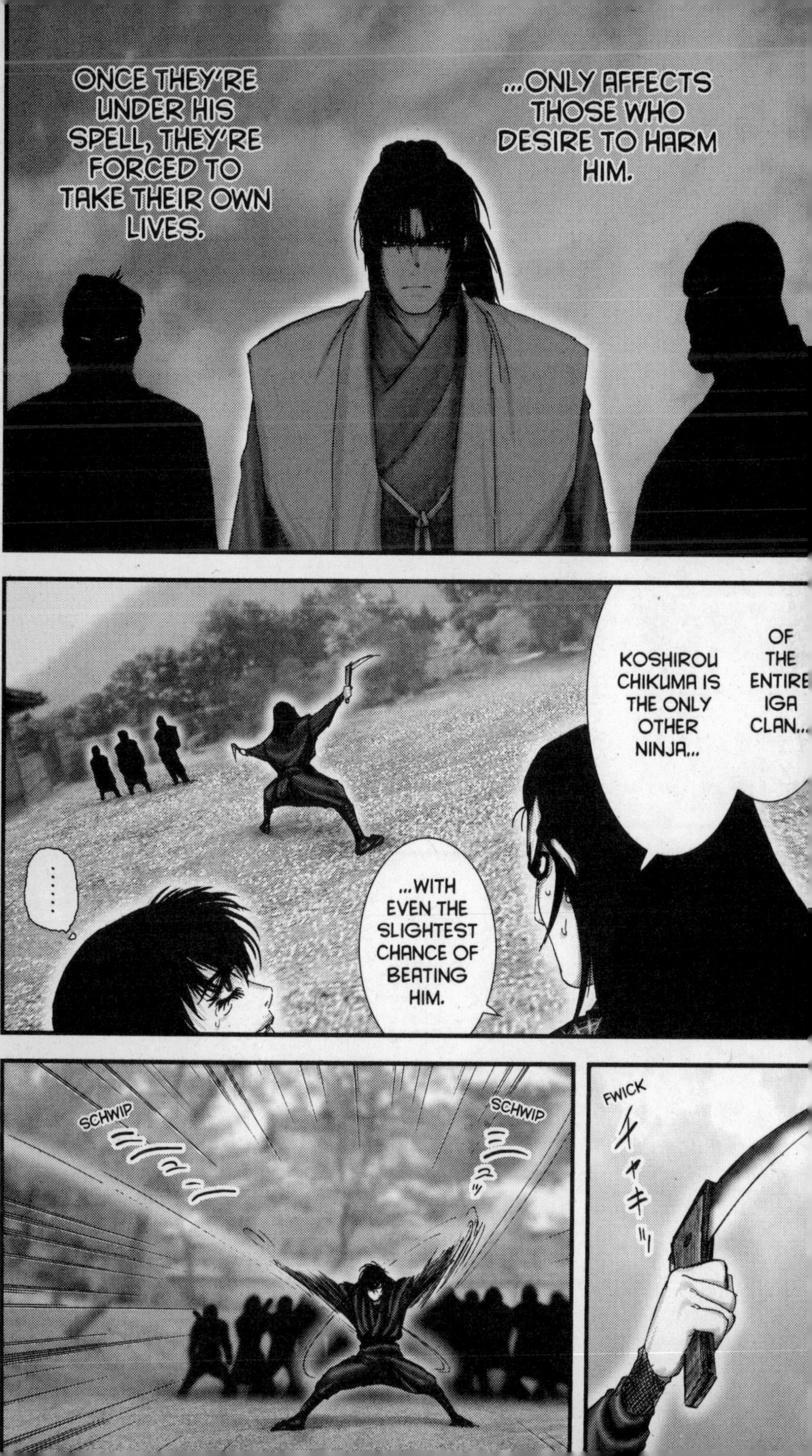
...ONLY AFFECTS THOSE WHO DESIRE TO HARM HIM.
ONCE THEY'RE UNDER HIS SPELL, THEY'RE FORCED TO TAKE THEIR OWN LIVES.
KOSHIROU CHIKUMA IS THE ONLY OTHER NINJA...
OF THE ENTIRE IGA CLAN...
...WITH EVEN THE SLIGHTEST CHANCE OF BEATING HIM.
......
FWICK
SCHWIP
SCHWIP

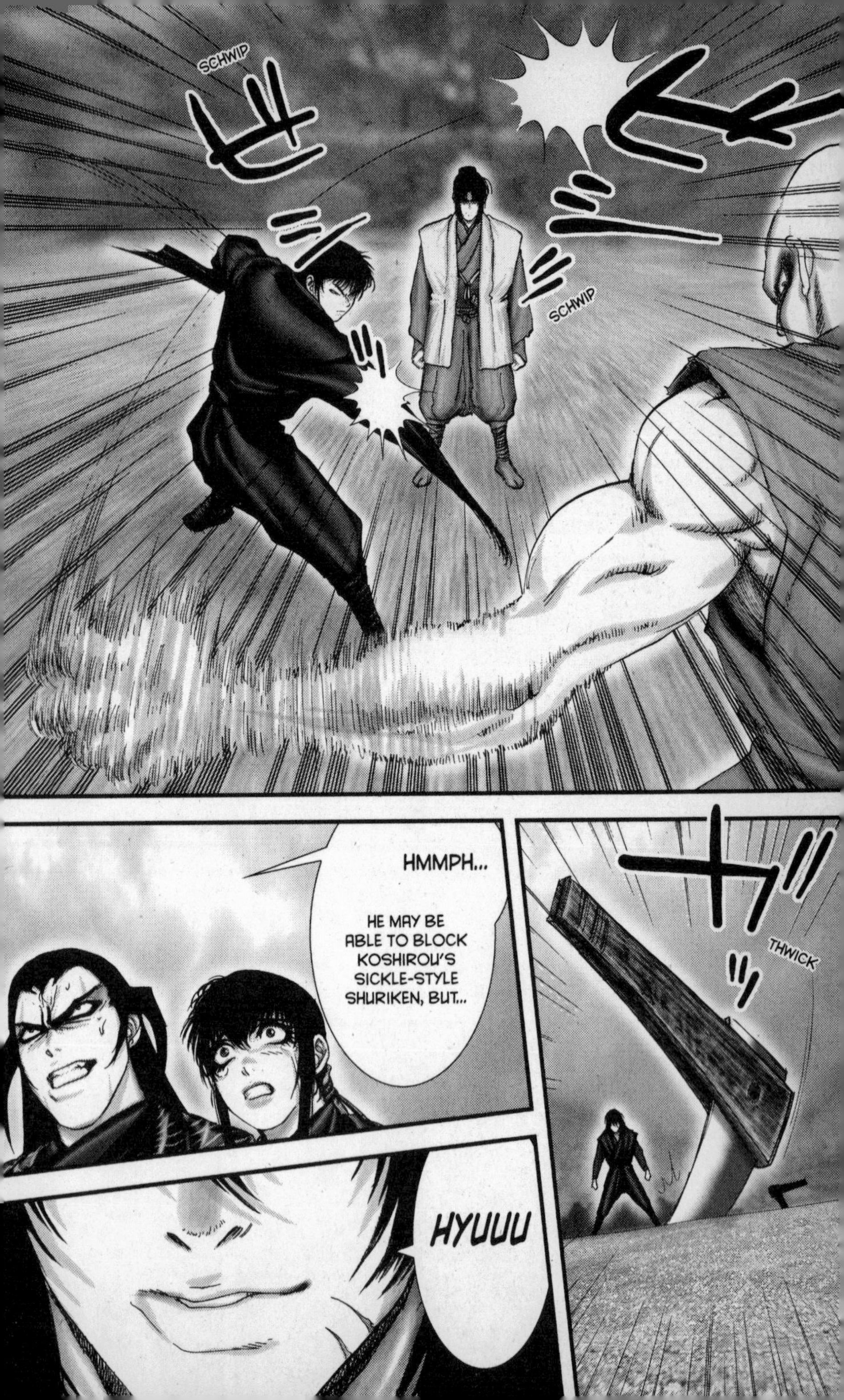
SCHWIP
SCHWIP
THWICK
HMMPH...
HE MAY BE ABLE TO BLOCK KOSHIROU'S SICKLE-STYLE SHURIKEN, BUT...
HYUUU

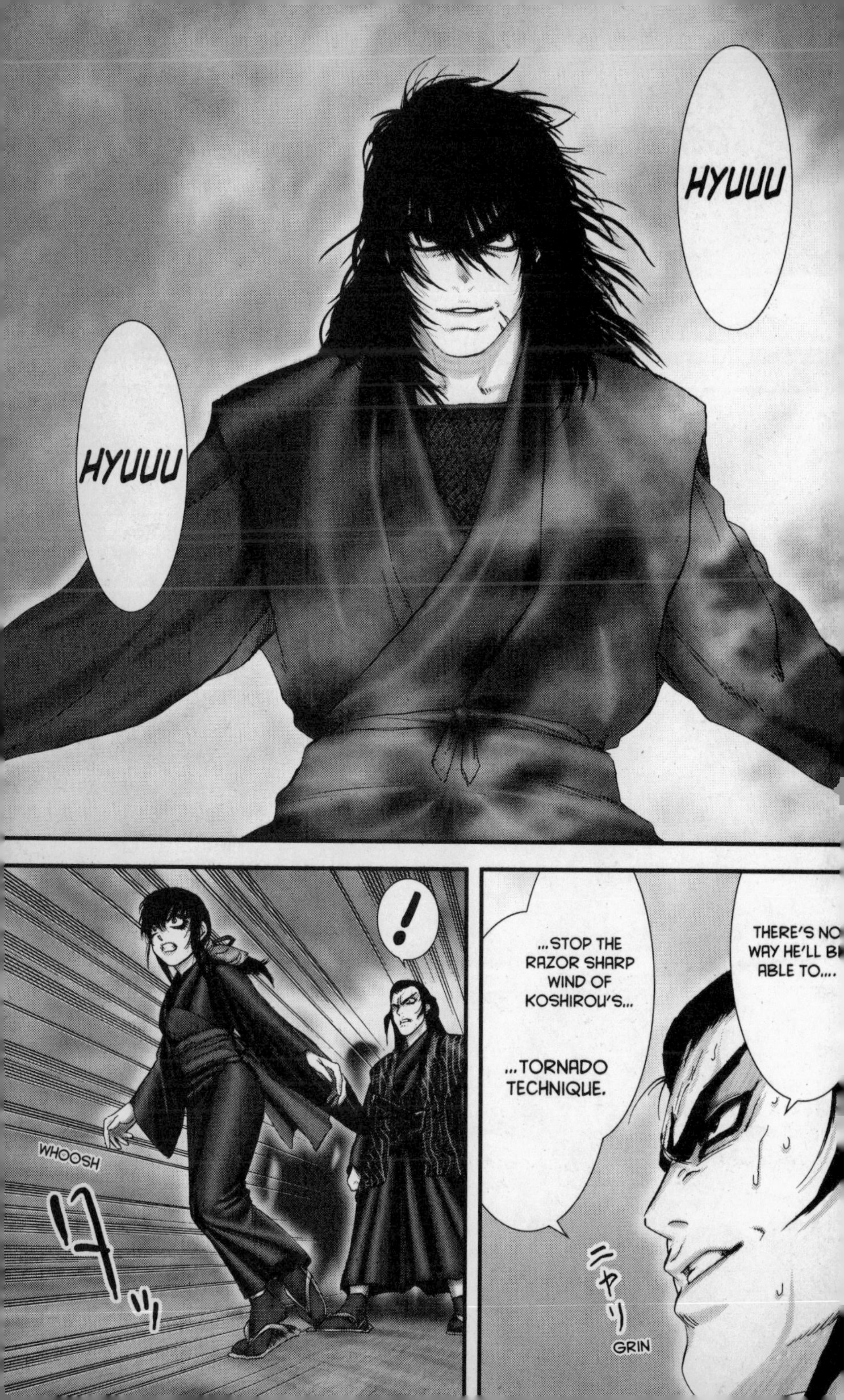
HYUUU
HYUUU
THERE'S NO WAY HE'LL B ABLE TO....
...STOP THE RAZOR SHARP WIND OF KOSHIROU'S...
...TORNADO TECHNIQUE.
GRIN
!
WHOOSH

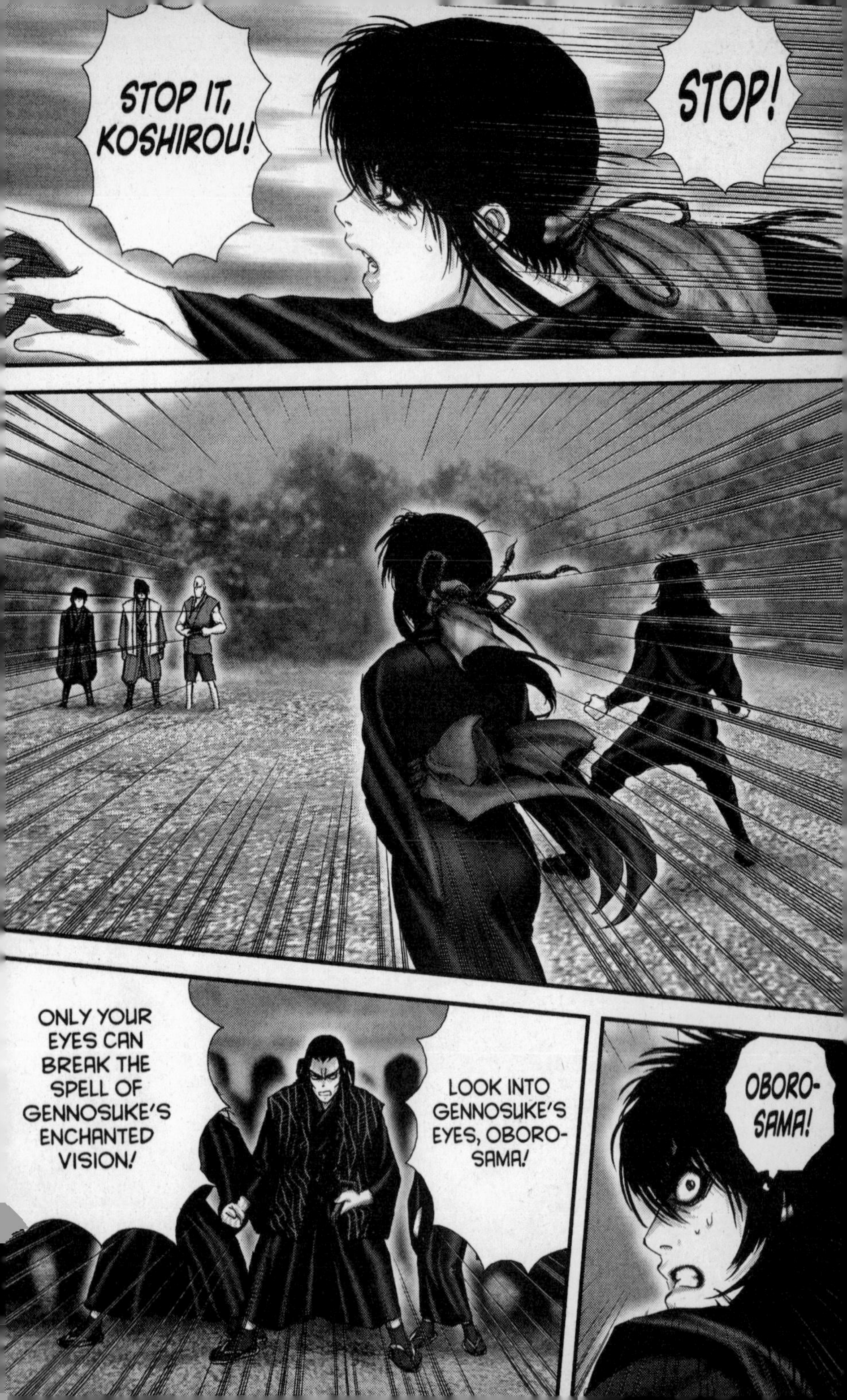
STOP!
STOP IT, KOSHIROU!
OBORO-SAMA!
LOOK INTO GENNOSUKE'S EYES, OBORO-SAMA!
ONLY YOUR EYES CAN BREAK THE SPELL OF GENNOSUKE'S ENCHANTED VISION!

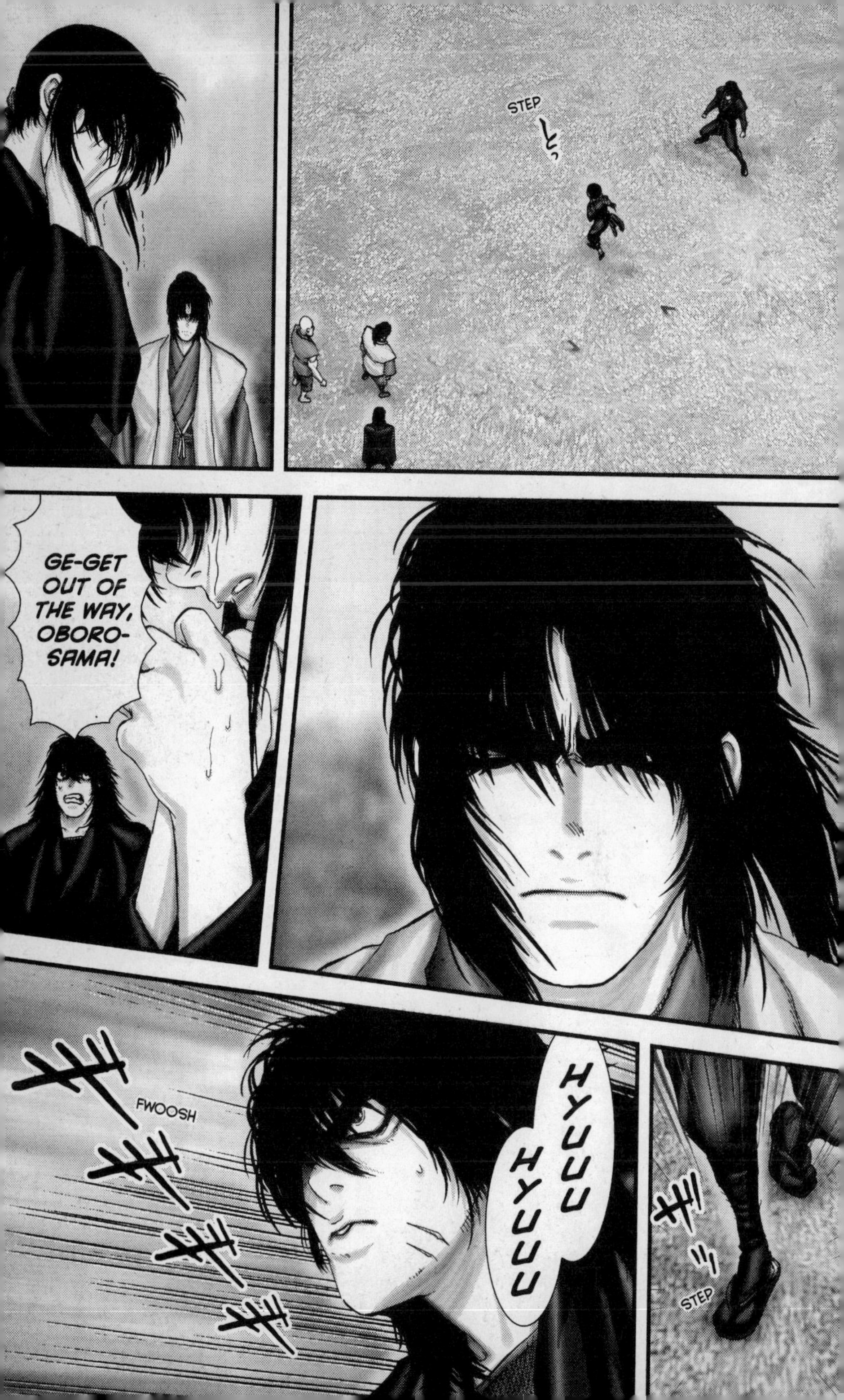
STEP
とっ
GE-GET OUT OF THE WAY, OBORO-SAMA!
STEP
HYUUUU HYUUUU
FWOOSH

STOP!
KOSHIROU!

WHOOSH

SWIP

GOT TO...

TURN AWAY...GOT TO TURN AWAY!

NO! OBORO-SAMA'S EYES!

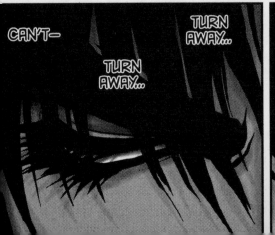

CAN'T—

TURN AWAY...

TURN AWAY...

GOT TO... TURN AWAY!

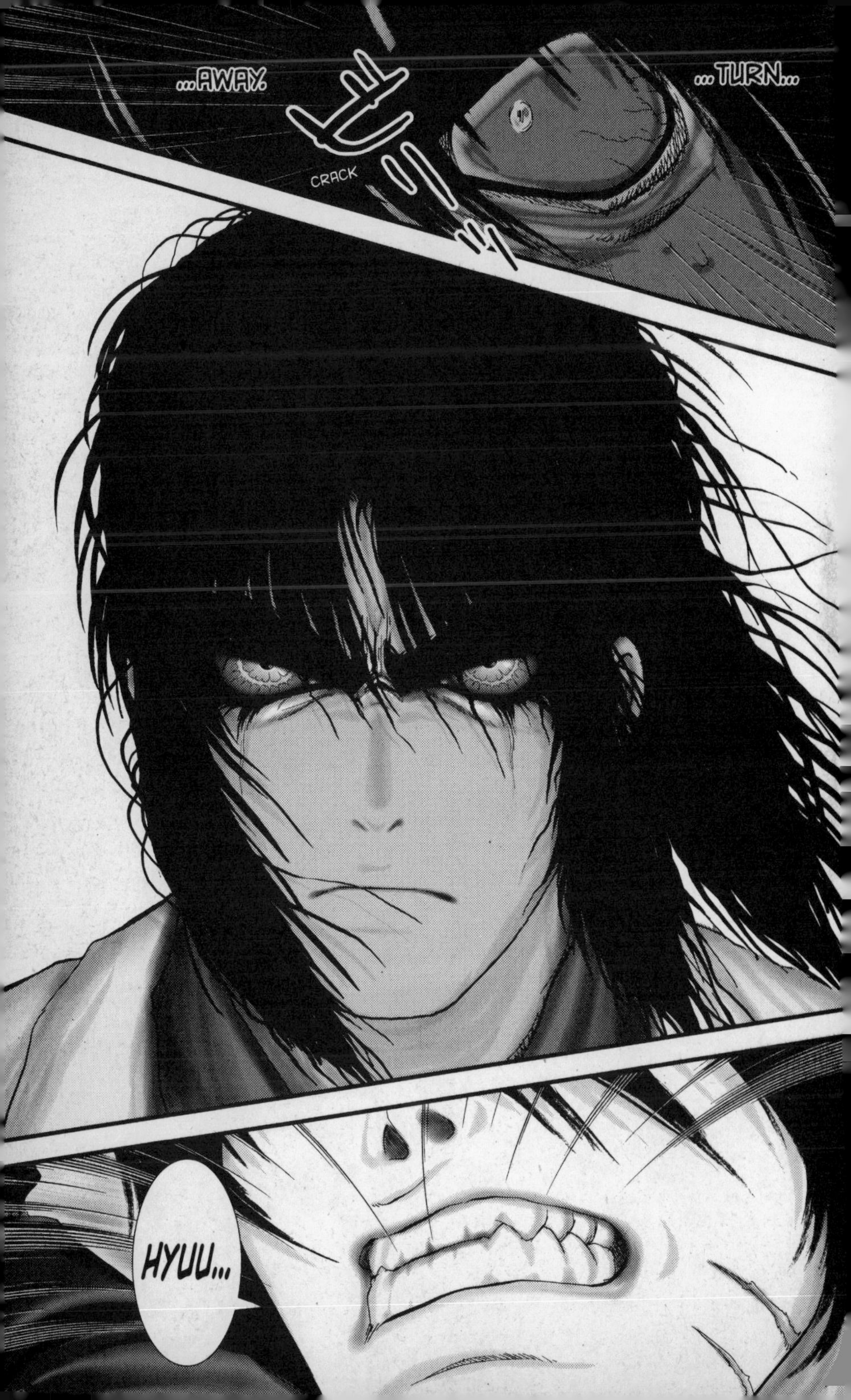
...TURN...
CRACK
...AWAY.
HYUU...

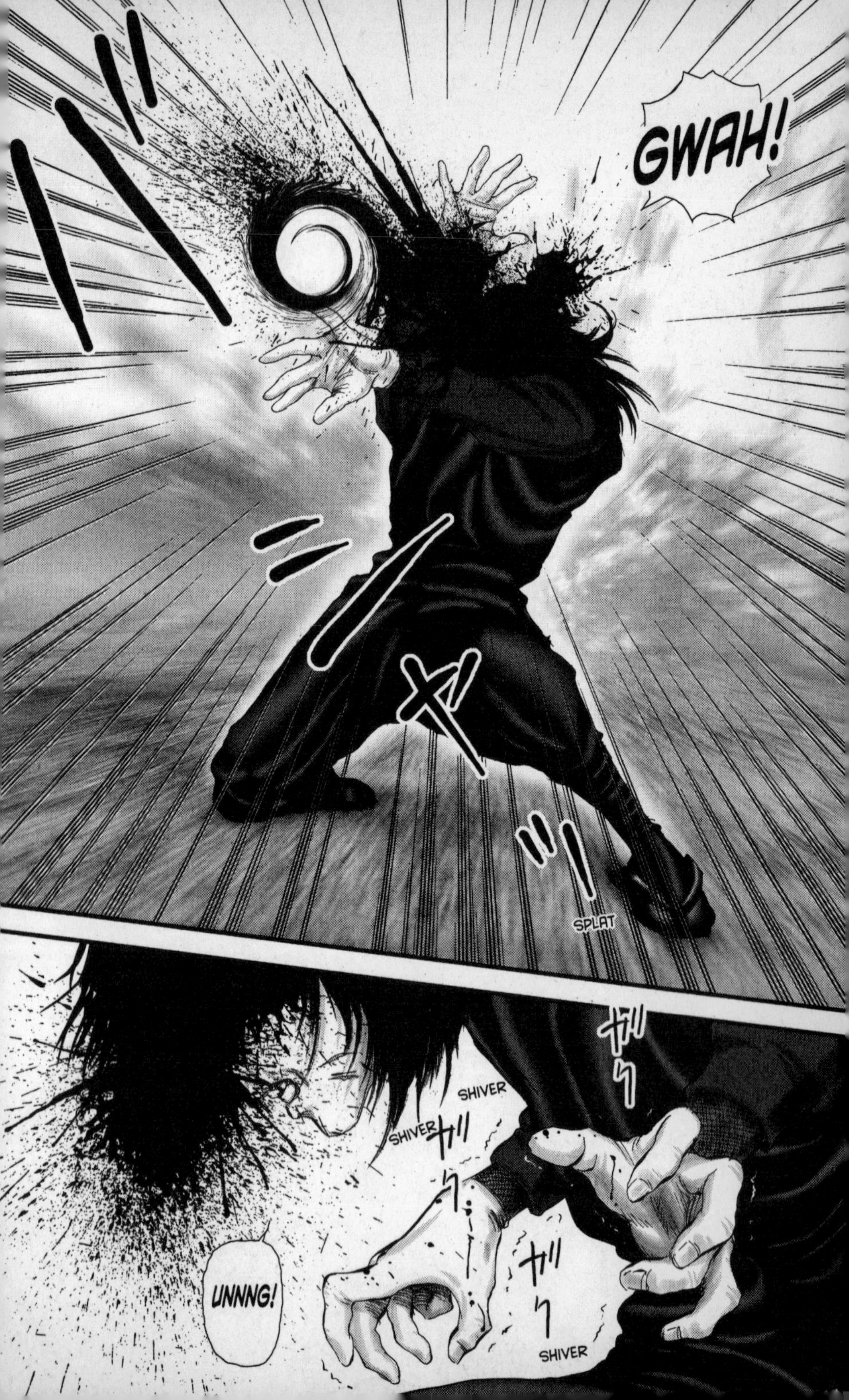
GWAH!
SPLAT
SHIVER
SHIVER
SHIVER
UNNNG!

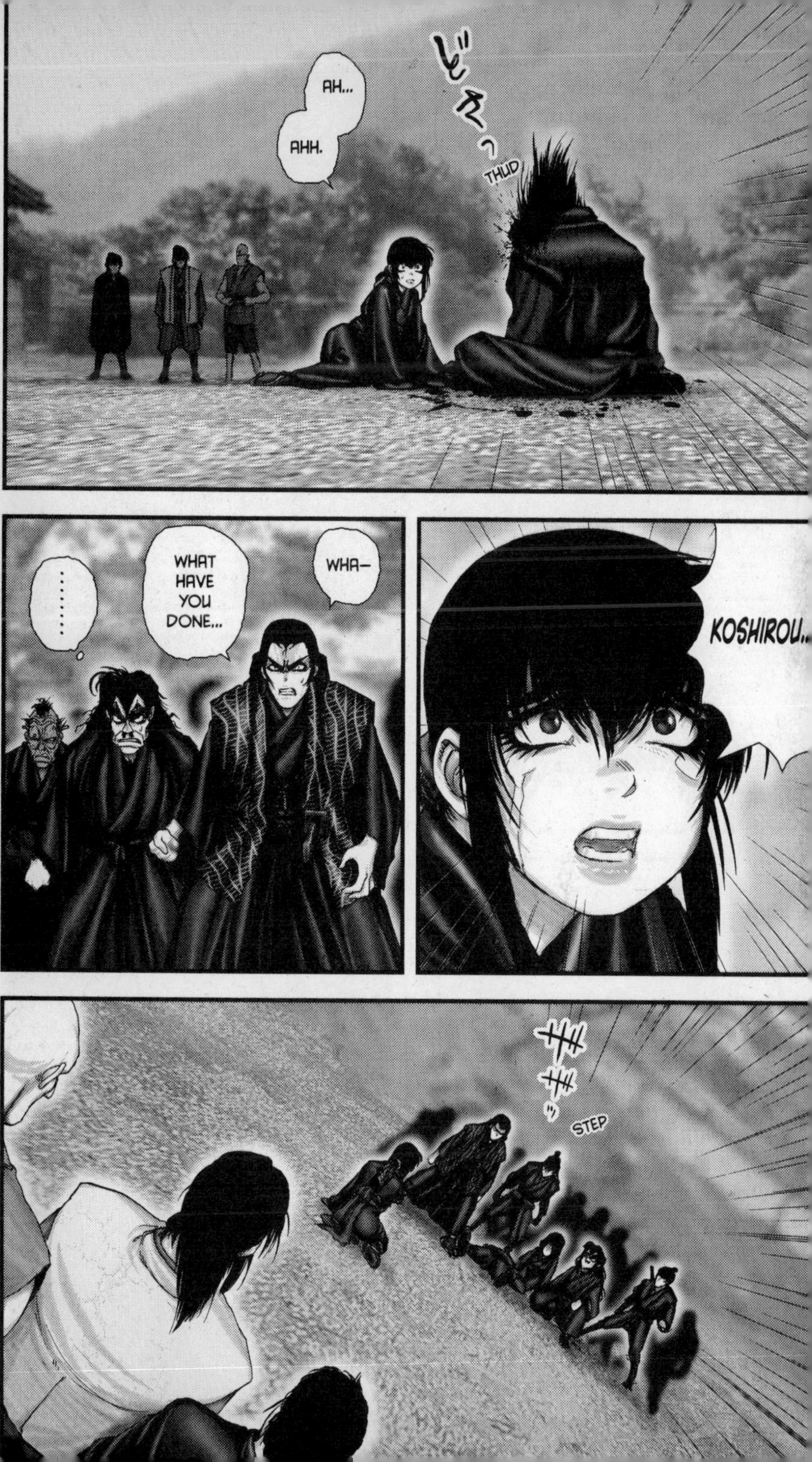
THUD
AH...
AHH.
KOSHIROU...
WHA—
WHAT HAVE YOU DONE...
....
STEP

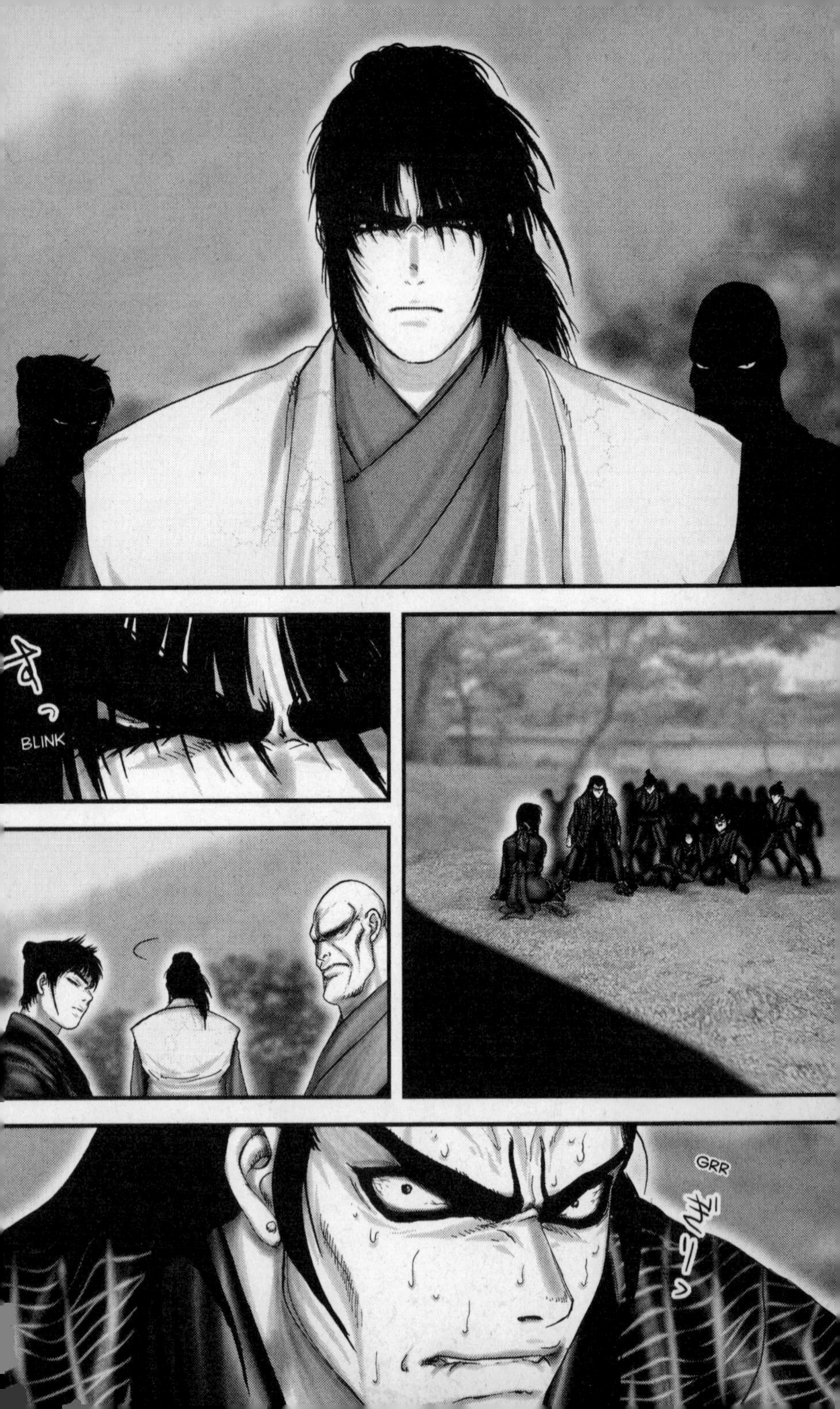
BLINK
GRR

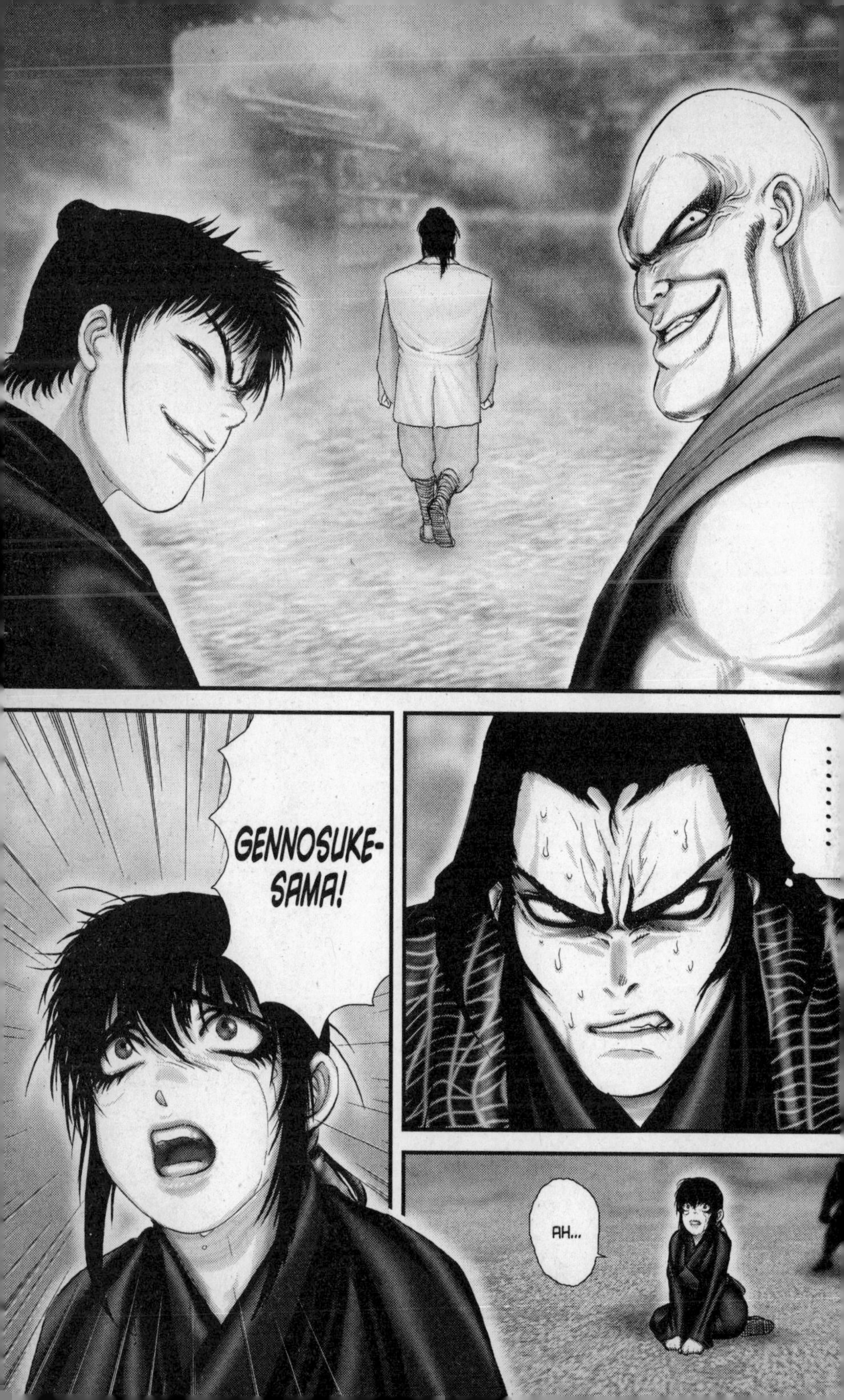

......
GENNOSUKE-SAMA!
AH...

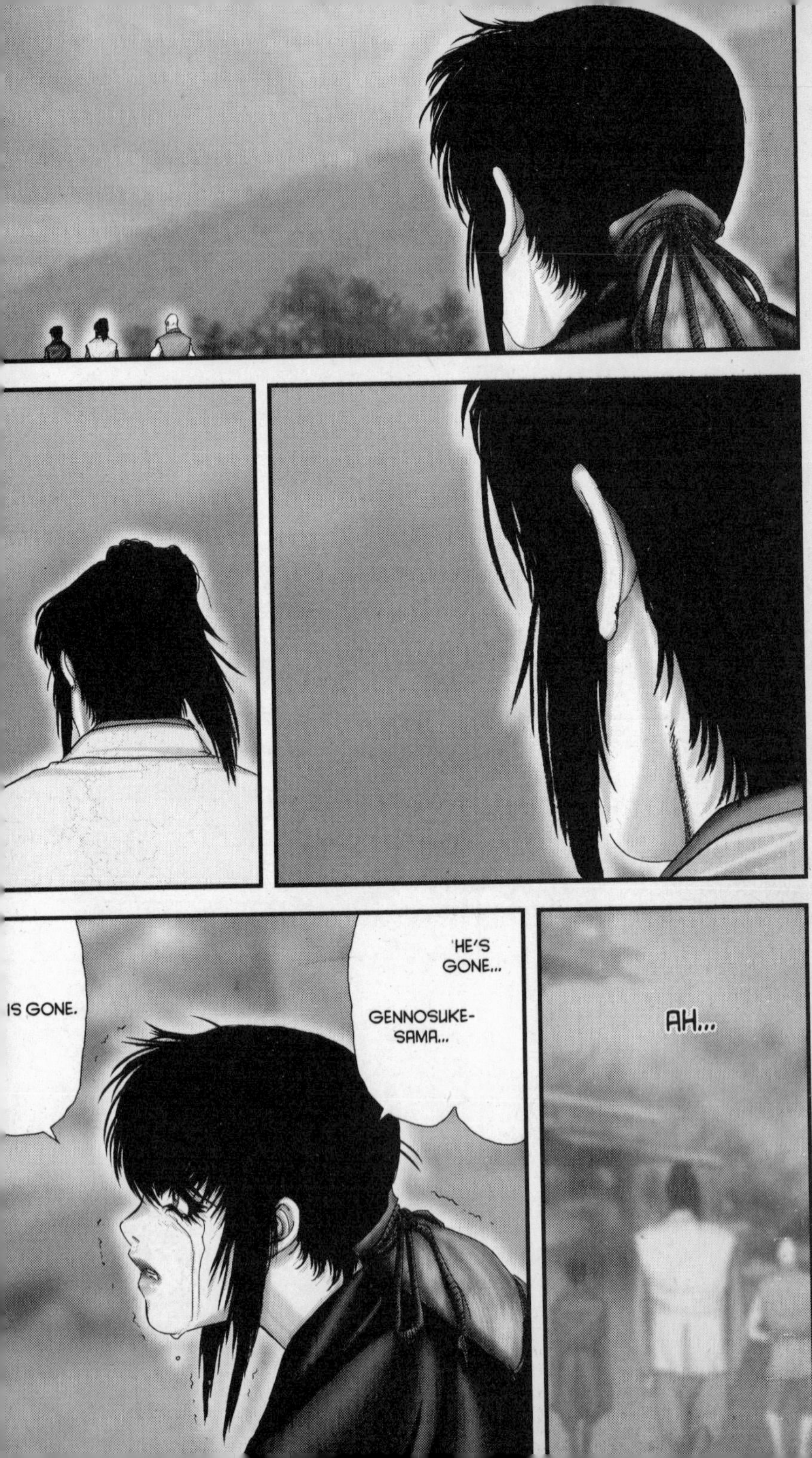
AH...
'HE'S GONE...
GENNOSUKE-SAMA...
IS GONE.

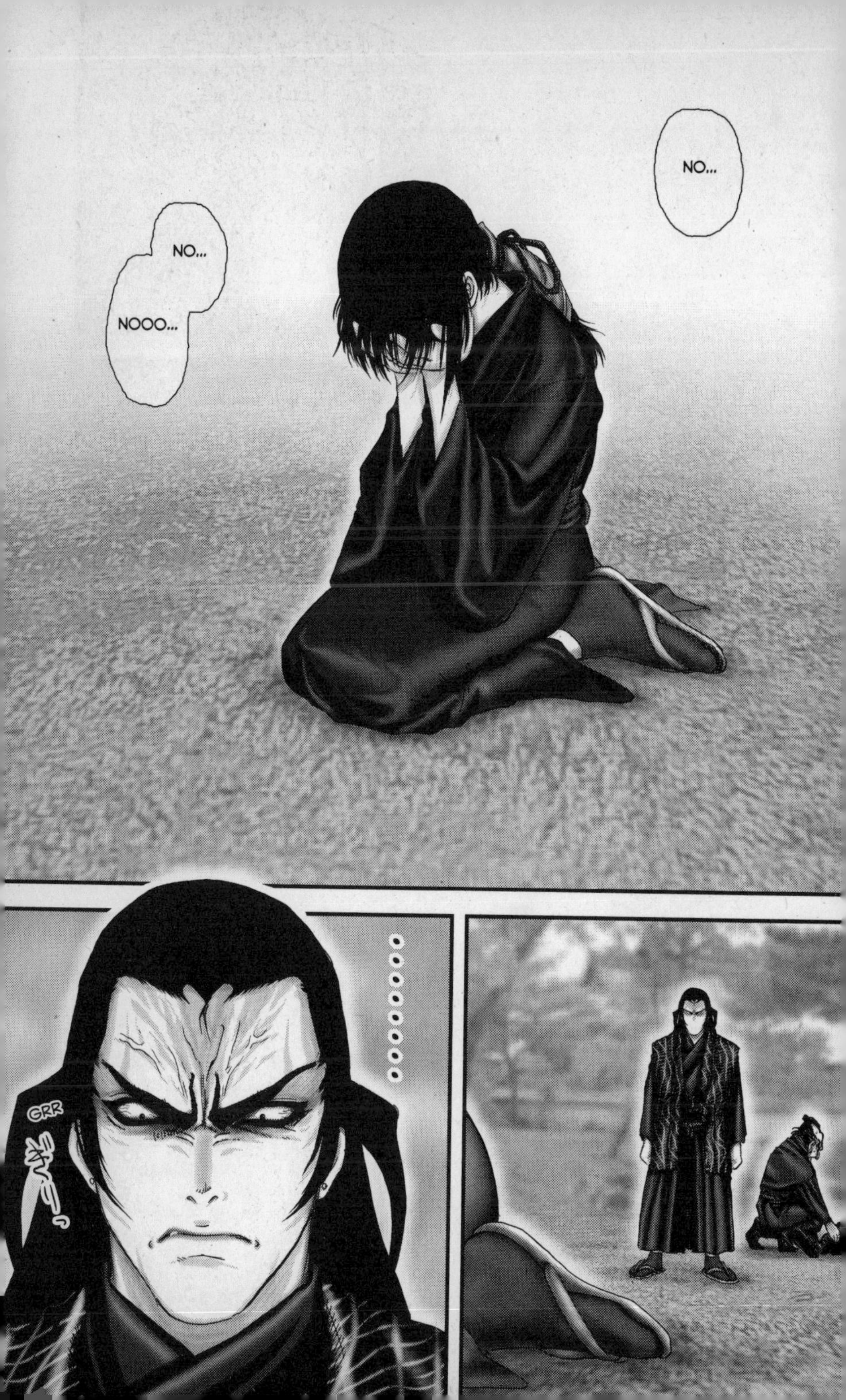
NO...
NO...
NOOO...
....
GRR

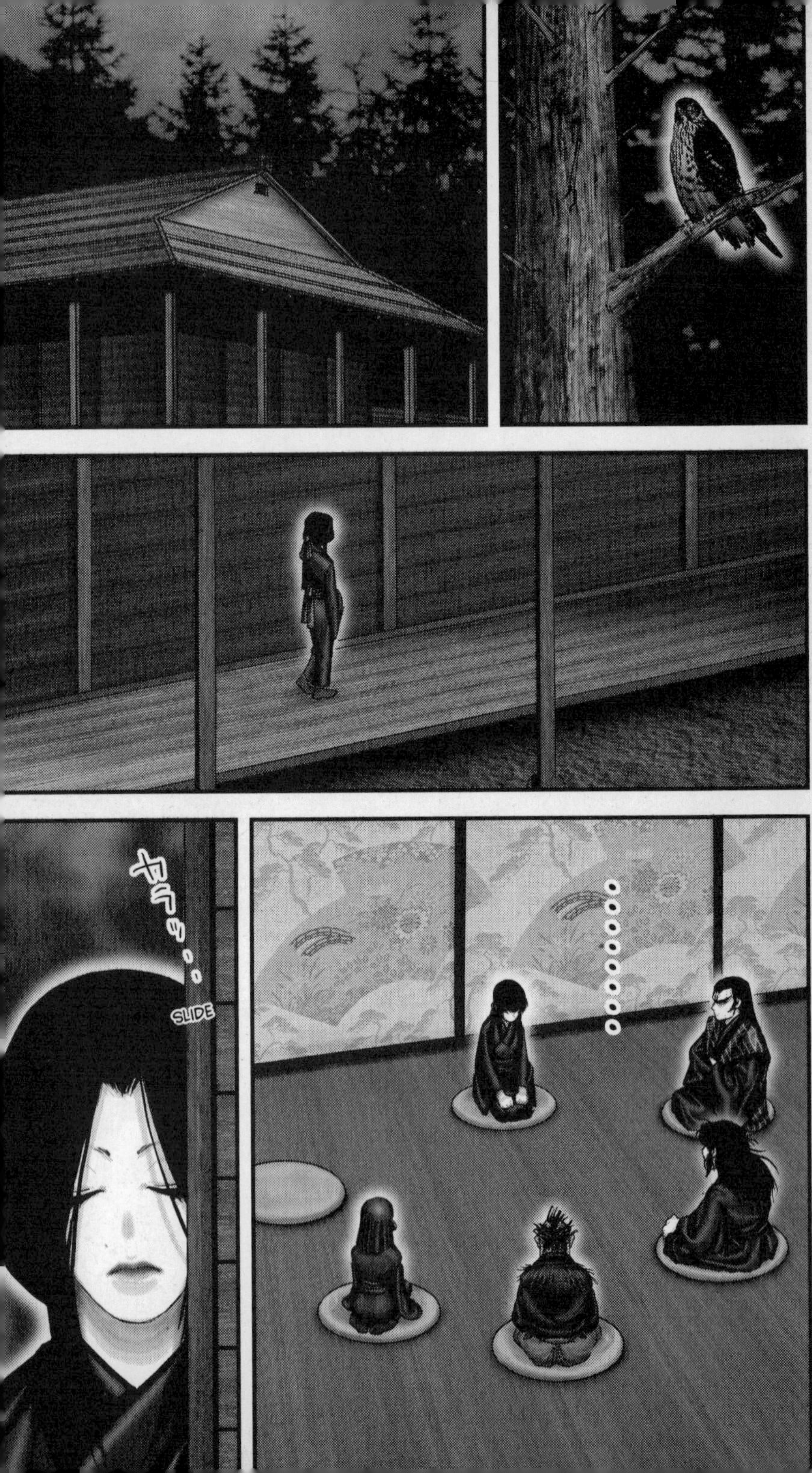
....
SLIDE

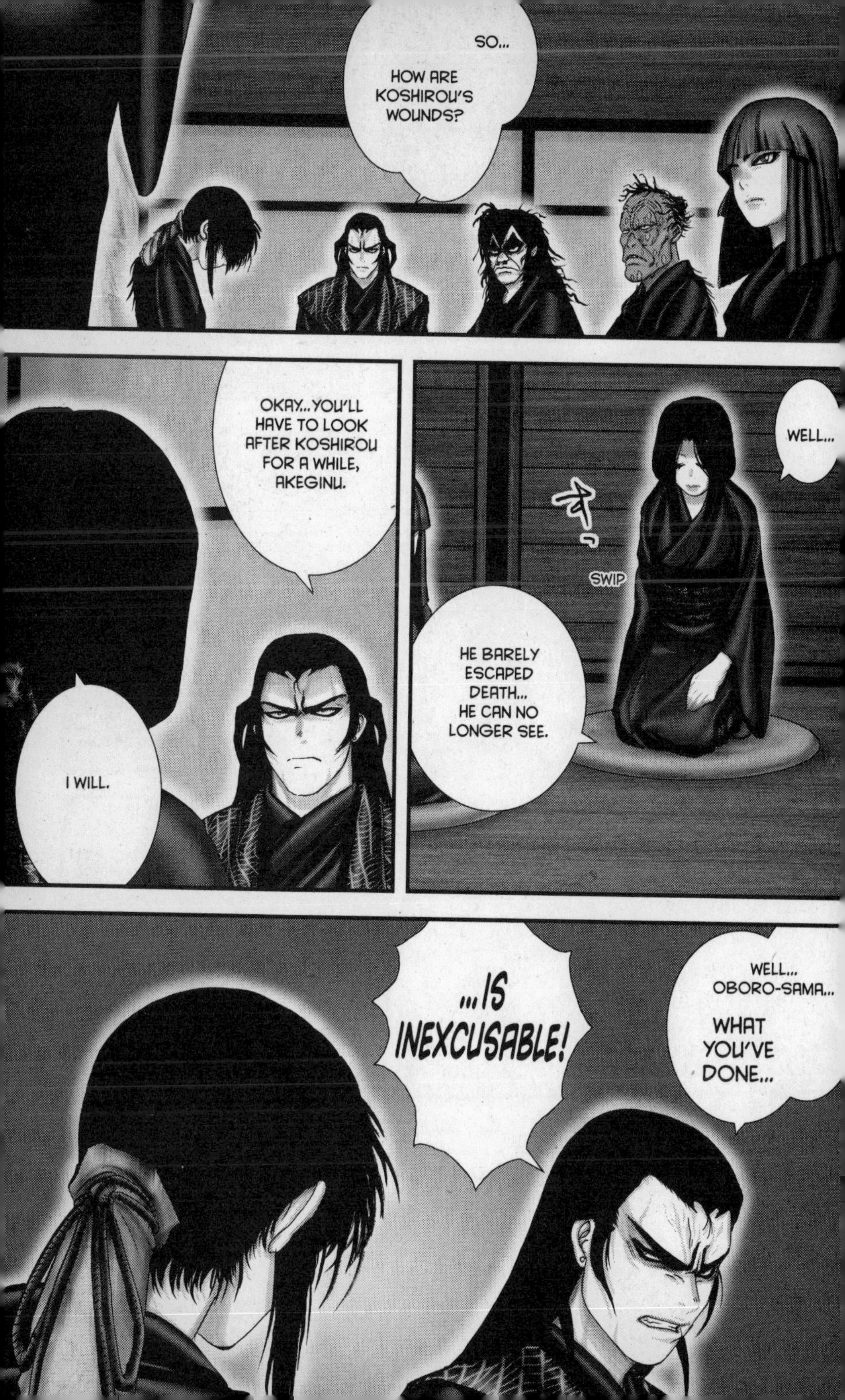
SO... HOW ARE KOSHIROU'S WOUNDS?
WELL...
SWIP
HE BARELY ESCAPED DEATH... HE CAN NO LONGER SEE.
OKAY...YOU'LL HAVE TO LOOK AFTER KOSHIROU FOR A WHILE, AKEGINU.
I WILL.
WELL... OBORO-SAMA... WHAT YOU'VE DONE...
...IS INEXCUSABLE!

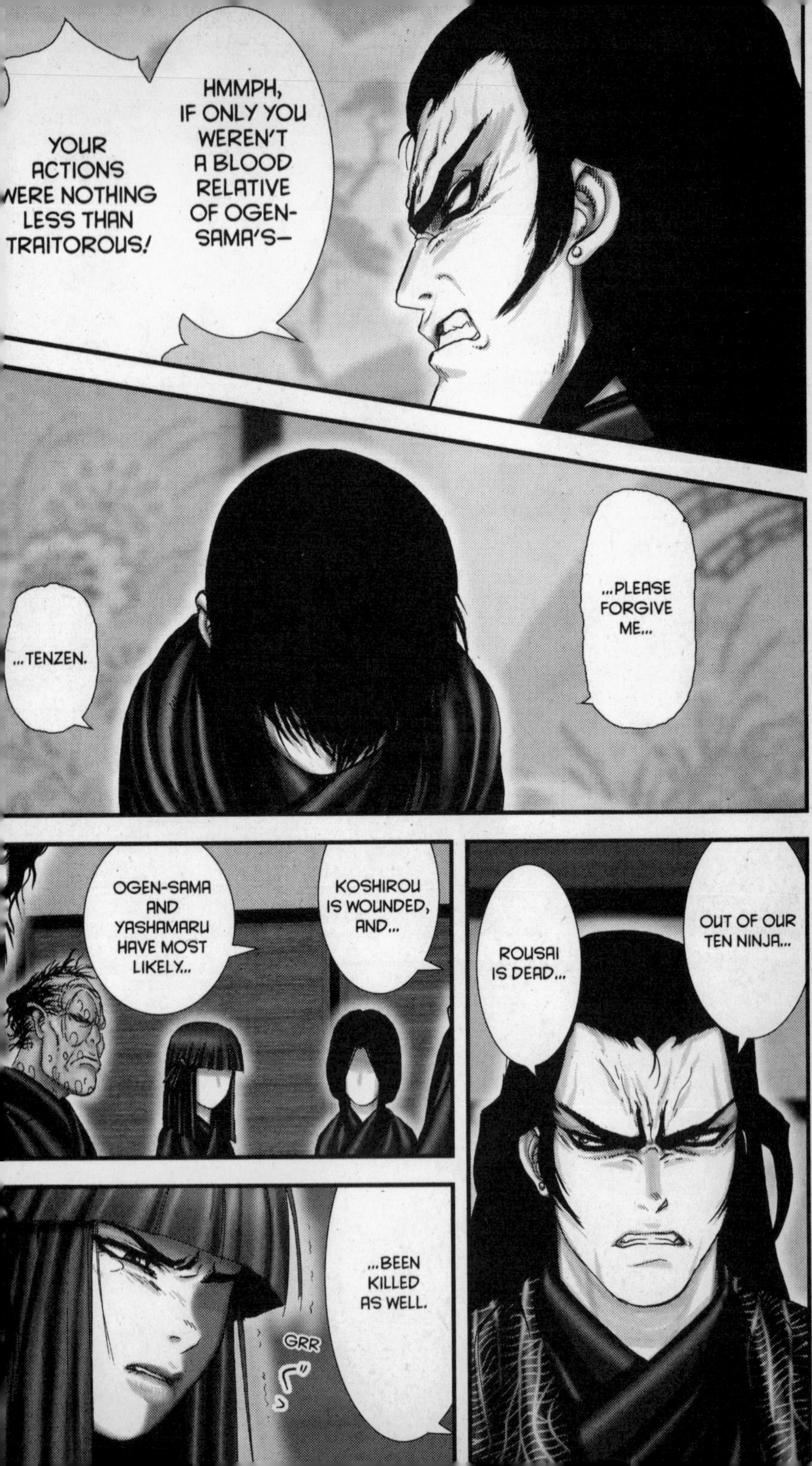
HMMPH, IF ONLY YOU WEREN'T A BLOOD RELATIVE OF OGEN-SAMA'S—
YOUR ACTIONS WERE NOTHING LESS THAN TRAITOROUS!
...PLEASE FORGIVE ME...
...TENZEN.
OUT OF OUR TEN NINJA...
ROUSAI IS DEAD...
KOSHIROU IS WOUNDED, AND...
OGEN-SAMA AND YASHAMARU HAVE MOST LIKELY...
...BEEN KILLED AS WELL.
GRR

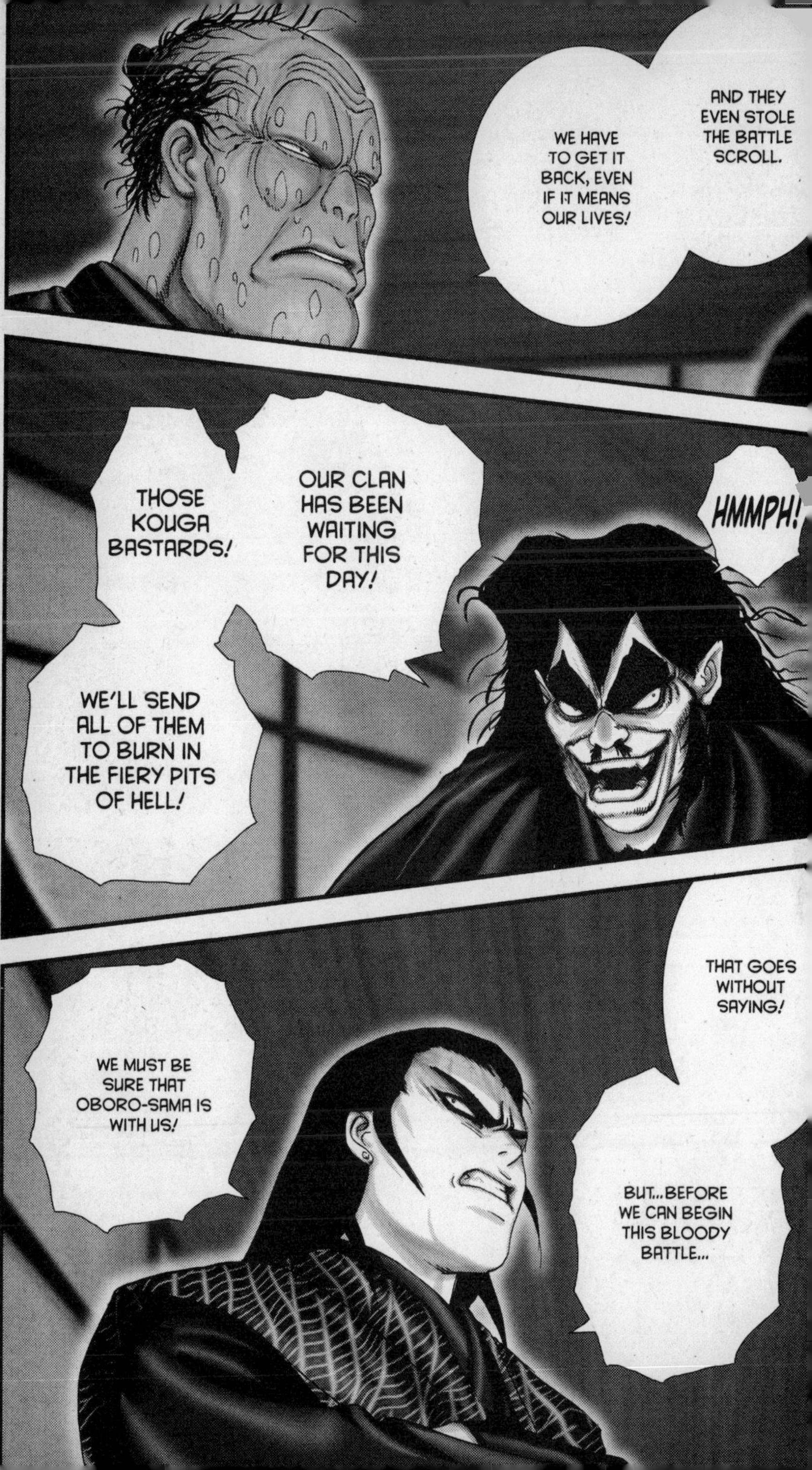
AND THEY EVEN STOLE THE BATTLE SCROLL.
WE HAVE TO GET IT BACK, EVEN IF IT MEANS OUR LIVES!
HMMPH!
OUR CLAN HAS BEEN WAITING FOR THIS DAY!
THOSE KOUGA BASTARDS!
WE'LL SEND ALL OF THEM TO BURN IN THE FIERY PITS OF HELL!
THAT GOES WITHOUT SAYING!
BUT...BEFORE WE CAN BEGIN THIS BLOODY BATTLE...
WE MUST BE SURE THAT OBORO-SAMA IS WITH US!

SO...
OBORO-
SAMA!
CAN YOU
SWEAR
TO US...

...THAT
ENNOSUKE
OUGA WILL
DIE BY
YOUR
HAND?

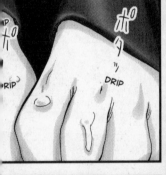

DRIP

DRIP

DRIP

. . . .

DRIP

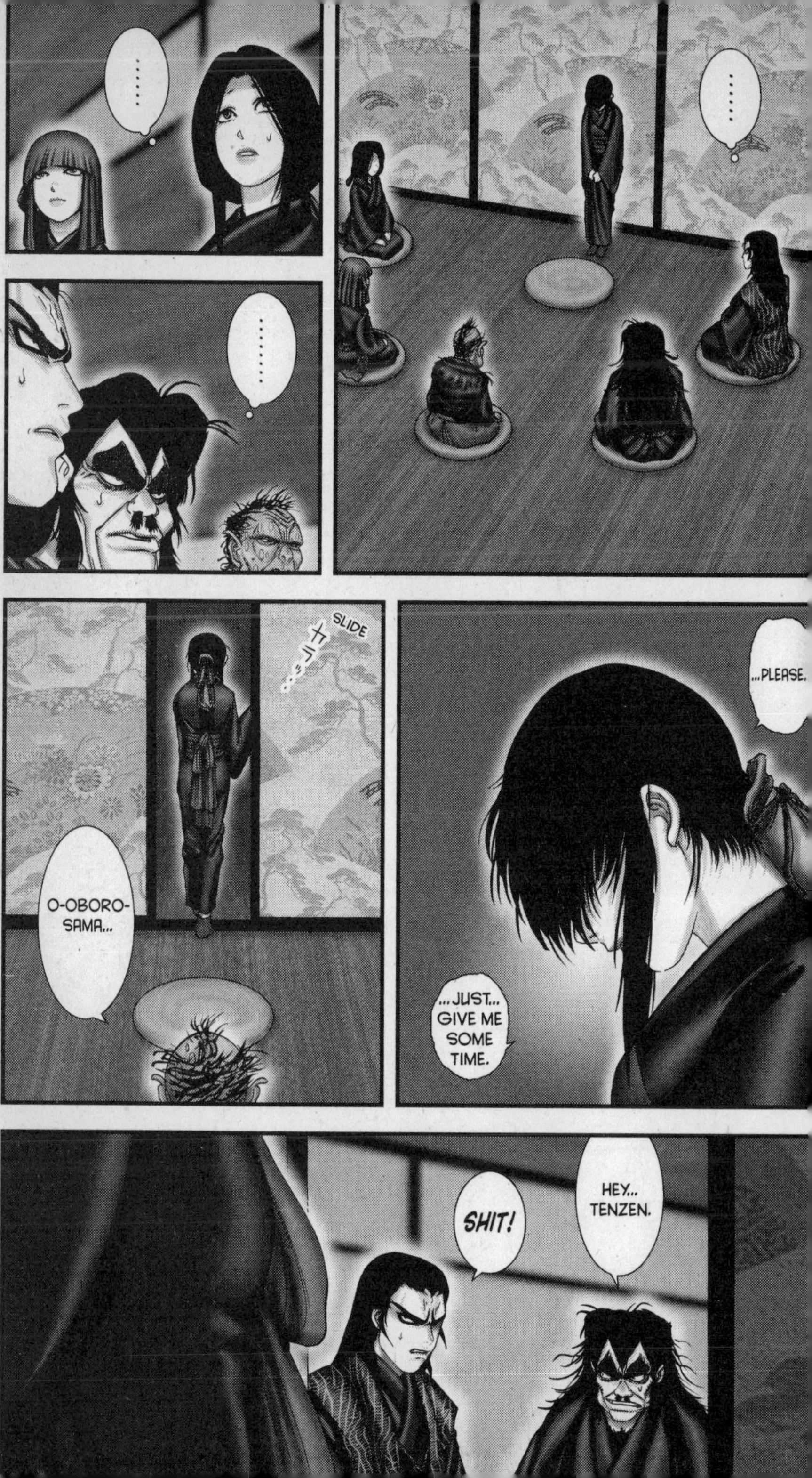
......
......
......
...PLEASE.
...JUST... GIVE ME SOME TIME.
SLIDE
O-OBORO-SAMA...
HEY... TENZEN.
SHIT!

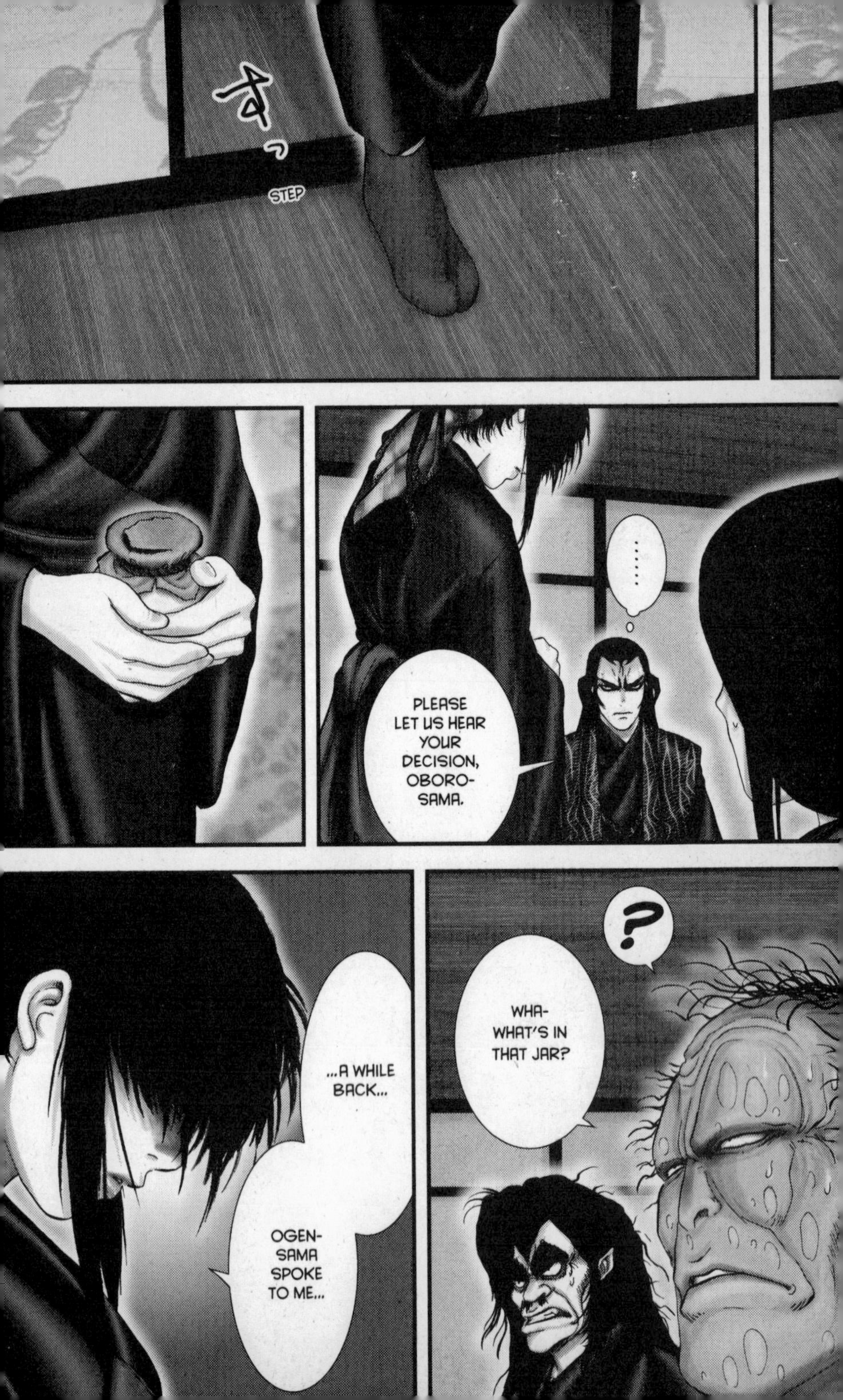
すっ
STEP
......
PLEASE LET US HEAR YOUR DECISION, OBORO-SAMA.
?
WHA- WHAT'S IN THAT JAR?
...A WHILE BACK...
OGEN-SAMA SPOKE TO ME...

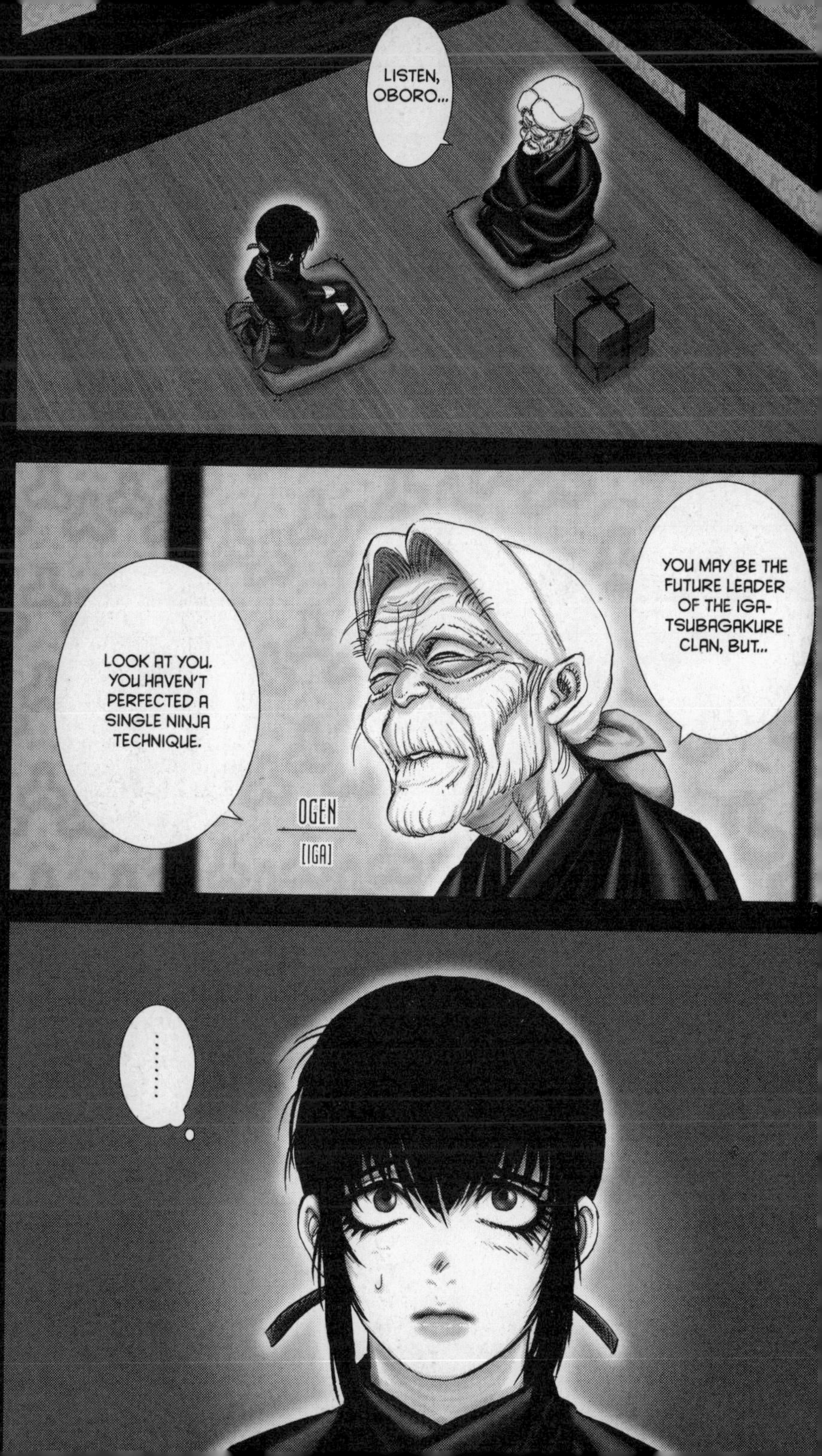
LISTEN, OBORO...
YOU MAY BE THE FUTURE LEADER OF THE IGA-TSUBAGAKURE CLAN, BUT...
LOOK AT YOU. YOU HAVEN'T PERFECTED A SINGLE NINJA TECHNIQUE.
OGEN
[IGA]
......

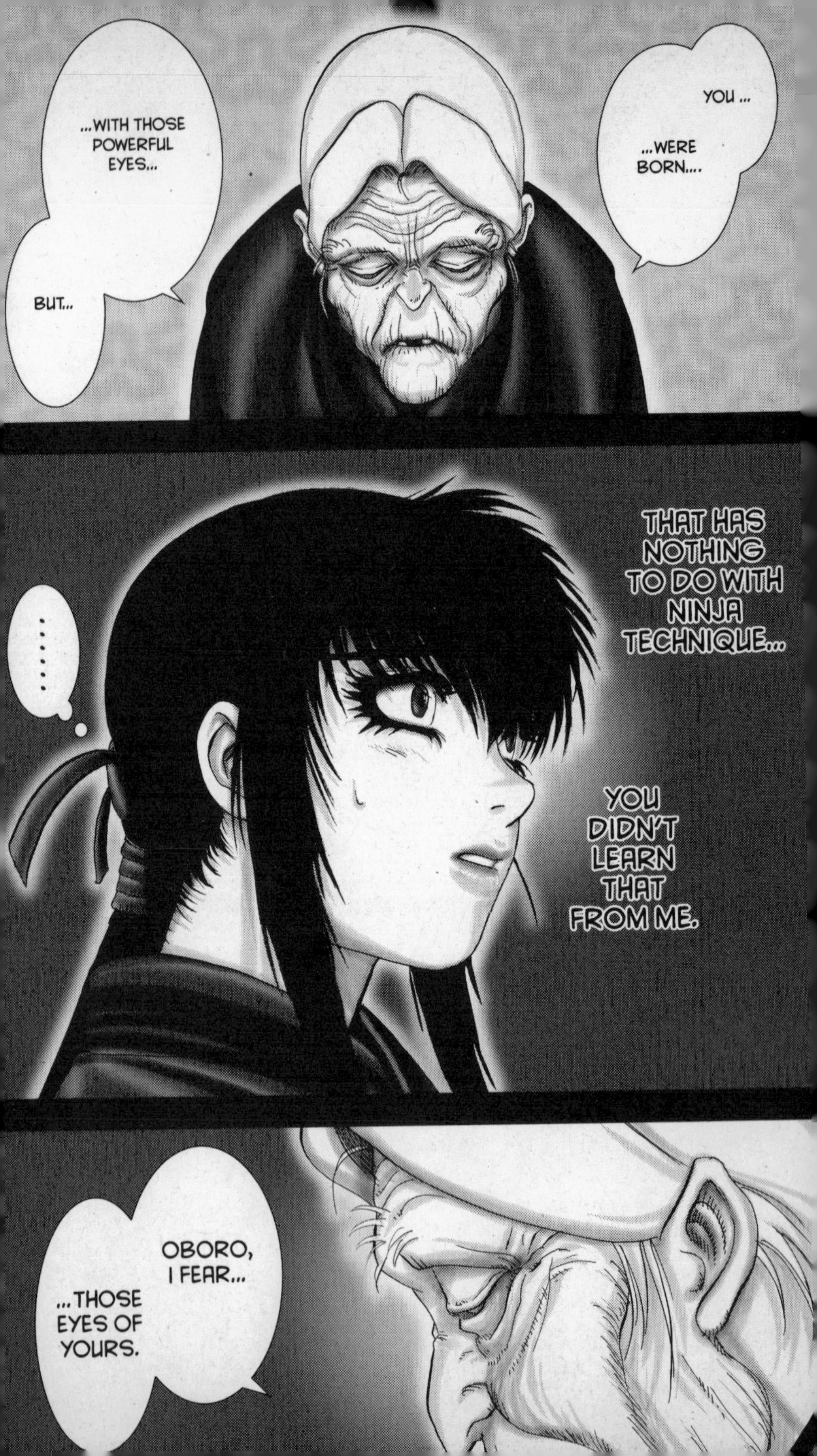
YOU ...
...WERE BORN....
...WITH THOSE POWERFUL EYES...
BUT...
THAT HAS NOTHING TO DO WITH NINJA TECHNIQUE...
YOU DIDN'T LEARN THAT FROM ME.
......
OBORO, I FEAR...
...THOSE EYES OF YOURS.

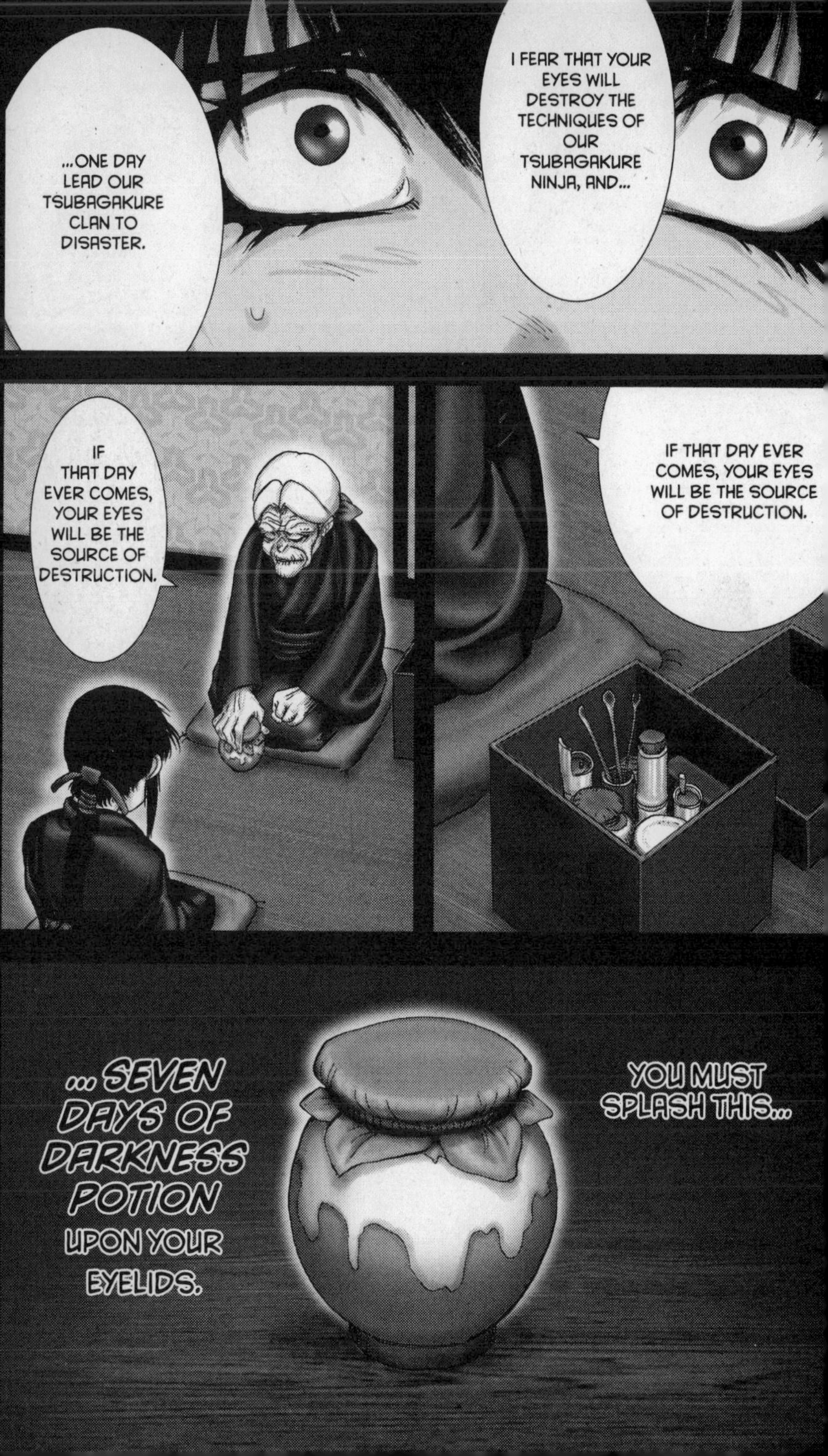
I FEAR THAT YOUR EYES WILL DESTROY THE TECHNIQUES OF OUR TSUBAGAKURE NINJA, AND...
...ONE DAY LEAD OUR TSUBAGAKURE CLAN TO DISASTER.
IF THAT DAY EVER COMES, YOUR EYES WILL BE THE SOURCE OF DESTRUCTION.
IF THAT DAY EVER COMES, YOUR EYES WILL BE THE SOURCE OF DESTRUCTION.
YOU MUST SPLASH THIS...
...SEVEN DAYS OF DARKNESS POTION UPON YOUR EYELIDS.

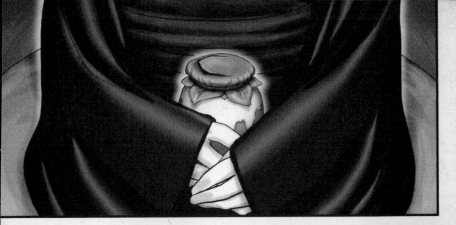

AND THEN... WHAT WILL HAPPEN?

YOU CAN'T MEAN—

AND—

IF...

I POUR THE SEVEN DAYS OF DARKNESS POTION UPON MY EYELIDS...

...MY EYES WILL BE SEALED SHUT...

...FOR SEVEN DAYS AND SEVEN NIGHTS.

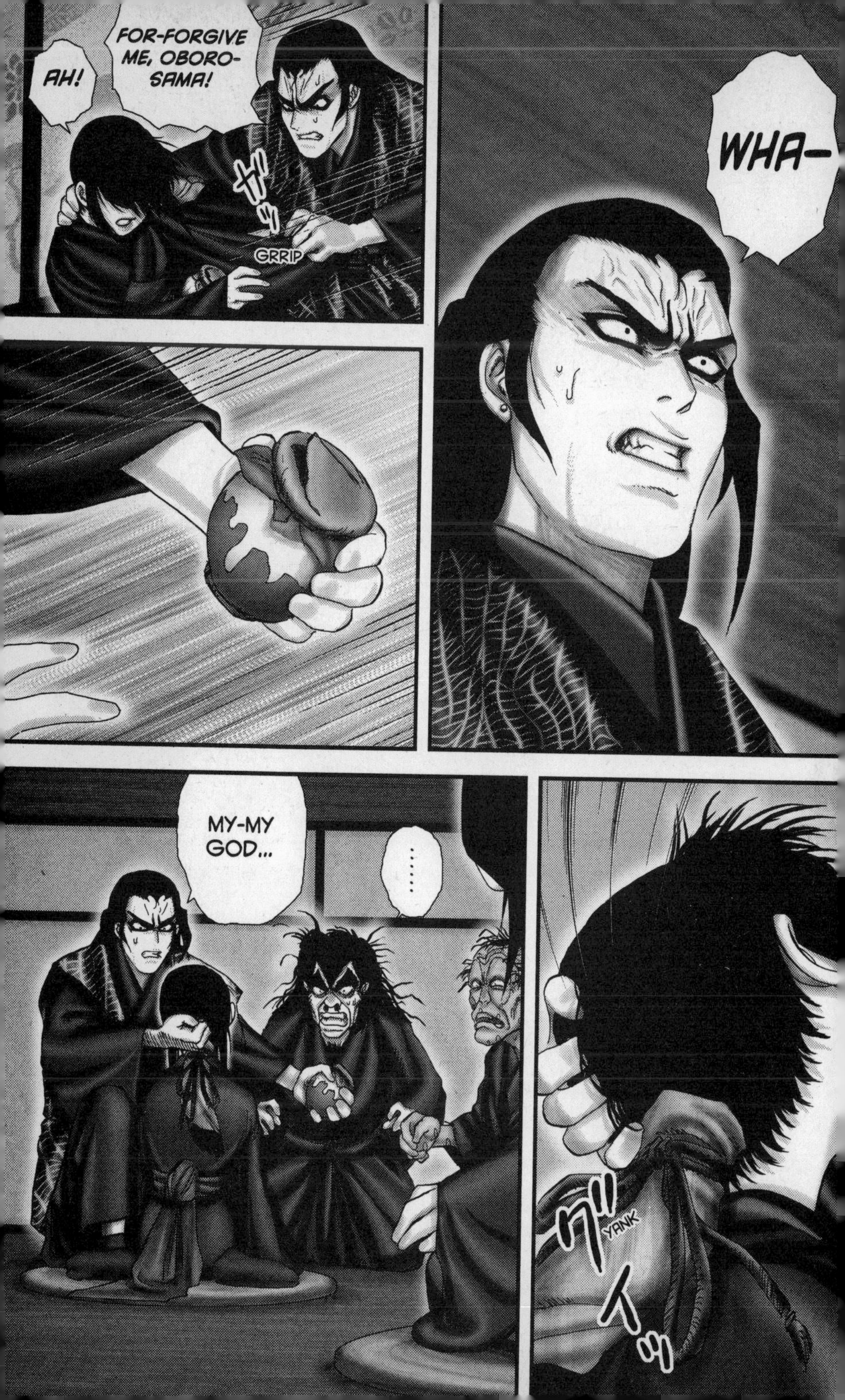
WHA-
FOR-FORGIVE ME, OBORO-SAMA!
AH!
GRRIP
YANK
......
MY-MY GOD...

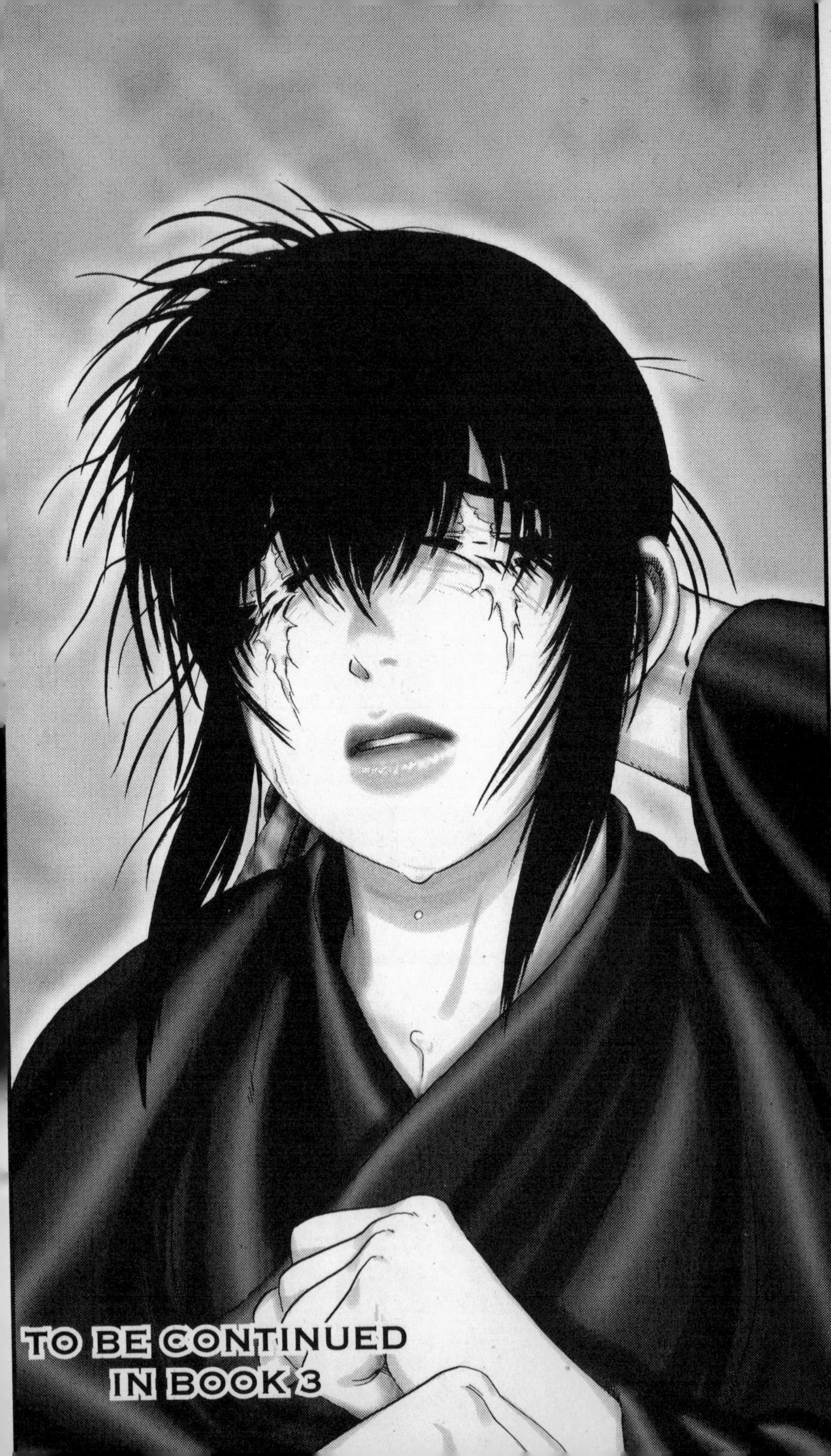
TO BE CONTINUED IN BOOK 3

FŪTARO YAMADA

Born in 1922 in Hyogo Prefecture, Fūtaro Yamada made his debut as a novelist while still a student at Tokyo Medical University. Yamada was known for his mystery novels such as *Ganchuu No Akuma*. Later, his Ninja Scrolls series became wildly popular. He penned a wide body of literature, including the period piece *Makaitensei*, as well as several collections of essays such as *Ato Senkai No Banmeshi* and *Ningen Rinjyuu Zukan*. He passed away on July 28, 2001.

MASAKI SEGAWA

Masaki Segawa made his debut in 1997 with the series Senma Monogatari, which ran in the weekly comic *Morning*. In 1998, he began his long-running *Uppers* magazine series Onigiri Jyuuzou, which ended in the year 2000. This is his second long-running series, and his first adaptation. He loves cats and watermelon.
He currently resides in Funabashi.

Translation Notes

Japanese is a tricky language for most Westerners, and translation is often more art than science. For your edification and reading pleasure, here are notes on some of the places where we could have gone in a different direction in our translation of the work, or where a Japanese cultural reference is used.

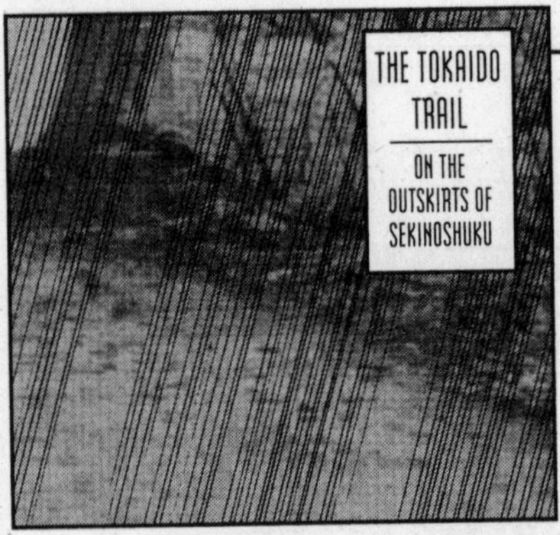
THE TOKAIDO TRAIL
ON THE OUTSKIRTS OF SEKINOSHUKU

THE TOKAIDO TRAIL, PAGE 63

The Tokaido Trail was a famous 300-mile coastal road linking Kyoto and Tokyo during the Tokugawa Era. The road was used by the shogun to maintain control over the country, but it soon became a major commercial route. The fifty-three stations along the Tokaido route were depicted in wood block prints by the famous Edo Era artist Hiroshige. Today several train lines make the journey from Kyoto to Tokyo along parts of the Tokaido Trail.

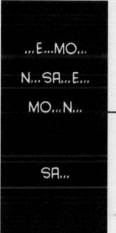

...E...MO...

N...SA...E...

MO...N...

SA...

ANISAMA, PAGE 148

Okoi is actually calling her brother "anisama," or "older brother." In Japanese, siblings are commonly referred to as "older brother" or older sister." We chose to translate this using Saemon's name, since it sounds unnatural in English to refer to someone as "older brother." "Anisama" is actually a very formal, and somewhat antiquated, term. "Oniisama" is the modern equivalent, and "oniisan" and "oniichan" are less formal variations.

SHURIKEN, PAGE 194

Shuriken are the throwing stars used by ninja. Goshiro's shuriken is shaped not like a star but like a sickle, or scythe.

HMMPH...

HE MAY BE ABLE TO BLOCK KOSHIROU'S SICKLE-STYLE SHURIKEN, BUT...

Preview of Volume 3

We're pleased to present you with a preview from volume 3. This volume will be available in English on November 28, 2006, but for now you'll have to make do with the Japanese!

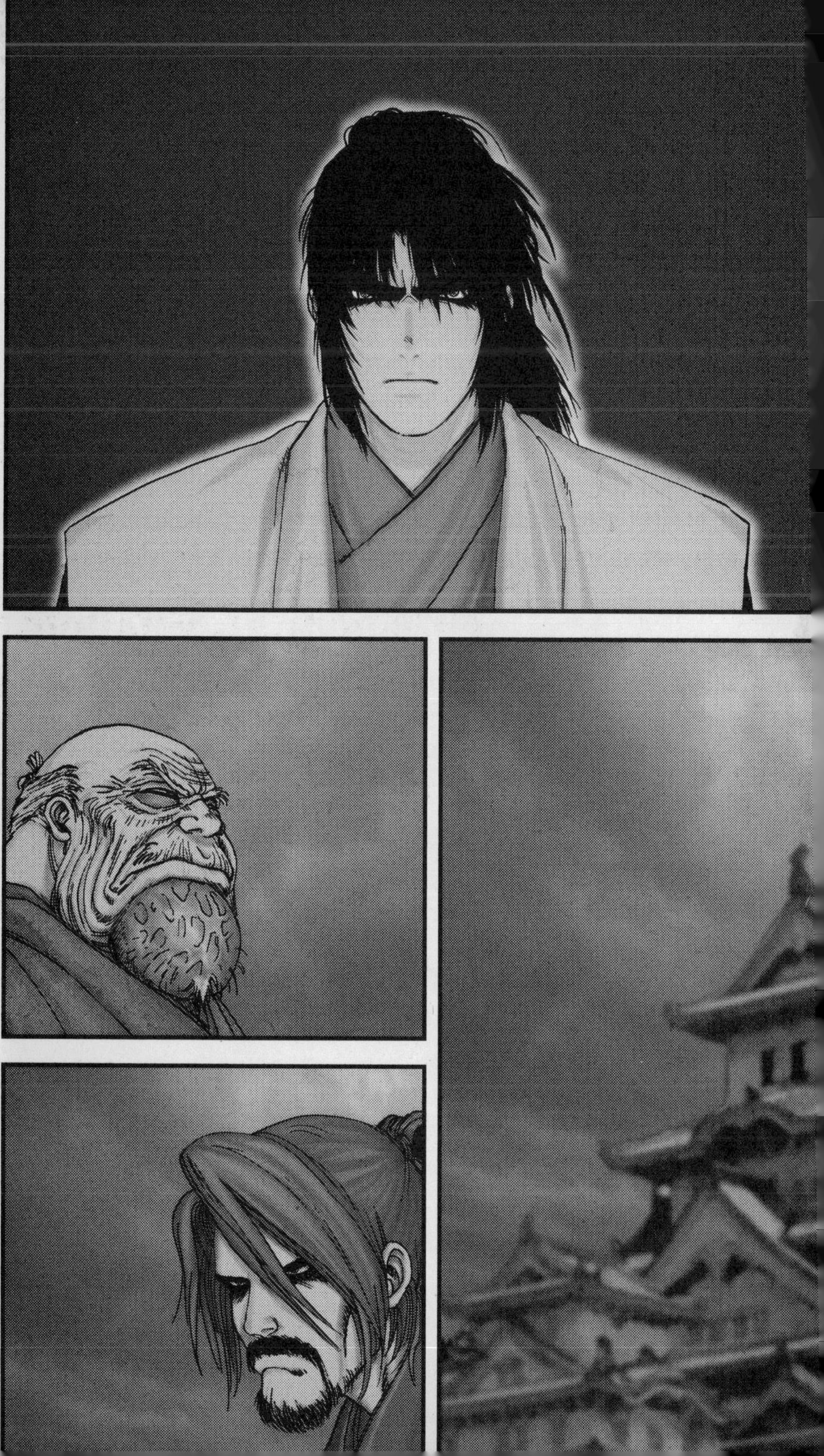

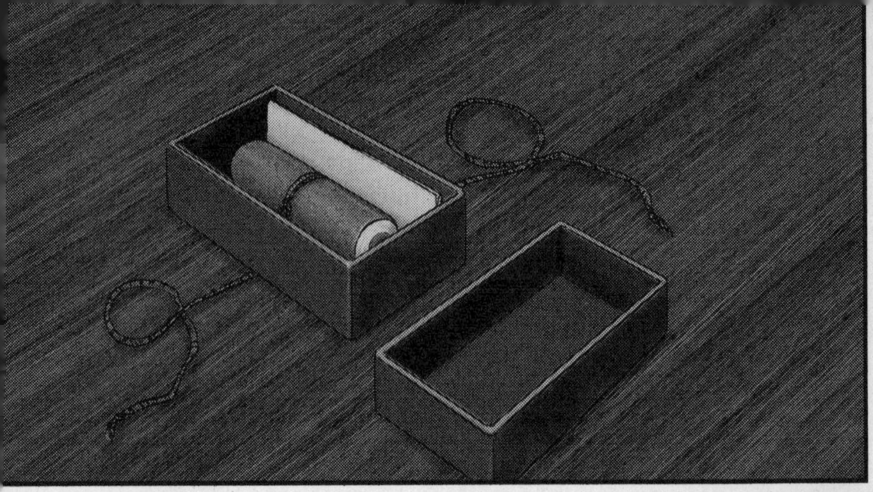
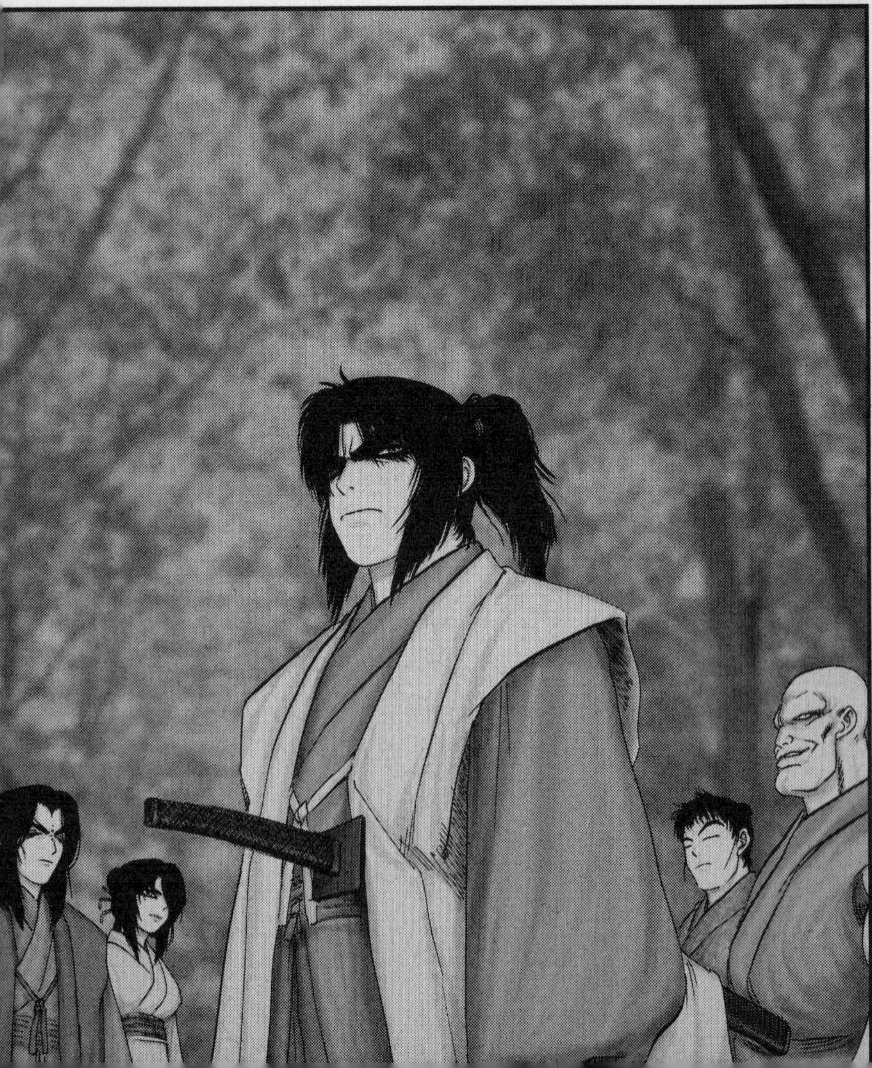

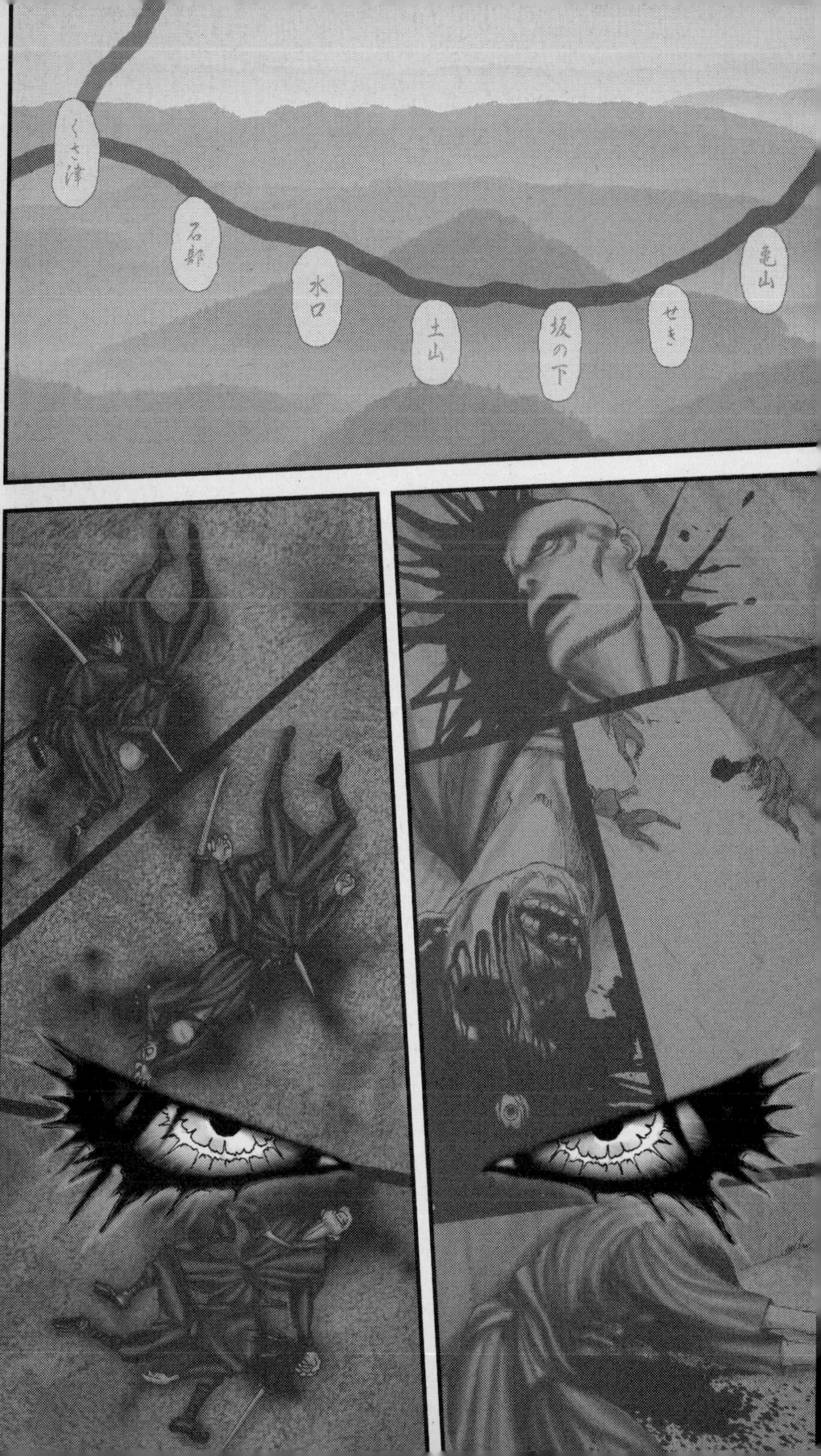
亀山
せき
坂の下
土山
水口
石部
くさ津

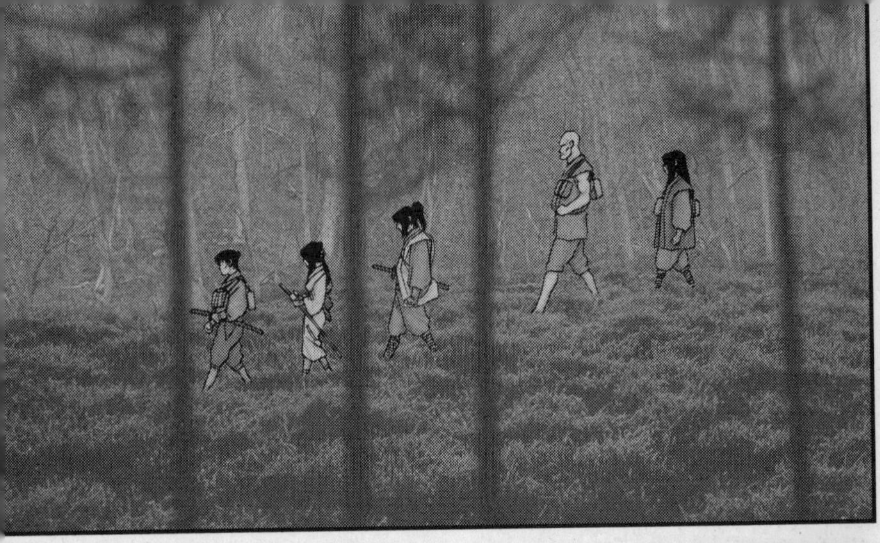

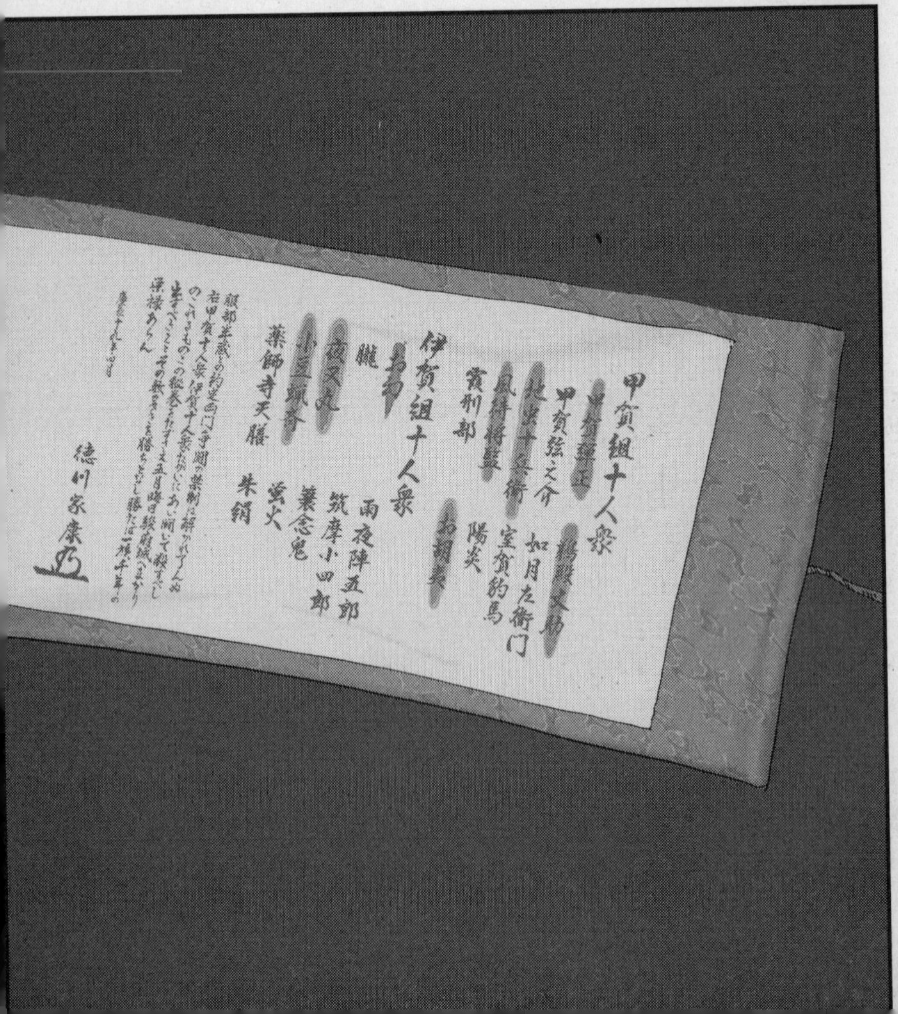

甲賀組十人衆
甲賀弾正
甲賀弦之介
地虫十兵衛
風待将監
霞刑部
鵜殿丈助
如月左衛門
室賀豹馬
陽炎
お胡夷
伊賀組十人衆
お幻
朧
夜叉丸
小豆蝋斎
薬師寺天膳
雨夜陣五郎
筑摩小四郎
蓑念鬼
蛍火
朱絹
服部半蔵との約定両門争闘の禁制は解かれ了んぬ
右甲賀十人衆伊賀十人衆たがいにあい闘いて殺すべし
のこれるもの この秘巻をたずさえ五月晦日駿府城へまかり
出ずべし その数多きを勝ちとなし勝たば一族千年の
恩禄あらん
徳川家康

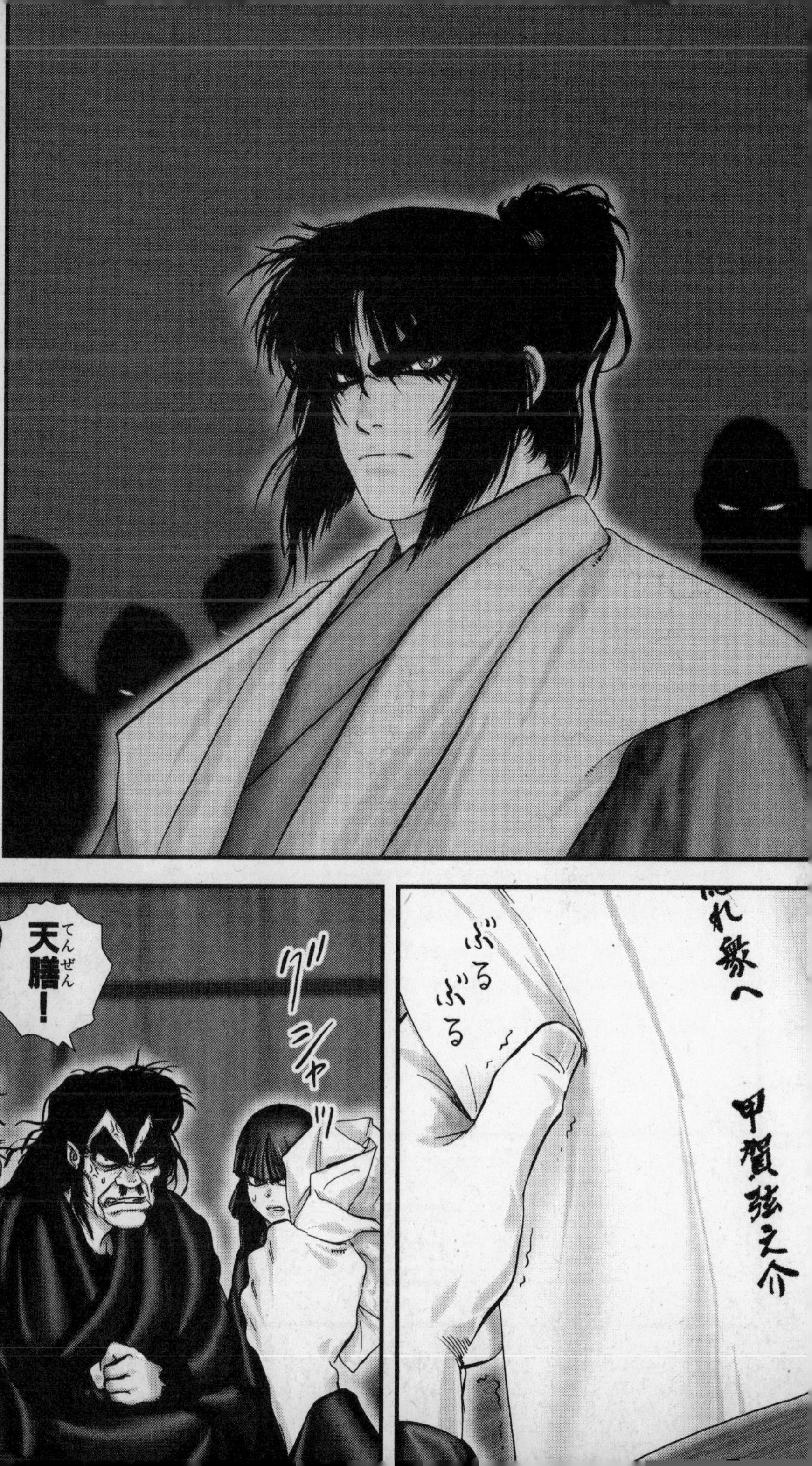
れ衆へ
甲賀弦之介
ぶるぶる
天膳(てんぜん)！
グシャッ

School Rumble

BY JIN KOBAYASHI

SUBTLETY IS FOR WIMPS!

She . . . is a second-year high school student with a single all-consuming question: Will the boy she likes ever really notice her?

He . . . is the school's most notorious juvenile delinquent, and he's suddenly come to a shocking realization: He's got a huge crush, and now he must tell her how he feels.

Life-changing obsessions, colossal foul-ups, grand schemes, deep-seated anxieties, and raging hormones—School Rumble portrays high school as it really is: over-the-top comedy!

Ages: 13 +

Special extras in each volume! Read them all!

BY OH!GREAT

Itsuki Minami needs no introduction—everybody's heard of the "Babyface" of the Eastside. He's the strongest kid at Higashi Junior High School, easy on the eyes but dangerously tough when he needs to be. Plus, Itsuki lives with the mysterious and sexy Noyamano sisters. Life's never dull, but it becomes downright dangerous when Itsuki leads his school to victory over vindictive Westside punks with gangster connections. Now he stands to lose his school, his friends, and everything he cares about. But in his darkest hour, the Noyamano girls give him an amazing gift, one that just might help him save his school: a pair of Air Trecks. These high-tech skates are more than just supercool. They'll enable Itsuki to execute the wildest, most aggressive moves ever seen—and introduce him to a thrilling and terrifying new world.

Ages: 16 +

Special extras in each volume! Read them all!

VISIT WWW.DELREYMANGA.COM TO:
- Read sample pages
- View release date calendars for upcoming volumes
- Sign up for Del Rey's free manga e-newsletter
- Find but the latest about new Del Rey Manga series

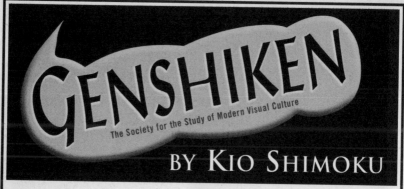
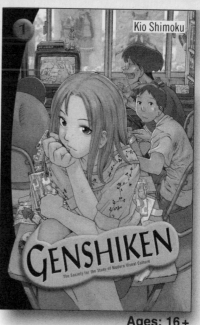

BY AKIRA SEGAMI

MISSION IMPOSSIBLE

The young ninja Kagetora has been given a great honor—to serve a renowned family of skilled martial artists. But on arrival, he's handed a challenging assignment: teach the heir to the dynasty, the charming but clumsy Yuki, the deft moves of self-defense and combat.

Yuki's inability to master the martial arts is not what makes this job so difficult for Kagetora. No, it is Yuki herself. Someday she will lead her family dojo, and for a ninja like Kagetora to fall in love with his master is a betrayal of his duty, the ultimate dishonor, and strictly forbidden. Can Kagetora help Yuki overcome her ungainly nature . . . or will he be overcome by his growing feelings?

Ages: 13 +

Special extras in each volume! Read them all!

KURO GANE

BY KEI TOUME

AN EERIE, HAUNTING SAMURAI ADVENTURE

Avenging his father's murder is a matter of honor for the young samurai Jintetsu. But it turns out that the killer is a corrupt government official—and now the powers that be are determined to hunt Jintetsu down. There's only one problem: Jintetsu is already dead.

Torn to pieces by a pack of dogs, Jintetsu's ravaged body has been found by Genkichi, outcast and master inventor. Genkichi gives the dead boy a new, indestructible steel body and a talking sword—just what he'll need to face down the gang that's terrorizing his hometown and the mobster who ordered his father's hit. But what about Otsuki, the beautiful girl he left behind? Steel armor is defense against any sword, but it can't save Jintetsu from the pain in his heart.

Teen: Ages 13+

Special extras in each volume! Read them all!

Compare!

STOP!

YOU'RE GOING THE WRONG WAY!

**MANGA IS A COMPLETELY DIFFERENT
TYPE OF READING EXPERIENCE.**

**TO START AT THE *BEGINNING*,
GO TO THE *END*!**

THAT'S RIGHT!

AUTHENTIC MANGA IS READ THE TRADITIONAL JAPANESE WAY—
FROM RIGHT TO LEFT. EXACTLY THE *OPPOSITE* OF HOW AMERICAN
BOOKS ARE READ. IT'S EASY TO FOLLOW: JUST GO TO THE OTHER
END OF THE BOOK, AND READ EACH PAGE—AND EACH PANEL—
FROM RIGHT SIDE TO LEFT SIDE, STARTING AT THE TOP RIGHT.
NOW YOU'RE EXPERIENCING MANGA AS IT WAS MEANT TO BE